D1593861

Israel, Jordan,
and the Peace Process

Yehuda Lukacs

Syracuse University Press

Library of Congress Cataloging-in-Publication Data
Lukacs, Yehuda.
    Israel, Jordan, and the peace process / Yehuda Lukacs. — 1st ed.
      p.   cm. — (Syracuse studies on peace and conflict resolution)
    Includes bibliographical references (p.   ) and index.
    ISBN 0-8156-2720-3 (cloth : alk. paper) — ISBN 0-8156-2855-2 (pbk. : alk. paper)
    1. Israel—Foreign relations—Jordan.   2. Jordan—Foreign relations—Israel.
    3. Jewish-Arab relations—1967–1973.   4. Jewish-Arab relations—1973–
    I. Title. II. Series.
    DS119.8.J67L85   1996
    327.569405695—dc20   96-20089

For my wife Louise Noakes-Lukacs
and daughter Vera Ellen Lukacs

I have never been used to standing, except with you next to me, speaking of peace, speaking about dreams and hopes for generations to come that must live in peace, enjoy human dignity, come together, work together, to build a better future which is their right. Never in my thoughts would it have occurred to me that my first visit to Jerusalem and response to your invitation, the invitation of the Speaker of the Knesset, the invitation of the President of Israel, would be on such an occasion. . . . Let's not keep silent. Let our voices rise high to speak of our commitment to peace for all times to come, and let us tell those who live in darkness who are the enemies of life, and through faith and religion and the teachings of our one God, this is where we stand. This is our camp. . . . [W]e are not ashamed, nor are we afraid, nor are we anything but determined to fulfill the legacy for which my friend fell, as did my grandfather in this very city when I was with him but a young boy.

—**King Hussein,** from "Eulogy for late Prime Minister Yitzhak Rabin." Mt. Herzl, Jerusalem. November 6, 1995

Yehuda Lukacs is director of the Center for Global Education, George Mason University, Fairfax, Virginia. He also serves as associate professor of international transactions, International Institute, George Mason University; adjunct associate professor of international relations, School of International Service, the American University, Washington, D.C., as well as adjunct faculty of Judaic studies, University of Maryland, Baltimore County. He has published several articles and books dealing with contemporary international relations and Arab-Israeli affairs including *Documents on the Israeli-Palestinian Conflict; The Arab-Israeli Conflict: Two Decades of Change,* with Abdalla M. Battah; and *The Israeli-Palestinian Conflict: A Documentary Record.*

Contents

Tables

Preface

Numerous individuals have guided and helped me through the long and lonely process of writing this book. The late Alan Ros Taylor, a gentleman, true friend, and my mentor, who stood by my side and provided moral and intellectual support, unfortunately will not see this book published. I would also like to acknowledge the support of Louis W. Goodman, dean of the School of International Service, American University, for his encouragement and support. Rex Brynen, Louis Kreisberg, and Don Peretz have examined this manuscript with fine-tooth combs and contributed dozens of useful comments; I am indebted to them for their valuable insights.

The Lady Davis Foundation of the Hebrew University, which provided a generous research fellowship, deserves special thanks as does Edy Kaufman, the executive director of the Harry S Truman Institute at the Hebrew University who facilitated my research there.

I owe my deepest gratitude to the dozens of Israelis and Palestinians who shared with me their insights and valuable information on Jordanian-Israeli relations. I am especially grateful to Ady Keidar of the Israeli Labor party, who helped me enormously by arranging many interviews with Israeli officials.

My friend, Andrea Barron, who has written widely on the Middle East, provided numerous useful comments, both substantive and editorial. Jill MacNeice, who is not a specialist on the subject, nonetheless, offered a refreshing perspective. Smadar Hochberg from Tel Aviv University was a useful assistant in locating archival material and in providing translations. My two graduate assistants at American University, Sara Labelle and Paul Kengor, did a superb job of providing material about Jordanian-Palestinian confederation and developments since the Gulf War. Michael S. Lee deserves special thanks for painstakingly constructing the index.

In Israel, I interviewed numerous government officials, members of the Knesset, military officials, and others who have been involved in Israeli-Jordanian relations. I also interviewed scores of Palestinians who shared with me their intimate knowledge of Jordanian involvement in the West Bank, such as banking agreements, trade and commerce across the Jordan River bridges, and more. In some cases, I cannot name my Israeli and Palestinian sources. I have, however, presented publicly available material to support my analysis.

Because of the sensitivity of the subject matter in Jordan, especially before its peace treaty with Israel was signed, I could not conduct research in the Hashemite Kingdom. Because I hold dual American and Israeli citizenship, Jordanian officials at the embassy in Washington, D.C., told me in 1987 that if I entered Jordan to conduct research, I would be expelled immediately because of my Israeli passport. After the Israeli-PLO agreement was signed in September 1993 and Israel and Jordan subsequently signed a formal agenda for negotiations, travel restrictions on Israelis holding dual citizenship were removed. But because I carried out my research before these dramatic breakthroughs, I worked only in Israel and the occupied territories.

Israelis and Palestinians, many of whom were former Jordanian officials, were quite eager to tell the story. I greatly benefited from these interviews. Now that the two countries have signed a formal peace treaty, more information is available, especially from Jordanian sources. The next person to research this subject, I hope, will reap the benefits of such openness.

This book is divided into two parts and follows the dual-track approach that has characterized Jordanian-Israeli relations since 1967. In part 1, comprising the first three chapters, I examine emerging Israeli attitudes toward the occupied territories, withdrawal, and peace with Jordan, and the "open bridges" policy and functional cooperation between the two countries in areas of mutual concern. In part 2, chapters 4 and 5, I focus on the formal peace process and its relationship to the ongoing cooperation between the two countries from the end of the Six-Day War until King Hussein's July 1988 administrative and legal disengagement from the West Bank. In chapter 6, I examine Israeli-Jordanian relations since Jordan's 1988 administrative and legal disengagement from the West Bank.

Finally, I dedicate this work to my life-partner, confidante, and loving wife, Louise, and to my daughter, Vera, whose joie de vivre fills my heart. Most of the research and writing were done before Vera's arrival; without Louise's love and continuous support this book would not have been completed.

Yehuda Lukacs

November 1995
Manassas, Virginia

Israel, Jordan, and the Peace Process

1

Introduction

On September 25, 1973, three years after Israel saved the Hashemite monarchy during the 1970 Jordanian-Palestinian civil war and twelve days before the outbreak of the Yom Kippur War, King Hussein bin Talal and Israeli Prime Minister Golda Meir met secretly in a government guesthouse outside Tel Aviv. This urgent meeting was the ninth encounter between the two heads of state since Golda Meir assumed office in early 1969. During the meeting King Hussein explicitly warned his Israeli hostess that units of the Syrian army were deployed offensively along the border with Israel "in pre-jump positions."[1] Israel's leaders, however, did not heed the king's warning, and on October 6, 1973, the Syrian and Egyptian armies launched coordinated attacks on two fronts and caught Israel ill-prepared.

In March 1992 the Israeli government unilaterally adjusted its telephone system so Israelis would be able to dial directly to the Arab world. The country that most vehemently objected to this act was Jordan, which responded by blocking the lines. The Jordanian minister of communication characterized the Israeli action as a "telephone rape."[2] He argued that Jordan objected to any formal ties with Israel as long as no significant progress had been made in the peace process.

Immediately after the signing of the Israeli-Jordanian peace accord on October 26, 1994, thousands of Israelis traveled to Jordan as tourists. Jordanian tour operators have since bitterly complained to their Israeli counterparts that Israeli tourists return to their homes in Israel without staying overnight in Jordan, thus depriving Jordanians of the much anticipated "peace dividend." Distances between the two countries are negligible, so many Israelis prefer one-day excursions without the need for hotel accommodations. But as Israelis discover Jordan's archeological treasures, more opt to stay in Jordan for several days. Since the signing of the treaty, 200,000 Israelis visited Jordan; over 84,000 Jordanians visited Israel.

Each of the first two episodes capture, albeit differently, the essence of Israeli-Jordanian relations that existed from Israel's establishment in

1

1948 to the convening of the 1991 Madrid international peace conference: maintenance of a formal state of war that precluded any overt
contacts and ties while the two countries forged an extensive network
of sub rosa relationships, approximating an alliance, as a result of the
convergence of interests in several areas.[3]

The Jordanian complaint about the frugality of Israelis now attests
to the transformation of the relationship from a de facto to a public de
jure peace.

The foundations of Israeli-Jordanian relations date back to 1921
when Transjordan was created. Since then, the two sides have maintained
a constant dialogue over a range of issues emanating from their overlapping interests. The convergence of Zionist-Hashemite interests during
the British mandatory period peaked when the two sides arrived at
an explicit agreement in 1947 to divide Palestine after the mandate
terminated. As Avi Shlaim demonstrates in his groundbreaking study,
Collusion Across the Jordan, this agreement was aimed at frustrating the
1947 United Nations partition plan that called for the establishment of
an Arab Palestinian state alongside Israel.[4]

This study, by emphasizing the 1967–88 period, provides an example
of the discrepancy between announced policy and actual behavior in
international politics. Jordan maintained a technical state of war with
Israel (until the signing of the Washington Declaration in July 1994)
and, after 1967, it took issue with nearly every aspect of Israeli policy in
the occupied territories. On an unofficial pragmatic level, however, Jordan was willing to establish a working relationship with its formal enemy.
Similarly, Israel regarded Jordan's 1950 annexation of the West Bank
as "unlawful," yet this legal perspective did not prevent several successive
Israeli governments from supporting the "Jordanian option"—the designation of the Hashemite Kingdom as the sole interlocutor in negotiations with Israel about the future of the West Bank in the post-1967
period. As is often the case in international relations, states tend to
operate in terms of actual interests rather than their ideological commitments.

In this work I probe the foundations, forms, and impact of Israeli-
Jordanian relations from the 1967 war until the signing of the Israeli-
Jordanian Treaty of Peace in October 1994. I particularly emphasize the
period from the end of the Six-Day War until King Hussein's July 31,
1988, announcement of administrative and political disengagement from
the West Bank. The thrust of my argument is that, despite the formal
state of war between Israel and Jordan, the two countries have engaged
in a policy of functional cooperation resulting from a perception of
shared interests. Specifically, I divide my argument into three parts.
First, Israeli-Jordanian relations can be best understood in terms of their

interdependence and corresponding interests. These arose from the need to maintain tranquility on the common border, mutual reliance on natural resources, and a desire to subordinate and marginalize the Palestinian national movement. Second, after the 1967 war, as a result of these mutual interests, a pattern of functional cooperation developed between the two countries, culminating in a state of de facto peace. This functional cooperation reflected the functionalist position within the Israeli government on relations with Jordan and the future of the West Bank. The functionalist position that supported Jordanian involvement in the West Bank through the open bridges policy resulted in trade, movement of people and capital, and, above all, coordinated efforts by both countries to contain the Palestine Liberation Organization (PLO) in the West Bank. Third, I argue that Jordanian-Israeli functional cooperation greatly contributed to the status quo and to lack of progress in the formal diplomatic Arab-Israeli peace process. It allowed both countries to put aside their fundamental disagreement on a number of issues (e.g., Israeli withdrawal from the occupied territories or Jordanian formal recognition of Israel) and to address their immediate concerns secretly without having to sign a formal peace accord that would necessitate negotiating these thorny matters.

The nature of the two countries' relations, however, changed as a result of Jordan's July 1988 announcement of an administrative and legal disengagement from the West Bank. Jordan was no longer the party with whom Israel expected to negotiate over the Palestinian question. This issue was left to Israel and the PLO, and Jordan began to pursue bilateral issues with Israel, such as water, refugees, and final boundaries (outside the West Bank), culminating in the October 1994 treaty.

I argue that with the signing of the formal peace agreement both sides are now able to capitalize upon a plethora of past common practical experiences that constituted sub-rosa peace and to refashion the relationship from a clandestine to an open partnership.

Israeli-Jordanian interests converge in a number of areas: the two countries share their longest border; both derive their water from the same sources (the Yarmuk and Jordan rivers); and both share the Dead Sea, with its rich mineral deposits. Additionally, the two countries are situated along the Gulf of Aqaba as are their two adjacent cities, Eilat and Aqaba.

Zionist-Hashemite contacts date back to 1918 when King Faisal of Iraq explored with the Zionist leader Chaim Weizmann the possibility of Jewish-Arab cooperation, culminating in the famous 1919 Weizmann-Faisal agreement. Faisal's brother, Abdullah, the amir of Transjordan who became king of Jordan in 1946, maintained a dialogue with the leadership of the Yishuv in order to find a modus vivendi between the two sides. In the 1947–49 period the Jewish agency and King Abdullah reached an understanding to circumvent the establishment of a Palestinian state as called for by the 1947 United Nations partition plan. In 1950 the two sides negotiated a treaty of amity and nonaggression, but it was never implemented because the Jordanian monarch was assassinated in 1951. After 1963, when King Hussein first secretly met Ya'acov Herzog of the Israeli foreign ministry, he participated in dozens of clandestine gatherings with Israeli leaders.[5] The meetings took place in London, on an Israeli missile boat in the Gulf of Aqaba, and in a "safe house" near Tel Aviv.[6] Most of the encounters focused on the question of the West Bank (in the post-1967 period) and on the possibility of reaching a formal understanding between the two countries regarding a contractual peace. The meetings also focused on issues of bilateral concern. One of the best examples of Israeli-Jordanian convergence of interests took place in 1970 when Israel mobilized its military to deter the Syrian army from advancing toward Jordan's heartland and threatening the regime during the civil war between Hussein and the PLO. By doing so, Israel demonstrated its willingness to risk a war against Syria to protect its vital interests—preservation of the Hashemite monarchy and opposition to the establishment of a Palestinian state on either bank of the Jordan River.

Other issues of mutual concern between Israel and Jordan included agriculture; transfer of Israeli irrigation technology to Jordan; sale of Israeli medical supplies to Jordan during the 1970 civil war; sharing the Yarmuk waters; banking in the West Bank; communication links between the Aqaba and Eilat airports to prevent accidents; joint energy projects in the Dead Sea; Jordanian financial and administrative involvement in the West Bank; and even joint efforts against insects and mosquitos in the Gulf of Aqaba.

According to Aaron Klieman, one of the leading scholars of Israeli-Jordanian relations, the underlying interest that helped galvanize the interdependence between Israel and Jordan "has been the parallel quest for security through the exclusion and subordination of the Palestinian national movement."[7] This aspect of Israeli-Jordanian relations found particular expression in the 1967–88 period when the West Bank, which Jordan annexed in 1950, became the focus of attention.

The ascendance of the PLO after 1967 to center stage in regional and international politics posed a challenge to both Israel and Jordan. Before the secret Israeli-PLO negotiations in Norway in early 1993 and the ensuing peace agreement signed on September 13, 1993, Israel formally regarded the PLO as its mortal enemy, sparing no effort to discredit the Palestinian organization. Similarly, before King Hussein's

1988 disengagement, the PLO and Jordan were engaged in an overt and covert battle over the question of who represented the Palestinians. The Arab world formally recognized the PLO as the "sole legitimate representative of the Palestinian people" in the 1974 Rabat resolution. Jordan, however, attempted to bypass the formal endorsement of the Palestine Liberation Organization by continuing its financial and administrative links to the West Bank and by attempting to persuade the Palestinians to accept Jordan as their representative. Israel, as part of its strategy in the territories, encouraged these attempts to "Jordanize" the West Bank and to minimize the influence of the PLO.[8] These efforts were ultimately aimed at creating an Israeli-Jordanian condominium, or joint rule, in the West Bank. All these undertakings, however, came to an end as a result of the Palestinian uprising that began in December 1987 and led to King Hussein's July 1988 announcement in which he severed Jordan's connections with the West Bank.

The second part of my argument is that Israeli-Jordanian interdependence led to a policy of functional cooperation after the 1967 war. Functional cooperation is defined here as an interest-driven type of cooperation that takes place in the context of a formal state of war between the two countries.[9] As demonstrated throughout this work, functional cooperation has involved political, economic, and administrative aspects.

For this purpose functional cooperation should not be confused with the theory of Functionalism in the study of international relations. Functional cooperation is not a school of thought as is Functionalism with its ongoing research agenda but is a conceptualization that helps to elucidate the multifaceted scope of Israeli-Jordanian relations. For example, according to the father of Functionalism, David Mitrany, Functionalism claims that "social and economic cooperation between states will (and should) erode the 'ubiquitous' yet 'anachronistic' place held by the territorial states in the modern world."[10] According to Mitrany, the result of this erosion would and should lead to a more peaceful world. Further, Mitrany argues that political problems which separate states can be broken down into technical issues, which then results in a cumulative process that breaks down the barriers between states.[11]

Israel and Jordan understood that a degree of interdependence bound them together, which necessitated collective action in a number of areas. Furthermore, given this interdependence, Israel and Jordan concluded that they had no choice but to cooperate. The aim of this cooperation, however, should be viewed in tactical terms; it was not directed at conflict resolution but at conflict management with the hope of preventing open military conflict and of addressing mutual interests. In other words, because their functional cooperation was secret, neither

Israel nor Jordan expected that the fundamental disagreements between the two countries over Israeli withdrawal from the territories would disappear as a result of their cooperation. Rather, the overlapping of interests dictated a policy of limited objectives: both attempted to prevent the establishment of a Palestinian state on the West Bank and both decided to address Israeli-Jordanian bilateral problems through tacit and secret arrangements. These arrangements, which were intended primarily to reach a modus vivendi between the two countries, were based, according to Klieman, on three constants:

> For Israel, the need to have Jordan's assistance in moderating the inevitable stresses of an awkward, prolonged military administration [of the West Bank]; for Jordan, the renewed invitation to act more assertively in extending its influence at the expense of the PLO; and for both Israel and Jordan, the only apparent alternative to an unpleasant but also unavoidable confrontation over the two issues confirmed through secret diplomatic discussions to be basically unresolvable given the position of the two parties—the final status of the disputed territories, and the shape of a real peace settlement.[12]

To understand the evolution of Israeli-Jordanian functional cooperation one must examine Israeli attitudes toward the West Bank as they developed in the 1967–88 period.

After the Six-Day War, four dominant positions or schools of thought emerged within the Israeli government on the question of peace with Jordan and the future of the occupied territories: the functionalist, territorialist, annexationist, and reconciliationist.[13]

The functionalist approach was clearly an instrumentalist position that helped guide Israeli policy in the short run while leaving the question of withdrawal in abeyance. The other three positions were ideological, focusing on the degree and desirability of an Israeli withdrawal. Thus, a proponent of the functionalist school, for example, could also belong to any of the other ideological camps.

The first school of thought, the functionalist, was championed by Moshe Dayan and Shimon Peres of the Rafi Party (Israel's Workers List, which later was incorporated into the Labor Party). Dayan was very pessimistic about the prospects of formal peace with Jordan. Hence, he advocated the "creation of facts" in the territories, largely in the form of Jewish settlements, for he viewed the West Bank as part of Israel's biblical heritage. Yet, he also wanted to maintain Jordanian influence in the West Bank through the open bridges policy, which enabled the West Bank to have an outlet to the Arab world, especially to Jordan. This policy was intended to serve as a "pressure release valve" for the West Bank Palestinians who were living under Israeli occupation. The

Palestinians were allowed to maintain their ties to Jordan, which both the Israeli and Jordanian governments hoped would fulfill their nationalist aspirations. Dayan argued that as long as there was no peace treaty Israel should create an economic infrastructure in the West Bank that would be linked to Israel, thus enabling the Palestinians to coexist with Israel.[14] Dayan coined the phrase "waiting for the phone call from the Arabs," which expressed Israeli expectations that it was up to the Arabs to seize the initiative because Israel was in possession of the territories and could live with the status quo. With regard to formal peace with Jordan, Dayan proposed a peace treaty on September 3, 1967, that would empower Jordan to exercise civil administration over the West Bank while Israel maintained military control.[15] This proposal was rejected by Jordan because it did not include references to total Israeli withdrawal from the territories occupied in 1967 as demanded by the Hashemite Kingdom.

Dayan's biographer, Shabtai Teveth, argues that before 1967 Dayan believed that a confederation should be established between Israel, Jordan, and the West Bank people. Teveth argues that Dayan tried to implement this scheme after the 1967 war.

> [A]n Arab from Jerusalem and an Arab from Nablus, though belonging to the same demographic and cultural group, could belong to different political entities. Both would work in the same economy but would vote for representatives in different countries and enjoy different civil rights. Dayan's overall aim was to blur the identification between the geographic and the demographic lines of demarcation. He therefore proposed that the government establish four Jewish cities along the mountain ridge extending from Hebron and Nablus, thereby breaking up the Arab demographic continuity.[16]

Dayan, however, never clearly articulated a consistent position on whether Israel should withdraw from the West Bank. Although he supported the idea of "territorial compromise" (the exchange of territories occupied by Israel for contractual peace with the Arabs), Dayan made contradictory statements on the issue. On the one hand, he supported the right of Jews to settle anywhere in the Land of Israel. On the other hand, he opposed Israeli annexation of the territories.[17] Therefore, the functional solution that Dayan developed also reflected his ambivalence regarding the final status of the territories.

After his resignation as defense minister in 1974, Dayan received a personal note from King Hussein who wished to thank the Israeli leader for the special friendship that had developed between the two (the contents of the letter were published by Dayan's confidant, Naftali Lavie, in April 1993). It read, "I shall always cherish your wisdom and foresight; your imaginative, creative and constructive approach towards the problems facing us; and the fact that you always had the courage to act in accordance with your conviction when you handled these problems."[18]

Shimon Peres, the other proponent of the functionalist school of thought, attached even less ideological significance to the West Bank. For Peres security considerations were of utmost importance. As noted by Abba Eban, Peres does not "brandish the Holocaust or appeal to biblical roots when making a point. The national style [since Peres became prime minister] has changed."[19] For Peres, like Dayan, supported the idea of "territorial compromise" in the West Bank without specifying the extent to which Israel ought to withdraw in exchange for peace. Until Jordan's 1988 disengagement he also was the most vocal supporter of the "Jordanian option," which opposed an independent Palestinian state on the West Bank but supported returning part or all of the West Bank to Jordan. Peres also played a key role in supporting substantial Jordanian involvement in the West Bank to counter the influence of the PLO. While he was prime minister between 1984 and 1986, Peres, along with King Hussein, attempted to establish an Israeli-Jordanian power-sharing or condominium arrangement on the West Bank whereby the two countries would comanage the territories.[20] Further, in April 1987 in a secret meeting in London, Peres, who was Israel's foreign minister as a result of the famous "rotation" agreement with Likud leader Yitzhak Shamir, reached accord with King Hussein on convening an international peace conference. The accord, however, was rejected by Shamir and, thus, was never ratified by the Israeli government.

Although Peres played a key role in Israel's rapprochement with the PLO in 1993, he still viewed Jordan as an essential player. Peres, for example, traveled to Amman on November 3, 1993, after the signing of the Israeli-PLO accord, hoping to persuade, without success, his old friend King Hussein to sign a peace agreement that would codify, regulate, and bring to light the decades-old functional cooperation. Despite Peres's enthusiasm and pleading the Jordanian monarch preferred at that time to continue his low-profile policies on formal relations with Israel. By the summer of 1994, however, King Hussein had changed his mind regarding formal peace with Israel, and on October 26, 1994, the two countries signed a peace treaty.

The second school of thought was the territorialist, established by Yigal Allon of the Ahdut Ha'Avoda Party (Unity of Labor, which together with Rafi and Mapai formed the Labor Party Alignment in 1969).[21] Yitzhak Rabin, the late prime minister, and a sizable portion of the Labor party supported this view.[22] This school advocated that territory is an essential component of security and, therefore, parts of the West Bank must be kept by Israel. Specifically, the territorialist position, which became synonymous with the Allon Plan, called for retaining the nonpopulated areas of the West Bank for security reasons. It also called for maintaining an Israeli military presence along the Jordan River and for returning the rest of the West Bank to Jordan. During the 1992 elections campaign, when Rabin a distinguished between "political" and "security" settlements in the West Bank, he clearly based this differentiation on the Allon Plan. For Rabin "security settlements" constituted part of the territory that Israel was supposed to retain under the plan's provisions. In contrast, "political settlements," built by the Likud Party for ideological reasons, were located outside the boundaries of the plan in areas heavily populated by Palestinians. During Israel's negotiations with the United States over the $10 billion housing loan guarantee in August 1992 Rabin promised to stop building "political settlements" that were not essential to Israel's security as a prerequisite for the loan guarantees. The Israeli government has, to a large extent, adhered to this promise, especially in light of its agreement with the PLO.

The Allon Plan never became official governmental policy. It was submitted to the Israeli government on July 27, 1967, but was never formally discussed.[23] The Allon Plan, however, became the unofficial doctrine of the Labor Party regarding peace with Jordan in subsequent years but was not formally adopted in its platform until 1977.[24] By the June 1992 elections, which culminated in a Labor victory, the Allon Plan as an official doctrine of the party had been replaced in favor of a more reconciliationist view that emphasized the centrality of the Palestinians in any negotiated agreement on the West Bank.

The 1993 Israeli-PLO accord further modified the territorialists' perspective by introducing the concept of a PLO-controlled interim period of self-rule although its core doctrine—the need to retain permanently a portion of the West Bank for security—remained intact.

The territorialist position called for retention of about 30 percent of the West Bank's territory. When this position was introduced, it was rejected by Jordan, which opposed any territorial changes in the status quo ante.[25]

In addition to worrying about Israel's security needs, Allon was also concerned about the so-called demographic problem. If the territories were to be annexed, Israel could lose its Jewish character because the territories were populated by more than one million Arabs, who had a much higher birth rate than did the Jews. Allon, however, advocated the building of many Jewish settlements in the area along the Jordanian border, which he believed Israel needed to control for security reasons. He also advocated drawing up a new map of Israel as quickly as possible, indicating "what we should keep for ourselves and what we should leave for others. . . . The guiding test should be Israel's security needs: we prefer secure borders that are not agreed to, to agreed borders which are not secure."[26] Allon believed that peace should be pursued relentlessly: "My line is to meet with everyone, regardless of the outcome. Peace is not an exact science."[27] Furthermore, Allon did not have a pro-Jordanian orientation per se. For him the West Bank's relations with the East Bank were a function of Jordan's annexation of the West Bank in 1950. Thus, negotiations had to be conducted with West Bank Palestinians and with Jordan. Allon's plan, thus, should be viewed as one that kept options open, including the possibility of autonomy for the West Bank with a possible confederal linkage to Jordan as was envisaged by Jordanian, Israeli, and PLO officials after the September 1993 accord.

By the mid-1970s Allon had modified his views. Initially, after 1967, he had advocated several options for the solution of the Palestinian problem. These options included a neutral Palestinian state that could not ally itself with any actors hostile to Israel or return of the territory to Jordan if the West Bank was demilitarized.[28] Allon's preferred solution, a Jordanian-Palestinian confederation, became clear during the mid-1970s.[29]

Allon did not oppose the functional division of the West Bank with Jordan. On the contrary, he supported Dayan's position if it would not lead to a permanent stalemate.

> A functional division, resulting from arrangements with Jordan and public representatives from Judea and Samaria, as an "interim agreement" is entirely possible. To a certain extent this reality exists today as a result of lack of formal peace. This has been achieved through the "open bridges" policy and the relative municipal autonomy [in the West Bank]. However, one should not compare an interim arrangement resulting from a war forced upon Israel, and a permanent settlement which aims to end the state of belligerency once and for all and to bring peace and normalization of relations.[30]

The third school of thought—the annexationist—was represented by Menachem Begin. Begin was the leader of the Gahal bloc, composed of the Herut (freedom) and Liberal parties which later fused into the Likud party in 1973. Those that adhered to this position comprised the right-wing spectrum of the Israeli body-politic, including most religious parties. Begin wanted the West Bank incorporated into Israel as part of his idea of Eretz Yisrael, or Land of Israel. Immediately after the war Begin called for the establishment of numerous settlements in the West Bank as the first stage toward formal annexation.[31] Begin opposed negotiations with Jordan because he did not think there was anything to negotiate.[32] He once refused to even recognize Jordan as a nation. During the first years after the establishment of the State of Israel, the Herut Party's official publication placed quotation marks around the word Jordan because the party considered Jordan part of the historic Land of Israel. In the post-1967 period, however, Begin changed his views on this matter and lent support to Dayan's functionalist policies because they did not foreclose the option of annexing the West Bank. Begin drew a distinction between the principle of a nation's historic right and concrete political reality; the former can be achieved in the long run, whereas the latter must be dealt with in the present. Thus, he opposed making Jordan into a Palestinian state because such a move would forfeit Israel's historic right to the East Bank.[33]

After his Likud Party won the 1977 elections, Begin presented an autonomy plan for the West Bank and Gaza. The plan was later incorporated into the Camp David Accords although it was never implemented because of conflicting interpretations by Israel and Egypt over the meaning of autonomy. The Likud supported autonomy for the population but not for the territory. This meant that Israel would maintain its presence in the territories although Jordan would be invited to play a role along with the Palestinian inhabitants. Clearly, this proposal also had a functionalist component that involved a Jordanian role in the territories.

The position of the Likud party vis-à-vis the West Bank has remained rigid since 1967; its basic stance against Israeli withdrawal has been consistent. The 1977 Likud party platform, for example, states:

> The right of the Jewish people to the Land of Israel is eternal and is an integral part of its right to security and peace. Judea and Samaria will therefore not be turned over to any foreign rule: between the sea and the Jordan will be only Israeli sovereignty. Any plan that involves surrender of part of Western Eretz Yisrael militates against our right to the Land, will inevitably lead to a Palestinian state, threatens the security of our civilian population, endangers the existence of the state and defeats all prospects for peace.[34]

A variation of the annexationist position can be found in Ariel Sharon's views toward Jordan. Sharon, a prominent member of the Likud Party, believed Israel should overthrow the Hashemite monarchy and replace it with a Palestinian government.[35] The "Palestinianization of Jordan" idea surfaced during the 1970 Jordanian civil war when some members of the Israeli military advocated toppling Hussein rather than helping him survive. Sharon saw no need to create a "second Palestinian state" on the West Bank because the Palestinian state already existed in Jordan as a result of the size of the Palestinian population there. Israel could then justify annexing the West Bank and the pressures for the creation of a Palestinian state would find expression on the East Bank.

Former Israeli Prime Minister Yitzhak Shamir also supported the "Jordan is Palestine" idea. In a 1982 article in *Foreign Affairs* Shamir wrote:

> On the subject of political entity, a homeland for the Arabs of the former British mandated Palestine, the facts speak for themselves. The state known today as the Kingdom of Jordan is an integral part of what was once known as Palestine (77 percent of its territory); its inhabitants are therefore Palestinian—not different in their language, culture or religious and demographic composition from other Palestinians. . . . That homeland is Trans-Jordan or eastern Palestine.[36]

Shamir, however, changed his mind on this issue after the Gulf War. According to Adam Garfinkle, one of the important consequences of the Gulf War was that the "Jordan is Palestine" idea championed by Israeli annexationists was largely discredited: "[If] Jordan [had] become a Palestinian state before the crisis . . . what would have stopped the creation of a real, as opposed to a limited and largely phony, Iraqi-Jordanian alliance?"[37] Apparently, Jordan's renewed strategic importance to Israel as a buffer on its eastern border was chiefly responsible for Shamir's volte-face.

The views of Prime Minister Benjamin Netanyahu, leader of the Likud Party, who assumed the premiership as a result of his victory over Shimon Peres in the elections held on May 29, 1996, are noteworthy. He considered Jordan to be a de facto Palestinian state as the result of demographics but, unlike Sharon, Netanyahu avoided calling for the elimination of the Hashemite regime.

> For strategic reasons, many people in Israel prefer the continuation of a Jordan under the less aggressive Hashemites. But this in no way alters the fact that a national home, indeed a sovereign state, exists for Palestinian Arabs. Even now, many of the principal functionaries of the Jordanian regime have been Palestinian Arabs who originated on the West Bank, including Prime Minister Zaid al-Rifai and Foreign Minister Taher Masri, both from Nablus. If the inhabitants of this Palestinian state wish to replace the head of government with a Palestinian as well, that should be up to them.[38]

Furthermore, Netanyahu opposed Israeli withdrawal from the territories, but he supported granting their Palestinian inhabitants a permanent autonomy based upon a modification of the Camp David framework. He proposed granting Gaza first the "fullest possible autonomy" because self-rule in Gaza did "not pose an extraordinary security risk for Israel."[39] With the Gaza-First idea Netanyahu was in line with Yitzhak Rabin and the majority of Israelis who opposed permanent control of the violent Palestinian enclave because of the high number of Israeli casualties and who, consequently, supported the Gaza portion of the Gaza-Jericho agreement with the PLO. Regarding the West Bank, he suggested an interim system of limited autonomy for "four self-managing Arab counties: Jenin, Nablus, Ramallah, Hebron," comprising the majority of the Palestinian population but only one-fifth of the land, and leaving the rest of the territory open for Jewish settlement. The Camp David Accords called for negotiations on the final status of the territories to be based on the implementation of United Nations Security Council Resolution 242 to determine the location of the boundaries and security arrangements and a final outcome that took into account "the legitimate rights of the Palestinian people and their just requirements." But for Netanyahu, negotiations about the final status would focus only on "the question of whether to grant Israeli citizenship to the residents of the counties."[40] No mention was made of a territorial compromise in the West Bank. At most, Netanyahu and his annexationist colleagues supported the idea of *peace for peace*, which precluded any territorial compromise on Israel's part but expected, nonetheless, that Israel's Arab neighbors would recognize it and sign peace treaties. Hence, Netanyahu expressed strong support for the peace agreement with Jordan, which did not involve any territorial compromise in the West Bank. On December 6, 1994, Netanyahu, in a meeting with King Hussein and Crown Price Hassan in Amman, disavowed the "Jordan is Palestine" idea and gave his blessing to increased economic cooperation between the two countries.[41] Following his election as Israel's prime minister, Netanyahu has sought close ties with Jordan and met King Hussein several times. He regards the king as Israel's strongest and most reliable partner in the Arab world and has enlisted the Jordanian monarch to help persuade Syria to renew its negotiations with Israel even though Netanyahu opposes Israeli withdrawal from the Golan Heights. While Netanyahu has accepted Israel's agreements with the PLO as a fait accompli, he is opposed to the establishment of a Palestinian state in the West Bank and Gaza as well as surrendering any part of Jerusalem to the Palestinians. By pursuing a pro-Hashemite policy, Netanyahu hopes to undermine the PLO by capitalizing upon the traditional rivalry and mistrust between Jordan and the Palestinians in the territories.

The fourth school of thought—the reconciliationist—was initially supported by Foreign Minister Abba Eban and Finance Minister Pinhas Sapir of Mapai, among others. Many members of the Labor Party, along with representatives from Meretz and other leftist parties, which now form what is known as the "peace camp," adhere to this school. (Meretz, now part of Israel's governing coalition, was created in 1992. It comprises Mapam, the Citizens Rights Movement, and Shinui.) Most supporters of this perspective, but clearly not all, called for substantial Israeli withdrawal from the territories with only minor alterations in the boundaries to accommodate Israeli security needs.[42]

Representatives of this position initially believed that the territories should be returned to Jordan. But because of the intensification of Palestinian nationalism in the West Bank and Gaza and the demand for independent statehood many began advocating negotiations with Palestinian representatives rather than with Jordan. Those who adhered to this position believed that morality and justice rather than the Bible or *blind security* considerations should dictate the terms of the settlement. They believed that Israel could give up the territories and still maintain its security. Moreover, they argued that unless peace was reached, Israel could not forever maintain its democratic character while forcibly ruling more than one million Palestinians.[43] They also put forth the demographic argument advanced by proponents of the territorialist position, namely, that if the status quo were maintained, Israel would lose its Jewish character and become a de facto binational state.[44]

In the 1970s several proponents of this position began advocating negotiations with the PLO based on the belief that peace is to be negotiated with one's enemy. Hence, they began supporting the creation of a Palestinian state in the West Bank and Gaza provided that the PLO recognized Israel and renounced terrorism against Israeli targets. Peace rather than maintenance of the status quo was the goal of the advocates of this perspective. Abba Eban, according to Michael Brecher, advocated "keeping all options open to settlement against the growing mood of 'fortress Israel'."[45] Unlike the territorialists, most reconciliationists did not think it was absolutely necessary for Israel to maintain a military presence on the West Bank to guarantee its security interests. They defined security as a positive sum process, entailing social, cultural, political, and, most importantly, economic exchanges that would then lead to interdependence between Israel and her neighbors and eliminate the need to rely only on military measures to guarantee Israel's survival.

Other advocates of the reconciliationist position argued that realism should dictate Israeli withdrawal to the 1967 border and negotiations with the PLO. A leading figure who argued for this position was the late General Yehoshafat Harkabi, former director of Israeli military intelligence and one of the leading intellectual critics of the policies of the Likud government in the early 1980s.[46]

Moreover, Harkabi criticized Israel's rejection of Arab overtures. He believed that before 1967 the Arab states called for the elimination of Israel but that this position changed after the war. Israel, by contrast, was flexible in its approach toward the Arab world before 1967, and until the Madrid conference it preferred the status quo.

> Just as the first signs of flexibility appeared in the Arab position, the Israeli position became absolute. The danger is that if the new Israeli absolutism persists it will lead to concomitant change in the Arab position. An Israeli demand for all the territory west of the River Jordan will encourage the Arabs to claim the entire area of Israel, thereby ending any incipient tendency to be satisfied by a return to the 1967 borders. The conflict will become an existential conflict, a fight to the death, and all possibility of resolving it peacefully will disappear. . . . Many Israelis do not understand the extent to which peace is in the Israeli interest. . . . [I]t threatens Israel's very existence. In making peace, including paying the price for peace, Israel would not be doing the Arabs a favor, but doing itself a favor.[47]

To understand Israel's emerging policy vis-à-vis Jordan, one must examine the interplay of the functionalist, territorialist, annexationist, and reconciliationist positions toward peace with Jordan. I argue here that the functionalist school of thought, which avoided the question of a territorial settlement with Jordan but opted for de facto arrangements with Jordan in the West Bank, was the position that was actually implemented. In his capacity as defense minister Dayan was responsible for day-to-day policies in the territories, and his authority to dictate policies was rarely challenged. Indeed, for all practical purposes, Dayan became the "sovereign authority, especially in the West Bank and Gaza."[48]

The fact that the Israeli political landscape was full of factionalism and ideological cleavages, resulting in a lack of consensus on the final status of the West Bank, was detrimental to settlement of the conflict. It was not surprising, therefore, that Dayan's policies were supported by the other three positions; as long as there was no formal peace with Jordan, the functionalist position did not contradict either the territorialist, reconciliationist, or annexationist positions. Support for Dayan's policies was reached through a process of default. Although the territorialists and reconciliationists hoped for an eventual agreement with Jordan or the Palestinians, the lack of serious negotiations over the West Bank during the 1967–88 period also contributed to the fact that the functionalist position was implemented and was never seriously challenged. The territorialist and reconciliationist schools of thought did not regard the functionalist position as detrimental to the peace process in the short run. The functionalist approach was regarded as a convenient interim arrangement until a formal peace treaty was signed. Even the annexationists valued cooperation with Jordan because they hoped that through joint Israeli-Jordanian efforts Palestinian nationalism would be weakened in the territories. The annexationists also regarded the functionalist approach as consonant with Israel's interests in general. As maintained throughout this study, Israel's indecisiveness about withdrawal guided many of its policies during the 1967–88 period. This has resulted in the maintenance of the status quo, which was aimed at conflict management and preservation of de facto peace with Jordan rather than at conflict resolution, which would have necessitated a withdrawal from the territories.

Faced with Israel's indecisiveness, Jordan had no choice but to accept the reality imposed by Israel. Hussein always maintained that the Palestinians and the Jordanians are the same people, part of the East Arab nationalist ideal of which his great-grandfather was the first titular head. Nevertheless, he was often forced by circumstances to pursue a pragmatic approach designed to protect his dynastic power. To enter into an open, public dialogue with Israel (before the Madrid conference), King Hussein needed Arab backing, Palestinian passivity, and, above all, Israeli willingness to return all the territories, including East Jerusalem. In the absence of such willingness Hussein chose to participate in the "functional game" because clearly he had very little to lose by endorsing this approach. He could try to maintain Jordanian influence in the West Bank and, at the same time, engage in a secret dialogue with Israel, hoping that eventually the impasse would be broken and Jordan would regain its lost territory. The fact that neither Jordan's secret meetings with Israel nor Jordanian-Israeli cooperation in the territories was public knowledge allowed Hussein to accept the functionalist approach, albeit by default. Because the king could not get what he really wanted, he settled for second best. The formal state of war with Israel provided Hussein with a patina of "plausible deniability" of contacts with his formal enemies.

Jordan's policy toward Israel and the West Bank has been shaped by a number of factors. First, the historical links between the East and West Bank were extremely important in shaping Jordanian policy after the 1967 war. The removal of Transjordan from the provisions of the British Mandate in 1922 was never fully accepted by Hussein's grandfather, Abdullah, who sought to establish the Kingdom of Greater Syria under his rule. Abdullah was also the first Arab leader who attempted to negotiate a peace agreement with Israel after the 1948 war. Moreover, it was the Arab Legion under Abdullah's leadership that secured the Old City of Jerusalem during the 1948 war and prevented an Israeli takeover of the city.[49] When King Abdullah was murdered in 1951 at the

Al-Aqsa mosque in Jerusalem, Hussein was standing by his grandfather's side. The loss of Jerusalem in 1967, the city that his grandfather secured, has never been fully accepted by Hussein, who has regarded the question of Jerusalem as a top priority.[50] Even after Jordan's administrative and legal disengagement from the West Bank in July 1988, King Hussein remained the protector of the Muslim holy places in Jerusalem. In its peace treaty with Israel, Jordan was granted a "special role in Muslim holy shrines in Jerusalem." Demographic factors also have played a crucial role in shaping Jordanian foreign policy. Because the 1948 war forced seven hundred thousand Palestinians to flee from Palestine to the East and West Banks, Jordan now has a sizable Palestinian population. After the Six-Day War, more than two hundred thousand Palestinian refugees crossed from the West to the East Bank, thus increasing the Palestinian population on the East Bank. The Palestinian population grew further after the Gulf War when approximately three hundred thousand refugees fled to Jordan.

Valerie Yorke, in her 1988 book, *Domestic Politics and Regional Security,* cites Jordanian data which show that only 40 percent of Jordan's population is Palestinian, contrary to the commonly held view that the East Bank Palestinians constitute the majority. She maintains that Jordanian sources claim that Hussein had a vested interest in not revealing the exact number of Palestinians in the East Bank so the Transjordanians would remain loyal to the Hashemite regime.[51] Whereas Hussein's power base rests on the Transjordanians, who are the most loyal to the regime, the Palestinians themselves have been integrated into the mainstream of Jordan's social, political, and economic life. Although Palestinians are not fully represented in key political positions such as the army and security services, they have, nonetheless, acquired a real stake in the continued stability and security of the regime. As long as the final status of the territories has yet to be determined, few desire to jeopardize what has become a second home and risk returning to a precarious situation. The best testimony to the Palestinians' stake in the status quo was their relative noninvolvement in the Jordanian 1970 civil war when Hussein fought the PLO.[52] Although the Jordanian security services kept a close watch on the Palestinians during the war, most of them did not join the PLO in their struggle against the regime. In addition, the king's support of Iraq during the gulf crisis and war has earned him high respect among the Palestinians living in Jordan, most of whom were ardent supporters of Iraq's Hussein. In the wake of the Israel-PLO and Israeli-Jordanian agreements, respectively, East Bank Palestinians are generally supportive of the peace process but uneasy about the slow pace of implementation of the Oslo Accords with the PLO. Some, however, are vocal opponents of the process as a whole, reflecting dissatisfaction among Jordan's professional class that the agreements with Israel did not yield any peace dividends—largely, government promises of foreign aid and investment that did not materialize.

Although the relative stability characterizing the East Bank since 1970 helped foster a distinct Jordanian identity on the East Bank, the close familial, social, and economic ties between the two Banks have been maintained (the West Bank was annexed by Jordan in 1950 and remained under Jordanian sovereignty until 1967). These ties precipitated a high degree of Jordanian and East Bank Palestinian involvement and identification with the West Bank, which was occupied by Israel in 1967. These ties have been facilitated through the open bridges policy, which has allowed travel to and from the West Bank and helped to maintain the strong ties between the two Banks. These ties are exemplified in the idea of the "unity of the two Banks." The West Bank was regarded as part of the Jordanian patrimony, and, as such, Jordan believed it would assume control of it once Israel evacuated the territory. This idea received particular political expression in 1972 when Hussein introduced the United Arab Kingdom Plan. The plan called for an East-West Bank federation and autonomy for West Bank Palestinians who would live under Jordanian rule.

From an economic perspective the loss of the West Bank in 1967 negatively affected the Jordanian economy. East–West Bank trade was an important factor in Jordan's economic life. In addition, the loss of Jerusalem and Bethlehem meant that substantial revenues from tourism were lost.

Third, Jordan's small size and its relative lack of natural resources have placed constraints on its freedom of action. Jordan cannot publicly deviate from the Arab consensus on the Palestine question. Surrounded by powerful neighbors—Syria, Iraq, and Saudi Arabia—Jordan has pursued a pro–status quo–oriented policy in order not to antagonize its neighbors. Before the Gulf War, Jordan relied on economic assistance from Saudi Arabia and the oil-rich gulf states, which limited the kingdom's maneuverability. Therefore, on the question of a formal peace settlement with Israel Jordan abided by the Arab consensus. The only major exception to this position occurred during the gulf crisis and the ensuing war when Jordan supported Iraq largely because many of the Palestinians residing in Jordan and elsewhere identified strongly with the Iraqi leader and because the Jordanian and Iraqi economies are intertwined.[53] Nevertheless, immediately after the war, Jordan joined Syria, Egypt, Lebanon, the Palestinians, and other Arab states in attending the October 1991 Madrid peace conference and the subsequent bilateral and multilateral negotiations with Israel that resulted in the signing of a bilateral peace treaty in October 1994.

Emile Sahliyeh maintains that Jordan's policy toward the West Bank was shaped by the interaction of three different approaches to the problem.[54] The first view argued against the reintegration of the West Bank into Jordan because the continuous support for the Palestinian cause drained Jordan's resources and, above all, because the West Bank Palestinians were anti-Jordanians who could not be trusted. The second approach argued that the Palestinian issue was a Jordanian problem and that disengagement from the West Bank was an unrealistic course of action because of the strong ties between the two Banks. Those who adhered to this approach called for coordination of action with the PLO, which was considered the representative of the Palestinians. Thus, once Israel evacuated the West Bank, a Jordanian-Palestinian confederation consisting of two states ought to be established. A corollary of this view supported Palestinian autonomy in the West Bank in the context of a Jordanian federation as articulated by Hussein in his 1972 United Arab Kingdom proposal. This approach, however, was publicly modified after the 1974 Rabat declaration, which granted the PLO the status of "sole legitimate representative of the Palestinian people." Notions of a Palestinian-Jordanian confederation/federation were revived in 1993 after the Israeli-PLO accord, which called for negotiations about the final status of the West Bank and Gaza to begin in May 1996, thus raising the specter of West-East Bank formal linkage.

The third position maintained that Jordan and the Palestinians could not reach a settlement with Israel by themselves. Adherents to this position mistrusted the PLO and believed that it could not deliver on its promises. Consequently, a pan-Arab approach was recommended whereby a political strategy was to be coordinated with Syria, Israel's most powerful adversary, which could veto a peace settlement if its interests were not met.[55]

Thus, in the 1967–88 period Jordan pursued a dual-track approach in its dealings with Israel, reflecting the constraints on its freedom of action and the ambivalence that characterized its relationship with the Palestinians. Since 1967, when Israel occupied the West Bank, Jordan has faced the dilemma of how to incorporate Palestinian national aspirations within a Jordanian framework without jeopardizing the delicate balance that underlay Hashemite supremacy on the East Bank. Despite the official adherence to the Arab consensus on the need to establish an independent Palestinian state on the West Bank Jordan was extremely uneasy about such a development. An independent Palestinian state might inspire irredentist tendencies among East Bank Palestinians, who would then attempt to destabilize the regime as was the case during the 1970 civil war between the Hashemite monarchy and parts of the PLO.

As part of the first track, between 1967 and 1988, Jordan attempted to check the influence of the PLO in the West Bank by using the open bridges policy, which provided for a link between the two Banks so Jordanian influence could be exerted on the West Bank. The Jordanians had an additional motive in maintaining a modicum of involvement in the West Bank. By aiding the Palestinians in the West Bank, Jordan hoped to stem emigration from the West Bank because it feared that movement of Palestinians to Jordan would undermine the already precarious demographic balance in the East Bank.[56]

The second track entailed consistent involvement in the peace process, attempting to bridge the gaps between the Arab and Israeli positions so a formal peace could be signed. In this context Hussein met secretly with Israeli leaders for hundreds of hours in search of an Israeli agreement to withdraw.[57] Publicly, however, Jordan abided by all Arab League resolutions concerning peace with Israel, and King Hussein was at the forefront of Arab efforts to secure an Israeli withdrawal. This position included active encouragement of all international and, particularly, American efforts to resolve the conflict. Jordan participated in both the Geneva and Madrid international conferences held in 1973 and 1991, respectively. It also took part in the negotiations with Israel after the Madrid conference that culminated in a peace treaty. The only major effort in which Jordan refused to participate was the Camp David process for reasons that are detailed below. Adnan Abu Odeh, Jordan's former minister of information, commenting in 1981 on Jordan's position regarding peace with Israel, noted:

> Jordan continues to believe in the necessity of reaching a peaceful solution to the Middle East crisis. Such a solution must be based on the total withdrawal of Israel from the occupied Arab lands, especially East Jerusalem. In return, reasonable security guarantees acceptable to Israel and the other Arab countries must be provided. Jordan considers such a peaceful solution possible only if the basic issues of the conflict are addressed.[58]

On the question of recognition of Israel, King Hussein declared: "[W]e say this Arab commitment offers mutual recognition of Israeli and Palestinian national rights. To those in the West who seek security for Israel, we say this Arab commitment would guarantee the security of Israel . . . within the context of a final comprehensive peace based on justice for all."[59]

The third part of my argument maintains that functional cooperation, rather than promoting a formal Israeli-Jordanian peace, in fact, contributed to the status quo between 1967 and 1988. It effectively forestalled resolution of the Arab-Israeli conflict because it met the immediate needs of both countries without necessitating an end to the state. Sub-rosa interaction certainly contributed to a quiet border, reduced tensions, and helped foster habits of cooperation between the two formal enemies. But, de facto peace with its eastern neighbor was perceived by Israel's leaders as *yielding the benefits of peace without having to decide on the fate of the occupied territories* and, thus, prolonged the diplomatic status quo. Likewise, Jordan was unwilling to forfeit or expose its clandestine relationship with Israel and engage in a public diplomatic process that would endanger the regime and yield few benefits, given Israel's position vis-à-vis the territories. Neither Israel nor Jordan was willing to take a major risk to open a public dialogue because of the lack of societal consensus in Israel over the question of withdrawal and Jordan's reluctance openly to break Arab ranks over recognition, negotiations, and peace with Israel.

The nature of the two countries' relations, however, was transformed in the wake of the Palestinian *intifadah* and Jordan's July 1988 administrative and legal disengagement from the West Bank. Jordan was no longer the party with whom Israel was expected to negotiate over the Palestinian question. This was left to the PLO. Consequently, Jordan, unburdened by the weighty issue of the West Bank, began to pursue bilateral concerns such as water, refugees, and Israeli withdrawal from Jordanian territories outside the West Bank, a pursuit that culminated in the October 1994 peace treaty.

The Gulf War, the end of the cold war, the demise of the Soviet Union, and the persistence of Secretary of State James Baker in starting an Arab-Israeli dialogue were largely responsible for the Madrid conference and the ensuing bilateral and multilateral talks. The new regional and international climate coupled with Jordan's need to rehabilitate its image as a result of the support it gave to Sadaam Hussein during the Gulf War, propelled the kingdom to enter talks with Israel, initially as part of a joint Jordanian-Palestinian delegation. Israel started the negotiations with the joint team over West Bank autonomy but had no intention of making any significant concessions to the Palestinians. Former Prime Minister Shamir, for instance, admitted that he sought to prolong the negotiations for as long as ten years until the West Bank would be totally populated by Israeli settlers.[60]

This rejectionist position was eclipsed when the Labor Party, led by Yitzhak Rabin, won the June 1992 elections and pursued the negotiations with vigor and flexibility. The Labor Party, after all, is dominated by reconciliationists and territorialists, both of whom are supportive of a peace agreement with Jordan and the Palestinians. The Israeli-PLO Declaration of Principles (DOP) and the Israeli-Jordanian Treaty of Peace are, therefore, part of a new approach toward Arab-Israeli reconciliation.

For Jordan and Israel what was once considered the building blocks of sub-rosa peace—water sharing, joint energy projects, health, and education, to name but a few areas of cooperation—now are the foundations of the de jure peace. Decades of secret functional cooperation are expected to reinforce and galvanize the formal accord. Both sides are now able to capitalize upon a plethora of common practical experiences and refashion the relationship from a clandestine to an open partnership, unlike in the past when Israeli-Jordanian cooperation in effect hindered progress on a formal peace treaty. Full realization of the benefits of Israeli-Jordanian peace, however, still is contingent upon Israel and the PLO agreeing on and implementing a peace treaty, as well as Israel, Lebanon, and Syria concluding peace accords. With the May 1996 victory of the Likud party and the election of Prime Minister Benjamin Netanyahu, the likelihood of reaching such a comprehensive Arab-Israeli peace has decreased considerably, thus diminishing prospects of a warm Israeli-Jordan peace.

2

The Open Bridges Policy

> Israeli [and Palestinian] products are marketed to the largest food transit in Amman. From there, they are sent to other Middle Eastern countries including Iraq, Syria, and the Persian Gulf. . . . The Israeli economy is greatly affected by the price fluctuations in the Amman transit because we are the largest food supplier in the Middle East. . . . Today, Israel exports to Amman 55,000 tons of tomatoes, 72,000 tons of [cooking] oil, 80,000 tons of citrus, and 20,000 tons of vegetables. . . . Regular meetings between Israeli and Jordanian officials are taking place in order to improve marketing techniques and trade routes.[1]

This statement in 1989 by former Israeli Minister of Agriculture Avraham Katz-Oz refers to Israeli exports to the Amman food market as if Israel and Jordan were not in a formal state of war at that time. The movement of goods, people, and capital from Israel and the West Bank to Jordan and vice versa has taken place over the bridges of the Jordan River since the 1967 war. These bridges, which the Israelis called Allenby and Adam, and the Jordanians called King Hussein and Prince Mohammad, have symbolized Israeli and Jordanian functional interaction since 1967. Understanding the origins and subsequent developments of the open bridges policy elucidates the multifaceted dimensions of Israeli and Jordanian policies that have molded economic, social, and political life in the West Bank since 1967. The bridges are the meeting places where the triangular relationship between Israel, Jordan, and West Bank Palestinians is best expressed. Each party has sought to use the open bridges policy to its own advantage. Israel had hoped that by linking the Palestinians in the West Bank with those in the East Bank, a "pressure release valve" would be created that would deflect Palestinian resistance to the Israeli occupation. Through the open bridges Jordan has attempted to reassert its influence in the West Bank by regulating trade, the movement of people, and financial assistance to various institutions. The Palestinians have used the open border as a channel to the Palestinian diaspora and to the Arab world to solicit financial and moral support in their quest for independence and to export goods to Jordan and the Arab world.

Aims of the Policy

What began as illegal crossings by West Bank trucks transporting agricultural products to the East Bank after the 1967 war later became institutionalized by the Israeli government as the open bridges policy. The bridges over the Jordan River were destroyed during the war, and the accumulation of summer crops became a serious problem for West Bank farmers. Defense Minister Dayan permitted Palestinians to cross the river, which was dry during the summer. But the bridges had to be rebuilt for crossings during the rainy winter season.[2] By October 1967, after Israel's coordination with Jordan, the Jordanian military had built two Bailey bridges over the Jordan River.[3]

The aims of the open bridges policy were rooted in Dayan's philosophy vis-à-vis the territories, developed in the wake of the 1967 war. He believed that functional cooperation with Jordan in the West Bank was the best *temporary* policy until a permanent solution was found. He sought to separate the question of ultimate sovereignty over the West Bank from the issues associated with the future of the Israeli military administrative apparatus in the territories. He believed that if the inhabitants of the territories had as much autonomy as possible, a structure of peaceful coexistence would develop between Arabs and Jews.[4] Dayan's initial instructions to the newly appointed military commander of the West Bank were, "Don't set up an Israeli administration. Use the existing Jordanian apparatus. Don't make the same mistake that the Americans made in Vietnam. See to it that the essential services return to normal as quickly as possible, but they must be run by the Arabs themselves."[5]

Dayan, who coined the phrase "living together forever," believed that pragmatic interests rather than ideology would eventually dictate the terms of an Arab-Israeli peace settlement. On the one hand, Dayan viewed the West Bank as part of Israel's biblical heritage. Thus, he regarded Israeli settlements in the West Bank as emanating from Israel's moral right to the territories: "We have returned to the mountains, to the land of our fathers, the land of the Judges, and to the glory of David's kingdom."[6] On the other hand, he opposed Israeli annexation of the territories. Although he understood that Israel was facing an indigenous Palestinian nationalist movement in the territories, he refused to address these aspirations in a territorial context, that is, by returning the West Bank to Jordan or by supporting the establishment of a Palestinian state. He hoped that a solution would evolve naturally out of the daily interaction between the two peoples. This functional solution was based on long-term considerations and did not satisfy the demands put forward by the territorialists, reconciliationists, and annexationists. They agreed to Dayan's policy by default, however, because the Israeli government lacked a political consensus on the future of the territories.

The open bridges policy allowed Jordan to continue to pay salaries to its employees in the West Bank, to subsidize and supervise the education system, and, above all, to prevent entry into the East Bank of any Palestinians suspected of anti-Jordanian activities. Moreover, the Jordanian dinar was allowed to remain as the legal currency along with the Israeli lira (the predecessor of the present shekel). The legal system and the local courts continued to be regulated according to Jordanian law although Israel substantially modified this law through military orders. Above all, it was hoped that "Jordan would continue to exercise the sociopolitical influence it had wielded so effectively during the years of its rule. This entailed preserving the traditional leadership, reinforcing localism, and co-opting newcomers through traditional *hamula* [familial] channels— elements of a political control that Israel as a non-Arab occupier, could not contrive."[7]

From an operational perspective this policy was aimed at achieving a number of objectives. Shlomo Gazit, the government's coordinator of the Territories, notes in his book *ha-Makel veha-gezer* (The carrot and the stick) that the policy had four components. First, it was an attempt to mold Israeli-Palestinian relations in the West Bank. By breaking down the barriers between Israel, the West Bank, and Jordan through trade, transfer of capital, and free movement of people and goods, mutual interests in maintaining a modicum of functional coexistence might develop. The policy also was aimed to break down the psychological wall that had separated Israel and her Arab neighbors since 1948. By allowing the free movement of people, Gazit argues, Israel hoped to allow the population of the Gaza district to reunite with its Palestinian brethren in the East and West Banks, thus giving the Palestinian Gazans a feeling of belonging to a greater Arab entity.

Second, Israel hoped that the open bridges policy would help resolve the problem of Jerusalem. On June 27, 1967, Israel's Knesset proclaimed Jerusalem a single city under Israeli administration and officially announced free access to all the holy places and freedom of worship to people of all religions. By doing so, Israeli policymakers wanted to demonstrate to the inhabitants of East Jerusalem that despite the annexation Arabs could maintain their ties to the East and West Banks. (In reality it was not easy for Arabs outside Israel and the territories to visit Jerusalem.) By breaking down the barriers Israel hoped to send a message to the Palestinians in the West Bank that they could maintain their former life style and still be linked to the Arab world through trade, family visits, and education. In other words, Israel hoped that the policy would become a "pressure release valve" for the Palestinians who were facing the prospects of a prolonged military occupation.

Third, Israel's ability to close the bridges so the Palestinians "would have something to lose" became a powerful instrument in containing anti-Israeli activities on the West Bank. In other words, the open bridges policy was meant to address the problem of a long-term resistance to Israeli rule by the local population. Israel hoped to be able to use the bridges as a "carrot and stick" to deny exit visas and import and export permits to individuals, groups, cities, and regions as a deterrent against anti-Israeli activities.

Fourth, Israel attempted to use the policy as a propaganda tool in the Arab world and abroad. By allowing the free movement of people and goods across the bridges Israel hoped to demonstrate to the world that its occupation policies were benign compared to other occupations in history.[8]

There was an additional motive underlying the open bridges policy. The policy created a golden opportunity for Israel to break the Arab states' boycott of its products. Over the years, Israel used the bridges as a channel for West Bank exports and to market its products in the Arab world. In addition to the bridges, Israel now uses a multiplicity of outlets to market its products to the Arab countries, including its border with Lebanon, and a number of states in Europe. According to Gad Gilbar of Tel Aviv University, Israel exports between $1 billion and $2 billion worth of goods annually to the Arab world, including to such unlikely customers as Iraq, Syria, Libya, Sudan, and the Gulf states.[9] In a sense, Israel broke the boycott by exporting goods to the Arab world. Although neither Israel nor its Arab clients were interested in publicity about this matter, Israeli officials occasionally alluded to it. Chaim Herzog, the first military governor of the West Bank and later president of Israel, noted, for example, in 1970, "We have finally arrived at a situation in which a definite flow of commerce crosses over from the areas under Israeli control to the Arab world and back again, and from Israel itself, too, although I will not say much more about that aspect of it."[10]

With progress in the Arab-Israeli peace process, most Arab states formally relaxed their adherence to the provisions of the boycott. For example, the Gulf Cooperation Council declared in 1994 its intention to ignore the secondary and tertiary aspects (products manufactured by countries that conduct business with Israel) of the Arab boycott. Moreover, the Middle East/North Africa Economic Summit convened in Casablanca, Morocco, in October 1994, declared its intention to move toward ending the Arab boycott altogether. In July 1995 the Jordanian parliament approved a new law that terminated all limitations on trade and economic relations with Israel. This official legislation ended Jordanian participation in the Arab boycott against Israel and paved the way for the October 1995 signing of the bilateral trade agreement.

Each of these five goals was intended, in essence, to ease the problems associated with Israel's military occupation of the West Bank. By allowing a measure of Jordanian involvement in the West Bank Israel hoped that the Palestinian nationalist elements associated with the PLO would not be able to gain the upper hand. Israel and Jordan viewed Jordanian-Palestinian relations in zero-sum terms. If Jordan gained the upper hand in the struggle for the hearts and minds of the West Bank Palestinians, PLO influence would decrease.

Israel's West Bank policy can be divided into five periods: from 1967 to 1977 when the Labor Party was in power; from 1977 to 1984 when the Likud bloc controlled the government; from 1984 to 1988 when a national unity government comprising Likud and Labor was in power; from 1988 to 1993 from the beginning of the *intifadah* until the 1993 signing of the Israel-PLO Declaration of Principles; and since the establishment of the Palestinian Authority and implementation of the Gaza-Jericho agreement in 1994.

During the first period Israel attempted to implement Dayan's principles of "nonintervention" although in numerous instances the military government in the territories exercised a strong hand: removal of the Arab mayor of Jerusalem and other notables, expulsion of the president of Bir Zeit University and the Mufti of Jerusalem, and textbook censorship, among other actions. In 1972 and in 1976 during the first phase of occupation two municipal elections were held in the West Bank. Both elections were held in accordance with Jordanian law although the law was amended in 1976 to allow women to vote.[11] The three principles of Israeli military rule were enunciated by the defense ministry in *Three Years of Military Government, 1967–1970:* nonvisibility, nonintervention, and open bridges.

> Every sign of Israeli rule—buildings of the military administration, the Israeli flag, a sign posted on the building of the military headquarters—could constitute a source of friction [with the Palestinian population] and could result in clashes between the population and the [Israeli] authorities. The policy that was decided was unequivocal—whenever possible—no visibility should be attained. A military and foreign rule, if it is not felt and seen, is easier to live with. In principle, the aspiration of the administration was that an Arab from the area could be born in a hospital, receive his birth certificate, grow up, get educated, get married, raise children and grandchildren—he could do all this, without the need to rely even on one

> Israeli person. . . . Except for areas that could have a direct impact
> on Israel (health or economic activity that could negatively affect
> the Israeli economy)—the military administration does not interfere
> and does not want to force development on the population against
> its will. . . . The third area . . . is the policy of the military adminis-
> tration that little harm could be caused by renewing contacts be-
> tween the Arabs of the territories and the surrounding Arab states.[12]

Of the three principles of nonvisibility, noninterference, and open bridges, only the last principle was upheld after 1977. By 1977 it had become apparent that Dayan's nonintervention policy was incompat-ible with the realities of military occupation and Israel's interests— establishment of new facts intended to integrate much of the West Bank's infrastructure, such as the road system, water supply, electrical grid, and trade and commerce with Israel.[13] Moreover, during the first tenure of the Likud between 1977 and 1984 numerous new Jewish settlements were established in the West Bank. Until 1977 there were 4,200 settlers in 36 settlements, mostly in the area designated under the Allon Plan. By June 1981 the number had risen to 30,000 settlers in more than 100 settlements.[14] By 1986 there were 60,500 settlers in 118 settlements.[15] By 1991 there were 98,500 Israeli settlers in the West Bank, excluding East Jerusalem.[16] In 1995 that number had increased to more than 140,000.

Between 1977 and 1984, particularly after the second Likud victory of 1981, a strong anti-Jordanian attitude characterized Israeli policy in the territories. This policy was associated with the 1982 appointment of Menachem Milson as the head of the newly established civilian adminis-tration. Milson attempted to cultivate the Village Leagues as an alterna-tive West Bank leadership. Under Likud an Israeli interventionist policy attempted to control every aspect of life in the West Bank and encour-aged the growing assertiveness of the Israeli settler population.[17] This policy was manifested in frequent issuing of military orders that regulated life in the territories. Raja Shehadeh, a Palestinian lawyer, calculated that between 1967 and 1988 more than twelve hundred military orders were issued.[18]

During the third period, from 1984 to 1988, Israel and Jordan closely coordinated their policies and attempted to combat the growing influ-ence of the PLO by trying to establish a Jordanian-Israeli condominium. This attempt failed, however, when the Palestinian uprising began.

The intifadah that started in December 1987 was a direct response to a host of factors. First, the strong interventionist policies Israel pursued in attempting to regulate all spheres of Palestinian life in the territories backfired. "Creeping annexation" was best exemplified by the establish-ment of Jewish settlements that led to constant friction between the

Israelis and Palestinians; the takeover of land and water resources and the linking of roads to those in Israel; control of marketing and agriculture; and special benefits to Israeli investors in the territories. Second, the peripherialization of the West Bank and Gaza economies did not give the Palestinians a stake in the maintenance of the status quo. Third, the attempts to establish a Jordanian-Israeli condominium, in effect, brought the Palestinians closer to the PLO rather than alienating West Bank Palestinians from the PLO. Fourth, the Arab world was preoccupied with the Iran-Iraq war and, hence, did not pay much attention to the plight of the Palestinians in the West Bank. The Arab world's ambivalence toward the Palestinians was demonstrated during the Arab League's November 1987 summit convened in Amman. The deliberations during the summit and the final communiqué deemphasized the Palestinian question.[19] The Palestinians regarded the summit's outcome as evidence of the Arab world's neglect and, thus, felt that they ought to pursue an independent course of action. Fifth, West Bank Palestinians viewed the manner in which the Shiite population of southern Lebanon resisted Israeli occupation of Lebanon after the 1982 war as having direct application to the West Bank. In other words, the Palestinians believed that Israel withdrew from Lebanon because of the large number of casualties it suffered. Consequently, the Palestinians hoped that an uprising would increase the pressure on Israel to reassess its West Bank policies and begin to negotiate the final status of the territories. Once the uprising began, Jordan realized that it could not attain its dream of regaining the West Bank. It also feared that the uprising would spread to the East Bank as well. Therefore, on July 31, 1988, King Hussein announced that Jordan would disengage from the West Bank.

The Emerging Economic Policy

Israel's economic policy vis-à-vis the territories after 1967 was predicated on a number of factors. As Larry L. Fabian notes:

> every Israeli cabinet since 1967, while insisting that there would be no return to the June 1967 borders, has decided not to decide the political future of the West Bank and Gaza Strip. But government policy, including economic policy, was grounded on three understandings. Israel would not formally annex the territories, Israel could not withdraw from them. And Israel would not allow them to become a net budget burden.[20]

The West Bank economic policy was debated in two specially designated forums. The first, the Va'adat ha-Mankalim (Directors Committee), was formally appointed on June 25, 1967. Initially, it was composed of the directors-general of the ministries of finance, agriculture, interior, trade and industry, and representatives of the defense ministry and the general staff. Later, representatives of other ministries joined the committee.[21] The committee was headed by Ya'akov Arnon, the director-general of the ministry of finance. The second committee, the Va'adat ha-Sarim le-Kalkala (Ministerial Committee for Economics), was headed by Pinhas Sapir, minister of finance. The Directors Committee requested the Economic Planning Authority at the prime minister's office to prepare a study on alternative economic policies in the territories.[22] The report examined three different economic scenarios. The first was a complete integration of the West Bank and Israeli economies with no restrictions on trade, factors of production, and labor. The second was the total segregation of the two economies. The third called for maintaining separate economies while conducting trade between Israel and the West Bank, including allowing a selective movement of labor from the territories to work inside Israel.[23] Additionally, the committee asked a number of Israeli economists from various universities to submit their recommendations to the committee.[24] The committee of experts based its recommendations on two assumptions: that the aim of Israel's overall policy was to raise the level of West Bank economic activity to the status quo ante and that the standard of living of the Palestinian population should approximate the prewar level. The committee's main recommendations included, inter alia, the following: "We recommend the creation of free trade in goods and services while maintaining full control of labor movement between Israel and the administered territories. . . . As part of this free trade regime, we recommend the use of the Israeli lira as the only legal currency in the administered territories."[25]

In the absence of a political consensus regarding the final status of the territories, however, the Israeli government failed to produce a coherent economic policy toward the West Bank and Gaza and refused to adopt the recommendations of the committee of experts.[26] Five years after submitting the committee's report, Michael Bruno, the chair of the committee, complained about the lack of a coherent Israeli economic policy vis-à-vis the territories. In the report Bruno and his colleagues called for the infusion of government funds to create an economic infrastructure for the West Bank. Yet this recommendation was not carried out.

The most vocal opposition to the development of an infrastructure in the territories came from Finance Minister Pinhas Sapir, whose opposition to the retention of the territories was based on economic considerations: "The addition of a million Arabs means, in effect, that we would take on ourselves a fifth task as if we are not burdened enough with the problems of defense, absorption of immigrants, closing the gaps between rich and poor, and developing the economy. Some among us are now demanding the "absorption of Aliyah" [ascent or immigration to Israel] of a million Arabs with all its implications."[27]

As time passed, the economic development of a Palestinian infrastructure was neglected by Israeli policymakers. Israeli fears that the West Bank would become an economic burden did not materialize. Instead, the territories became an enormous *political* burden.

The economies of Israel, the West Bank, and Gaza were interdependent, supplying cheap Palestinian labor to Israel's economy and providing a market for Israeli products in the territories.[28]

Undoubtedly, the standard of living for the Palestinian population rose considerably after 1967. The gross domestic product (GDP) for both the West Bank and Gaza grew at an average annual rate of 15 percent between 1968 and 1972; 9 percent between 1973 and 1976; 7 percent between 1977 and 1980; and 4 percent between 1981 and 1986.[29] The gross national product per capita (GNPPC) also rose considerably from $552 in 1968 to $1,880 in 1987 although it dropped in 1991 to $1,715 as a result of severe disruptions from the Gulf War and several closures imposed by the Israeli military.[30]

In a 1993 study the World Bank distinguishes between four phases in the growth pattern of the occupied territories since 1967: meteoric growth until the mid-1970s; deceleration to the early 1980s; followed by stagnation until 1987 when the intifadah erupted; and decline thereafter.[31] The initial increase in the economic growth of the territories was largely the result of the significant number of Palestinians working in Israel and remittances sent by Palestinians employed in the Gulf region. For example, in 1970, of 114,300 employed persons, 14,300 worked in Israel. By 1986 the labor force had risen to 167,000, 51,000 of whom were employed in Israel, an increase of 37 percent.[32] After the outbreak of the intifadah, however, the number of Palestinians working in Israel decreased significantly. Following several Palestinian suicide attacks inside Israel in 1996, Israel placed severe travel restrictions on Palestinian laborers. A lengthy closure of all the territories prevented Palestinians from traveling to Israel at all. Only in July 1996, following the election of Benjamin Netanyahu in May, was the closure partially lifted, but the number of Palestinians working inside Israel has been reduced dramatically.

The rise in the Palestinian standard of living was largely the result of the extensive acquisition of household items such as appliances. For example, between 1970 and 1991 household ownership of refrigerators (mostly purchased second or third hand) increased from 11 to 85 percent.[33] But only 2 percent of West Bank localities had proper sewerage, and most Palestinians did not have telephones.[34]

The data about the Palestinian standard of living are somewhat problematic. Israeli as well as Palestinian data must be consulted when determining the economic status of the occupied territories or the Palestinians' standard of living. Life under military occupation resulted in serious economic dislocations for the Palestinians on the individual and macro levels. The overall economic infrastructure of the territories, as noted throughout this work, remained gravely underdeveloped as a result of conscious Israeli policies.

Trade with Jordan

Estimates vary about the role of the West Bank in Jordan's prewar economy.[35] Eliyahu Kanovsky argues that Jordan's loss of the West Bank had a minimal economic impact because the Jordanian government's prewar allocation of economic resources was directed at the East rather than the West Bank.[36] He notes, for example, that 80 percent of Jordan's main crop, wheat, was in the East Bank. Israel's occupation of the West Bank, however, resulted in a considerable loss of fertile land.[37] Fouad Hamadi Basayso notes additional effects on the Jordanian economy. In 1966, for example, the West Bank's population reached 981,000, about 47 percent of the total Jordanian population. Additionally, before 1967 80–90 percent of Jordan's tourist income came from tourism to the West Bank; in 1966 revenues for tourism and remittances from West Bankers working abroad reached 68 percent of the total revenues of exported services. Basayso also notes that the West Bank had been a market for industrial products, oil, cement, and textiles.[38]

Based on his research Kanovsky concluded that "from an economic point of view, the pressure on Jordan to reach a political settlement with Israel [was] nowhere as strong as with Egypt [which lost the oil fields in Sinai]."[39] He then concluded that Jordan would eventually recover from the economic loss of the West Bank. During the 1970s Jordan developed the agriculture of the Jordan valley, which became the agricultural center of the East Bank. Moreover, because after the 1967 war trade with the West Bank continued without interruption through the open bridges policy, the initial shock waves experienced by Jordan after the war were absorbed.

In 1966 the West Bank's exports to the East Bank and other countries (see table 2.1) amounted to 4,300,000 Jordanian dinars (or $15,351,000 based on the exchange rate of $0.357 to the dinar) of which 77.9 percent were agricultural products and 22.1 percent were industrial goods. By 1987 total West Bank exports amounted to $251.9 million, $63.4 of which

Table 2.1

West Bank Exports by Commodity Types, 1966

EXPORTS	THOUSANDS OF DINARS	PERCENTAGE
Agricultural Products		
To the East Bank	1,600	47.8
To Other Countries	1,750	52.2
Total	3,350	100.0[a]
Industrial Products		
To the East Bank	400	42.1
To Other Countries	550	57.9
Total	950	100.0[b]
Grand Total	4,300	100.0

[a] 77.9 percent of the total.
[b] 22.1 percent of the total.
Source: State of Israel, Prime Minister's Office, Economic Planning Authority, *Ha-Gada ha-Ma'aravit: skira klalit* (The West Bank: A general overview) (Jerusalem, 1967), p. Gimel-4.

were exported to the East Bank. Exports included olive oil, samna (liquid margarine), dairy products, soap, and building stones.[40] Jordanian imports in 1966 totaled 68 million Jordanian dinars ($243 million) of which the West Bank imports totaled 20 million Jordanian dinars ($71.4 million).[41] West Bank imports from Jordan in 1987 were $8.7 million of a total of $709 million in imports, or 8 percent. Imports included paper, printed material, films, textiles, and cotton goods.[42]

The West Bank's trade with Jordan between 1967 and 1993 was influenced by a number of factors. First, West Bank products could not be easily exported into Israel because of Israel's protection of its homeland agriculture. Second, Israel became the West Bank's main trading partner although most of the trade was in one direction with the West Bank importing mostly from Israel (see table 2.2). Of $709 million in total imports in 1987 the West Bank imported $650.6 million from Israel. The West Bank's trade imbalance between 1968 and 1987 totaled over $3.13 billion, indicating a severe dependence on Israel for imports. Third, Jordan imposed a number of import restrictions on West Bank trade, including a limit of 50 percent of the total estimated agricultural production; only trucks that were registered before 1967 were allowed to cross the bridges into Jordan.[43] In addition, the Arab boycott of Israeli products stipulated that raw materials that were either

Table 2.2

Import and Export of Goods: *The West Bank*

(millions of dollars)

Year	TRADE WITH JORDAN			TOTAL[a]		
	Imports	Exports	Balance	Imports	Exports	Balance
1968	5.1	14.7	9.6	51.3	27.5	−23.8
1969	7.1	18.4	11.3	63.9	31.1	−32.8
1970	3.6	13.8	10.2	64.9	30.5	−34.4
1971	3.8	18.8	15.0	75.8	40.2	−35.6
1972	4.5	25.5	21.0	98.4	51.5	−46.9
1973	3.9	15.8	11.9	132.3	57.8	−74.5
1974	4.8	26.2	21.4	192.1	89.7	−102.4
1975	5.0	34.7	29.7	230.1	109.0	−121.1
1976	3.7	42.6	38.9	247.8	123.2	−124.6
1977	4.7	43.8	39.1	266.5	118.4	−148.1
1978	5.0	61.6	56.6	250.9	140.8	−110.1
1979	5.0	57.9	52.9	348.1	148.0	−200.1
1980	5.5	76.0	70.5	403.7	189.0	−214.7
1981	7.3	74.2	66.9	427.7	205.2	−222.5
1982	8.9	90.5	81.6	418.5	200.6	−217.9
1983	6.8	65.9	59.1	452.7	201.0	−251.7
1984	8.2	83.5	75.3	406.8	184.5	−222.3
1985	8.7	69.3	60.6	386.5	166.4	−220.1
1986	10.9	81.8	70.9	512.0	238.6	−273.4
1987	8.7	63.4	54.7	709.0	251.9	−457.1
Total	121.2	978.4	857.2	5,739.0	2,604.9	−3,134.1

[a] Including trade with Israel, Jordan, and other countries.

Sources: State of Israel, Central Bureau of Statistics, *National Accounts of Judea, Samaria and Gaza Area, 1967–1986* (Jerusalem: Central Bureau of Statistics, 1988), 137; Israel, Central Bureau of Statistics, *Judea, Samaria and Gaza Area Statistics* 18, no. 1 (Mar. 1988): 6.

partially or totally processed in Israel or were imported through Israeli intermediaries and facilities were prohibited.[44] Fourth, Israel also imposed a number of restrictions on West Bank exports to Jordan. The trucks that transported the products to the East Bank were especially remodeled so Israeli inspection officers at the border could easily inspect them.

Moreover, Israel also imposed custom duties on imports from Jordan, which were added to Jordanian custom duties imposed on exports

Table 2.3

West Bank Trade with Jordan by Commodity Type

(percentage)

	IMPORTS			EXPORTS		
Year	Agricultural Products	Industrial Products	Total	Agricultural Products	Industrial Products	Total
1968	73.0	27.0	100	48.4	51.6	100
1969	68.2	31.8	100	43.0	57.0	100
1970	40.3	59.7	100	52.4	47.6	100
1971	35.7	64.3	100	36.7	63.3	100
1972	20.9	79.1	100	49.1	50.9	100
1973	25.0	75.0	100	52.1	47.9	100
1974	15.4	84.6	100	49.9	50.1	100
1975	14.9	85.1	100	54.0	46.0	100
1976	6.0	94.0	100	28.5	71.5	100
1977	5.8	94.2	100	48.6	51.4	100
1978	5.0	95.0	100	42.2	57.8	100
1979	7.1	92.9	100	63.1	26.9	100
1980	7.1	92.9	100	71.7	28.3	100
1981	3.6	96.4	100	31.9	68.1	100
1982	4.8	95.2	100	33.4	66.6	100
1983	3.7	96.3	100	33.9	50.1	100
1984	1.0	99.0	100	40.1	59.9	100
1985	3.9	96.1	100	46.8	43.2	100
1986	1.4	98.6	100	29.0	71.0	100
1987	0.2	99.8	100	34.7	65.3	100

Sources: Derived from State of Israel, Central Bureau of Statistics, *Judaea, Samaria and Gaza Area Statistics* (various issues); Arie Bergman, *The Economy of the Administered Areas, 1974–1975* (Jerusalem: Bank of Israel, Research Department, 1976), 51; Raphael Meron, *Economic Development in Judea: Samaria and the Gaza District, 1970–80* (Jerusalem: Bank of Israel, Research Department, 1983), 58–59.

to the West Bank. Clearly, West Bank–Jordanian trade was influenced by Israeli and Jordanian policies. Jordan remains an important market for West Bank products. Jordan's control over the flow of goods from the West Bank to its territory has not prevented the West Bank from maintaining a positive trade balance with Jordan (see table 2.3). Israeli policies were, however, the detrimental factor that shaped the fate of the West Bank economy. The West Bank served as a satellite of the Israeli economy, providing cheap manual labor and an outlet for Israeli goods.

The Palestinian uprising somewhat altered this pattern. The flow of labor from the territories into Israel was greatly curtailed by Israeli restrictions on movement and the refusal of many Palestinians to come to work in Israel on a regular basis. Israeli exports to the territories also decreased because many Palestinians boycotted Israeli products. Moreover, since the implementation of Palestinian self-rule and because of several suicide attacks by Palestinians against Israelis in 1994 and 1995, Israel placed additional restrictions on Palestinian laborers entering Israel and even began to import guest workers from several countries such as Thailand and Romania.

Since 1967 all Israeli governments have claimed credit for improving the Palestinian standard of living. For example, in *An Eighteen Year Survey of Judea, Samaria and the Gaza District*, the Defense Ministry boasted that

> the administration diligently develops services for the welfare of the population and encourages local and external services for the welfare of the population, and encourages local and external initiatives in the economy and the development of new projects—this, of course, provided that there is no such conflict with the security and economic interests of Israel. Where no such conflict exists, there is total and unrestricted freedom of movement.[45]

Yet the West Bank could be described as structurally underdeveloped and peripheralized. This situation was largely the result of Israeli policies but also of the lack of infrastructural development under Jordanian rule before 1967.[46] Israeli economic planners ascribed the West Bank's trade deficit with Israel not to Israeli policies but to indigenous factors. For example, a Bank of Israel report said that "the sizable gap between imports and exports of goods, and the high share of industrial goods in total imports stems, among other things, from the paucity of natural resources, from a low level of technology in the production of intermediate inputs, from the absence of local inputs for industrial products, and from an archaic production system."[47]

As discussed earlier, various recommendations for an Israeli economic policy that could have helped to create an infrastructure were not followed. Clearly, from a purely economic point of view the economic status quo that prevailed in the West Bank in the 1967–88 period suited Israel's interests well. From a Palestinian perspective the outlet to the East Bank, albeit limited, was an important way to maintain a degree of economic activity.

There are no data on exports from Israel proper to Jordan because such data were considered a state secret. Now that the two countries have signed a peace treaty, open trade is encouraged, albeit, it still is very limited. Before 1993 Israel, however, maintained an extensive export program to Jordan and the Arab world. Israeli Minister of Agriculture Avraham Katz-Oz estimated in 1987 that his country had exported about $1 billion in goods to Jordan and the Arab world annually.[48] This revelation by the minister led to strong protests by Israeli farmers who accused the minister of jeopardizing a vital trade link. In a letter to the editor of *Yediot Aharonot* an Israeli farmer wrote: "I do not know how much you [the minister] know about agriculture, but you do not understand a thing in international trade. With one slip of the tongue, you have destroyed what others have built for years."[49] In another episode Israeli Minister of Science Gideon Pat estimated that Israel annually exports $500 million in goods to Jordan. He said that Jordanian dinars flow into the West Bank where they are converted into Israeli shekels. The shekels are used to buy Israeli goods that are transported across the open bridges to Jordan.[50] Eliyahu Kanovsky, an expert on the Jordanian economy, speculated that although the figure of $1 billion worth of annual exports to Jordan might be exaggerated, Israel had marketed its products to Jordan. Because the official Israeli *Statistical Abstract of Israel* does not contain any references to trade with the Arab world (except for the West Bank's trade with Jordan), it is probable that trade with the Arab world is included under the ambiguous category "trade with other countries," which does not specify the destination of Israeli exports.

Other examples of previous direct trade include a 1974 sale of high-quality sheep each capable of yielding 200 liters of milk annually compared with the 30–40 liter yield of the average Jordanian sheep.[51] In addition to selling Israeli irrigation technology to Jordan (see chap. 3) Israel also exported a variety of animals and products, including potatoes, fruits, biscuits, textiles, peanuts, sandals, soap, and horses.[52] Moreover, in a study at Tel Aviv University researchers claim that Israel gave Jordan aerial photographs of crop areas in the West Bank and Gaza as part of their functional cooperative activities in the sphere of agriculture.[53]

With the signing of the 1994 Israeli-Jordanian Treaty of Peace the two sides began to negotiate a trade agreement that would govern all commercial ties between them. The agreement, signed on October 25, 1995, culminated nearly one year of negotiations. It established a protocol in which the two sides agreed to work toward removing all trade barriers, boycotts of goods, and economic discrimination. In addition, preferential treatment was granted to a list of products. Israel agreed to give preferences to most Jordanian industrial products, including cement, furniture, foodstuffs, antennas, pharmaceuticals, toys, and other products. Jordan agreed to give import preference to Israeli products, including plywood, tires, foodstuffs, pharmaceuticals, electronic compo-

Table 2.4
Arrivals and Departures: *Jordan River Bridges, 1968–1986*

Year	ARRIVALS Residents	ARRIVALS Visitors	DEPARTURES Residents	DEPARTURES Visitors
1968	183,495	26,482	203,477	23,411
1969	100,766	5,486	59,386	6,719
1970	75,990	3,561	77,524	3,885
1971	79,589	91,474	79,758	88,356
1972	144,504	152,467	157,922	144,796
1973	209,595	111,942	204,107	110,231
1974	240,411	123,958	253,687	120,979
1975	275,074	119,562	276,859	119,606
1976	291,584	119,843	306,414	119,344
1977	302,338	131,383	313,270	126,378
1978	314,027	137,220	327,566	131,512
1979	337,776	130,062	354,264	126,842
1980	342,003	109,642	360,627	108,255
1981	385,257	110,656	404,704	109,331
1982	350,339	61,843	361,985	57,573
1983	315,674	65,056	319,010	60,222
1984	347,287	68,692	355,671	66,968
1985	326,357	50,509	336,541	61,693
1986	294,923	45,862	312,983	45,664
Total	4,916,989	1,665,700	5,065,755	1,631,765

Sources: State of Israel, Central Bureau of Statistics, *Administered Territories Statistical Abstract Quarterly; Judaea, Samaria and Gaza Area Statistics; Statistical Abstract of Israel,* (various issues).

nents, medical equipment, communication equipment, locks and safes, and other goods. The agreement took into account the disparities between the two economies as it attempted to preserve local industries. Special preference was given to those products that did not compete with Jordanian industry, such as tires, plywood, and so on.[54]

Travel Across the Bridges

An important component of the open bridges policy was the movement of people across the Jordan River. Between 1968 and 1993, 17,744,410 individuals crossed the bridges in both directions (see tables 2.4, 2.5).

Table 2.5

Arrivals and Departures: *Jordan River Bridges,*
1987–1993

YEAR	ARRIVALS AND DEPARTURES
1987	921,983
1988	522,294
1989	565,858
1990	660,868
1991	474,043
1992	600,556
1993	900,599
Total	4,464,201

Source: Israel Information Service (on-line), "Israel and the Territories: The Jordan Bridges," February 1994. Available by
e-mail: Gopher israel-info.gov.il

The bridges became a major port of entry for both Israel and Jordan.
Travel across the bridges was restricted to residents of the West Bank
and Gaza, tourists from the Arab world who had relatives in the territories, regular tourists, and Israeli Muslims who traveled to Mecca for their
annual Hajj, or pilgrimage.[55] Until 1993 Israeli Jews were forbidden to
travel to Jordan because of the existing state of war between the two
countries, but since the signing of the Jordanian-Israeli peace treaty
Israelis and Jordanians cross the border with very few restrictions. As of
August 1, 1995, Israelis can travel to Jordan via two border-crossing
points that were opened to traffic after the bilateral peace treaty was
signed: in the north, the Shaikh Hussein crossing located south of the
Sea of Galilee and the southern Arava border crossing located north of
Eilat and Aqaba. Travelers are allowed to cross the border with their
private vehicles. The Israeli-Jordanian transportation agreement signed
on July 9, 1995, also provides for the opening of uninterrupted passenger
bus service between several destinations in both counries. Before the
agreement was signed, travelers were required to switch busses at the
border. Bus lines now connect Tel Aviv and Amman, Haifa and Irbid,
Acre and Zarka, Eilat and Aqaba, and Nazareth to Amman and Irbid.
The agreement also permits commercial trucks to transport shipments
between the two countries and between the territories and Jordan.[56]

Since 1968 Israel has allowed visits of citizens from Arab countries
into the territories. In many cases these tourists also visit Israel. Usually,
these visitors come during the summer months. In 1981 Israel prohibited

tourists who entered Israel via the bridges from leaving the same way. This move was intended to protect the Israeli national airline El Al from competition by the Jordanian airline Alia, which had offered lower fares than had the airlines flying to Israel.[57] Once the regulations went into effect, the number of tourists crossing the bridges from Jordan decreased substantially. Hence, in October 1982 the Israeli government reinstated its previous policy.[58] Tourists coming from Jordan to Israel, including visitors from the Arab world, comprised about 10 percent of the total number of tourists who came to Israel in 1985, an important source of revenue for the Israeli tourist industry. Because of the importance of tourism, both countries coordinated their efforts on this issue in several instances. For example, *Ha'aretz* reported that in June 1988 a group of Jordanian travel agents visited Israel to discuss tour packages that would include visits to Israel, Jordan, and Egypt. The Jordanians had to come to Israel because coordination through East Jerusalem travel agencies was no longer feasible after the Palestinian uprising.[59]

Since the fall of 1993, after the signing of the Jordanian-Israeli agenda, several delegations of Jordanian tour operators visited Israel to negotiate tourist packages to both countries in anticipation of the lifting of travel restrictions. As a symbol of the changing relationship between the two countries, in August 1994 King Hussein, an accomplished pilot, flew a Jordanian jetliner through Israeli airspace escorted by Israeli air force F-15 fighters while he talked on the radio with Prime Minister Yitzhak Rabin.

El Al and the Royal Jordanian Airlines are actively planning several joint ventures, including the formation of a regional air charter service to Tel Aviv, Jerusalem, Amman, and Petra. The Jordanian airline was granted permission to fly over Israel en route to Europe. In return, Israeli civilian aircraft now fly over Jordan and the Gulf states en route to the Far East. On April 7, 1996, the Royal Jordanian Airline's subsidiary Royal Wings inaugurated its first direct flight from Amman to Tel Aviv. Israel's El Al began flying to Amman in late April 1996.

In the past, restrictions on the movement of people and goods were imposed by both parties. Israel sometimes, as punishment, banned groups of individuals (mostly young people) or people from specified areas, towns, and villages from traveling to Jordan.[60] The military government ruled that West Bank residents in their twenties and thirties could not return home until nine months from the date of their departures. People who did not return within three years lost their right to reside on the West Bank.[61] All these measures were taken to encourage young Palestinians to emigrate. In addition, those who were classified as "undesirable" could not enter the West Bank.[62] Between 1983 and 1985 Jordan prevented young Palestinians from staying in Jordan for more than one month in order to prevent emigration.[63]

In 1980, after thirteen years of inactivity, Jordan decided to reopen its passport offices in the West Bank so passports could be issued and renewed. The offices are located within the various Chambers of Commerce and the municipalities. But in the wake of Jordan's 1988 decision to disengage from the West Bank certain restrictions were placed on those holding Jordanian passports. These passports became valid for two years instead of the normal five years.

In the Jericho-Gaza agreement Israel and the PLO agreed that the Palestinian National Authority would be authorized to issue travel documents that had both "laisser passer" and "passports" written on them. Thus, Israel's concerns that the travel documents not become a symbol of Palestinian sovereignty and the PLO's insistence that it issue the documents were addressed simultaneously by the use of both titles.

The Pilgrimage to Mecca (Hajj)

West Bank Palestinian Muslims who want to travel to Mecca, Saudi Arabia, face few difficulties in crossing the bridges in their annual pilgrimages. Until 1978, however, Israeli Muslims had to travel to Mecca via a third country such as Cyprus.[64] By 1977 Saudi Arabia had given permission to Israel's Muslim population (within the pre-1967 boundaries) to travel to Mecca.[65] Travel by land also required Jordanian consent for Israeli citizens to cross the bridges en route to Saudi Arabia. The only condition stipulated by the Israeli Ministry of Interior was that for security reasons only those over the age of thirty-five could make the journey.

The crossing of Israeli Arabs over the bridges began in 1978 and has lasted ever since. Between 1978 and 1988, of 41,567 applications submitted to the Israeli ministry, 39,290 were approved (see table 2.6). The pilgrims receive an exit visa valid for one month, and all travel arrangements are handled by a private travel agency.

In March 1995 Israel's religious affairs minister announced that his ministry had completed new arrangements to enable Israeli Muslims to travel to Mecca. These included dropping the limitations on age and the number of pilgrims and instituting a special registration procedure. Those with valid Israeli passports would be allowed to cross the Jordanian-Saudi border.

Capital Movement Across the Bridges

The transfer of funds from the East to the West Bank has been an important component of Jordan's strategy to maintain its influence in

Table 2.6

Israeli Muslim Pilgrimage to Mecca

YEAR	APPLICATIONS SUBMITTED	APPLICATIONS APPROVED
1978	2,450	2,438
1979	4,350	2,435
1980	4,702	4,688
1981	4,302	4,276
1982	2,563	2,554
1983	4,019	3,989
1984	2,295	2,260
1985	3,166	2,994
1986	3,405	3,381
1987	4,687	4,661
1988	5,638	5,614
Total	41,567	39,290

Source: Letter to author by Yoseph Tov, deputy director of Population Administration, Israel, Ministry of Interior, Jerusalem, Aug. 22, 1988. Reasons were not given as to why some of the applications were not approved by the Israeli authorities.

the West Bank. The movement of capital forms the third leg in the triad that comprises the open bridges policy along with trade and the movement of people. In the West Bank, as elsewhere, money and political influence go hand in hand. Therefore, since 1967 Israel and Jordan have used money both as a political weapon and as an incentive to co-opt or punish the Palestinians. Israel has tried to control the flow of funds to the territories as part of its attempt to contain the influence of the PLO. At times, particularly when the Likud was in power, it also prevented Jordanian funds from entering the territories. After the Palestinian uprising, which started in December 1987, Israel tried to curtail the flow of capital into the territories. Also, after the uprising, the number of Palestinians who work in Israel decreased substantially. Thus, reliance on outside sources of funds has become extremely important. Some Israeli leaders believed that the best way to stop the intifadah was by interrupting the flow of funds to the West Bank. This attempt did not succeed.

In addition to Jordan, a variety of sources funnel funds into the territories, including Arab, private, governmental, nongovernmental, and private voluntary organizations.[66] Of these various sources, Jordan was the most important provider of capital to the West Bank before the signing of the Declaration of Principles, after which the World Bank, International Monetary Fund, and several countries, including the United States, the European Union, and Japan committed to providing monetary and economic aid. The most salient Jordanian institutions that provided assistance to the territories before Jordan's disengagement were:

1. *Supreme Committee for Occupied Territory Affairs.* This policy-planning body, established in 1980, was responsible for the formulation of economic, administrative, and social policies in the West Bank. It was abolished in 1987 in the wake of the disengagement.

2. *Ministry of Occupied Territories Affairs.* Established in 1980, this ministry was responsible for coordinating all activities related to Jordan's involvement in the West Bank. After the disengagement, this ministry was abolished.

3. *Jerusalem Committee.* This consultative group consisted of experts and dignitaries whose main task was to report to and advise the government on all issues concerning Jerusalem.

4. *Joint Jordanian-PLO Committee.* This committee was established after the 1978 summit in Baghdad to support the "steadfastness of the Palestinian people." The committee's work was suspended after the Jordanian-PLO rift in 1986. The committee disbursed funds to individuals and institutions in the territories.[67] Most of the funds coming from Jordan covered wages and pensions of Jordanian civil servants, rent paid on government premises, subsidies to municipalities, guarantees on bank loans to public institutions, direct grants, education, and health services.[68]

Before the establishment of the Joint Committee in 1978, Jordan had a free hand in selecting the individuals and institutions it wished to support. But after the Baghdad summit, with the establishment of the Joint Committee, Jordan was required to obtain the approval of the PLO for money spent in the West Bank. Although the Joint Committee was an important channel to transfer funds to the West Bank, Jordan was able to bypass the committee and directly subsidize its supporters. This way it did not have to depend on the PLO, which would have limited its freedom of action. This was done through the Awqaf, or Supreme Muslim Council, located in East Jerusalem.[69] According to Jordanian law, the council is responsible for all Islamic property in the West Bank. The Awqaf owns fifteen thousand dunams of land, one thousand mosques, and hundreds of stores, and it has a large staff responsible for the maintenance of the mosques. By transferring money directly to the Awqaf, Jordan was able to support its clients without having to rely on the PLO.[70] After Jordan severed legal and administrative

Table 2.7

Distribution of Money Changers in the West Bank,
April 1986

TOWN	NUMBER OF MONEY CHANGERS
Nablus	64
Jerusalem	34
Ramallah	22
Bethlehem & Bet Sahour	22
Tulkarem	15
Qalqiliya	14
Hebron	7
Jericho	2
Total	196

Source: UNCTAD, *The Palestinian Financial Sector under Israeli Occupation*
UNCTAD/ST/SEU3, July 1987, 78. Before 1967 only forty-two money
changers were in the West Bank.

ties from the West Bank, the Awqaf became Jordan's main representative
in the territories.

The Chamber of Commerce, another important institution that was
directly linked to Amman, had eight branches in various West Bank
cities. The eight chambers were responsible for issuing export licenses
that certified that the product was manufactured or produced in the
West Bank and not in Israel. As stated earlier, Jordan, until it signed
the Washington Declaration in July 1993, formally adhered to the provisions of the Arab boycott, which prohibited the export of products manufactured in Israel. The Chambers of Commerce became particularly
important after the 1976 elections, which resulted in a victory for the
pro-PLO forces in the West Bank. These chambers were staffed by pro-
Jordanians who used this powerful institution to counter the influence
of the PLO. Jordan continued to use the chambers even after its 1988
disengagement to issue export certificates, although these offices today
maintain a lower profile than they held before the disengagement.

The Money Changers

Money changers, those individuals who own currency exchange kiosks,
operated in the West Bank and Jordan before 1967 (see table 2.7). After
the Six-Day War, in the absence of a proper banking system because of

the closure of Jordanian banks in the West Bank, the number of money changers grew substantially. Since 1967 they have played an instrumental role in the monetary system of the West Bank.[71]

A dual currency system has existed in the West Bank since 1967, whereby Israeli shekels and Jordanian dinars are allowed as legal tender. Because Israeli currency was much weaker than the Jordanian dinar before 1988, most West Bank Palestinians accumulated dinars and tended to hoard them.[72] Almost all Arab financial assistance to the West is transmitted in dinars. The money changers play a crucial role in bringing the money across the bridges, either legally or illegally. In the absence of a relationship between Israeli and Jordanian banks at that time (except for the 1986 Cairo-Amman Bank agreement) and given Israeli foreign exchange controls on the amount of cash that could be carried across the bridges (controls that were tightened and relaxed at different times), currency smuggling became an important element in transferring money between Amman and the West Bank.[73] The opening of the Cairo-Amman Bank in the West Bank in 1986 somewhat diminished the role that the money changers play in formal transactions. Yet after the beginning of the intifadah, smuggling money into the West Bank became extremely vital because the PLO attempted to infuse cash into the territories to finance the uprising. Money changers also handle transfers of remittances from Palestinians working abroad and transfers related to imports and exports and regular money exchanges as well.[74]

With the signing of the Gaza-Jericho agreement in May 1994 the money changers' role has further eroded. Transfer of money to the West Bank is now done legally either through the Cairo-Amman Bank or other Jordanian banks that resumed their West Bank operations in April 1994, having been closed since 1967. Several Jordanian banks now operate in the West Bank after the December 2, 1993, signing of an Israeli-Jordanian memorandum on reopening banks in the West Bank.

The financial base underlying the activities of money changers is derived from deposits accepted by individuals and institutions. Because Israeli banks refused to pay interest on deposits in Jordanian dinars, the money changers filled the role of quasi banks.[75] They have also provided check-cashing services to the West Bank.

The total amount of transfers, including those that are illegal, is not available although some partial data is available on the official cash flow from the East to the West Bank.

The activities of the money changers are allowed by Israel if they conduct transactions in shekels or dinars. The illegality of the money changers' other activities was tolerated by Israel in the 1967–88 period if they did not conflict with Israel's macroeconomic policies.[76]

Unilateral Transfers

As seen in table 2.8, the West Bank's capital movement is flowing in Israel's direction because of the huge trade deficit. The export surplus with Jordan and the remittances and the unilateral transfers by Jordan, the Joint Committee, and other agencies do not exceed the capital outflow. The Jordanian government's transfer of funds for salaries and pensions is a large component in the total aid to the West Bank. Between 1978 and 1984 total unilateral Jordanian transfers to individuals, municipalities, and institutions amounted to $127.4 million. The Joint Committee in the same period actually disbursed $405 million of an allocation of $462 million. The difference is the result of unfulfilled commitments by the Arab states.[77] Through its technical bureau in Amman the Joint Committee receives project proposals and disburses the money on the West Bank through Jordanian channels (see tables 2.8, 2.9).[78] As noted earlier, the Jordanian government is the main source of financial assistance to the West Bank municipalities (see table 2.10). Between 1968 and 1984 Jordan transferred 5,378,077 dinars, or about $17 million, to the municipalities. During the 1979–85 period funds for the municipalities were transferred through the Joint Committee.[79] When Jordan issued its ambitious $1.25 billion development plan for the West Bank in 1986, it intended to finance the municipalities directly.

There are no estimates regarding capital movement from the West to the East Bank although some experts believe that before the Palestinian uprising started, capital movement was increasing.[80]

The Dual Legal System

When Israel occupied the West Bank in 1967, it perceived itself as a "lawful belligerent occupier." Because international law requires the occupier to maintain the legal system that existed before the occupation, Israel acted accordingly. Military Order No. 2 of June 7, 1967, stated that "the laws that were in force in the territory on June 7, 1967, shall remain in force."[81]

Israel regarded Jordanian annexation of the West Bank as "unlawful." This position was summarized by Raja Shehadeh and Jonathan Kuttab in *The West Bank and the Rule of Law* as follows:

> Israel considers that since the Jordanian annexation of the West Bank in 1950 was recognized only by Great Britain and Pakistan, the question of sovereignty of the area is undecided. Therefore, Israel considers itself as the present power administering these territories until their status is resolved by negotiations. Consequently, it

Table 2.8

Net Capital Movements Between the West
Bank, Jordan, and Israel

(Israeli shekels)

YEAR	ISRAEL	JORDAN
1968	−5.8	10.8
1969	−7.7	8.7
1970	−5.9	10.6
1971	−0.4	10.5
1972	−1.7	11.1
1973	−12.1	5.7
1974	−23.6	8.9
1975	−43.8	23.4
1976	−49.1	42.2
1977	−96.0	59.6
1978	−117.1	141.2
1979	−304.1	172.4
1980	−994.3	604.3
1981	−1,560.9	870.9
1982	−3,211.9	2,352.7
1983	−5,977.0	3,996.7
1984	−34,203.9	23,509.3
Total	−46,615.3	31,839.0

Sources: Raphael Meron, *Economic Development in Judea-Samaria
and the Gaza Strip, 1970–1980* (Jerusalem: Bank of Israel, Research Department, 1983), 63; Dan Zakai, *Economic Development
in Judea-Samaria and the Gaza District, 1983–1984* (Jerusalem:
Bank of Israel, Research Department, 1986), 69.

considers that the various Geneva Conventions governing enemy
territory do not apply to the West Bank, and that Israel has the role
of an administrator rather than occupier of the territories.[82]

The international conventions governing the conduct of an occupy-
ing power—the 1949 Geneva and 1907 Hague Conventions—were only
partially accepted by Israel. Israel's position on the Geneva Convention
was that although it did not accept the convention in toto, "it decided
to act de facto in accordance with the humanitarian provisions of the
Convention."[83] As Don Peretz observes, the partial acceptance of the
international conventions "obviated an automatic transfer of sovereignty

Table 2.9

Estimates of Private and Official Arab Transfers
to the West Bank, 1978–1985

(millions of dollars)

YEAR	JGT[a]	JNGO[b]	ARIS[c]	JJPC[d]	TAIA[e]
1978	26.9	2.0	4.25		33.0
1979	20.6	2.3	4.25	42.7	70.0
1980	21.4	2.7	3.6	82.1	110.0
1981	20.1	2.7	3.6	76.2	103.0
1982	19.6	2.8	2.0	93.8	118.0
1983	19.6	2.7	2.0	37.9	62.0
1984	19.2	2.6	10.0	33.0	65.0
1985				40.0	
Total	147.4	17.8	29.7	415.7	561.0

[a] JGT: Jordanian government salaries and pensions to West Bank residents. Jordanian government rent paid for premises in the West Bank; other transfers, including aid to municipalities, guarantees on loans by commercial banks, direct grants, education, and health.
[b] JNGO: Aid from Jordanian nongovernmental organizations.
[c] ARIS: Arab and Islamic States' aid.
[d] JPJC: Jordanian-Palestinian Joint Committee grants and loans.
[e] TAIA: Total transfers.
Source: UNCTAD, *The Palestinian Financial Sector under Israeli Occupation* UNCTAD/ST/SEU/3, July 1987, 143, 145.

to the State of Israel.''[84] Although Israel rejected Jordan's legal claim to the West Bank, it chose not to institute Israeli sovereignty on the West Bank because of the political divisions inside Israel regarding the future of the territories. Moreover, as in other aspects of the relationship, a dual approach was maintained vis-à-vis Jordan: upholding the unlawfulness of the pre-1967 Jordanian rule of the West Bank, while, concomitantly, successive Israeli governments had pursued the "Jordanian option" that regarded Jordan as the only interlocutor in negotiations over the West Bank.

The West Bank's legal structure conforms with Jordanian law although the Israeli military government has amended Jordanian law through the extensive issuing of military orders that cover all aspects of life in the West Bank. Since 1967 more than twelve hundred orders have been issued.[85] These orders have had the cumulative effect of establishing a new body of law that only theoretically purports to rely on Jordanian law.[86] Further, the Israeli High Court of Justice and the military govern-

Table 2.10

Transfers by the Jordanian Government
to West Bank Municipalities, 1968–1984
(Jordanian dinars)

YEAR	TOTAL REVENUES
1968	695,597
1969	449,259
1970	288,314
1971	354,793
1972	443,583
1973	370,064
1974	409,632
1975	402,173
1976	598,161
1977	618,827
1978	594,194
1979	61,492
1980	1,466
1981	49,221
1982	5,110
1983	17,232
1984[a]	18,959
Total	5,373,077

[a] Until Sep. only.
Source: Royal Scientific Society and Jordanian-PLO Joint Committee, *Al-Ahwal al-Maliyya w᾽l-masrafiyya fi᾽l-diffa al-gharbiyya wa-qita᷾ gazza al-muhtalaym* (Financial and banking conditions in the occupied West Bank and Gaza Strip) (Amman: Royal Scientific Society, 1985), Table 3.3.

ment have frequently locked horns over the myriad changes enacted by the military in the West Bank. For example, when Israel attempted to take over the Jerusalem District Electric Company, the High Court ruled against such a move. Notwithstanding the court's decision, the modification of Jordanian law by Israel has had a long-lasting effect on the legal, social, economic, and political life in the West Bank.

Raja Shehadeh notes four legislative stages in the history of Israel's occupation of the West Bank.[87] The first was from 1967 to 1971, during which Israeli rule was consolidated. During this period the military government issued some two hundred military orders, which gave it full authority in all aspects of life, ranging from control over issuing driver's licenses to the extension of military courts to civilian matters, which were under the domain of the civilian courts during Jordan's rule. During the 1971–79 period the number of Jewish settlements in the West Bank increased. For example, order no. 418 amended the Jordanian planning law to make possible the zoning of larger areas in the West Bank for the benefit of Jewish settlers.[88] From 1979 to 1981 Israel cemented the dual legal system in the West Bank, which placed Jewish settlers under the jurisdiction of the Israeli legal system and placed the Palestinians under Jordanian law as amended by the military government. In 1981, also, the Israeli government replaced the military government with the Civilian Administration, whose purpose was to implement the Autonomy Plan as envisaged in the Camp David Accords (Military Order No. 947). (The Civilian Administration in the territories was abolished after the signing of the Declaration of Principles and the establishment of Palestinian self-rule in Gaza and Jericho.) During the fourth period, from 1981 to 1988, regulations were issued that allowed the acquisition of additional lands for use by the settlers. Moreover, many orders were issued to control the flow of funds into the territories, including the institution of the value-added tax (VAT), which was created to increase revenues from the territories into Israel.

The establishment of the Civilian Administration in 1981 was particularly noteworthy. Menachem Milson, a professor at the Hebrew University, was named as the first head of the Civilian Administration. With the abolition of the military government, the West Bank was no longer a separate military district but one controlled by the Central District Command with the West Bank as one area where Israeli troops were stationed. Notwithstanding these semantic changes, the military commander of the Central Command continued to hold the same power as his predecessor, the military governor of the West Bank.

Milson was appointed by Likud Defense Minister Ariel Sharon, who had been impressed by Milson's article in *Commentary* magazine that attacked the Dayanist approach to the West Bank. Milson argued that Israeli policies in the territories had led to the PLO's success in winning the hearts and minds of the Palestinian population.

Milson's views were embraced by Sharon and the Likud government. Milson believed that Dayan's "noninterventionist" policies were largely responsible for the ascent of the PLO during the 1976 local elections in the West Bank. To counter the influence of the PLO Milson attempted to use the urban-rural cleavage that existed in the West Bank to his advantage. Milson argued that the PLO derived its strength from the urban areas, and so he began cultivating the Village Leagues. The Leagues were established in 1978 to promote rural development and were used by Milson in his quest to create an alternative leadership to the pro-PLO urban nationalists.[89] Milson attempted to co-opt the Village Leagues by giving them myriad privileges as a prize for cooperating with the Israeli authorities. Concomitantly, he pursued a harsh policy against both PLO and Jordanian supporters in the West Bank. Milson attempted to neutralize the pro-Jordanians in the West Bank to make them dependent on the Civilian Administration.[90] As Don Peretz observed: "Within a few months, the mayors of the largest West Bank cities were dismissed, the pace of expulsions was increased, and curfews, demolition of houses, seizure of property, and imprisonment without trial were used with increased frequency."[91]

Israel's attempt to arm members of the Village Leagues eventually backfired. Jordanian Prime Minister Mudar Budran termed the Village Leaguers "collaborators with the Israeli occupation." He issued a military order calling on the Leagues to end their support of the Civilian Administration or face severe consequences if they ever came under Jordanian jurisdiction.[92] Jordan issued the threat once it became apparent that Israel was cultivating a leadership that depended on neither the PLO nor Jordan but on Israel. Jordan considered such a development dangerous. Under Sharon's leadership, in fact, the thrust of Israel's policies was both anti-Jordanian as well as anti-PLO. The cornerstone of Sharon's approach was an attempt to impose unilateral autonomy in the West Bank based on the Camp David approach that called for the establishment of a self-governing authority in the West Bank. The effort to establish an alternative leadership failed when it became apparent that the Village Leagues lacked support among the Palestinian population. After the Lebanon war started in June 1982, this attempt came to a halt. Milson resigned his post, acknowledging that he could not pacify the local population and that the popularity of the PLO during and after the war had reached new heights.[93] Moreover, Israel invaded Lebanon to destroy the PLO's infrastructure in order to cement its control of the territories. Sharon told Samuel Lewis, the American ambassador to Israel, that Israel had invaded Lebanon so the PLO would no longer be able to intimidate the West Bank Palestinians, who would then agree to autonomy under Israeli conditions.[94]

From 1977 to 1984 when the Likud was in power Israel pursued an extreme activist policy to try to eradicate support for the PLO in the West Bank. When a National Unity Government was established between Labor and Likud in 1984, attention was fully directed at Jordan. It was hoped that Israel and Jordan would be able to maintain a condominium over the West Bank so that Jordanian influence would counter that of the PLO.

The legal system that Israel created after 1967 was described as a mongrel of Israeli and Jordanian law as amended by the military government.[95] The large volume of military orders that govern life in the West Bank attests to the changes that Israeli policy has undergone since the occupation began. They reflect the trend of a relative noninterventionist policy under Labor to an activist posture under Likud that attempted to regulate all aspects of Palestinian life in the territories. Although legally Israel has not annexed the West Bank, for all practical purposes, the military orders have become a substantive body of law that reflects "Israel's creeping annexation" of the West Bank.

With Palestinian autonomy, the legal system erected by Israel since 1967 was gradually rolled back. With an elected Palestinian Council empowered to legislate in most spheres of civilian life coupled with authority transferred from the Civilian Administration, the Palestinians in the West Bank and Gaza, for the first time in their history, governed themselves.

Education

Nowhere in the West Bank was Jordan's profile as high as in the sphere of education. This area was also one of the finest examples of the division of labor between Israel and Jordan. Even after it disengaged from the West Bank in 1988, Jordan continued to supervise the high school matriculation exams called *Tawjihi*, supply textbooks, and provide the curriculum. With the signing of the Declaration of Principles, one of the first areas for which the Palestinian Authority assumed responsibility was education although Jordan still continues to exercise a measure of influence in curriculum and matriculation requirements.

There are three types of schools in the West Bank (see table 2.11): United Nations Relief and Works Agency (UNRWA) and government and private schools. The government schools were those operated by Jordan before 1967. UNRWA cares for Palestinian refugees and runs elementary, preparatory and vocational schools, and teachers colleges as well. Elementary and secondary private schools comprise the smallest sector in the system.[96]

The West Bank education administrative structure is based on the structure that existed before the 1967 war. The highest administrative authority is the Examination Committee in Nablus, which includes the directors of the six education districts—Jenin, Tulkarem, Nablus, Ramallah, Bethlehem-Jericho, and Hebron. This committee, which was linked directly to the Jordanian Ministry of Education in Amman, supervised the *Tawjihi* exams that were written and graded in Amman.[97]

Before the transfer of authority from Israel to the Palestinian Authority, actual control of government schools rested in the hands of the Israeli Civilian Administration, whose specially designated staff officers

Table 2.11

Number of Students and Institutions in the West Bank

Year	GOVERNMENT		UNRWA[a]		PRIVATE		TOTAL	
	Schools	Students	Schools	Students	Schools	Students	Schools	Students
1967–68	884	107,332	142	23,425	162	11,459	1,188	142,216
1986–87	831	235,398	100	40,678	268	34,441	1,199	310,517

[a] UNRWA: United Nations Relief and Works Agency.

Sources: State of Israel, Ministry of Defense, Coordinator of Government Operations in Judea and Samaria and Gaza District, *An Eighteen Year Survey (1967–1985)* (Tel Aviv: Ministry of Defense Publishing House, 1986), app. no. 16. State of Israel, Central Bureau of Statistics, *Statistical Abstract of Israel, 1988* (Jerusalem: Central Bureau of Statistics, 1989), 754.

coordinated all the educational activities in the West Bank. All schools in the West Bank followed the Jordanian curriculum.[98] Education in East Jerusalem was especially problematic. Because it annexed East Jerusalem in 1967, Israel sought to apply its curriculum to the Jerusalem schools. This action would have prevented students from pursuing higher education in the Arab world because the Israeli matriculation exams were not recognized by any Arab government. The Israeli policy caused many students to transfer to private institutions that used the Jordanian curriculum. In 1976 the Israeli government gave the East Jerusalem students an option to pursue either the Israeli or Jordanian tracks. Not surprisingly, they chose the Jordanian.[99] The elementary schools, however, used the Israeli curriculum.

The best example of this bifurcated system was found in the village of Beit Tzafafa, near Jerusalem, which until 1967 was evenly divided along the Israeli-Jordanian border. The high school students on the Israeli side took the Israeli *Bagrut* matriculation exam, whereas students in the same village in the West Bank took the Jordanian Tawjihi exam.[100]

The textbooks used by the West Bank schools were Jordanian although they were censored by the Israeli military government authorities. Initially, after the 1967 war, the Israeli Ministry of Education tried to introduce to the West Bank government school system the same texts used in the Arab sector in Israel. This attempt, however, was abandoned in response to the objections of the local population. The result was an Israeli-Jordanian agreement mediated by the United Nations Education, Scientific, and Cultural Organization (UNESCO) by which Jordanian books could be used provided that all anti-Israeli and anti-Jewish passages were deleted.[101] In other words, Jordan agreed to censor its own textbooks that Israel regarded as offensive. (The Jordanian texts used in the East Bank were not affected.)[102]

There are five universities in the West Bank: Al-Najah in Nablus, founded in 1977; Bir-Zeit in Ramallah (1972); Bethlehem University (1973); Hebron University (1980), which was previously an Islamic seminary; and Al-Quds University, composed of the Abu Dis College of Science (1982), a religious college in Beit Hanina (1978), and the El-Bireh School of Nursing (1979).[103] Jordan does not regulate the universities in the West Bank. They are governed by an independent Council of Higher Education, which, during Israel's occupation of the West Bank, was not recognized by the Israeli authorities. Israel viewed the West Bank universities as hotbeds of Palestinian nationalism and closed them for lengthy periods.[104] The West Bank universities remained closed between 1987 and 1992 when Israel alleged that nationalist activities were taking place there. In 1992 all universities were allowed to reopen provided that no political activities occurred at these institutions.

Education on the West Bank was particularly problematic because of the difficulties associated with the military occupation. The fact that Israel and Jordan were jointly responsible for different aspects of the system caused the education system to be more underdeveloped than it should have been. For example, after 1967 the number of students more than doubled while the number of schools increased insignificantly (see table 2.11). The education system was a good example of how Israeli and Jordanian interests were maintained, often at the expense of the Palestinian students, to support the status quo.

Evaluation of the Policy

The utility of maintaining the open bridges policy was a subject of fierce debate in Jordan in the summer of 1987, one year before Jordan officially disengaged from the West Bank. Two schools of thought arose on the subject. One called for the termination of the policy while the other supported the status quo.[105] The debate took place on the pages of the daily *al-Ra'i* and should be understood in the context of the different perspectives on Jordan's relations vis-à-vis the West Bank as discussed earlier. Those who called for terminating the policy argued that it was in Jordan's national interest to reduce Jordanian ties to the West Bank.

In the *al-Ra'i* article, "The Open Bridges Policy: Reevaluation and Adjustment," the anonymous economic editor of the paper listed a number of adverse effects that the policy had on Jordan. First, he claimed that because of the emigration from the West to the East Bank Jordan was facing an increasingly volatile demographic problem: How and to what extent should it absorb the Palestinian immigrants? Second, the Jordanian economy suffered because of the restrictions Israel placed on exports to the West Bank. Third, the net flow of capital to the West Bank "represents the exact net deficit of the East Bank as a result of its dealings with the West Bank across the bridges." Consequently, "We must not allow the occupation to transform the West Bank into an easy source of hard currency or to use the West Bank to influence the Jordanian economy in a negative way. . . . We must limit and ration the movement of trade, finance, and people across the bridges in a way that [e]nsures the national interest."

Fouad Hamadi Basayso, the author of numerous studies on the open bridges policy, argued in favor of maintaining the policy.[106] Basayso, former executive-director of the Jordanian-Palestinian Joint Committee and now the head of the Palestinian Authority's Palestinian Monetary Authority (PMA), wrote earlier in an article published in 1971 that the benefits of maintaining the policy exceeded their costs. In his response to the *al-Ra'i* article Basayso maintained that the policy should have been evaluated in light of two considerations. The first was the need to maintain ties to the Palestinians struggling against the Israeli occupation.

> Because the policy is connected to the strategic objectives of national steadfastness in the occupied territories, it is necessary that we look at that policy from a broad regional perspective and not from *a short-term one-country perspective* [emphasis mine] which may utilize a cost/benefit calculus (such as looking at the trade deficits or financial and human flows). . . . Therefore, we must consider these bridges not as "open bridges," but as "bridges of resistance, unity and steadfastness."[107]

The second, according to Basayso, was that support of the Palestinians in the West Bank should have been balanced with the requirements of the Arab League's boycott of Israeli products. "The boycott," Basayso maintained, "is the weapon which matured and proved effective in facing the Israeli technological and economic infiltration of the Arab world." When balancing these two objectives, Basayso concluded that the policy should continue because of the greater need to support the Palestinians in the territories. Regarding the Arab boycott, he recommended that attention be directed toward developing a Palestinian infrastructure in the territories so disengagement from the Israeli economy would take place. As such, Israeli products would no longer be exported to the Arab world disguised as Palestinian products.

A study by the Arab League of the open bridges policy supported Basayso's recommendations.[108] This study, which acknowledged the fact that Israel used the bridges to market its products in the Arab world, contended that "keeping the bridges open, even if Israel would gain a measure of economic benefit, would serve as a motivation for the Palestinians to steadfastly resist the arbitrary Israeli occupation."[109] The position of the PLO regarding the policy was ambiguous. Despite the claim made by the *Palestinian Encyclopedia* that the PLO had rejected the open bridges policy, Basayso maintained that the organization took no such position.

The open bridges policy generated intense debate in Israel as well. The debate in Jordan naturally followed the uneasy interaction between Jordan and the Palestinians in the West Bank.

The open bridges policy was debated in the Knesset only once, in February 1970. Opposition to the policy was expressed by Shmuel Tamir, a member of the Free Center List, which espoused annexationist policies. Tamir argued that the policy damaged Israel's security and interests in three areas. First, he said the bridges were the channel through which explosives and terrorists entered the territories. Further, he argued that after a terrorist operation had been conducted against Israel, the perpetrators returned in many cases to their bases on the East Bank. Second, both Jordan and the PLO used the bridges to transfer money into the territories and to support anti-Israeli activities. Additionally, the export of products from the West Bank to Jordan had created a dependency on the East Bank that was intolerable from an Israeli perspective because Jordan was in a formal state of war with Israel. Third, Tamir opposed Jordan's involvement in West Bank affairs because it had "created confusion about in whom supreme authority was vested in the West Bank." In other words, Tamir argued that the open bridges policy was undermining Israeli attempts to pacify the Palestinians because they had a link with the Arab world.[110]

Dayan, the architect of the policy, disagreed with Tamir's call to close the bridges because he believed that its benefits outweighed the costs and that the danger to Israel's security could be contained: "The main reason for having the "open bridges" policy is . . . to maintain the affiliation of the Arabs in the territories with the Arabs across the border. . . . The basic question facing us as an alternative [to the policy] is Do we want to isolate them or try to force on them Israelization, culturally and socially, or are we willing to allow them to maintain these ties?"[111]

The most consistent and vocal critic of the open bridges policy was Zvi Elpeleg, former military governor of Nablus. He rejected Dayan's thesis that through the open bridges policy a structure of coexistence would develop between Jews and Arabs. According to Elpeleg, by pursuing a noninterventionist policy Israel made it more likely that the PLO would be supported by the West Bank Palestinians. Elpeleg argued that allowing Jordan a modicum of influence in the territories was unworkable because Jordan was unable to deploy its security forces against anti-Hashemites as it did before 1967. Therefore,

> when Israel pursued its non-interventionist policies, and Jordan was prevented from effectively controlling political behavior, a political vacuum was created. This vacuum was quickly filled by the PLO. If we add the fact (which is inexplicable in my view) that Israel decided to impose on the local population municipal elections in 1972 and 1976—during which pro-PLO elements won over Jordan's supporters—we will better understand how the PLO became the almost sole authority among the population.[112]

Furthermore, Elpeleg argued that Israel's attempt to present its occupation policies as "benign" had failed because the local Palestinian population failed to appreciate gestures such as the open bridges policy.[113] Elpeleg also criticized the policy of the Civilian Administration, which "has allowed the PLO to maintain its anti-Israeli activities" through the transfer of monies from the East Bank to support such activities. Above all, Elpeleg maintained that the biggest failure was Israel's inability to make the Palestinians dependent on Israel.[114] Instead, Elpeleg proposed a model of social and political control that characterized Israeli rule over its Arab citizens (within the pre-1967 borders) before 1967. During that period Israeli Arab contacts with the Arab world were nonexistent, and, thus, they were "integrated" into Israeli society.[115]

Other critics of the policy have argued that the bridges served as a channel to transport weapons and explosives into the West Bank for use against Israel. Reuven Mroz, a columnist in the now defunct newspaper *Al-Hamishmar* who supported Elpeleg's thesis that the bridges should have been closed, called in 1974 for implementation of an "iron fist" policy in the territories.[116]

Despite these calls to close the bridges Israel resisted the temptation because it believed that the open bridges policy was the best method of pacifying the Palestinians in the territories. Were the intended objectives of the open bridges policy that were listed in the beginning of this chapter achieved? First, the barriers that were broken down between Israel, the West Bank, and Jordan did not lead to the emergence of a structure of Jewish-Arab coexistence, as Dayan had hoped. The fact that the bridges had remained open since 1967 (they were even open during the 1973 Yom Kippur War) meant that the West Bank Palestinians had little incentive to associate themselves with Israel either politically or psychologically.[117] Moreover, the contacts between the Palestinians inside the territories and the PLO on the outside and with the Arab world in general helped strengthen the Palestinian national identity and helped resist Israeli military occupation. The renewed contacts between residents of the Gaza Strip and the West Bank created a situation in which the fate of Gaza became linked with developments in the West Bank.[118] From an official Israeli perspective this was counterproductive because resistance to the occupation was coordinated by the residents of the two areas. The Palestinian uprising is a case in point: activities in Gaza were inseparable from those in the West Bank. In fact, the intifadah first started in Gaza. Second, despite Israel's annexation of East Jerusalem its Palestinian residents have never considered themselves part of Israel. This attitude became evident during the uprising; disturbances and riots occurred in East Jerusalem just as they did in the rest of the territories. Third, restrictions applied to the free movement of people, goods, and capital across the bridges did not help to reduce anti-Israeli activities. On the contrary, the Palestinians became radicalized as the occupation continued, and Israel's harsh policies in the territories contributed to the growth of militancy, culminating in the intifadah. Fourth, the open bridges policy as a propaganda tool did not convince world public opinion that Israeli occupation policies were "liberal" compared with other occupations in history. If anything, the cumulative effect of Israeli measures against the Palestinians, particularly after the uprising, dispelled the myth of a liberal occupation. Fifth, although no accurate data were available, Israel was able to bypass the Arab boycott against its products by exporting goods to Jordan and the Arab world across the bridges. The objective of circumventing the Arab boycott was, indeed, successful.

The record of the open bridges policy after almost three decades of Israeli occupation, therefore, is mixed at best. The greatest achievement resulting from the policy was to buy time in the absence of a political decision regarding the fate of the territories. Former Government Coordinator of the Territories Binyamin Ben Eliezer summed up this realization:

> In essence, closing the bridges would have meant separate development of Jordan and the West Bank populations. And, I believe, this would have led to a South Africa type of a rebellion against Israeli rule. This in turn, would have forced us to take the necessary steps to control violence. In a year or two or 10, this might have made annexation easier. But, as it stands, without a clear decision by the Israeli government on the future of the territories, the "open bridges" policy has helped give Israel 19 years of relative quiet on the West Bank.[119]

Those were Ben Eliezer's words in 1986, exactly one year before the Palestinian uprising began. Paradoxically, the intifadah started in spite of the open bridges policy, a policy meant to prevent a violent eruption in the territories.

The uprising caught Israel by surprise. A number of individuals, however, warned as early as 1985 that an explosion on the West Bank was imminent. In May 1985 an intra-agency committee was established to formulate a set of recommendations on policy toward the West Bank. The committee included specialists from the Mossad (Israel's external intelligence services), Shin Bet (General Security Services, internal security), defense intelligence, the research division at the Foreign Ministry, representatives of the Civilian Administration, and academic experts. In a number of reports that it submitted to the top Israeli leadership the committee called for a revision of Israel's policy vis-à-vis the territories.[120]

The first set of recommendations was presented on May 15, 1985. Its main point was to recommend reevaluation of the pro-Jordanian stance of the government.

> In contrast to the innovative dynamism of the PLO structure, the Jordanian structure is characterized by conservatism and lack of

initiative, as well as unwillingness to establish organizations for mass mobilization. This explains why Jordan had lost its influence even in the institutions it had established. . . . In the last six months, there are signs that the Jordanian leadership is reassessing its policies vis-à-vis the territories. The break with the PLO has led to a conflict over influence [in the territories]. . . . The [Jordanian] leadership was deeply shocked when the meek response to Hussein's February speech became apparent, even among those whose salaries are paid by Jordan. The illusion that Jordan has a solid clientele was shattered. [What became clear] is the institutional strength that the PLO had built for years. In the conflict with the Jordanian structure which is based on old dignitaries and is built top to bottom, the PLO has won with its structure which is based on mass participation from bottom up.[121]

The Israeli government chose to ignore these warnings and the changes taking place on the ground as well. For example, one year before the outbreak of the uprising, Shimon Peres boasted to visiting U.S. senators about the success of Israeli-Jordanian cooperative efforts to transform the political orientation of the inhabitants of the territories into pro-Jordanian.[122] Other reports called on the government to assist in the creation of an economic infrastructure and to transfer jobs gradually from the Civilian Administration to local personnel. This, it was argued, would give the Palestinians a stake in preserving a modicum of stability in the territories.[123] Yet none of these recommendations was implemented by the government. By the time the Palestinian uprising started these proposals had become irrelevant, but not forgotten.

One of the annexes of the 1993 Israeli-PLO accord focuses on Israeli-Palestinian economic cooperation and regional development programs. At last, Israeli decision makers have acted upon the cumulative advice of those who have advocated since 1967 the building of a Palestinian infrastructure as a necessary, but not sufficient, condition for peace.

After the signing of the Israeli-PLO accord, attention was also given to various aspects of the open bridges policy, especially the physical control of the bridges. The Palestinians had expected that, given the close proximity of the Allenby Bridge to Jericho, they, rather than Israel, would exercise full authority over it. Israel, however, refused to relinquish its control over this indispensable link to its eastern neighbor, Jordan, until the final status of the territories was agreed upon. Meanwhile, Palestinian police officers are stationed at the Allenby Bridge crossing and work side by side with Israeli border guards. Palestinian police are responsible for Palestinians and tourists visiting the self-rule areas while Israel remains responsible for overall security and for tourists entering Israel.

With the signing of the interim Israel-PLO agreement and the Israeli-Jordanian peace accord the bridges, once again, have come to symbolize the painfully complex but hopeful triangular relationship between Israelis, Palestinians, and Jordanians.

3

De Facto Peace

After the signing of the October 26, 1994, Treaty of Peace between Israel and Jordan, open, formal cooperation between the two countries no longer seemed elusive. Israeli, Jordanian, and other Arab entrepreneurs and officials have started to plan for the borderless map of the future Middle East. As stipulated in the various articles in the peace treaty, cooperation between the two countries is planned in most areas, including, inter alia, economic development, water sharing, cultural and scientific exchanges, police and scientific cooperation in combating crime and drug trafficking, transportation and roads, civil aviation and maritime transportation, telecommunications, tourism, environment, energy, Jordan Rift Valley development, health, agriculture, and the joint development of Aqaba and Eilat. Several cooperative agreements have already been negotiated between the two governments to implement the various aspects of the peace agreement, among them: linking the electrical grids of Israel, Jordan, and Egypt to save hundreds of million of dollars annually; marketing tour packages that include visits to Israel and Jordan; joint extraction of mineral deposits in the Dead Sea; opening their border to private vehicular traffic; creating a Free Tourist Zone (Red Sea Riviera) along the Red Sea coasts of Israel, Jordan, and Egypt; joint use of the Eilat and Aqaba ports and granting Jordan rights to use Israel's Mediterranean Port Ashdod; sharing Jordan's Aqaba international airport; joint development of agricultural products; constructing highways to connect all major cities in the Middle East; increasing trade between Israel and the Arab world by opening Jordan's border with Israel; establishing a regional bank for development; using Israel's ports as outlets for natural gas and oil transported from the Gulf states to Israel via Jordan; and environmental, scientific, and educational joint projects. With the signing of a peace agreement between Israel and Jordan and the establishment of low-level diplomatic relations between Israeli and several Arab countries, it is very likely that many of these projects will be realized, given the Israeli-Jordanian past record of functional cooperation.

In this chapter I examine several cooperative ventures that constituted the backbone of sub-rosa peace before formal Arab-Israeli negotiations in Madrid began in October 1991. After 1967 Jordanian-Israeli relations were predicated on a mutual understanding whereby the formal state of war was maintained while, concomitantly, the two countries continued an ongoing dialogue on issues of mutual concern ranging from water sharing to the return of missing persons. Given the myriad formal diplomatic breakthroughs between Israel and her neighbors, many of these past examples of functional cooperation seem trivial at best, but in the 1967–88 period they were meaningful, and, most importantly, Israelis and Jordanians regarded them as genuinely significant and beneficial.

Although the open bridges policy laid the foundation for the functional relationship that developed between Israel and Jordan after 1967, cooperation took place in other areas. Aaron Klieman attributes this cooperation to three factors: complementary needs, corresponding interests, and tangible benefits.[1]

As defined earlier, functional cooperation is an "interest-driven" type of cooperation. Examples of this type of cooperation have focused on the mutual needs and interests of the countries in narrowly defined areas without necessarily substantially impacting the larger issues that separate them, such as Israeli withdrawal from the territories or Jordan's formal recognition of Israel. This cooperation continued despite the formal state of war between Israel and Jordan.

In this chapter I cover seven areas in which cooperation has occurred: repatriation of refugees, the transfer of medical and food supplies, the Cairo-Amman banking agreement, the transfer of Israeli irrigation technology, the modus vivendi reached between the cities of Eilat and Aqaba, the agreement on the Jerusalem District Electric Company (JDEC) concession, and the sharing of the Jordan and Yarmuk rivers. In addition, I discuss the complementary/competitive interaction between Jordanian and Israeli television. In all these areas, with the exception of the media, cooperation arose out of mutual needs and interests and resulted in tangible benefits for both countries.

In addition to the areas of cooperation discussed in this chapter, numerous forms of purely practical cooperation have occurred. For example, in 1987 the authoritative Israeli paper, *Ha'aretz*, reported that Israeli engineers had helped Jordanian engineers to extract phosphates from the Dead Sea by using new Israeli techniques. The meetings took place along the Israeli-Jordanian border.[2] Moreover, the two countries secretly embarked on a new project to use oil shales as a possible alternative energy source.[3]

Operation Refugee

As a result of the 1967 war, an estimated 250,000 Palestinians fled to the East Bank of Jordan. This number included 93,000 refugees from the 1948 Arab-Israeli war, almost all of whom had been living in the refugee camps in the Jordan Valley, and residents of the West Bank and Gaza who had been considered displaced persons.[4] This exodus presented a real problem to many Palestinians from the West Bank and to the Jordanian government as well. Before the 1967 war a large number of West Bank Palestinians worked in Jordan because of the relative scarcity of jobs in the West Bank; many of them sent their salaries back home in the form of remittances. After Israel occupied the West Bank, many of these families feared a permanent separation from their relatives and a possible halt to those remittances. This was one reason why many West Bank families fled to the East Bank during the first months after the 1967 war. In addition, the refugees also posed a problem for Jordan, which had to provide them with food and shelter. The refugees themselves pressed the Jordanian government to help them return to the West Bank.[5]

Israeli and Arab explanations for the reasons why the refugees fled varied. The Arab states charged Israel with "forcible expulsion," whereas Israel denied these allegations. On June 29, 1967, the Israeli government decided to require those wishing to move to Jordan to produce written approval from the mayors or the village heads (*mukhtar*) of their places of residence.[6] A study of one hundred refugee families conducted by the American University of Beirut reported that these families left because they feared the Israelis and believed that "staying under Israeli rule would compromise their honor and dignity."[7]

The United Nations emissary who investigated Arab charges stated in his report that he had

> received no specific reports indicating that persons had been physically forced to cross to the East Bank. On the other hand, there are persistent reports of acts of intimidation by Israel armed forces and of Israeli attempts to suggest to the population, by loudspeakers mounted on cars, that they might be better off on the East Bank . . . . The truth seems to lie somewhere between an Israel statement that "no encouragement" was given to the population to flee, and the allegation about the use of brutal force and intimidation. . . . The inevitable impact upon a frightened civilian population of hostilities, as such, particularly when no measures of reassurance were taken, has clearly been a main factor in the exodus.[8]

After international pressure on Israel to allow the refugees to return, including Security Council Resolution 237 of June 14, 1967, the Israeli government decided on July 2, 1967, to accept their repatriation. United Nations Secretary-General U Thant appointed Nils-Goran Gussing of Sweden as a special representative to deal with the refugee problem. He stayed in the Middle East from July 11, 1967, until September 1, 1967. Israel regarded the question of repatriation as a humanitarian issue and wanted to deflect international pressure on this matter. The name that the Israeli government gave this project was "Operation Refugee." Israel's acceptance of the project, however, stipulated that all the refugees must return by August 10, 1967.[9]

The official Jordanian reaction to Israel's decision was presented on July 3, 1967, and stipulated that the return of those who had left their homes be facilitated unconditionally.[10]

One of the immediate problems confronting Israel was to determine the type of administrative apparatus it needed to install to facilitate the return. In addition, an orderly return of the refugees required the tacit approval and cooperation of the Jordanian government.

The humanitarian nature of this issue led to the involvement of the International Red Cross. Subsequently, the Red Cross took it upon itself to serve as the intermediary between the Jordanian and Israeli governments. Initially, Israel had proposed that refugees who wanted to return should complete an official application form that bore the Red Cross emblem. Jordan rejected this form because it also bore Israel's name.[11]

Finally, the Red Cross brokered an agreement between Israeli and Jordanian representatives. The meeting took place at the Allenby Bridge over the Jordan River on August 6.[12] The Israeli-Jordanian agreement stated that:

> 1. The application forms, serving those wishing to return, will bear the names of the two countries and the Red Cross.
> 2. The final date for returning to the West Bank is postponed to August 31.
> 3. As stated in the application forms, the applicants must present their passports, or UNRWA identification cards, or Jordanian identification cards, issued before July 1, 1967, or any other documents that will be deemed necessary by the government of Israel.[13]

The dispute between the two parties—a dispute not over substance but over the form that the prospective returnees would have to complete—was finally resolved. The form included the names of three parties: Israel, Jordan, and the Red Cross. This dispute symbolized how Israel and Jordan viewed each other. Israel, on the one hand, viewed the refugee problem in pragmatic terms and did not want to allow the return of *all* refugees. Jordan, on the other hand, initially feared that accepting a form with Israel's signature would be interpreted as an Israeli ploy to secure Jordanian recognition of Israel.[14] Yet pragmatic considerations on Jordan's part overruled, and an agreement on the form was reached. The final agreement also stipulated that all Palestinians who had permanent residence on the West Bank on June 5, 1967, and had crossed to the East Bank between that date and July 4, 1967, were entitled to return.[15]

Once the decision of the Israeli government became public, the International Red Cross began registering eligible refugees. The Jordanian government, though, faced a dilemma. On the one hand, Jordan wanted to encourage as many Palestinians as possible to apply to return because of the mounting pressures at home by the refugees. And about 120,000 refugees did complete the applications.[16] On the other hand, Jordan placed obstacles before those who planned to return because it did not want to be seen as according legitimacy to Israel's occupation of the West Bank. Jordan resolved this dilemma by allowing the refugees to return, but it also encouraged them to start resisting the Israeli military government in the West Bank immediately.[17]

A debate erupted in the Israeli government over this issue with a number of ministers from the Liberal and Herut parties wanting to cancel the accord.[18] The Liberal Party issued the following statement, calling for an end to Operation Refugee: "In light of the Jordanian government's declaration that the duty of the repatriated refugees was to harm Israel's security, and in light of the incitement which is directed by the Jordanian propaganda, the Liberal Party demands that the return of the refugees should be stopped."[19]

The Israeli government, however, did not yield to the Liberal Party's pressure and issued a communiqué, stating that "while the Cabinet is aware of the incitement by Jordanian authorities of the West Bank and the refugees and is not prepared to ignore this campaign, nevertheless it does not see fit to change the decision to permit the return of the refugees."[20] Israel did decide to prioritize the categories of the refugees who would be admitted. This decision, which was not made public, stipulated that first priority would be given to Palestinians seeking to reunite with their families. The second priority was given to permanent residents of the West Bank, and the third, to the residents of the refugee camps. Israel also decided to use certain security precautions to screen the refugees before their return to counter Jordan's attempt to incite them. U Thant feared that the propaganda war between Israel and Jordan would lead to the termination of Operation Refugee. The Israelis charged the Jordanians with incitement while the Jordanians argued that Israel was overreacting. Emissary Nils-Goran Gussing shuttled between

Amman and Jerusalem, attempting to diffuse the crisis. He was able to reduce the tensions, and, indeed, the first refugees were expected to arrive on August 18, 1967.

To facilitate the return of the refugees the Jordanian government allowed an advance team of the Israeli police to cross the Allenby Bridge to the East Bank to check the applications of the returnees. The Israeli representatives were surrounded by a unit of the Jordanian army that provided protection for them. Throughout this process, Israeli and Jordanian representatives regularly held meetings at the bridge. Jordan's ambivalence toward this newly established contact with the Israelis was exhibited when a disagreement erupted between the two sides over the military uniform of the Israeli officer, Captain Touvia Navot. Navot was the liaison between the Israeli Defense Forces (IDF) and the Jordanians, along with Myer Silverstone, the director general of the Israeli Ministry of the Interior. Both were allowed to cross back and forth over the bridge. The Jordanian officer in charge of the Allenby Bridge did not object to Navot crossing into Jordan wearing the IDF uniform. The Jordanian officer in charge of the crossing at the Umm Shart Bridge, the second bridge for refugee crossing, however, objected to Navot wearing the "enemy's uniform" in Jordan and insisted that Navot cross wearing civilian clothes.[21] Notwithstanding these difficulties, the direct contacts between the two adversaries continued throughout Operation Refugee and were even formally acknowledged by Israeli Foreign Minister Abba Eban.[22]

According to the agreement, each day refugees from different regions of the West Bank would be allowed to cross the bridges. On the first day, for example, residents from the northern West Bank towns of Jenin, Nablus, and Tulkarem crossed over, whereas on the second day residents from Ramallah and Hebron Mountain would cross over.

Once the first refugees had begun to cross the bridges, the issue of the daily quota allocated by the Israelis became a bone of contention between Israel and Jordan. The Israelis argued that the Jordanians were not filling their daily quota, which was initially set at 2,500, then raised to 3,000. By August 31, the last day of the operation, of 20,000 applications that had been approved by the Israeli government, only 14,056 refugees had returned.[23] The Israelis argued that most refugees did not want to return to the West Bank and that those who applied to return "were forced to do so by the Jordanian authorities."[24] In addition, the fact that only 20,000 applications were approved by the Israeli government clearly attests to Israel's unwillingness to allow all the refugees that fled to return to the West Bank. By allowing 120,000 Palestinian applicants to return, Israel would have created a precedent that could have been used by 1948 Palestinian refugees who wanted to be repatriated to Israel. Furthermore, Israel also used the screening procedure to deny return on security grounds. Although Israel had legitimate security concerns in screening the returnees, it also used this procedure to reduce the number of refugees allowed to return. The Jordanians, by contrast, argued that Israel should be blamed for the slow pace of the refugee return. Jordan insisted that it did not have sufficient time to round up all the refugees before the August 31 deadline. At Jordan's request the United States and the United Nations both asked Israel to extend this deadline but to no avail.

Israel did, however, extend the deadline for the seven thousand refugees whom it had already approved but who had been unable to cross the bridges by August 31. The government also decided that only those refugees who had immediate family members in the territories would be allowed to return. This family reunification principle was also applied to the 1948 refugees.[25]

Israel had agreed to extend the August 31 deadline for some refugees partly because of a request by Dean Rusk, the American secretary of state. Rusk sent a letter to the Israeli government, requesting an extension of the deadline. Rusk argued that an increase in the number of refugees in Jordan would have necessitated an increase in UNRWA's budget. Because 40 percent of UNRWA's budget comes from the United States, this would have meant an increase in American assistance to UNRWA. Israel wanted to prevent this increase, fearing that an increase in the U.S. allocation for UNRWA would come at Israel's expense.[26]

Although Operation Refugee should not be considered a milestone in Israeli-Jordanian relations, it was, nevertheless, one of the first instances of functional cooperation in the context of the open bridges policy after the Six-Day War. Israel and Jordan had interests that were divergent, yet overlapping. The interests proved to be a backdrop for future functional interaction between the two formal enemies.

Israel certainly did not wish to reopen the issue of the right of the 1948 refugees to return. On the one hand, a strong consensus existed in Israel not to allow these Palestinian refugees to be repatriated even though U.N. Resolution 194 called upon Israel either to repatriate them or to compensate those not wishing to return. On the other hand, Israel wanted to demonstrate to the inhabitants of the newly acquired West Bank that humanitarian issues could be resolved on an ad hoc basis. In the first instance Israel refused to allow the Palestinian refugees who had either fled or been evicted to return because their original residence was within the pre-1967 boundaries of the state. In 1967 the refugees fled from the West Bank and Gaza, thus Israel felt it could show a degree of flexibility on the matter.

The American connection with Operation Refugee was also important. Israel needed American support and did not want to risk antagonizing the United States over this relatively minor issue. Furthermore, Operation Refugee was part of the overall open bridges policy that was engineered by Moshe Dayan. The various meetings between Israeli and Jordanian representatives at the bridges laid the groundwork for the functional interaction and the comanagement of the occupied territories between Israel and Jordan. This relationship was founded on the understanding that there were issues of mutual interest that could be dealt with pragmatically.

The agreement on the application form, which initially was a source of friction between the two countries, showed that despite diverging interests Israel and Jordan could cooperate in certain areas. This agreement did not mean that the propaganda war between the two countries ceased. On the contrary, in the case of Operation Refugee the war of words served as a self-absolving mechanism, particularly for the Jordanians, who did not want to be viewed as "cooperating with the enemy."

For the Jordanians the addition of an estimated 250,000 refugees was a real problem. Jordanian Premier Sa'ad Juma'a had acknowledged this problem: "Jordan with its limited resources will not be able to provide for them [the refugees] . . . the services they need."[27] Consequently, the Jordanians pressured the refugees to return, even though some feared an uncertain future under Israeli occupation and preferred to remain in the East Bank.

Twenty-eight years after the Six-Day War, the issue of the Palestinian refugees who left the West Bank and Gaza in 1967 came to the fore again. With the signing of the Jericho-Gaza agreement and the Israeli-Jordanian Treaty, Israel, the PLO, Jordan, and Egypt began talks on the return of Palestinian refugees from 1948 and those displaced in 1967. Several rounds of talks produced no concrete results. Israel and the PLO were unable to agree on the number of displaced Palestinians: Israel claimed that their numbers did not exceed 250,000, whereas the PLO argued for the return of a minimum 875,000 displaced Palestinians. Israel defined a displaced person as someone who had fled during the four months after the June 1967 war. The PLO stipulated that not only the refugees themselves should be allowed to return but also their descendants, a total between 875,000 and 1.5 million Palestinians. During the March 1995 negotiations in Amman over the question of the displaced Palestinians, Israel completely rejected the PLO position. Israeli officials viewed those who wished to return as a potential security threat: Israeli officials were skeptical about the absorption and integration of those wishing to return in terms of employment, housing, education, and soon Israel feared that if a large number of Palestinians were allowed to return to the West Bank and Gaza, given the prevailing economic malaise and the scarcity of available resources, it was likely that they would join the ranks of the unemployed and, perhaps, join the opposition to the PLO and the peace process, thus potentially constituting a security risk for Israel. Moreover, Israel was afraid that if the 1967 refugees were allowed to return to the West Bank, pressure would mount on Israel to allow refugees from 1948 into Israel proper. Another issue that complicated the talks was the Jordan demand that it receive financial compensation for the twenty-eight years of "hosting" the displaced Palestinians. Undoubtedly, the sensitive issue of Palestinian refugees, both from the 1948 and 1967 wars, will continue to cast a shadow over the normalization process between Israel and Jordan and on Israeli-PLO relations once the negotiations over the final status of the territories begin.

Israeli Aid to Jordan During the Civil War

One of the most interesting instances of overt Israeli-Jordanian functional cooperation occurred during the 1970 civil war when Israel and the West Bank Palestinians sent medical aid and food supplies to Jordan. This project coincided, not surprisingly, with the strategic umbrella that Israel provided Hussein in deterring Syria. According to an official report published by the Israeli military, three steps were taken during the civil war:

> 1. The eight [Israeli-controlled] government general hospitals [in the West Bank] were nearly completely evacuated and placed on an emergency footing after the offer of the Israeli government to accept wounded children, women, and elderly civilians. In case of an "overflow" or possible need for specialized treatment, arrangements were also made for transfer of cases to Israel hospitals. This state of readiness—hospitals, ambulances and special medical teams—was maintained for a period of twelve days but was not used.
>
> 2. Three teams of physicians and nurses from Judea and Samaria were organized and equipped with emergency drugs and instruments—in great part paid for by local contributions and supplied by the health authorities. These teams were organized and prepared to be sent over in case they were needed, but this proved to be unnecessary.
>
> 3. Together with the large convoys of trucks containing food and other essentials donated by the population of Judea and Samaria and the Israeli Government, which were sent to Jordan, a sizable consignment of emergency drugs and materials was sent by the health authorities, one of the first such aids to reach the affected area in Jordan.[28]

The most authoritative account of the supply of aid to Jordan comes from Brigadier General Shlomo Gazit, then the Israeli Defense Ministry coordinator of activities in the territories. Gazit describes the entire process as a "co-production between the Israeli government and the inhabitants of the territories," who wanted to aid their Palestinian brethren on the East Bank.[29] The initial request to send medical supplies and personnel was submitted to the military government on September 18 by the director of the hospital in Nablus and by the Nablus City Council. This appeal was also transmitted to the International Red Cross (IRC), which became the intermediary throughout the entire operation. While the IRC was getting ready to respond to the request, the Israeli government took unilateral steps to address the problem. Israeli Minister of Health Victor Shemtov announced that, as a goodwill gesture, Israel would be willing to hospitalize the wounded in Israel and in the West Bank. This step, according to Shemtov, was contingent upon Jordanian approval. At the same time, he gave permission for medical staff in the West Bank to travel to Jordan.[30] Some technical difficulties were associated with Shemtov's plan because the Jordanians had temporarily closed the Jordan River bridges to traffic.

After a September 23 meeting with a Jordanian officer on the Allenby Bridge, a formal Jordanian request was made through the mayor of Nablus for food and medical supplies. The Jordanian officer claimed that there was a severe shortage of both supplies in Jordan at that time.[31] The first convoy of Israeli supplies crossed the Allenby Bridge on September 26. The convoy consisted of thirty-two trucks that carried basic foodstuffs: flour, oil, sugar, beans, rice, and potatoes. On the Jordanian side, the Jordanian army unloaded the trucks and immediately began their distribution. The Jordanian army became involved in this project because the Israeli government requested that the Jordanians provide security arrangements for the trucks once they reached Jordanian territory.

According to accounts of the Arab truck drivers, there was a severe food shortage in Jordan, and Jordanian requests for additional supplies were transmitted to the West Bank.[32] The largest supply was sent on September 27 when three convoys passed the bridge that was opened specifically for the operation. The third convoy also contained fuel needed for cooking. In addition, the Jerusalem-based Hadassah Medical Center sent a large shipment of medical supplies at the request of the IRC (see table 3.1).

On September 30 the Jordanian authorities said they would not accept any more aid from Israel. Because the Jordan River bridges opened for traffic in early October, regular shipments of goods donated by the inhabitants of the West Bank were continued.[33] As noted in the

Table 3.1

Medical Supplies Sent to Jordan During September 1970

QUANTITY	DESCRIPTION	PRICE (ISRAELI LIRA)
22 doz.	vaseline gauze	1,056.00
1,000 m.	gauze	600.00
1,000 rolls	leukoplast (5 cm)	1,900.00
500 ampules	morphine	50.00
10,000	bandages (7 cm)	2,000.00
20,000 tablets	APC	80.00
100 kg.	dettol	300.00
100 kg.	alcohol	270.00
50 kg.	cotton wool	275.00
12,000 tablets	chloramphenicol	420.00
28 × 36	infusion sets	1,431.36
40 × 12	saline solution (1,000 cc)	2,160.00
30 × 12	glucose-saline solution (1,000 cc)	1,080.00
20 × 12	glucose-saline solution (500 cc)	540.00
1,000	disposable syringes (5 cc)	230.00
400	streptomycine (1 gm)	528.00
500 ampules p	ATS (1,500 U each)	310.00
4	plastic containers (50 l)	120.00
Subtotal		13,350.36
Expenses for packing and transport		3,631.20
Total		16,981.65

Source: State of Israel, Ministry of Defense, Military Headquarters, Judea and Samaria, Health Department, *Statistical Report,* 1968–1970 (Israel, 1971), table 27.

Israeli medical report published by the Israeli health authorities, no organized effort to transmit the wounded to Israeli hospitals was allowed by the Jordanians.[34] This brought the operation to an end.

The reaction to the Israeli moves on the West Bank was mixed. Wasfi al-Masri, a prominent Nablus lawyer, termed the Israeli actions "more humane than the butcher sitting in Amman."[35] Other Palestinians ascribed political motivations to the Israeli aid efforts, claiming that "the aid was only a means to hide the fact that the slaughter of the guerrillas served its [Israel's] interests."[36]

With the signing of their bilateral peace treaty in 1994, issues pertaining to cooperation in the health area were also agreed upon.

Table 3.2

Jordanian Commercial Banks and Branch Locations
in the West Bank, May 1967

BANK	LOCATION
Arab Bank	Nablus, Jerusalem, Hebron, Ramallah, Jenin, Tulkarem
Cairo-Amman Bank	Nablus, Jerusalem, Hebron, Ramallah, Jenin
Ottoman Bank[a]	Nablus, Jerusalem, Ramallah, Bethlehem
Jordan National Bank	Nablus, Jerusalem, Jericho
Jordan Bank	Nablus, Jerusalem, Jericho
Arab Real Estate Bank	Nablus, Jerusalem
British Bank of the Middle East	Jerusalem
Bank Intra	Nablus, Jerusalem

British owned.

Source: UNCTAD, *The Palestinian Financial Sector under Israeli Occupation,* UNCTAD/ST/SEU3, July 8, 1987, 45.

A joint health committee was established and members agreed to ex-change information about environmental health and medicine, in-cluding animal-transmitted diseases, methods to treat them, and the possibility of establishing a joint testing center; to cooperate during nat-ural disasters and accidents; and to collaborate about poisons, for exam-ple, by trading samples and training personnel. They also agreed to share medical information regarding standardization, immunization, and other health-related matters. In August 1995 an additional health agreement was signed between the two countries, which included the licensing of physicians and joint projects to combat diseases.

The Cairo-Amman Bank Agreement

Before the announcement on September 17, 1986, by Shmuel Goren, Israel's coordinator for the occupied territories, that the Cairo-Amman Bank would reopen for the first time since 1967, a number of Israeli and Palestinian officials visited the Nablus branch of the bank. When they entered the bank's gate, they found it to be exactly the same as it had been in 1967. The large calendar showed June 3, 1967; files and forms were lying on the dusty tables. Nobody had touched anything since 1967.[37]

The opening of the Nablus branch was the culmination of the Israeli-Jordanian secret negotiations that took place in Jerusalem and London with American mediation. Before 1967, eight commercial banks oper-ated in the West Bank with twenty-six branches (see table 3.2). By June

1967 the total assets of the West Bank branches amounted to about 15 million Jordanian dinars (JD), one-fifth of the total assets of Jordan's commercial banks, with deposits of 14 million JD and 10 million JD credit.[38]

The closure of the banks by Israel after the 1967 war prompted Jordan to complain to the Security Council. At the same time Jordan began several rounds of secret negotiations with Israel on reopening the bank branches in the West Bank. An initial effort to reopen the banks, whose assets were frozen by Jordan, was undertaken from August 16–18, 1967, when a Jordanian delegation visited Jerusalem and negotiated an agreement on reopening the banks. The Jordanian delegation consisted of Abdalla Boshnak, assistant general manager of the Arab Bank, and M. E. Constant, a British national and regional manager of the Ottoman Bank in Amman.[39] Israel was represented by Eliyahu Shimoni, controller of banks in Israel and the West Bank; Baruch Yekutieli, chief of the economic branch of the newly established West Bank Command; and Ze'ev Sher, legal adviser to the Bank of Israel. An agreement was eventually reached whereby Jordan would retain control over the West Bank branches while Israel would have authority over the Arab banks in Jerusalem. After additional negotiations, the delegations agreed that Arab oil would be transported to the Haifa refineries and made provisions for Israeli-Jordanian trade exchanges.[40]

When the agreement was presented to the Israeli government for approval, Ministers Shimshon Shapira (Justice) and Pinhas Sapir (Finance) convinced Israeli Prime Minister Levi Eshkol to veto the agreement. They contended that because they expected formal peace with Jordan to be signed in the near future, there should be a government-to-government agreement rather than one signed by banking officials. Moreover, they objected to Jordan controlling the monetary sector because this would give it a degree of economic leverage.[41] Thus, the agreement was never ratified, and Israeli banks began operations in the territories, replacing the Jordanian banks.

The second round of negotiations took place in the mid-1970s, but no agreement was reached because of a number of outstanding issues, including:

> 1. Israeli authorities would permit the opening of all branches except those in East Jerusalem, and this had serious political implications unacceptable to the Arab Bank;
> 2. Legal reserves of more than 70 percent were to be kept at the Bank of Israel (in Jordanian dinars) at no interest;
> 3. Deposits that were held in banks outside the country would have to be transferred back to local branches;

4. Reopened banks would be asked to generate more equity capital so that they would maintain their finances on an autonomous basis independent of their main offices in Amman.[42]

In subsequent Israeli-Jordanian negotiations numerous attempts to arrive at an agreement included mediation by the International Monetary Fund (IMF) and the United States. According to Ze'ev Sher, who participated in these efforts, several main issues separated the two countries. First, the parties could not agree whether liquidity should be kept in Jerusalem or Amman. Second, an agreement could not be reached on the supervision and regulation of the banks. The illegal transfer of funds was the third major obstacle to an agreement.

These outstanding issues were not resolved until 1986 when the political climate became markedly different from that of previous years. When Shimon Peres became prime minister in 1984, he emphasized the importance of expanding the functional ties between Israel and Jordan. He hoped to establish an Israeli-Jordanian condominium in the West Bank, which was expected to lead to a formal peace between the two countries. One of Peres's top priorities when he assumed office was to reopen a Jordanian bank in the West Bank.[43]

The 1986 Israeli-Jordanian accord signed in London in August was reached after two years of negotiations with American help. The Jordanian negotiating team included Hasan Shukry, deputy director of the Jordanian Central Bank, and Juwadad Sha'sha, the managing director of the Amman branch of the Cairo-Amman Bank. The Israeli delegation included Amnon Neubach, Shmuel Goren, and Galia Maor, the supervisor of banks. The agreement stipulated joint Israeli-Jordanian control whereby Jordanian dinars and Israeli shekels would be legally used in transactions. The Bank of Jordan was to supervise transactions in JD while the Bank of Israel supervised Israeli shekels and other foreign currencies.[44]

One of the issues that delayed the opening of the bank was whether Israeli citizens would be permitted to open accounts in the bank. The dispute focused on the Arab residents of Jerusalem who became Israeli residents after Israel annexed East Jerusalem in 1967. Finally, it was agreed that they would not be allowed to use the bank's services.[45]

The banking agreement clearly showed how Jordanian and Israeli long-term interests overrode short-term considerations. Although a major stumbling block in the post-1967 negotiations was the question of supervision, the agreement called for comanagement of the Cairo-Amman Bank. Until the agreement was signed, Israel feared that if it allowed Jordan to reopen its banks in the West Bank, Jordan would have economic leverage beyond what Israel considered acceptable. Yet in 1986 Jordanian influence in the territories was welcomed by Israel.

In addition to Peres's emphasis on improving the quality of life for the Palestinians in the West Bank the policies of the two countries converged in a number of areas. After the February 1986 cancellation of the Amman accord, Jordan attempted to woo West Bank Palestinians away from the PLO. Jordan closed the PLO offices in Amman and expelled PLO activists from Jordan. During the same period Israel placed pro-PLO activists in the territories under town arrest and encouraged pro-Jordanian elements. Many Palestinians attributed these arrests to joint Israeli-Jordanian efforts to undermine the PLO. Moreover, the opening of the Cairo-Amman Bank in Nablus was intended to help Jordan implement its $1.3 billion five-year development plan for the West Bank.

The Cairo-Amman Bank was selected to reopen among the eight commercial banks that operated in the pre-1967 period for two reasons: the Egyptian government that signed a peace treaty with Israel owned 12 percent of the bank, and the other owners included some traditional Palestinian families who were perceived to be political moderates. The response by the people in the territories to the opening of the bank was positive, but some were cynical. A Nablus businessman commented, "It is nice of you to have reopened the bank. But, this is not what will regain us Palestine."[46] The Cairo-Amman Bank today has branches in the West Bank, including Nablus, Ramallah, Hebron, Jenin, and it also has a branch in Gaza. The bank continued to operate even after Hussein's disengagement from the West Bank in July 1988.

On December 2, 1994, representatives of the Central Bank of Jordan and Israel's supervisor of banks signed a new memorandum, replacing the August 1986 agreement that allowed the Cairo-Amman Bank to reopen. The new accord provided for the reopening of all Jordanian banks that had been closed in June 1967.

In January 1994 Jordan and the PLO signed an agreement that governed the monetary and banking relationship between the two. In April 1994 the Bank of Jordan had opened a branch in Ramallah followed by additional branches in Gaza, Hebron, and Nablus. By 1996, fifteen banks with fifty branches were operating in the territories, including two Israeli, three locally incorporated, eight Jordanian, one Egyptian, and one Joint Australian-British bank. Further, the two sides agreed that the Jordanian dinar was to remain the legal tender in the territories along with the Israeli shekel as had been true since 1967.[47]

In December 1995, Israel turned over responsibility for banking supervision in the areas controlled by the Palestinian Authority. The new Palestinian Monetary Authority (PMA), headed by Fouad Hamadi Basayso, will perform the banking supervisory function.

Transfer of Drip-Irrigation Technology to Jordan

Drip-irrigation technology was invented by Israel in the 1960s. Israel successfully used this technology at home and exported it to numerous countries around the world. Drip-irrigation saves 30 to 50 percent of the water used in conventional irrigation. The water drips directly into the roots, and different fertilizers can pass through the system ensuring that nutrients reach the roots directly.[48] The technology is manufactured by the Netafim Company in three kibbutzim—Magal, Hatzerim, and Yiftah—and by Plassim, a company located at Kibbutz Merhavia. On its twenty-fifth birthday Plassim revealed that it sold its drip-irrigation technology directly to Jordan.[49]

The Israeli manufacturer in search of new markets sent a Nablus businessman to Amman to explore the possibility of Jordanian purchase of the irrigation system. Eventually, the system was sold for $36,000 to King Hussein's uncle, Sharrif Nasser (who visited Israel for this purpose). Nasser said he would purchase the system only if it neither carried any Hebrew letters nor stated the country where it was manufactured.[50] The irrigation system was shipped via the bridges of the Jordan River, which were declared a closed military area by the Israeli military authorities while the operation lasted.[51]

Subsequently, a factory that manufactures the drip-irrigation system was built in Jordan with French help. Initially, the Jordanians had some difficulties in successfully applying the technology because the water was not filtered before use. Israel had developed a granule filter to address this problem. The filter was also transferred across the border and incorporated into the Jordanian system.[52] Jordanian agricultural development was so successful that Israeli farmers began to fear competition. Because Jordanian agricultural surpluses were occasionally sent to the West Bank, some Israeli farmers had to lower their prices in response to the competition.[53]

Israeli Agricultural Minister Arye Nehamkin acknowledged the transfer of Israeli technology to Jordan: "Before 1967 the Jordan Rift was barren and nothing was growing. Today their side [Jordan's] seems to be greener than ours. This is thanks to the professional aid they received from extension services advisers trained in Israel, and the use of the latest agricultural technologies which we have sold them."[54]

Nehamkin explained that after the 1967 war Israel trained Jordanian employees in the West Bank in agricultural technologies who then took them to Jordan. Additionally, agricultural advisers from other Arab countries, including the Gulf states, also received training. Israel continues to export greenhouses and irrigation equipment to a number of Arab countries. Nehamkin summed up the benefits from the functional cooperation between Israel and Jordan, "It has made the border quiet, and now that they are working land up to the Jordan River, they have an interest in peace."[55]

Eilat and Aqaba

When Israeli Premier Yitzhak Shamir visited the city of Eilat in 1987, he asked Mayor Rafi Hochman whether he had recently met Jordanian representatives.[56] Shamir's question showed that contact between Eilat and Aqaba officials had become so routine that the prime minister saw no need to be informed on a "real time" basis.

The two resort cities lie adjacent to the Red Sea and their close proximity has made it necessary for them to maintain regular contacts between officials.[57] Aqaba and Eilat are vital to the economies of Jordan and Israel, respectively. Aqaba is Jordan's only port, and Israel heavily relies on Eilat, which is the country's outlet to Asia and to Africa. As long as the Suez Canal remained closed, Israel used Eilat extensively. The gulf was protected not only by Israel's navy but also by Jordanian patrol boats stationed off the coast of Aqaba, to prevent Arab terrorist infiltration into Eilat.[58] This joint defense arrangement was a function of a 1968 agreement between the two countries, which guaranteed that no hostile acts would be initiated on either side of the border.

Over the years before Israel and Jordan signed their peace treaty in 1994 the close proximity of the two cities offered several opportunities for functional cooperation. Jordan complained that the border marking in the Arava region, north of Eilat, was not accurate because Israel had illegally occupied a few square kilometers in 1948. Israeli Prime Minister Yitzhak Rabin agreed in 1976 to return the territory to Jordan.[59] The close proximity of the Eilat and Aqaba airports led to an agreement mediated by the International Civil Aviation Organization (ICAO) for the two countries to monitor each other's airport communications and to exchange information about flight arrivals and departures to prevent accidents. Meir Amit, Israel's minister of transportation and communications, revealed that he held talks with one of Hussein's advisers on possible development of the Aqaba airport for international flights to Israel and Jordan.[60] Moreover, the two countries jointly fight mosquitoes; when it is mosquito-spraying time along the border in Eilat, it is mosquito-spraying time along the Jordanian border in Aqaba. Spraying teams show up simultaneously on both sides of the border to ensure that the mosquitoes do not find temporary refuge across the frontier.[61]

There has also been intensive Israeli-Jordanian dialogue to preserve the ecology of the Gulf of Aqaba. Measures have been taken on each side to warn the other of oil spills.[62] A source of friction developed between the two countries when Jordan began to build a sewage-treatment plant near Aqaba in 1983. Because the plant was built only a few hundred meters from Eilat's resort hotels, Israeli authorities feared that the plant would emit foul smells, pollute the beaches, and harm Eilat's tourist industry, the city's main source of income. This occurred when the Likud party was in power and Israeli-Jordanian contacts were maintained at a minimal level. Because the plant was built with a $15 million grant from United States Agency of International Development (AID), the Environmental Protection Agency (EPA) and the State Department attempted to mediate the dispute. At one point, according to Amnon Neubach, a confidant of Shimon Peres, Prime Minister Shamir even contemplated taking military action against the plant in Jordan.[63] Finally, the issue was resolved after Israel received Jordanian assurances that the treatment plant would not affect Israel and the United States promised to train Jordanian engineers in pollution prevention methods.[64] Yet the treatment plant still causes some concern in Eilat that discharged water could pollute the pure water aquifers under the city.

The best testament to the level of coexistence between Eilat and Aqaba is the fact that King Hussein maintains one of his residences near the border with Israel. This villa reportedly has served as a secret meeting place for Israeli and Jordanian officials.

Article 23 of the Treaty of Peace stipulates that the joint development of the two cities must be undertaken "as soon as possible." Consequently, several agreements were signed with that aim in mind. For example, Israel accepted Jordan's offer to use Aqaba's new international airport until the new Israeli-Jordanian airport, the International Peace Airport, was completed. In November 1994 the first shipping agreement was signed to allow free passage of small vessels to both countries in the Gulf of Aqaba. One month later the European Union agreed to subsidize the building of a railroad to link Irbid and Haifa and Eilat and Aqaba. Moreover, because the port of Eilat was unable to process cargo, Israel was forced to transport the salt it extracted from the Dead Sea via its northern port in Haifa. The two countries negotiated an agreement that enabled Israel to export its cargo through the port of Aqaba and Jordan to use Eilat for passenger traffic. In addition, in July 1995 Jordan agreed to open a free tourism zone in Aqaba and Eilat for tourists from both countries. The agreement provides for one-day visits by Israeli and Jordanian citizens to respective neighboring cities without having to stay overnight. Special permits will be issued to enable free movement throughout the legal boundaries of each city. Officials envisage the gradual transformation of the entire Eilat/Aqaba region into the Gulf Riviera. In 1996, the two countries signed an agreement to constitute Eilat and Aqaba as a single district for cooperation in tourism, industry, trade, environment, and infrastructure. Also, they agreed to build an ocean park on both sides of the gulf.

The two countries agreed to implement an environmental project to fight pollution in the Gulf of Eilat/Aqaba. In the framework of this project three stations have been set up in Aqaba, Eilat, and Nuweiba. The three stations, which will be linked by a joint communications network, will together deal with pollution in the waters of the gulf. The project is also being financed by the European Union and the Japanese government.

The Boundless Air Waves

On May 19, 1977, Jordanian radio broadcast a special program on the Israeli elections. It analyzed the election results and presented interviews with Israeli politicians that were produced by Israel's Arabic radio service. It was the first time that any Arab radio station had aired a program prepared by Israeli radio.[65] An editorial in the Jordanian weekly, *Al-Anbah,* went even further and congratulated Israeli radio for a professional and successful all-night Arabic broadcast of election results.[66]

Middle East media, especially in the Arab-Israeli zone, is reflecting the sea change in Arab-Israeli relations. Although in the past most media were mouthpieces for governmental propaganda, in the 1990s newspapers and television are becoming, in some cases, facilitators of improved communication and understanding among Israel and its neighbors.[67]

In the Israeli-Jordanian context communications have played an important role. Each side closely scrutinizes the other party's media and, thus, receives instant feedback on policy issues. Because of the close proximity of the two countries, a number of television and radio programs are frequently watched and listened to. Jordanian television began its Hebrew broadcast in 1972. It includes a half-hour news program that is aired every night at 7:30 P.M. A sizable portion of the Israeli public watches the Hebrew, English, and French news programs on Jordanian television (see table 3.3). Whenever Israeli television is on strike, even more people tune in to Jordanian television. All Israeli newspapers carry a daily listing of programs shown by Jordanian television, and in 1988 56.3 percent of all households in Israel were able to receive Jordanian TV's signal.

Although no comparable surveys are available for Jordanian viewing of Israeli television, there are many indicators that Israeli programs are quite popular. Visitors from Jordan or West Bank Palestinians who spent time in Jordan have attested to the popularity of Israeli TV.[68]

Table 3.3

Survey of Jordanian Television Viewing among
Israeli Jews

VIEWERS	PERCENTAGE
Adults 18 years old or older	
Watch every day or almost every day	11.9
Watch at least once a week	10.9
Watch on an irregular basis	18.3
Do not watch at all	15.2
Cannot receive Jordanian television	43.7
Youths 12–17 years old	
Watch every day or almost every day	12.1
Watch at least once a week	17.1
Watch on an irregular basis	20.4
Do not watch at all	10.4

Source: Survey conducted by PORI (Israel) in 1988, based on a representative sample of 1,200. *Otot,* Sept. 1988.

Israeli observers of Jordanian television note that Jordanian coverage of developments in Israel, before the Madrid peace process, was presented within "a tolerable bias." Israeli right-wing nationalists objected to some of the terminology used by Jordanian TV in its broadcasts. For example, the West Bank was "the occupied Arab lands" and not Judea and Samaria; and the Israeli military was the "arm of the occupation." During the 1982 Lebanon war Jordanian television scored heavily among the Israeli public. Because many military operations were heavily censored by Israel, many Israelis tuned in to Jordanian TV for information.[69]

In 1987 a great scandal erupted in Israel when it was learned that a correspondent for Jordanian television was working in Israel and sending back to Jordan interviews with Israeli politicians that were later shown on Jordanian TV. The reporter, Ziad Darwish, an Israeli Arab from Acre, was a freelancer employed by the Jordanians to cover developments in Israel. Because he used the technical services of a British network (Visnews), however, it was announced before each broadcast that the program was produced by Viznews. Darwish presented himself to the Israelis as an employee of the Jordanians, yet Jordanian TV did not admit his affiliation. If it had, Jordan could have been accused of formally recognizing Israel.

After interviews of Israeli members of Knesset were shown on Jordanian TV, Prime Minister Shamir ordered a formal investigation into whether Jordanian television was formally represented in Israel and whether granting interviews to an enemy's state television reporter was a criminal offense. Geula Cohen from the right-wing party Techiya termed the interviews "political sabotage." The dovish parliamentarian Yossi Sarid responded by saying "Jordanian TV is TV like any other and I will use any outlet to express my views. If it is [the TV] of an enemy state, then all the more so."[70]

The charges and countercharges of bias and propaganda presented by the two countries in their respective media do not prevent the population from watching the television and listening to the radio programs of their formal enemy.[71] In 1988, Israeli television broadcast a new situation comedy called *Neighbors,* which dealt with Jewish-Arab relations. Jordanian media immediately called the program propaganda: "The new Israeli series (Neighbors) expresses a new direction in Israeli propaganda. Its aim is to brainwash the minds of the Arab viewers and to intoxicate them through laughter, entertainment, song, and dance."[72]

The two television stations also compete for the same audience. For example, as Dov Shinar, the Israeli media analyst, notes:

> "Dallas" . . . has been broadcast on Jordan TV at the same time as the popular "Mabat" Hebrew news bulletin on Israel TV. The Jordanian news in Hebrew intends to break the monopoly on news in this language that was previously enjoyed by the Israeli broadcasting service. A second expression of this competition/complementarity is that each station pirates news items broadcast by the other whenever such items are unavailable locally due to political and military limitations.[73]

A Doctor Behind the Microphone

One of the programs that had helped foster Israeli-Arab cooperation before the peace process that was inaugurated in Madrid in October 1991 was Israel's Arabic radio program, "Doctor Behind the Microphone." Since 1971, Ilana Basri, the Iraqi-born producer for Israeli radio, has interviewed Jewish and Arab doctors twice a week on medical issues and the latest technological breakthroughs in medicine. Because there are no direct postal links between Israel and the Arab world, letters from all over the Arab world arrive in Israel via a post office box in Geneva or over the Jordan River bridges. According to Basri, about three hundred letters arrive in Israel every month with questions about medical problems addressed to the Israeli medical specialists.[74] Letters arrive from Jordan, Syria, Lebanon, Kuwait, Bahrain, Qatar, Iraq, Libya, Tunisia,

Morocco, and Saudi Arabia, all countries that are officially at war with Israel. Seventy-five percent of the letters are concerned with skin ailments and infertility. Israeli medical specialists are consulted and give advice over the air waves. Those who also send their medical records to Israel and whose ailments are considered treatable are invited to Israel at their own expense.

Basri estimates that about 120–150 patients per year actually come to Israel for treatment. Most Arabs enter Israel either through the open bridges or via a European country, where entrance visas to Israel have been prepared in advance.[75]

The Israeli paper, *Ma'ariv*, reported that a special meeting of the Arab ministers of health was convened in early 1987 in Khartoum to join efforts in combating the phenomenon of Arabs coming to Israel for medical treatment. The Arab ministers regarded the success of the Israeli program as an "insult to Arab medicine."[76]

Basri claims, however, that in most cases the patients consulted with their physicians in their country before coming to Israel and that these doctors encouraged their patients to be treated in Israel.

With the signing of the Israeli-Jordanian treaty and the establishment of low-level diplomatic relations with several Arab countries, Arab patients now routinely come to Israel for medical treatment.

The Jerusalem District Electric Company

The Jerusalem District Electric Company (JDEC) was established in 1914 by Euripedes Mavromatis, a Greek national, when a concession for generation and distribution of electricity was granted by the Ottoman rulers of Palestine. The concession extends for twenty kilometers from the point regarded by medieval cartographers as the center of the world—the dome of the Church of the Holy Sepulchre. When the British occupied Palestine in 1917, they refused to recognize the concession issued by the Ottomans.[77] The Greek entrepreneur, however, appealed to the Permanent Court of International Justice at the Hague, which upheld the concession. In 1926 a British firm bought the concession from Mavromatis and built a power station in Jerusalem. Just before their departure from Palestine in 1948 the British extended the concession retroactively for sixty years from January 1, 1926, until December 31, 1987. After the establishment of the State of Israel in 1948 and the War of Independence, Jerusalem was divided into two parts, Israeli and Jordanian. The concession was also divided between the two countries. In 1954 Israel and Jordan conducted secret negotiations that culminated in the purchase of the West Jerusalem concession by the Israeli Electric Company (IEC).[78] The Jordanian government bought the company in

1957 from its private owners, and JDEC became a public company. Its board of directors was composed of two thousand private shareholders and representatives of West Bank municipalities: Beit Sahor, Beit Jallah, Ramallah, El-Bireh, Bethlehem, and Jerusalem. In 1962 the concession was also extended to Jericho, which sent a representative to the company's board of directors.

With the 1967 occupation of East Jerusalem and the West Bank by Israel JDEC became a focal point for political maneuvering and power struggles between Israel, Jordan, and the Palestinians. The question of control of the company became of paramount concern because it was the largest employer in the West Bank and was regarded as a national institution by most Palestinians. The company was transformed from a purely economic unit into a nationalist symbol, part of the Palestinian quest for an independent infrastructure that would pave the way to an independent state. In a sense the struggle over control of the company was a microcosm of the conflict between Israel and the pro-Jordanians and Palestinian nationalists in the West Bank. The erosion of Jordan's ability to control events inside the company attested to its gradual loss of power in the West Bank. From an Israeli perspective control of the company became an important aspect of Israel's West Bank policy, which sought to contain Palestinian nationalism.

When Jerusalem was unified in 1967, Israel decided to uphold the status quo because nationalization of the company would be interpreted as an attempt to alter the Arab character of East Jerusalem.[79] It was not until the end of the concession in 1988 that Israel disconnected West Jerusalem and its West Bank settlements from the East Jerusalem company.

From a legal perspective an anomaly was created. Because East Jerusalem was annexed by Israel in 1967, Israeli law applied to the company in the Jerusalem area. Hence, the company was required to register as an Israeli company in 1968. But according to Israeli Military Order No. 2, Jordanian law regulated the company's activities in the West Bank.[80] This meant that the concession that existed under the Jordanians remained intact. The Israeli settlements and military outposts in the West Bank were linked to the Arab electric company. JDEC insisted on providing electricity to the Jewish settlements and military installations in the West Bank because of fear that it would lose its concession altogether. After intense negotiations between Israel and the company after the 1967 war, the Israeli government agreed to the company's demands with the provision that it accept Israeli tariffs and send its bills and notices to its Jewish customers in Hebrew.

The increase in Jewish construction and the growth of Jewish settlements in the concession area led to a substantial increase in service by the company. Between 1969 and 1977 JDEC had an annual growth rate of 25–30 percent compared with 8 percent for the Israeli Electric Company.[81]

JDEC was unable to meet the demand and began buying electricity from JEC. By 1986 it was serving one hundred thousand customers, thirty thousand of whom were Jews, and was buying 90 percent of its electricity from IEC, incurring a debt of $12 million.[82]

After the Yom Kippur War, the energy crisis, and the 1974 Rabat decision to grant the PLO the status of "sole legitimate representative of the Palestinian people," the power struggle inside the company between the supporters of Jordan and those of the PLO intensified. Because the company's board of directors mainly came from the West Bank municipalities, the 1976 elections, which resulted in a victory for pro-PLO nationalists, were reflected in the company as well. For example, among the board members were Bishara Daoud of Beit Jallah, who was close to Fatah; Karim Khalaf of Ramallah, who was identified with the radical Democratic Front for the Liberation of Palestine (DFLP); and Ibrahim Tawil of El-Bireh, also a Fatah supporter. Pro-Jordanians, such as Elias Freij, the mayor of Bethlehem, were on the defensive. Eventually, Jordan's supporters—the mayors of Bethlehem, Beit Jallah, Beit Sahur, and Jericho—were forced to resign.[83] By 1981 the company's board was composed of a majority of pro-PLO individuals.

As a result of the 1978 Baghdad Arab summit, which established the Joint Jordanian-PLO Committee, Jordan was no longer considered the only party responsible for supervising and regulating the company. In 1979 Elias Freij, mayor of Bethlehem, and Israeli Minister of Energy Yitzhak Modai agreed on a plan to disconnect all Israeli military installations and Jewish settlements from the JDEC. Yet the agreement was torpedoed by Anwar Nusseibah, the newly appointed chairman of the JDEC board. Nusseibah, a former defense minister in the Jordanian government, was expected by the Israeli and Jordanian authorities to represent Jordanian interests in the company. But he did not meet these expectations. Instead, he proved to be an ardent supporter of the pro-PLO elements in the company.

Nusseibah, on the one hand, believed that once part of the concession was taken away Israel would use the precedent to take over the company. Freij, on the other hand, believed that the agreement should be signed, saying that "there is no logic in investing Arab money in illegal Jewish settlements."[84] The company's labor union also opposed the deal because it feared that once part of the concession was lost, the company's labor force would also be reduced. As a sign of protest against the deal, the company's employees began a strike. In August 1979 the Israeli government decided to purchase the company by January 1, 1981, because of its poor productivity, its growing debt to Israel, and the dependence of Israel's military bases in the West Bank on Arab electricity, which was considered unwise from a security point of view.

JDEC challenged Israel's decision to purchase the company at the Israeli High Court. The High Court rejected Israel's claim that the minister of energy had "absolute discretion" under the terms of the original concession without having to provide any reasons for his decision.[85] The court also rejected the state's argument that the purpose for purchasing the company was solely rooted in economic and technical reasons. The company argued that Israel's real motives were aimed at controlling the largest Palestinian institution on the West Bank. The court sided with JDEC and ruled in favor of maintaining the status quo.[86]

Thus, the court barred Israel from proceeding with its takeover bid in the West Bank. The court, however, did rule that Israel could purchase the concession in the Jerusalem area. It based this decision on the distinction it made between Jerusalem, which was under Israeli sovereignty, and the West Bank, which it regarded as occupied territory. The decision to allow Israel to purchase the Jerusalem concession was merely deemed impractical. Although the generators were in Jerusalem, all the electrical lines were in the West Bank. Consequently, Israel decided to wait until the concession ended in 1987 before taking further action.

By 1986 the company was facing a serious financial crisis. Its debt to IEC had reached $12 million, and it was operating at a deficit. Despite repeated appeals by the company's directors for Jordanian help, Jordan refused to help as long as JDEC refused to accept its conditions for restructuring the company. Jordan viewed the struggle mainly in political terms. It had no interest in assisting a company controlled by pro-PLO elements. The Jordanian decision to withhold funds occurred at a time when its relationship with the PLO had reached its nadir. By placing a number of conditions on the company, Hussein sought to demonstrate to the Palestinians in the territories who was stronger and whom they should support in the dispute with the PLO.[87]

The Jordanian conditions were stated in a letter addressed to the company's board of directors (indirectly addressed to Israel) by Taher Cana'an, the Jordanian minister of the occupied territories, on March 16, 1986. It stated that Jordan would be willing to aid the company if it implemented a recovery plan based on the recommendations of Yehezkel Flomin (an accountant and a former Israeli official). The second condition was that the concession be extended beyond 1987. Flomin provided JDEC with a detailed assessment of its financial status.[88] He discovered that JDEC had incurred a staggering debt because of its old equipment and the insufficient price differential between JDEC's buying price and IEC's selling price. Flumin recommended that JDEC reduce the large number of employees (five hundred) and modernize its equipment and that Israel reduce its selling rate to JDEC by 20 percent to correspond to the real operating conditions of the company.

When JDEC Chairman Anwar Nusseibah died in December 1986, his brother, Hazam, arrived from Jordan for the funeral. Hazam Nusseibah, a former Jordanian foreign minister and a close confidant of Hussein, was able to reach an agreement with Israeli Minister of Energy Moshe Shahal on the future of the company. The agreement stipulated that the company's concession be extended beyond 1987 until the year 2000. In return, it was agreed that the Jewish settlements, military bases, and Jewish residents of Jerusalem would be connected to the Israeli Electric Company. This agreement should be viewed as part of the Israeli-Jordanian attempt to create a West Bank condominium.[89] By August 1987 the Israeli government had voted to extend the concession until the year 2000 in the West Bank. Israel took over some of the company's old equipment in lieu of its debt to Israel and also reduced the staff by half.[90] All of the company's Jewish customers were connected to the national grid on December 6, 1987. Thus ended a power struggle over the largest Palestinian national institution in the territories. Jordan was satisfied with the renewed concession, Israel was no longer dependent on Arab electricity, and the Palestinians were able to continue to manage their largest institution as a symbol of their nationalist struggle.

Sharing the Water

Much ink has been spilled in the dispute over water in the Arab-Israeli conflict. The scarcity of water in the Middle East coupled with rapid development and population growth led to intractable conflict over the years, which was inextricably linked to developments in the Arab-Israeli conflict. As long as Israel and her neighbors were in a state of war, overt cooperation in developing a water-sharing regime was not feasible. Yet a number of tacit agreements were reached between Israel and Jordan that helped reduce tensions over this issue. In the absence of a formal agreement excessive water use with a disregard for the needs of other parties had the potential to aggravate the Arab-Israeli conflict.

The water issue, however, attests to the durability and quality of Israeli-Jordanian interdependence more than any other aspect of the relationship. Despite fundamental disagreements the two countries have adhered to a tacit regime of water sharing since the early 1950s. With the signing of the 1994 peace treaty a formal agreement on water sharing became a reality. Article 6 in the Treaty of Peace and Annex II to the treaty establish specific water allocation quotas from the Yarmuk and Jordan rivers, provide for cooperation in storage and protection of water quality, among other areas of concern, and establish a Joint Water Committee. (The article dealing with water was placed in the text immediately after "Diplomatic and Other Bilateral Relations," attesting to the importance of water for Jordan and Israel.[91]

The upper part of the Jordan River consists of a number of springs. The Dan Spring, which is located inside Israel, contributes about 50 percent of the Jordan's discharge.[92] The other two feeders are the Hasbani and Banias rivers. The Hasbani flows into the Jordan from springs located in Lebanon, whereas the Banias originates in Syria. These three systems form the upper Jordan River, which flows into the Sea of Galilee in Northern Israel. Just south of the lake, the Yarmuk River flows into the lower Jordan River from the east. The Yarmuk forms the border between Syria and Jordan for forty kilometers then becomes the Jordanian-Israeli border.[93] Each of these tributaries is an international water.[94] As Selig Taubenblat notes, the main reason for the persistence of conflict over water was the division of the river among four riparians: Jordan, Syria, Lebanon (all of which were in a state of war with Israel), and Israel. "In the case of the Yarmouk River, Syria is an upper riparian to Jordan, and Jordan is an upper riparian to Israel. In the case of the Jordan River, Syria and Lebanon are upper riparians to Israel, and Israel is an upper riparian to Jordan."[95]

In the lower Jordan River, below the Sea of Galilee, the river forms the international boundary between Israel and Jordan for 40 kilometers after which it forms the western boundary of the West Bank. The river ends where it flows into the Dead Sea. The total distance between the Sea of Galilee and the Dead Sea is 320 kilometers.

In 1964 Israel completed the construction of its National Water Carrier, which supplies water from the upper Jordan River to the arid Negev. This project, which lies totally within Israel's 1967 borders, caused much conflict with the Arab states. They objected to Israel's use of "Arab water" drawn from the Jordan River. The Arab states charged that "Israel preempted the clean waters of northern Lake Tiberias with the result that the only water Israel returned to the lower Jordan was primarily irrigation runoff."[96] Consequently, the Arab League devised a plan to divert the Hasbani and Banias Rivers to the Yarmuk.[97] Because the diversion was mainly carried out by Syria, Israel considered the project a hostile act against its sovereign rights to water.[98] Israel subsequently bombed the project, and construction came to a halt with the start of the 1967 war. It could be argued that the conflict over water was a major contributing factor to the outbreak of the 1967 war.

The basis for Arab-Israeli water sharing is found in the 1953–55 negotiations under the auspices of U.S. mediator Erik Johnston, who was appointed by President Eisenhower to devise a regional plan for water utilization in the Jordan River system. A number of plans submitted by various experts formed the basis for negotiations.[99] Discussions focused on the following major issues: the allocation of water quotas for the riparian states; the use of the Sea of Galilee as a storage facility; the use of water from the Jordan River for out-of-basin usage; the incorporation of the Litani River in southern Lebanon into the water regime; and international monitoring and guarantees.[100]

After some hard bargaining, a compromise solution was found on most issues. Israel was allotted 400 million cubic meters per annum (mcm/yr.), Jordan 720 mcm/yr., Syria 132 mcm/yr., and Lebanon 35 mcm/yr. The Sea of Galilee could serve as a reservoir, and water could be used for out-of-basin purposes. Israel agreed to forego its demand for the integration of the Litani into the system in exchange for an agreement by the Arabs to reduce their water quotas and to permit Israel to use the Jordan water for its coastal plan and the Negev.[101] This agreement, which became known as Johnston's Unified Plan, was never officially ratified by either the Arab states or Israel.[102] Nonetheless, the plan served as the basis from which the riparian states drew their water from the system. Occasionally, a violation on either side had occurred but in most cases the agreement was adhered to.

After the 1967 war, with the occupation of the West Bank and the Golan Heights, Israel's water resources were greatly expanded. Israel then controlled almost half of the Yarmuk River as well as two major aquifers in the West Bank, which provide most of the water within the pre-1967 boundaries. Israel is perceived by Palestinians as exploiting the water resources, pumping 600 mcm/yr., about one-third of its total supply, out of which 115 mcm/yr. is allocated to the 1.4 million Palestinians in the West Bank and 30 mcm/yr. to the 130,000 settlers, and the rest supplied water to Jerusalem and Tel Aviv.[103]

During the 1995 negotiations between Israel and the PLO on the implementation of the self-rule agreement in the West Bank the question of water allocation sharply divided the two sides. Israel demanded that the allocation regime that was in place during its occupation of the West Bank remain for the duration of the interim autonomy agreement, leaving questions pertaining to water rights and use to be discussed during the negotiations about the territories' final status. The Palestinians, however, vehemently objected to such an unfair arrangement and protested against the favorable treatment of Jewish settlements. The most important issue that divided the two sides pertains to the Yarkon-Taninim aquifer, an underground water basin that extends from Israel's coast near Tel Aviv to the West Bank towns of Tulkarem and Kalkilya, under the area designated as the Palestinian Autonomous Area. This is the largest and best source of water between the Jordan River and the

Mediterranean Sea. Israel's water consumption per capita is at least four times greater than the Palestinians; but the Palestinians insisted on their right to the water. In August 1995 an interim solution was found, guaranteeing access by both sides and taking the needs of each party into account. Israel agreed to recognize Palestinian water rights in the West Bank while the Palestinians agreed to postpone further discussions on this issue until the negotiations on the final status of the territories resume.

From 1968 to 1969 Palestinian guerrillas launched numerous raids from Jordan against Israeli targets, including water pumping stations and water projects. Nabil al-Sha'ath, a close adviser of Yasser Arafat, noted: "The water issue was the crucial one. We considered our [the PLO's] impact on this to be the crucial test of our war with Israel." Indeed, the first military action against an Israeli target after the establishment of the PLO in 1964 was carried out by al-Assifa, the military branch of Fatah. It was an unsuccessful attempt to sabotage Israel's National Water Carrier on December 31, 1964.[104]

Jordan began construction of the East Ghor Canal in 1959, diverting water from the Yarmuk River to the east side of the Jordan Valley. As part of its campaign against the PLO in Jordan, Israel sought to apply pressure on Jordan to curtail PLO activities against Israel by raiding and bombing the canal. Israel hoped King Hussein would act against the PLO.[105] These military exchanges led to secret Israeli-Jordanian negotiations in July 1969, producing an agreement whereby Jordan pledged to curtail PLO attacks and Israel allowed the canal to be repaired.[106]

After the 1970–71 civil war against the PLO in Jordan, which led to the expulsion of the organization from Jordan, calm was restored to the Israeli-Jordanian border. The two parties continued to adhere to the technical aspects of the Johnston Unified Plan concerning the water quotas from the Jordan and Yarmuk Rivers. In this regard several Israel-Jordanian meetings took place, which focused on the bilateral aspects of water sharing in the Jordan River system.[107]

During the 1967 war Israel occupied the northern bank of the Yarmuk River, which forms the Syrian-Jordanian border. One of the recurring problems that Jordan has faced since then has been the removal of accumulated silt, which interferes with the river's flow. According to Thomas Naff, a leading expert on the subject, in 1976 with the help of the United States. Jordan gained Israeli approval for silt removal.[108] This issue came to the fore again in 1979 when Jordan threatened to mobilize its army if Israel did not allow it to clear the intake canal. A severe drought affected the region in the summer of 1979 and Israel charged that Jordan was diverting additional water from the Yarmuk for cleaning efforts. Israel claimed that its part of the river had dried up. Consequently, Israeli tractors diverted the Yarmuk to its original path.[109] In another incident the United States midwifed an additional Israeli-Jordanian agreement to remove the rocks from the silt bar. Jordan charged that Israel had violated the agreement because it had placed the rocks so that scarcely any water reached the Jordanian canal. Here again, American mediation helped avert that crisis.[110] On the question of water allocation from the Yarmuk, several rounds of Israeli-Jordanian negotiations took place in 1979–80. In 1979 a high-ranking American delegation headed by Joseph Wheeler, senior assistant administrator of the Agency of International Development (AID), mediated between the parties.[111] In the fall of 1980 Philip Habib, U.S. special envoy to the Yarmuk River negotiations, visited the region. The talks centered around two issues: the building of the Maqarin Dam over the Yarmuk River and a large Jordanian storage facility and the allocation of the waters that would be harnessed.[112] Israel demanded that the water from the dam be allocated to the West Bank because its underground reservoirs had been almost totally depleted.[113] Although Jordan had a direct interest in reaching a tacit agreement with Israel about the use of the Jordan and Yarmuk rivers, it had minimal incentives to negotiate water supplies to the West Bank, a former Jordanian territory. Even before Hussein's July 1988 disengagement from the West Bank, Jordan was reluctant to reach an accord with Israel over the West Bank because Jordan feared that Israel would return the West Bank to the Palestinians. If an independent Palestinian state were established, the Jordanians reasoned, the agreement would have to be renegotiated anyway.[114]

The Maqarin Dam negotiations did not bear fruit because the project was canceled in favor of a smaller-scale dam—the Unity Dam—which became the focal point for negotiations in the mid-1980s. In 1984, as Thomas Naff notes, Jordan charged Israel with excessive use of the Yarmuk beyond the Johnston Plan quota. It claimed that Israel was using 100 mcm/yr., well above the 25 mcm/yr. allotted to Israel in the plan. Israel, however, offered its own interpretation of the plan, claiming that it was allowed to draw 25 mcm/yr. during the summer and unlimited amounts of water during the rainy winter season.[115]

Another constant irritant was the clearing of the intake to the East Ghor Canal, which required constant cleaning of the rocks that interfered with the water flow. Occasionally, both countries had moved the rocks to increase the water flow to their respective territories. This issue was partially resolved through American mediation, which enabled the parties to reach a modus vivendi.[116] Until the signing of the Israeli-Jordanian water agreement contained in the Treaty of Peace, regular contacts regarding the water issue were maintained between the two countries.[117] Jonathan Randal of the *Washington Post* maintained that once each month from May to October, Jordanian and Israeli hydrologists met along the Yarmuk River to discuss issues related to water sharing.[118] In April 1992 during the bilateral negotiations between the two countries Israel reportedly submitted a comprehensive proposal to Jordan regarding the establishment of a joint administration of regional water resources. This proposal was based on ongoing discussions held between officials from the two countries. Although the Jordanians embraced the suggestions with enthusiasm during the talks, they linked their implementation to progress in the talks held with the PLO.[119] The two parties also were concerned about the building of the Syrian dam at Sheikh Misk on the Yarmuk, which involved the building of dams in the Israeli-Syrian disengagement zone established after the 1973 war. This issue also concerned Jordan because Jordan shares the Yarmuk River with Syria.[120]

Yet the biggest source of potential conflict was the plan by Jordan and Syria to build the Unity Dam. It was expected to be 100 meters high with an annual storage capacity of 220 mcm and to provide Syria with electricity and greatly expand Jordan's irrigation system.[121] Israel, however, argued that any project dealing with the Yarmuk must also take Israeli interests into account. In return for its consent, Israel demanded that some of the Yarmuk waters be used to fill its depleted aquifers and even threatened to bomb the facility if an agreement was not reached.[122] The Syrian-Jordanian project, however, seems now to be on hold in light of the Jordanian-Israeli water agreement.

Water shortages will haunt the countries of the Middle East for years to come. Naff estimates that by the year 2000 Israel will face a deficit of 800 mcm/yr. and Jordan 170 mcm/yr.[123] Before they signed the water agreement as part of the peace treaty, the two countries had managed to maintain a water regime by adhering to the Johnston Plan and by conducting bilateral negotiations directly or through the United States.

The multilateral regional talks about water between Israel and her neighbors, which started in May 1992, provided momentum for the bilateral talks between Israel and Jordan. During the fourth round of talks held in November 1993 in Beijing much progress was made, including discussions of concrete proposals such as the construction of canals from the Mediterranean to the Jordan River; the establishment of a regional database about water; and Israeli-Arab cooperation in a process called cloud seeding.[124]

With the signing of the water agreement, Jordan's allocation of water increased by more than 25 percent and an elaborate bilateral water-sharing management regime was finally installed, thus alleviating a major burden, especially for Jordan. The vital concern about water has affected the relationship of the two countries since Israel's establishment.[125] The

Palestinians, however, claim that Israel made an agreement with Jordan about water that is Palestinian: water from the eastern basin of the mountain aquifer and water from the Jordan River that will be Palestinian in the future. Therefore, they seek compensation from both Israel and Jordan. In February 1996 in Oslo, Israel, Jordan and the PLO signed a regional water cooperation agreement as part of the multilateral Arab-Israeli peace negotiations. They pledged cooperation in developing new water sources and coordination of the water infrastructure in the Middle East.

These myriad examples of Israeli-Jordanian functional cooperation that took place over the years while the two countries were in a formal state of war played a major role in the 1994 peace treaty. It is not surprising, therefore, that seventeen of thirty articles in the Treaty of Peace concern Israeli-Jordanian cooperation in most aspects of life. By comparison, the 1979 Israeli-Egyptian peace accord contains no references to specific areas of Egyptian-Israeli cooperation. Unlike Israel's "cold" peace with Egypt, the Jordanian-Israeli treaty has the potential to lead to a "warm" peace, one based on genuine economic and political cooperation. If a comprehensive peace is achieved in the Arab-Israeli-Palestinian zone, then Israel and Jordan can capitalize upon their past clandestine cooperation and transform their relationship into an open partnership.[126] The experience gained during past decades of functional cooperation could serve as a foundation for and a model of Arab-Israeli reconciliation and mutual respect.

4

The Beginning of the Peace Process, 1967–1974

Having examined the substance of Israeli-Jordanian functional cooperation in the previous chapters, I focus here on the diplomatic peace process that unfolded during the 1967–88 period. As noted earlier, Israeli-Jordanian relations after the 1967 war were based on a dual-track approach. The first entailed the establishment and maintenance of functional cooperation aimed at furthering the two countries' converging interests in the territories and outside. The second track addressed the peace process either through secret Jordanian-Israeli meetings or through indirect public negotiations via third parties.

Routine clandestine rendezvous between Jordanian and Israeli officials took place throughout the period, including dozens of meetings among top leadership of the two countries. By 1977, when the Labor Party lost the election, all its leaders, including Yigal Allon, Abba Eban, Golda Meir, Moshe Dayan, Shimon Peres, and Yitzhak Rabin, had met King Hussein numerous times. King Hussein maintained that he held more than eight hundred hours of meetings with Israel's leadership. During the Likud's first term in office, between 1977 and 1984, only one meeting was held with King Hussein (with Moshe Dayan, who joined the Likud as its foreign minister). During the first tenure of the Government of National Unity, 1984–88, a number of encounters took place between Israeli and Jordanian leaders including several secret meetings between Shimon Peres and King Hussein that led to the signing of the April 1987 London Agreement. George Shultz, secretary of state under President Ronald Reagan, recounts in his memoirs that even Yitzhak Shamir, known for his anti-Jordanian views, met the king in July 1987. Two weeks after the 1992 election of Yitzhak Rabin to the post of prime minister, the first newspaper report (denied by both sides) about a secret meeting between King Hussein and the Israeli leader was published in the semi-official Egyptian paper *Al-Ahram*. In addition, Yitzhak Rabin,

Shimon Peres, and King Hussein met several times after the signing of the Israel-PLO accord in efforts to convince the king to sign a peace treaty and to enlist Jordan's support for the agreement with the PLO. The first public meeting between an Israeli and Jordanian leader took place when Peres and Crown Prince Hassan met at the White House on October 1, 1993, to announce the formation of a joint economic committee. Thereafter, numerous public meetings involving Israeli and Jordanian officials took place. King Hussein visited Israel twice in 1995, once when he attended Prime Minister Rabin's funeral in November.

The second track was based on a series of indirect public dialogues carried out through the good offices of a third party, such as those by United Nations Special Representative Gunnar Jarring and various American emissaries. Here the dialogue focused on the formal peace process and exploration of a possible Israeli withdrawal from the occupied territories in exchange for Arab recognition as stipulated in United Nations Security Council Resolutions 242 and 338.

After the 1967 war the United Nations, Israel, Jordan, and the United States initiated efforts to reach a formal peace settlement. An analysis of three watershed events is fundamental to an understanding of Israeli-Jordanian relations. The first was the 1970 civil war in Jordan in which King Hussein and the PLO, fought for control of the country. During the war Syria intervened militarily on the side of the PLO resulting in Israeli mobilization of its military to protect Hussein from being toppled, which provided the king with a strategic umbrella. The events of 1970 demonstrate the competitive/cooperative nature of Jordanian-Palestinian relations and attest to Israel's resolve to provide a strategic umbrella to Jordan to safeguard a vital Israeli interest, preventing the establishment of a Palestinian state on either bank of the Jordan River. In addition, during the fighting Israel provided Jordan with medical aid and food supplies—a testimony to the close functional cooperation that began to emerge between the two countries in the post-1967 period.

The second event was the unveiling of King Hussein's United Kingdom Plan in 1972. This plan offered to incorporate the West Bank into a federal system by creating a new entity—the United Arab Kingdom. It reflected the philosophical and political outlook that Hussein envisaged concerning Palestinian nationalism and the future of the West Bank. With the signing of the 1993 PLO-Israeli accord, the plan would become relevant to the discussions between Jordanian and PLO officials concerning the future relationship between the two banks once a formal peace treaty is signed between Israel and the PLO and the final status of the West Bank and Gaza is determined.

Israeli-Jordanian negotiations failed to produce a military disengagement agreement in the wake of the Yom Kippur War. Lack of a disengagement accord had far-reaching implications for both Jordanian-Israeli relations and the Arab-Israeli peace process.

As discussed earlier, after the Six-Day War, four dominant positions emerged in the Israeli national unity government on the question of peace with Jordan: the territorialist position, which advocated a partial Israeli withdrawal; the reconciliationist, which supported a return to the pre-1967 border in exchange for contractual peace; and the functionalist position, which did not address Israeli withdrawal from the territories per se but called for maintenance of a Jordanian presence through the open bridges policy. The fourth position, the annexationist, supported Israeli sovereignty over the West Bank, which it considered to be part of Greater Israel.

The lack of consensus on the future of the territories was manifested in the secret resolution reached by the Israeli government on June 19, 1967. This resolution called for a return to the pre-1967 borders in the Sinai Peninsula and the Golan Heights. The question of the West Bank and Gaza was left in abeyance and not mentioned in the resolution because of the conflicting positions within the government on this issue. Begin and Dayan pressured other members of the government to support the resolution because they opposed an Israeli withdrawal.[1]

Jordan's formal position on the terms of a peace settlement required a total Israeli withdrawal from the West Bank, including East Jerusalem. Israel's position was markedly different from that of Jordan. It aimed at securing public direct negotiations with the Arab states. Israel insisted on this policy because the Arab states refused to recognize it, and recognition meant legitimacy. This policy was officially declared by the Knesset in a resolution on August 1, 1967: "The Knesset confirms the government's stand that by means of direct negotiations between Israel and the Arab countries the conclusion of peace treaties should be brought about; and that until peace is achieved, Israel will continue to maintain fully the present situation as created by the cease-fire which the Israeli Defense Forces' successful repulsion of aggression effected."[2]

Although Hussein was willing to explore the possibility of a settlement directly with Israel in his secret contacts, publicly, he could not deviate from the overall Arab position that precluded direct negotiations with Israel. Hussein believed that moving alone was too risky; he constantly sought Arab backing for his public moves.

A united pan-Arab position began to crystallize in the Khartoum summit conference convened in late August 1967. Before the conference, Hussein declared: "I have repeatedly said that peace is quite possible, if there is justice. But, so long as Israel holds on to the Arab territories she has occupied since the 5th of June, then peace is un-likely."[3]

In preparation for the Arab League summit convened in Khartoum, Hussein traveled to Cairo in an attempt to solicit the approval of Egypt's President Nasser for negotiations with Israel, but Nasser refused. In addition, the King proposed that the summit adopt a position that provided for the demilitarization of the West Bank once it was evacuated by Israel. He also proposed that East Jerusalem be returned to Jordan and that the Wailing Wall could be an Israeli enclave inside Jordanian territory. These proposals were also rejected by the Arab leaders.[4] Instead, the resolution that was adopted by the Khartoum Conference contained the famous "three no's": "That there shall be no peace with Israel, no recognition of Israel, no negotiations with Israel, and that the Arab nations shall take action to safeguard the right of the people of Palestine to their homeland."[5]

Jordanian and Israeli interpretations of this resolution were mark-edly different. Israel viewed the "three no's" in the resolution as a total rejection of a diplomatic resolution of the conflict. Hussein believed that he had some room to maneuver. During a meeting with British Prime Minister Harold Wilson, Hussein was asked how he intended to proceed with the peace process after having said "no" three times. Hussein's response was that the Arab states said in the communiqué that there would be no *sulh*, or reconciliation, with Israel. The word *salaam*, or peace, was not used. In other words, Hussein meant that the Arabs were not opposed to peace with Israel but only to normalization of relations.[6]

Conflicting Interpretations of Resolution 242

A similar clash over interpretations occurred after the Security Council adopted United Nations Resolution 242 on November 22, 1967. This resolution became the cornerstone of most subsequent peace efforts to resolve the conflict by establishing the formula "land for peace." In other words, in exchange for Israeli withdrawal from the territories occupied in 1967, the Arab states would offer a contractual peace agreement.

The main difference between Israel and the Arab states on this is-sue was the interpretation of the withdrawal clause in the resolution. Israel insisted on the English language version, which called for "with-drawal . . . from territories," arguing that this did not mean withdrawal from *all* the territories. The Arab states, however, upheld the French language version, which uses the definite article *des* (the) *territoires occupées* (occupied territories) because the Arabs believed this meant Israel had to withdraw from *all* the territories.

Israel's official reaction to Resolution 242 was favorable. An Israeli diplomat commented, "We can live with it. . . . It is probably the best resolution we could have hoped for under the circumstances."[7] It should be noted, however, that the Israeli government did not officially accept 242 until August 1970 when it endorsed the Rogers Initiative, which called for an Israeli-Egyptian cease-fire agreement during the War of Attrition.

Israel's interpretation of Resolution 242 did not specify the details of the envisioned settlement nor did it accept Arab demands for its implementation without negotiations. But there was no consensus in the Israeli government on whether to accept the resolution. Dayan, for example, argued that "as long as the present situation exists—the way we are established in the territories must remain. . . . I suggest refraining from announcing that Israel accepts the Security Council Resolution of November 22 as a basis for a solution, because it means withdrawal to the June 4 boundaries and because we are in conflict with the Security Council on that resolution."[8] Eban, the reconciliationist, argued that "while the United States, Britain and many other Western states interpret the resolution as calling for new borders, why must Israel of all people come forth and say that the interpretation should be the one argued by the Soviet Union and Nasser? This was political defeatism."[9] When Israel's ambassador to the United Nations, Yoseph Tekoah, told the Security Council on May 1, 1968, that Israel accepted 242, an acrimonious debate erupted in the Israeli cabinet. Begin, the annexationist, led the attack against Eban for not seeking a prior authorization from the government over such a vital issue.[10] Subsequently, until Israel's official endorsement of 242 in 1970, this issue was feverishly debated, and each school of thought offered its own interpretation of the true meaning of the cabinet announcement.

The Jordanians took a favorable view of the Security Council Resolution even before it was officially adopted. While visiting the United States in early November, Hussein declared in a speech at Georgetown University: "Israel is a present fact of life. We may not like it, and we may choose not to recognize it, just as we choose not to recognize Red China."[11]

The Egyptians also supported the resolution. Mohammed Zayyat, the spokesman for the Egyptian government, announced that "the right of each party to security and freedom from fear of attack by the armed forces of the other shall be fully respected."[12] The only country bordering Israel that flatly rejected U.N. Resolution 242 was Syria, because it felt that the resolution "refers to Israel's right to exist and it ignores the right of the [Palestinian] refugees to return to their homes."[13] Iraq, Algeria, and Saudi Arabia were also vocal opponents of Resolution 242 at the time. The PLO denounced the resolution because it referred to the Palestinians merely as "refugees" and because the resolution accepted Israel's right to exist.

The initial support for the resolution by Jordan and Egypt apparently stemmed from their desire to have the United States work toward Israeli withdrawal. The Israelis went along because of the inherent ambiguities in the text that left them room to maneuver. As for an American commitment to a full Israeli withdrawal, Donald Neff maintains in *Warriors for Jerusalem* that during Hussein's visit to the United States in November 1967 the administration gave him assurances that Israel would withdraw from the West Bank within six months. "Thus by the first week of November the United States position was established—and made clear to the Arab states," writes Neff. "It would support adjustments to the armistice lines, but still it was assumed that they would entail only minor bits of land and that Israel's withdrawal would be nearly complete in return for peace."[14] Neff further argues that Eban also agreed to American assurances concerning an almost total withdrawal. Had Eban agreed to such a compromise, this would have contradicted Israel's June 19, 1967, resolution that called for the return of the Sinai and Golan Heights but never referred to the West Bank because there was no consensus on that issue. Hence, Eban's comment could not be considered a commitment by the Israeli government and should be viewed as private in nature.

What emerged toward the end of 1967 was a new consensus on the part of the Israeli government. On December 1, 1967, Israeli Premier Levi Eshkol outlined the new Israeli position that emphasized "secure and recognized borders which are different from those of 1949; and . . . direct negotiations."[15]

The first secret meeting between Israel and Jordan after the 1967 war took place in September 1967 in London, followed by several meetings in 1968.[16] In January 1968 the Israeli Labor Party was established, composed of Mapai, the reconciliationist party; Rafi, represented by Dayan and Peres, the functionalists; and Ahdut Ha'Avoda, represented by Allon and Yisrael Galili, the territorialists. By then it had become clear that the various Israeli positions canceled each other; when combined with the differences between Israel and Jordan on the vital questions of withdrawal and direct negotiations, the status quo became inevitable.

Consequently, Hussein had begun to sense that despite American promises that Israel would return the West Bank to Jordan the Israelis were divided on the question of peace with Jordan. His hopes of quickly recovering the territories began to fade. But on the public diplomatic level, indirect Israeli-Jordanian contacts continued through the efforts of United Nations mediator Gunnar Jarring.

During the Israeli-Jordanian secret meetings in 1968 functional ties and bilateral issues, rather than the peace process, dominated the discussion.[17] In the West Bank the process of "creating facts" was put into motion, and gradually, Dayan's functionalist position began to triumph.

The Jarring Mission

United Nations Security Council Resolution 242 called for the appointment of a special representative to promote a settlement. Secretary-General U Thant appointed Gunnar Jarring, the Swedish ambassador to the Soviet Union. Jarring shuttled between the capitals of the Middle East between 1967 and 1972, negotiating with representatives of Israel, Jordan, and Egypt. Syria did not participate because at that time it rejected 242.[18] Although negotiations did not produce any concrete results, some aspects of the Jarring mission need to be discussed in the context of Israeli-Jordanian relations. The opposing parties did modify their positions to some extent during the negotiations, but talks also highlighted the wide gulf that separated Israel, Jordan, and Egypt at that time.[19]

As Saadia Touval notes, "The negotiations were in fact about negotiations."[20] This was so because the parties themselves held divergent views on the purpose of the mission, all of which emanated from conflicting interpretations of 242. Israel demanded direct negotiations because this was the only way it could gain recognition from the Arab states. Israel interpreted the Jarring mission as one of "good offices" rather than mediation. The Arab states viewed the Jarring mission as procedural only. They wanted Jarring to bring about an Israeli withdrawal but did not want to recognize Israel or to sign a formal peace treaty with the Jewish state. Israel insisted on direct negotiations, whereas the Arab states were suspicious that Israel was using direct negotiations as an attempt to elicit recognition without making any substantive concessions. An additional problem that later haunted the negotiation process was Jarring's personal style of diplomacy, which was discreet and formal. As Abba Eban observed: "His mind moved strictly with the rational limits of European humanism. He assumed that nations, like individuals, guided their actions by reason. He later came to learn that logic played a very small part in the history of the Middle East."[21]

Israel's initial position was presented by Eban to Jarring on December 27, 1967. Although the proposal was specifically addressed to Egypt, its principles also applied to peace with Jordan. It included, inter alia, "The replacement of cease-fire arrangements by peace treaties ending the state of belligerency . . . [and] [t]he determination of agreed territorial boundaries and security arrangements.[22] A similar proposal for peace with Jordan was submitted to Jarring on January 7, 1968. It contained the aforementioned principles and included references to the "refugee problem" and access to the holy sites in Jerusalem.[23]

Jordan's rejection of the Israeli proposals coincided with Egypt's rejection as well because "the withdrawal of Israel's forces to the position held prior to June 1967 was a basic and preliminary step to a peaceful settlement in the Middle East."[24] In other words, the Arab states demanded a withdrawal before negotiations with Israel. As an attempt to break this initial deadlock, which contained both procedural and conceptual disagreements, Jarring sought to clarify each party's position. He hoped that the elimination of ambiguities would pave the way to negotiations. Jarring's efforts bore some fruit: Israel did change its view of 242 arguing that it was "a framework for agreement. It cannot be fulfilled without a direct exchange of views and proposals leading to a bilateral contractual commitment."[25] Israel also modified its views concerning direct negotiations. Abba Eban stated on February 19, 1968, that Israel would not object to an indirect approach to negotiations provided that it was designed to lead to direct negotiations and agreement. In other words, Israel accepted the indirect "Rhodes-type" formula if it would lead to a peace treaty. After Israel agreed to indirect negotiations, Jarring drafted an invitation for a conference to be held in Nicosia, Cyprus. Yet this effort failed because of Egypt's insistence that Israel give formal assurances that it would fully implement 242. The Jordanians issued a similar response. On March 14 they declared their readiness for indirect negotiations, provided that Israel made such a declaration.

The conflicting interpretations of 242 prevented the convening of a Rhodes-type conference in either Nicosia, or, as suggested later, in New York City. Jordan and Egypt held different positions on the conference. The Jordanians stated their readiness to come to such a conference on April 16. U Thant notes in his report that Jordan's acceptance depended upon Egypt's. Yet Egypt's response was markedly different: "I wish to reaffirm the readiness of our permanent representative to the United Nations in New York to meet with you to continue the contacts . . . in accordance with . . . 242."[26] Israel thought that, unlike Jordan, Egypt would agree merely to dispatch its United Nations representative "to continue the contacts" although the notion of a conference with Israel had disappeared. This was undoubtedly a missed opportunity. Two of the three parties were ready to come to the conference, yet Egypt's last-minute defection prevented the meeting from taking place. Consequently, Israel's response turned sour. As Eban notes, Israel's objection to coming to New York was rooted in its desire for an "Arab-

Israeli encounter." Dispatching the United Nations representative, from an Israeli perspective, was devoid of meaning.[27] Egypt obstructed the conference idea, but its position on the negotiations and withdrawal formula changed favorably. In March 1968 Egypt expressed a willingness for a "package deal," implying simultaneous negotiations and withdrawal provided that Israel did likewise. Although the tactical positions of the parties began gradually to change, some basic differences remained. On the most fundamental level, Egypt and Jordan were not ready at that stage to entertain the idea of a formal peace with Israel and continued to interpret 242 as requiring only the total withdrawal of Israeli forces without any reciprocity on their part. The conflicting strategic positions of the parties grew farther apart when Yoseph Tekoah, the Israeli United Nations delegate, declared before the Security Council on May 1, 1968: "[M]y Government has indicated its acceptance of the Security Council Resolution for the promotion of agreement on the establishment of a just and durable peace. I am also authorized to reaffirm that we are willing to seek agreement with each Arab state on all matters included in that resolution."[28] This statement, however, was flatly rejected by both Egypt and Jordan. Thus, the procedural and substantive stalemate continued.[29]

The Jordanian rejection of the various efforts—both private and public—frustrated the Israelis. Israel resented the fact that Hussein refused to abandon Arab solidarity and engage in a separate public dialogue. Israeli Premier Eshkol addressed this issue: "Jordan hitched its wagon to Egypt and Big Brother Nasser and could not take any step without the Egyptian leader's prior consent."[30] As a warning to Jordan, Abba Eban pointed out that "the longer Jordan repulses negotiations, the stronger will be the impulse on many Palestinian Arab leaders to work out the best settlement they can with Israel. The longer Jordan abstains from negotiations, the greater will be the tendency in Israel to explore that possibility."[31] Eban, however, reiterated Israel's position that it had not abandoned the idea of negotiating with Hussein.[32]

The American position on the Arab-Israeli conflict in the wake of the Six-Day War was based on President Johnson's five principles announced in June 19, 1967.[33] While Jarring's mission was alive, the United States kept a low profile and attempted to support it. In July 1968 George Ball, the American ambassador to the United Nations, was sent on a peace mission to Israel and Jordan. While in Israel, Ball was told by Eban that Israel was willing to return "most of the West Bank" to Jordan. Ball conveyed this message to King Hussein, who rejected it on the grounds that he wanted the entire West Bank, including East Jerusalem.[34]

In an effort to win over world public opinion Eban presented a nine-point peace plan to the United Nations General Assembly on

October 8, 1968, which contained the following principles: (1) the establishment of a contractual peace; (2) secure and recognized boundaries; (3) security arrangements; (4) an open frontier; (5) freedom of navigation; (6) settlement of the refugee problem; (7) Jerusalem's holy places under the responsibility of those who revere them; (8) acknowledgment and recognition of sovereignty, integrity, and the right to national life; (9) regional cooperation.[35] Moreover, during the speech, out of tactical concerns, Eban declared that Israel would accept a preliminary stage of indirect negotiations.

In response to the speech the United States decided on the following day to approve Israel's request to purchase fifty F-4 Phantom fighter bombers. This transaction was a dramatic shift in the American position after the 1967 war. For the first time the United States supplied Israel with sophisticated military equipment irrespective of progress on the peace process. In other words, the United States had begun to support the "thesis that Israel should hold on to the territories until the Arabs were prepared to make peace."[36] This shift, in turn, caused Israel to become more obstinate and to insist "on some territorial changes in order to place itself in a better position to defend itself against possible Arab bad faith."[37]

During this stalemate a number of attempts were made by the two (United States, Soviet Union) and four powers (United States, Soviet Union, France, United Kingdom) to move the peace process forward. The idea for four-power talks can be traced to French President Charles De Gaulle's call before the Six-Day War for a concerted effort by the four powers to solve the conflict. This call was repeated in October 1968 and again in January 1969.[38] While the French effort was underway, the Soviet Union presented a peace plan on December 30, 1968, that was based on implementing "all the provisions of 242."[39] The process of the two- and four-power talks, which will not be fully reviewed here, was based on the attempt to support the failing Jarring mission.[40] Initially, the United States and the Soviet Union held a number of meetings between March 18 and April 22, 1969. The two superpowers had different ideas about how to make progress.

The new American president, Richard Nixon, presented his position on the peace process during a press conference on February 6, 1969. Nixon made clear that he wanted to keep all options open and support all initiatives simultaneously.[41]

The Israeli government reacted negatively to these initiatives because it feared that the big powers would impose a solution. Golda Meir, who succeeded Premier Eshkol on March 17, 1969, vehemently opposed great power intervention in the conflict. The Israeli government declared its opposition to the four-power talks on March 30.[42]

The French involvement was particularly irksome to Israel. During the Six-Day War De Gaulle had imposed an arms embargo on Israel. Israel thus resented the involvement of France, which it considered partisan and pro-Arab.

Yet an imposed solution by the great powers was not part of the procedure upon which this effort was built. As U Thant described it in his memoir: "It was originally agreed that any plan initiated by the United States or the Soviet Union must first get the endorsement of both [countries], and then be presented to Britain and France. After all four powers agreed to it, the plan would be transmitted to me for transmission to Mr. Jarring for negotiations with Israel and the Arab states."[43] In addition, the United States made it clear that it did not intend to impose a solution. This was confirmed by Secretary of State William Rogers, who stated on April 7: "I regret that the Government of Israel is so strongly opposed to the idea of the four-power talks. We have made it perfectly clear to the Government that we are not—we do not intend and will not seek to impose a settlement on Israel. On the other hand, . . . we think that it may be that by this process we can influence the parties to come to some sort of a permanent settlement."[44]

Neither the two- nor the four-power talks produced any meaningful results. The gulf separating the parties was too wide to bridge. This was evident when Jarring sent a questionnaire to Israel, Jordan, Egypt, and Lebanon during the first week of March 1969 to try to clarify their positions. The formal responses, however, did not yield any breakthroughs or fresh ideas about how to move ahead.

While visiting the United States in April 1969, King Hussein attempted to inject some new blood into the decaying peace process. During a speech at the National Press Club in Washington, D.C., he said he was also speaking on Nasser's behalf and offered a six-point peace plan which stipulated that "Israel may have either peace or territory—but cannot have both."[45]

Golda Meir's response to the king's proposal was negative. She stated that Israel would not return to the pre-1967 boundaries.[46] Meir's opposition to Hussein's plan was rooted in an emerging Israeli conception that became known as the "oral law."[47] According to the oral law, which was adopted by the Labor-Mapam Alignment just before the 1969 elections, Israel would retain Jerusalem, the Golan Heights, the Gaza Strip, and Sharm al-Sheikh. The Jordan River would become a security belt, even if some parts of the West Bank were returned to Jordan. The oral law also demanded a contractual peace with the Arab states. Palestinian refugees were not considered an Israeli problem. Hence, the refugees were not to be included in the settlement. As Shlomo Aronson notes in *Conflict and Bargaining in the Middle East,* "Meir was to repeat this point often after becoming Prime Minister, stating that there was no such thing as a Palestinian nation.''[48] Although the oral law was not official governmental policy, the fact that the Alignment dominated the government made it a de facto political program. Clearly, this was a territorialist conception, similar to the Allon Plan. Because Hussein had never accepted the Allon Plan, it meant that no serious debate in the cabinet was necessary on the oral law and its relevance to a peace agreement with Jordan.[49]

During 1970 and 1971 there were several unsuccessful attempts by Jarring to break the stalemate. Israel's leaders believed that they had no incentive to move forward. The basic tenet of Israeli policy during the 1967–70 period was to rely on its military strength in the hope that the Arab states would eventually change their stance. From a Jordanian perspective King Hussein felt that he could not move without Arab backing. It was not until 1971, during an interview with *Newsweek*, that President Sadat hinted that he would be willing to negotiate a separate agreement with Israel.[50] The Israeli interpretation of the Sadat interview was that a possible "green light" might be given to Jordan to pursue a separate peace with Israel. But Hussein did not follow through. The failure of the Jarring mission prompted the United States to move ahead unilaterally in the form of the Rogers Plan. This decision was largely because America realized that it could not rely on either Jarring, the Soviets, or the Europeans to move the peace process forward.

The Rogers Plan

On December 9, 1969, American Secretary of State William Rogers officially announced a peace plan that laid out the American position on the Arab-Israeli conflict. The plan had been previously submitted in private on October 28 to Anatoly Dobrynin, the Soviet ambassador in Washington, in the context of the two-power talks and to Israel and Egypt as well in early November.[51] The plan was the first of a series of initiatives based on the determination of the United States to pursue an evenhanded approach toward the conflict. It was the most comprehensive and detailed plan that the United States had proposed since the 1967 war. Although the plan did not specifically address the Israeli-Jordanian front, it was, nonetheless, relevant to subsequent developments in the peace process.[52]

The Israeli, Egyptian, and Soviet reactions to the plan were negative. Jordan was the only party that never officially rejected the plan. Israel issued its official rejection of the plan on December 11, 1969.[53]

The Israeli rejection of the plan set in motion a collision course with the United States. The disagreement between the two countries was further exacerbated when the United States presented a follow-up plan that applied the principles of the Rogers Plan to the Israeli-Jordanian front. This plan was officially presented at the four-power talks on December 18 by Charles Yost, the American ambassador to the United Nations. The two plans together contributed to a major effort by the United States to try to bring about a settlement of the Arab-Israeli conflict.[54] It should be noted, however, that the unveiling of the Yost Plan was accompanied by an intense debate inside the U.S. administration. Henry Kissinger, the national security adviser, argued against issuing the plan. According to Kissinger, the plan constituted a grave mistake because "if we were not ready to impose our proposals, the mere presentation of them would gain us at most two to three weeks before we were again faced with the choice of offering more or letting the negotiations blow up."[55] Indeed, Kissinger was correct, because in spite of the emerging differences of opinion between Israel and the United States, the United States was unwilling to press the Israelis on the issue of peace. This attitude was evident when Nixon placated Israel by giving it private assurances that the United States would not push the Rogers and Yost proposals.[56] The introduction of the two peace proposals was clearly a function of the personal rivalry between Kissinger and Secretary of State Rogers and a clear example of bureaucratic politics. An additional motive for issuing the plans, according to William Quandt, was the upcoming Arab summit in Rabat. This was clearly an attempt to strengthen Hussein, who could have argued at the summit that an Israeli-Jordanian peace was a priority for the United States.[57]

The Yost Plan called for a contractual peace between Israel and Jordan to be concluded under the auspices of Ambassador Jarring in Rhodes-type negotiations. As was the Rogers Plan, the Yost Plan was the most comprehensive proposal yet that dealt with Israeli-Jordanian peace.

As David Korn notes in *Stalemate,* Israel's initial reaction to the Rogers plan was more a rebuke to the United States for trying to "appease" the Arabs than a flat rejection of the plan.[58] Two weeks later, upon the unveiling of the Yost plan, the cabinet issued a strong condemnation and rejection. This, of course, occurred because the Yost plan was the first international effort to deal with the question of the West Bank. A lack of consensus resulting from ideological divisions within Israel regarding the fate of the West Bank resulted in such an obdurate response. The annexationists led by Begin were able to form a negative consensus on this issue inside the government and lead the opposition against the American proposals. By December 29 the Knesset also rejected the Rogers and Yost plans.[59] The Soviet Union objected to the plans on the grounds that they were "one-sided pro-Israeli." It disagreed with the American concept of the de jure termination of the state of war between Israel and the Arab states once the agreement was deposited with the United Nations. The Soviets demanded a de facto cessation of hostilities that reflected the position of the Arab states.[60]

The Jordanian response to both plans was noncommittal. Jordan, however, did not officially reject the two plans. In an interview with the *New York Times* King Hussein called the plans "a step forward which renewed the chances of a political settlement. If there is a solution, it has got to be a general solution, not a piecemeal one."[61]

Although no apparent movement was taking place on the public level, the Israeli and Jordanian leaders met again in March 1970 while the clouds of civil war were gathering in Jordan. Just before the March meeting, on February 17, 1970, Hussein transmitted to Israeli Foreign Minister Eban an urgent message via Owen Zurhellen, the American deputy chief of mission in Tel Aviv. According to Yossi Melman and Moshe Zak, respectively, the message asked three questions: (1) Does Israel agree not to take advantage of the opportunity presented by Hussein's reduction of military forces on the Israeli-Jordanian border to deal with the growing Palestinian militancy at home? (2) Can Israel agree not to respond to provocations by the Palestinian guerrillas? (3) Can Hussein count on Israeli forces to assist him in the event the forces of neighboring countries come to the aid of the Palestinians while he tries to deal with them? Israel's reply to Hussein was basically threefold: (1) Israel will not take advantage of the situation and attack Jordan while Jordanian forces are engaged in fighting the Palestinians. (2) Israel will vigorously respond to any terrorist provocation. (3) Israel is willing to discuss the question of assisting Jordan should the need arise.[62] Zak wrote that Defense Minister Dayan had grave reservations about assisting Jordan because he did not believe that Hussein would survive a confrontation with the Palestinians. Moreover, Hussein's insecurity had made him decide to put the three questions to Israel via the Americans rather than directly to Israel. Perhaps Hussein wanted American assurances in case he faced difficulties in his fight against the Palestinians.[63]

During the March meeting between Israel and Jordan, Dayan, Eban, Herzog, and Israeli Chief of Staff Haim Bar-Lev represented Israel while the Jordanian delegation included Hussein and his military chief of staff, Zaid Bin Shakr. The conversation centered around the evacuation of the Israeli army from the al-Safi area located inside Jordanian territory, south of the Dead Sea. Israeli forces had occupied the area because it had become a PLO base that was being used to shell the Israeli civilian Dead Sea Works. The king demanded the withdrawal of Israeli forces from that area in exchange for Jordanian guarantees that no guerrilla activities would be carried out from the region. The Israelis agreed, and evacuated the military. The Jordanian official statement that followed the Israeli withdrawal described a military confrontation between Jordanian and Israeli forces that resulted in an Israeli retreat from the area. The Israelis did not challenge the Jordanian version even though it did not represent the truth. What mattered to Israel was that the area remain free of guerrilla activities.[64]

This incident, although insignificant in itself, demonstrated the emerging dynamics of Israeli-Jordanian relations. Publicly, Jordan presented the Israeli withdrawal as the result of fierce fighting between the two armies, but the reality was quite different. The withdrawal was reached through a secret mutual consent because the two parties had direct stakes involved. The Israelis wanted to stop Palestinian shelling of the Dead Sea Works, whereas Jordan wanted to regain control over its territory and, hence, prevent Israeli retaliation.

The Rogers Initiative

The Rogers and Yost plans caused an Israeli-American rift over the question of peace. Israel's rejection of the plans, irrespective of Egypt's rejection and Jordan's mild endorsement, made it difficult to move ahead. This stalemate occurred during the Israeli-Egyptian War of Attrition across the Suez Canal, which began in 1969. As the war over the canal escalated, Israel's Air Force carried out several attacks deep into Egypt's territory. This strategy, in turn, caused increasing Soviet military involvement in Egypt, which included a supply of ground-to-air SA-3 missiles and unprecedented military and economic aid that totaled about $4.5 billion by 1970.[65] The Israelis were conducting more than 150 sorties daily into Egypt, and Israeli casualties, although considerably lower than Egypt's, were, nonetheless, high.[66] In addition, certain segments of the Israeli public—intellectuals and high school students, in particular—began to challenge the wisdom of the government's policies with regard to the War of Attrition and the peace process in general. As a conciliatory gesture toward the United States, Premier Golda Meir announced to the Knesset on May 26, 1970, that Israel was willing to accept U.N. Resolution 242. This, indeed, was a sea change in Israel policy because the government until then had officially refused to accept the resolution. During the Knesset debate after Meir's speech, in order to keep the National Unity Government intact, permission was given to members of Gahal (composed of Herut and the Liberals)—the annexationists who opposed accepting Resolution 242—permission to abstain during the Knesset vote on the issue.[67]

As Michael Brecher notes, the concessions made by Israel, including the acceptance of the Rhodes-type negotiations, were part of the domestic pressure imposed by students and certain segments of the Israeli public over the casualties during the War of Attrition. But, above all, it represented a "concern about the possible loss of United States political and military support."[68] If this interpretation is correct, concern for the peace process, especially on the Israeli-Jordanian front, played a minor role in Israel's formal acceptance of Resolution 242. Moreover, the fact that Gahal did not resign from the National Unity Government to protest the endorsement of Resolution 242 could be viewed as evidence that Israeli acceptance was not directed toward the Arab states.

The escalating situation along the Suez Canal, including increasing Soviet involvement, prompted the United States to launch a second peace initiative on June 25, 1970, referred to either as the Rogers Initiative or Rogers Plan B.[69] Rogers sent letters to Egyptian Foreign Minister Mahmoud Riad, to Jordanian Foreign Minister Zaid Rifai, and to the Israeli government on June 19. It was publicly announced on June 25. The proposal contained two parts: a call for an Israeli-Egyptian cease-fire agreement along the canal and an attempt to move Israeli-Jordanian and Israeli-Egyptian negotiations forward based on U.N. Resolution 242.[70]

The initial Israeli response was negative. On July 21 the government voted to reject the initiative. In addition, the Israeli premier sent a harsh note to Washington, criticizing the initiative, although Yitzhak Rabin, the Israeli ambassador to Washington, refused to deliver it to the White House. Rabin thought the tone of the note was too harsh even though he agreed with its substance.[71] Israel's objections to the initiative can be explained at two levels. First, Gahal, which was then a partner in the coalition, objected to the withdrawal clause in the initiative that referred to the West Bank. Gahal's leader, Begin, objected to evacuating the West Bank, which he considered the "land of our fathers." He did not object in principle to a withdrawal from the Sinai, to which he did not attach any ideological significance. Begin was against the explicit linkage in the initiative between the Egyptian and Jordanian fronts. Consequently, he sought to separate the issues. In other words, applying 242 to the Egyptian front should not mean that it could be applied to the West Bank.[72] Dayan objected to the initiative on similar grounds.[73]

Second, Israel expected to link the fate of the Palestinian refugees to the cease-fire: "If the refugee problem was not resolved in accordance with Resolution 242 or the Rogers Plan, the Arabs might feel free to violate the cease-fire in order to extract more political and/or military advantages after having gained previous Israeli concessions."[74] Yet the United States was determined to get an affirmative answer from Israel. On July 24 Nixon sent Israel a letter clarifying the American position. In effect the Nixon letter invalidated the Rogers Plan.[75] While the Israeli government was reconsidering the initiative, both Egypt and Jordan accepted it. Just before Israeli official acceptance of the initiative, Israel was able to elicit from the United States additional military equipment and a promise that the Nixon note constituted the American policy toward the conflict and that the United States would veto any anti-Israeli resolution proposed by the Security Council.[76] With these guarantees, Israel then officially endorsed the initiative on July 31, 1970. Gahal, led by Begin, however, resigned from the National Unity Government on August 13. Clearly, the worsening military situation along the Suez Canal and the possible rift with Washington determined the Israeli response, even at the expense of breaking up the coalition.

The Israeli response to the second Rogers plan was based on its interpretation of the initiative. Plan B did not include the original reference to "having accepted and indicated their willingness to carry out Resolution 242 in all its parts." In addition, Israel's formulation of "withdrawal to secure, recognized and agreed boundaries" was not included in the original text of the initiative, so the original Rogers formulation of *withdrawal* was ignored. Nevertheless, this was the first time that Israel had used the term *withdrawal* in any official document.[77]

The Israeli-Egyptian cease-fire agreement went into effect on August 7, 1970. Immediately thereafter, Egypt moved its ground-to-air missiles closer to the Suez Canal. Israel responded to the move by charging Egypt with violating the agreement. On September 6 Israel decided not to participate in the forthcoming negotiations with Egypt that had been planned under Jarring's auspices.[78] Events in Jordan and in Egypt, however, changed the situation in the region. In early September clashes occurred between Jordanian forces and the Palestinians, leading to the outbreak of civil war. Egyptian President Nasser died at the end of September, and the Israeli-Egyptian border remained quiet until the 1973 Yom Kippur War.

Jordan's response to the Rogers Initiative followed Egypt's. Hussein did not want to accept the initiative on his own because he needed Egypt's backing. The Egyptian affirmative response was transmitted by its foreign minister on July 22. The Jordanian cabinet followed suit on July 26. In a letter written by Hussein to Nasser on July 26 Hussein explained his position: "You are the big brother, your armed forces are the strongest Arab forces in the fateful battle, and your dear country and dignified people are the big brother of the Arab nation. We accept what you accept and reject what you reject in the battle of our destiny and national prestige. . . . It pleases me to inform you that our Premier has informed us that the Jordanian Government has adopted an attitude fully in harmony with the UAR's wise political attitude toward the recent developments."[79] On the same day Jordanian Foreign Minister Antun Atallah sent his government's reply to Rogers, emphasizing two points:

full Israeli withdrawal in conformity with U.N. Resolution 242 and recognition of the "Palestinian people's full legal rights."[80]

The Jordanian acceptance, however, created an additional source of tension with the PLO, which totally rejected the initiative. Indeed, this issue became a bone of contention between the two parties, each of which was gearing up for an all-out confrontation. The Palestine National Assembly convened an emergency session, wherein it deplored the initiative and declared that "anyone who tries to speak on behalf of the people of Palestine or fraudulently claims to represent them or their will . . . is a traitor."[81] In addition, the PLO organized mass demonstrations in Amman to protest the acceptance of the initiative, including a general strike on July 30, "causing a complete standstill of trade and transport throughout the city."[82]

The 1970 Jordanian Civil War

In 1970 the PLO posed a grave challenge to Jordan's King Hussein by attempting to create a "state within a state" in Jordan.[83] This attempt eventually led to an overt Jordanian-Palestinian confrontation and to the outbreak of a civil war in what became known as Black September. Until February 1970 Jordanian-PLO relations had been governed by a November 1968 agreement that regulated the relationship. The agreement was signed after intermittent hostilities broke out between Jordanian forces and Palestinian guerrillas. The source of contention was Palestinian infiltrations from Jordanian territory into Israel after the 1967 war. These incursions led to retaliation by Israel against Jordanian and Palestinian targets in Jordan. In addition, Hussein saw the infrastructure the PLO had built inside his country as a direct challenge to Hashemite supremacy on the East Bank. Hence, on November 16, 1968, Jordan and the PLO reached a modus vivendi that "provided for both freedom of action for the Fedayeen [Palestinian guerrillas] and the safeguarding of Jordan's sovereignty."[84] The agreement was doomed from the start because it contained an internal contradiction. Palestinian freedom of action meant that Jordanian sovereignty would be compromised and vice versa. It could be argued that the 1970 civil war represented Hussein's inability to resolve this contradiction. The Palestinian attempt to form a "state within a state" constituted a serious problem and a grave challenge to Hussein's rule. He felt that if he did not stop the erosion of his power, his regime would eventually collapse. As matters worsened between the PLO and the Jordanians, the Jordanian government issued a special decree on February 10, 1970, which further restricted the PLO's freedom of action.[85]

Among the various Palestinian organizations operating in Jordan, the two groups that most threatened Hussein's regime were the radical Popular Front for the Liberation of Palestine (PFLP), led by George Habash, and the Democratic Front for the Liberation of Palestine (DFLP), led by Nayif Hawatmah. These groups, which both fell under the PLO umbrella, saw the creation of a Palestinian state in Jordan as the first step toward the establishment of a "secular democratic state in Palestine." The mainstream group, Fatah, led by PLO Chairman Yasser Arafat, was satisfied with the status quo in Jordan.[86]

After the decree was issued, fighting erupted in Amman for two days. The fighting stopped once Hussein agreed to suspend the decree, but the conflict between the two sides did not stop. When U.S. Under Secretary of State Joseph Sisco visited Jordan in April 1970, mass Palestinian demonstrations prevented him from visiting Amman. The king appeared to be losing control. The situation inside Jordan gradually deteriorated, and on September 1 there was an attempt to assassinate Hussein (attributed to the PFLP, which denied the accusation). Before the assassination attempt, King Hussein had accepted the peace initiative prepared by Secretary of State William Rogers, which called on Israel to exchange the land occupied in 1967 for peace with the Arabs. This became another bone of contention between the PLO and the king because the PLO strongly opposed acceptance of the Rogers Plan. In addition, the PFLP hijacked three Western planes on September 6 and held their passengers captive. The hijacking, almost more than any other act, showed that the Jordanian army was vulnerable, and, thus, the seeds of an open confrontation began to germinate.

In the northern part of Jordan Palestinian guerrillas enjoyed the support of their East Bank Palestinian brethren. The Irbid area in the north was proclaimed the "Liberated Land" by the guerrillas. Severe fighting erupted on September 16 between the army and the guerrillas, and a military government was formed on the same day. On September 18 the Syrian army crossed into northern Jordan with two hundred tanks to support the PLO against the king. But by September 22 the Syrian army was halted by a major Jordanian offensive coupled with an Israeli mobilization that deterred the Syrians from advancing toward the capital. The United States pressured the Soviet Union to force the Syrian troops to withdraw. Eventually, Hussein gained the upper hand, and the PLO power inside Jordan was greatly curtailed.

The civil war was a turning point in Israeli-Jordanian relations; Israel demonstrated that it was willing to go to war against Syria in order to save the Hashemite monarchy.

Israel's decision to mobilize its army and to deter Syrian forces from advancing towards Amman was the result of a number of factors. First,

Israel was afraid that a Syrian invasion of Jordan would tilt the regional balance of power against Israel. It did not want to face an additional front along the Jordan River, which would have placed it in a difficult strategic posture. Second, as will be shown below, Israel and the U.S. were in close contact throughout the crisis since the U.S. had decided that keeping Hussein on his throne was vital to American interests. Third, Israel needed Jordan in maintaining the open bridges policy; safeguarding the Hashemite regime would help Israel to control the West Bank. The possible Palestinianization of Jordan, with Syrian backing, was anathema to the Israeli decision makers, who feared that the West Bank would be radicalized; Jordan was also interested in containing Palestinian radicalism. During the crisis, Yigal Allon was Israel's acting prime minister because Prime Minister Golda Meir was in the United States at the time. Allon declared that the invasion of the Syrian army into Jordan constituted a threat to Israel, and it reserved the right to defend its interests on its eastern front.[87]

President Richard Nixon and National Security Adviser Henry Kissinger viewed the crisis in global terms. They believed that it was Soviet inspired and that its purpose was to inflict a loss on an American ally—Jordan. Henry Brandon maintained that "Nixon saw the situation in its broadest implications. Jordan to him was a microscopic spot on the map yet he viewed it as having far-reaching implications on the world stage and on American relations with the Soviet Union."[88]

The American response to the crisis can be understood at two levels. First, the United States attempted to address the problem of the American hostages being held by the PFLP. Second, it sought to protect Hussein's regime. The United States also held a dialogue with the Soviets during the crisis, hoping to prevent the Syrians from toppling Hussein. At the same time, the administration placed U.S. forces on alert and coordinated its moves with Israel. Initially, the aircraft carrier *Independence* and several destroyers were sent to the coast of Lebanon. A number of C-130's were stationed at a base in Turkey where they would be available to evacuate the hostages.[89] Writing about the 1970 Jordanian crisis in *White House Years,* Kissinger maintained: "American forces should be used for the evacuation of Americans. . . . [But] in case of a major conflict provoked by an Iraqi or Syrian move, I favored letting the countries most immediately concerned take the principal responsibility. Since I considered an Israeli response to an Iraqi-Syrian move almost certain, I thought the best use of our power in that contingency was to deter Soviet intervention against Israel."[90]

The notion of an Israeli military intervention was also endorsed by Joseph Sisco, who believed that American intervention would be detrimental to Hussein's interests in the long run.[91]

The hostage problem was resolved when the PFLP removed the hostages to a Palestinian refugee camp and then blew up the planes. All the hostages were freed during the following week except fifty-five Jewish passengers. The Jews were freed on September 29, a few days after the PLO's defeat in Jordan.

The situation in Jordan began to deteriorate on September 16 when Hussein imposed martial law. He thus showed his determination to confront the Palestinians with force if necessary. As a gesture to Israel on September 17, Nixon approved $500 million in military aid and promised to speed up the delivery of eighteen F-4's.[92]

On September 18 the Syrian army began invading the northern part of Jordan, prompting both Israel and the United States to place their forces on a high state of alert. On the same day Hussein sent an urgent request to the United States, asking the administration to pass along a message to Israel.[93] Kissinger reportedly told Yitzhak Rabin, "King Hussein has approached us, describing the situation of his forces, and asked us to transmit his request that [the Israeli] air force attack the Syrians in Northern Jordan."[94] The United States then took a number of steps that were interpreted as giving Israel a "green light" to intervene in Jordan. On September 20 Nixon endorsed an Israeli air strike against Syrian forces in Jordan. On September 21 the president supported Israeli armored actions against Syrian forces in principle although United States–Israeli consultations would have to take place and Jordan's attitude would have to be considered before such a move was made.

With the United States possibly backing its military deployment against the Syrians, Israel prepared a contingency plan that included an attack on Syria, using both its army and air force. According to Marvin and Bernard Kalb, "Israel was planning a pincer attack against Syrian forces concentrated in the Irbid area. Armored units stationed near the Golan Heights—two hundred tanks—would move east and then south toward Irbid. Israel would then count on Jordanian armor moving north from Amman. The Israeli air force would soften up the Syrian positions around Irbid. Coordination between Israeli and Jordanian forces would be necessary, and Hussein would be assured that Israeli forces would be withdrawn from Jordan the moment the operation was completed."[95]

On September 22 Israel was preparing to attack. But King Hussein, who had guarantees from both Israel and the United States, deployed his air force against the Syrian tanks and succeeded in stopping the Syrian invasion. At the same time, he was able to defeat the Palestinians and, subsequently, save his regime.

Finally, the crisis came to an end. The resolution of the crisis was formalized by what became known as the Cairo Agreement, signed on September 27, 1970, by Hussein, Arafat, and a number of Arab heads of state. The main provision of the agreement called for a cease-fire and freezing the military situation that existed on September 24.[96]

Hussein's victory in the civil war enabled him to consolidate his power inside Jordan and to focus on the West Bank. Concurrently, he began trying to be accepted as the legitimate representative of the Palestinians.[97]

Israel and the United States believed that their separate and joint efforts had helped Hussein win the war. Hussein's victory had far-ranging implications for both Israeli-American and Israeli-Jordanian relations. The Soviet-American dialogue also played an important role in diffusing the crisis although the extent of Soviet pressure on Syria is unknown.

The United States saw Israel in a new light as a result of the 1970 Jordanian civil war. Israeli decision makers used the 1970 episode as proof that Israel was fulfilling a strategic role for the United States in the Middle East by containing the Soviet Union and defending its allies in the region. As Quandt argues, the understanding reached between Washington and Jerusalem during the crisis "was a remarkable testimony to the new strategic relationship that existed between the two countries."[98] Some Israelis thought it had helped their country to show Hussein that Israel was not going to allow the disintegration of his kingdom. Other Israelis, including General Ariel Sharon, disagreed. In his autobiography, *Warrior,* Sharon outlined his position regarding aid to Jordan during the civil war: "If the P.L.O. unseated Hussein, Jordan would formally become a Palestinian political entity. . . . So if it had now become possible to resolve the most crucial . . . Palestinian problems, through the formal creation of a Palestinian state in Jordan, that is the direction I believe we should move in."[99] Sharon hoped that by toppling Hussein and creating a Palestinian state in Jordan, Israel would be able to annex the West Bank without much Palestinian resistance. Moreover, according to Yossi Melman, during the September crisis a senior official in the Israeli Defense Military Intelligence suggested in a top-secret memorandum that Israeli interests would be more enhanced by supporting the establishment of a Palestinian state on the East Bank than by helping Hussein. The memorandum said the creation of the state "would rectify the injustice done to the Palestinians in 1948." This memorandum, however, was rejected by General Aharon Yariv, head of military intelligence, and the Israeli decision makers were not even given a copy of it.[100] Sharon's recommendations were not accepted by the Israeli leadership.

Israel's leaders believed the country's interests were best served by maintaining the status quo. If the PLO had taken over in Jordan, the regional balance of power undoubtedly would have changed. Yet beyond grand strategic considerations, support for the Hashemites was also linked to developments in the West Bank. Israel felt that a PLO-dominated East Bank would radicalize the Palestinians in the West Bank and make it more difficult for Israel to maintain control of the territories. Dan Schueftan argues that the hidden message entailed in Israel's support of Jordan during the civil war was that Israel eventually sought an agreement with Hussein. Therefore, Israel was willing to intervene militarily on his behalf. A radicalization of the East Bank, with a possible Syrian military presence, and Iraq on Israel's eastern border would have given Israel an excuse to postpone indefinitely a withdrawal from the territories. This, Schueftan continued, put a weapon in the hands of those who opposed a withdrawal from the West Bank.[101]

It could also be maintained, however, that allowing Hussein to remain in power helped consolidate Israeli rule on the West Bank. After the crisis, Moshe Dayan wrongly asserted that if Hussein persevered, most of the population on the West Bank would support him without hesitation.[102] As long as Hussein remained in power, the costs of maintaining the occupation were bearable for Israel because of Jordanian involvement in the West Bank through the open bridges policy. The events of 1970 clearly demonstrated how Israel and Jordan both wanted to contain the PLO in the West and East Banks and opposed the creation of an independent Palestinian state on either side of the Jordan River. Israeli and Jordanian interests, therefore, converged on this issue. A rise in Palestinian nationalism in either Jordan or the occupied territories was going to be checked by both countries.

The civil war showed the PLO that there were limits on its freedom of action. After the civil war, the locus of Palestinian activism shifted to Lebanon, where one decade later, the Palestinian organization faced a predicament similar to the one it had confronted in Jordan. The establishment of a "state within a state" in Lebanon led inevitably to a confrontation with the host government, a war with Israel, and expulsion to Tunisia.

The majority of the Palestinian population supported the PLO against Hussein. It faced a dilemma, however, because many West Bankers had families living on the East Bank. Most identified with the Palestinian guerrillas who were fighting the king and viewed the war as a national struggle. But a quick victory for Hussein also meant that tranquility and order would be restored in Jordan and that their families living on the East Bank would be safe. There were several demonstrations against Hussein in the West Bank to protest the killing of Palestinians by the Jordanian army.[103] The local Palestinian leadership took an active part in the protests. Several petitions and memoranda were circulated that criticized both Hussein and the Arab states, whose "negligence had allowed the big criminal [Hussein] to slaughter the Palestinians."[104] Six of the twenty-two members of the Jordanian Parliament in the West Bank resigned to protest Hussein's actions. These resignations, however, were not accepted by the Parliament.[105] To calm the growing tide of anti-Hashemite sentiment on the West Bank Hussein had immediately after the war resumed the payment of salaries and pensions to Jordanian civil servants on the West Bank and maintained close contact with the local elite through a foreign consulate in East Jerusalem.[106]

The defeat of the PLO in Jordan prompted Yigal Allon to propose local autonomy for the West Bank Palestinians. This proposal was not received with enthusiasm either in the West Bank or in Israel. The Israelis argued that by granting autonomy to the West Bank Israel would forfeit its claim to the area. Prime Minister Meir termed the proposal "unworkable and impractical."[107] The Palestinian reaction was negative as well. Most Palestinians did not see any benefit in accepting such a proposal and were not prepared to sever their links with Jordan at that time.[108]

The 1972 United Arab Kingdom Plan

On March 15, 1972, King Hussein publicly announced a United Arab Kingdom Plan, or the Federation Plan.[109] This plan, the most detailed and ambitious Jordanian plan after the 1967 war, was a culmination of Hussein's efforts to consolidate his position vis-à-vis the Palestinians. It demonstrated the uneasy relationship between the two sides. In 1970 he fought them; two years later he offered them a federation within a Jordanian framework. In March 1972 Hussein attempted to reassert his power by proposing a plan based on the "unity of the two Banks" whereby the West Bank would be an autonomous region of the newly established United Arab Kingdom. Both Banks would be under the suzerainty of the Jordanian king. Autonomy for the Palestinians in the West Bank and hegemony for the East Bank were the foundations of the federation proposal.[110]

When analyzing the federation proposal, it becomes apparent that it outlined an *optimal* relationship, envisioned by Hussein, between Jordan and the Palestinians. The proposed linkage between the two Banks also underscored Hussein's philosophy concerning the nature of Jordanian and Palestinian nationalism. It implied that there were no significant differences between the two, and, therefore, there was no need for a separate Palestinian state on the West Bank. During the speech that unveiled the plan Hussein argued: "Foremost among the realities which the union of both Banks evolved day after day was that those living therein are one people, not two people. . . . The day came when it was impossible for anybody to distinguish between a person from the West Bank and one from the East, unlike the way a Palestinian is distinguished from a non-Palestinian in other parts of the Arab world."[111] Although King Hussein might have been correct about the similarity between the two peoples, he was unable to cope adequately with the question of ultimate political authority. The Palestinians had little interest in either the Hashemite dynasty or the institutions of monarchy because they were populist in their political outlook.

With regard to the administrative links between the two Banks, Hussein added, "[I]n Jordan, and under the auspices of the union of both Banks, the genuine Palestinian community found amongst the overwhelming majority of the people who live in both Banks, [is] the appropriate framework in which to live and move as well as the real starting point for the will of liberation and all the hopes it embodied."[112]

Furthermore, the origins of the Federation Plan could be placed in the context of developments in the East and West Banks, the Arab world, and Jordanian-Israeli relations. The historical justification for the "unity of the two Banks" idea was based, according to Hussein, on two Palestinian congresses that were held on December 1948 in the West Bank towns of Nablus and Jericho. These congresses were organized by King Hussein's grandfather, Abdullah, who sought the West Bankers' support for his scheme to annex the West Bank. (The West Bank was formally annexed by the Jordanian Parliament in April 1950.) Hussein presented the act of annexing the West Bank as a direct response to the "appeal of the [Palestinian] nation." These congresses, particularly the Jericho Congress, expressed support for "the union of Palestine with Transjordan as a prologue to complete Arab union" and recognized "his highness King Abdullah as the King of all Palestine."[113] In fact, the annexation of the West Bank by Jordan was very unpopular among the Palestinians of the West Bank.[114]

The plan constituted a solution that Hussein had devised in order to restore the status quo ante that had existed before 1967. Yet this time, Hussein hoped to gain Palestinian support for his plan. Regarding the East Bank, although the direct Palestinian threat on his throne was eliminated during the events of Black September, Hussein and the East Bank Palestinians still felt uneasy about each other. This plan "was intended to serve as a compromise between the Palestinians, who saw themselves as second class citizens, and the non-Palestinian Transjordanians who were uncertain as to the government's intentions towards the West Bank in view of some Jordanian politicians' support for separation [from the West Bank]."[115] By granting autonomy to the West Bank as part of the federation scheme Hussein also wanted to assure the East Bankers that any future Palestinian irredentism would be checked by the monarchy. The events of September 1970 were presented by the king as "a catastrophe, which if allowed to befall the country, would have resulted in the loss of the East Bank, and would have laid the stage for a final liquidation of the Palestinian cause forever. . . . This evil subversion was shattered on the rock of the firm national unity, which, born in 1950, grew and flourished, amidst the challenges which he had to face during the past twenty years."[116] In other words, Hussein viewed the challenge posed by Palestinian nationalism in zero sum terms. Had the PLO succeeded in 1970, it would have meant the end of the Hashemite monarchy. Consequently, the solution that Hussein devised could be interpreted as an attempt to co-opt the Palestinians in both Banks. He did, however, accept the West Bankers' demands for a separate Palestinian entity, provided it fell under Jordanian tutelage. Hence, the East Bank Palestinians would also have a stake in a system that provided for the expression of the national rights of their brethren on the West Bank.

This plan also was meant to address the problem of the West Bank. The events of 1970 had caused many West Bankers to distance themselves from the Hashemites. By introducing the Federation Plan Hussein hoped to restore his power and to check the growing ascendancy of the PLO as well. Clearly, Hussein was against an independent Palestinian state, which he feared would pose a direct threat to his rule on the East Bank. Granting autonomy to the West Bank was, according to Hussein, a real gesture to Palestinian nationalism. During a speech to the Jordanian Parliament on April 3, 1971, Hussein said that "it is impermissible and unreasonable that once Israel's rifles are withdrawn they should be replaced by other rifles."[117] The reference here to "other rifles" was obviously directed at the PLO. Hussein took a number of steps to convince the West Bank Palestinians that they should not support the PLO. For example, he prevented West Bank notables from entering Jordan and temporarily canceled entrance visas to Jordan that were issued by local West Bank municipalities. At the same time, he renewed paying the salaries of former Jordanian employees in an attempt to marshal support for Jordan in the territories. In other words, Hussein pursued a "carrot and stick" policy to show the West Bankers that their interests were best served by Jordan rather than by the PLO.[118]

Moreover, Israel planned to hold municipal elections in the West Bank at the end of March 1972. Hussein unveiled his plan in March so it would coincide with the upcoming elections. The king wanted to prevent the emergence of a local Palestinian leadership that would be hostile to him.[119]

The message to Israel was clear: do not attempt to cultivate a local leadership on the West Bank because only Jordan can sign an agreement with Israel. Although Hussein did not mention any specifics of the peace process in his speech, his position with regard to a settlement with Israel remained unchanged. He sought to recover all the territories that he had lost in 1967, including East Jerusalem. Section 2(A) of his proposal refers to "the Region of Palestine, and shall consist of the West Bank and any further Palestinian territories to be liberated and whose inhabitants opt to join."[120] The reference to "other Palestinian territories" is directed toward the Gaza Strip, which had been under Egyptian administrative control until 1967.[121] In other words, Hussein sought to incorporate in his United Arab Kingdom an additional territory—Gaza—that was inhabited by more than a half-million Palestinians.

Inter-Arab politics also played a role in the environment that led Hussein to issue the proposal. Hussein feared that after the August 1970 Israeli-Egyptian cease-fire agreement Israel and Egypt would sign an interim agreement on the opening of the Suez Canal, which had been closed since 1967. Additionally, Hussein perceived the Arab world to be in a state of disarray. He was afraid the Arab states would eventually give the PLO the legitimacy to represent the Palestinians. In an interview Hussein granted to Ada Luciani, a reporter for the Israeli daily *Ma'ariv*, the king expressed the view that "I think that the most severe and complex situation is here in Jordan, between Jordan and Israel, not in the Suez Canal. In my opinion, it is best to strive for a comprehensive agreement as opposed to an interim settlement." Yet he did not reject the possibility of the "right of any party to search for a solution to its own problem."[122] Hussein feared that the attention of the Arab world in pursuing a settlement would be shifted to the Egyptian-Israeli front. To deflect attention from Egypt the king hoped to inject momentum into the negotiations over the West Bank. Moreover, the Israeli-Jordanian border had been quiet since 1970, and, thus, no party, Israel in particular, saw any urgency in dealing with the Palestinian-Jordanian problem. In light of these factors, according to Dan Schueftan, Hussein faced two dangers: first, that the Arab world would regard the question of the West Bank as a bilateral matter that concerned only Israel and the PLO; and second, that Israel would try to settle the issue with the PLO instead of with Jordan.[123]

An additional factor that influenced the timing of the announcement of Hussein's plan was the king's planned trip to the United States. He had hoped that the United States would welcome the plan and, in turn, persuade Israel to accept it and begin negotiations with Jordan.[124]

The reaction of the Arab states to Hussein's proposed United Arab Kingdom was swift and negative. The plan was rejected by most states, and Egypt even broke off diplomatic relations with Jordan on April 6, 1972. The Arab states called the plan a unilateral Jordanian bid to sign a separate peace agreement with Israel. Moreover, they said the plan was inspired by the United States and coordinated by Israel as part of a conspiracy against the Palestinians.[125]

The most scathing criticism came from the presidents of the Federal Arab Republic (FAR) composed of Egypt, Syria, and Libya. Each country wanted to use its opposition to the plan for its own benefits. Zvi Elpeleg argues in *Tochnit hofederatzia shel Hussein* (Hussein's federation plan) that Iraq wanted to end its isolation in the Arab world and, thus, used its opposition to Hussein's Federation Plan as a justification for calling for a union with Egypt and Syria.[126] President Bakr of Iraq denounced the plan, saying that "the masses of the Arab world are looking to all of us for unified action against the reactionary plan for surrender to the Zionist enemy."[127] Some Arab states, however, initially did not reject the Federation Plan. Saudi Arabia and Kuwait, for example, took a cautious approach toward it. The Saudi newspaper, *Medina al-Munwara,* called the Arab attack on King Hussein "demagoguery." It said that the federation proposal was preferable to letting the West Bank Palestinians become "the victims of the municipal elections the Zionist authorities are planning in the occupied territories."[128] Yet as time went on, the condemnation of Hussein became almost universal in the Arab world.

The most vocal and vehement opposition to the plan was expressed by the PLO, which saw it as a negation of its entire raison d'être. If the West Bank again came under Jordanian control, it would mean the end of the Palestinian struggle as they saw it. The PLO could not agree to that result and, hence, attempted to discredit Hussein in the Arab world and among the Palestinians. The PLO's Executive Committee met immediately after the plan was announced and issued the following statement:

> The people of Palestine alone, and in the necessary atmosphere of freedom, can decide on their own future and the future of their cause. . . . And now the King is revealing himself and his collusion by announcing, though in different words, the birth of this "tiny entity," often bargaining with Israel that he should be a partner in it, in return for concessions in Jerusalem and in the Triangle and as regards real sovereignty and, of course, for recognition and peace with Israel, and the creation of a bridge over which it could cross into all parts of the Arab homeland.[129]

The Palestine National Council (PNC) even went so far as to call for the overthrow of the king's regime: "[We must] engage in a struggle to liberate Jordan from the subservient royalist regime which is a mask for the effective Zionist domination of the East Bank and acts as a hired guardian of the Zionist occupation of Palestine."[130] According to Helena Cobban, the Palestinian call for the overthrow of Hussein "was taken not in response to all the harsh military attacks to which the guerrillas and their supporters had been subject for 18 months in Jordan, but as a reply to the overt political threat posed by Hussein to represent a substantial part of the Palestinian constituency."[131]

Initially, the reaction in the occupied territories was mixed. According to Elpeleg, there were three types of responses to the plan.[132] The anti-Hashemites in the West Bank unequivocally rejected it. The traditional leadership was initially ambivalent about the plan. It was made up of the political and economic elites who wanted to maintain their ties to Hussein but, at the same time, wanted to avoid an open conflict with the PLO. The third group, the pro-Hashemites, openly supported the plan.

The anti-Hashemites claimed the plan constituted a negation of the Palestinian quest for self-determination. A letter signed by prominent West Bank Palestinians and sent to the PNC said:

> [The plan constitutes] acceptance of the principle that Palestine at best consists of the West Bank and the Gaza Strip, the consequent annulment of the Palestinian people's right to self-determination in the territory of their homeland, the abolition of the Palestine Liberation Organization and, in consequence of all this, the obligation to prevent the Palestinian struggle from being continued both now and in the future.[133]

Members of the second group—the traditional leadership—expressed qualified support for Hussein's Federation Plan. Hamdi Can'an, the former mayor of Nablus, responded sarcastically during a press interview, "We do not want a Palestinian entity; we do not want to stay with Jordan; what we really want is to stay with the Jews." In other words, the Palestinian entity is not within our reach; if we reject the federation plan, we will face only one alternative—staying with the Jews.[134]

The pro-Hashemites gave unqualified support to the plan. Fayyiq Barakat, the chairman of the East Jerusalem Chamber of Commerce, said that the king's speech was an important step that could lead to calm in the territories after the 1970 civil war in Jordan.[135]

As with the Arab world's reaction, as time went on, more and more Palestinians opposed the king's proposal. An Israeli official spokesman, who followed the West Bank reaction, commented that the "king's intention was to entice the Palestinians, but the opposite occurred: the plan caused further alienation from Jordan and deepened the hatred toward Hussein."[136]

The United States did not officially respond to the plan because the administration wanted to "avoid having the plan labeled as an American initiative, a label that would have further reduced its prospects of acceptance in the Arab world." The White House's deputy press secretary called the plan "a Jordanian matter" and said "it would not be appropriate for us to comment."[137]

Israel reacted immediately on the same day that Hussein announced his plan. A spokesman for Premier Golda Meir characterized the plan as "negating the cause of peace," and said it "creates obstacles on the roads to its achievement." Furthermore, he denied that there was any collusion between Israel and Jordan regarding the plan.[138] Israeli Defense Minister Moshe Dayan called Hussein's speech "mere words, which do not open a pathway to any agreement or solution."[139]

Because the Israeli reaction to the plan was of utmost importance, a Knesset debate was scheduled for the next day. After a heated debate, the Knesset drafted a resolution that, in effect, killed the king's proposal. Although the resolution did not specifically reject the Federation Plan, it stated inter alia that "the Knesset has duly noted the Prime Minister's statement of March 16, 1972, regarding the speech made by the King of Jordan on March 11, 1972. The Knesset has determined that the historic right of the Jewish people to the Land of Israel is beyond challenge."[140]

The reference to the "historic right of the Jewish people," although semantic, nevertheless could be interpreted as a turning point in Israel's official policy vis-à-vis the occupied territories. Although the Knesset did not adopt Menachem Begin's suggestion to annex the West Bank formally, the resolution still constituted a clear message to the Palestinians and especially to Hussein. In other words, the implicit message underlying the Knesset's resolution was that security was not the only determinant in Israel's relations with the West Bank but that there also was an ideological attachment, a "historic right." The Sinai Peninsula, on the other hand, was not accorded the same ideological or religious significance as the West Bank. Most Israelis did not regard the Sinai as part of Greater Israel, and, hence, the relationship between Israel and the Sinai was not based on a "historic right" but on the strategic significance it played in Israel's security doctrine. It could be argued, however, that the declaration lacked any operational meaning because, at that time, there was no substantial body of opinion in Israel that supported evacuation of the territories.[141]

During the Knesset debate, members of Mapam, the junior partner in the Labor-Alignment coalition bloc, and a few other dovish members of Labor who shared the reconciliationist perspective opposed the resolution. They argued that it would close the door on negotiations with Hussein. Yet their opposition was not accepted. The text of the resolution adopted by the Knesset was initially introduced by the annexationist Gahal. By being the first to introduce the resolution Gahal was able to entrap the Alignment, which initially sought to introduce a milder resolution. Members of the Alignment felt that they could not vote against a resolution that hailed the "historic right of the Jewish people to the Land of Israel." If the Alignment had voted against the resolution, Gahal could have accused it of being antipatriotic. More importantly, the Alignment feared that it could not allow Gahal to be the only champion of the cause of the territories. Consequently, the Alignment felt that it had no choice but to go along with the resolution.[142]

The only senior member of the government who was favorably disposed toward Hussein's plan was Yigal Allon. In an interview given to the same Israeli journalist who interviewed Hussein, Ada Luciani, Allon argued that although the boundaries that Hussein had proposed were unacceptable, the federation idea should not be ruled out. During the interview he elaborated on his territorial map, the Allon Plan, which turned out to be the unofficial political platform of the Labor party on a West Bank settlement.

Moreover, Allon added that Hussein's proposals were not necessarily incompatible with his plan. The only source of contention was the boundaries.[143] Yet Allon's views were not accepted by the Israeli government at that time. In fact, the government never even formally considered the plan. According to Golda Meir, the plan was "neither approved nor rejected."[144]

As stated earlier, the Israeli political landscape was filled with those who opted for the status quo. Most Israeli leaders in the period preceding the 1973 war were confident that "time was on Israel's side," and, hence, there was no need to focus on reaching a formal agreement with Jordan.[145] Shimon Peres, a proponent of the functionalist position, summarized this pro–status quo attitude during a debate in the Labor party's secretariat:

> Today, there is a relationship between us and Jordan. If we judge it by its substance, it is unlike anything that ever existed with any other Arab country, including Lebanon. This relationship is distinct not in a passive sense—nonaggression, nonbelligerency—but it also has an active component. This includes open bridges for people and goods, negations of war and terrorism, mutual dislike of the Russians, and an attempt to maintain a certain element of consistency in our relationship. What is interesting in the Israeli-Jordanian relationship is that all this is occurring while we do not have a formal peace agreement. Had we started formal negotiations with King Hussein, as the first and only representative of the Arab world, the question of Jerusalem and the boundaries of the West Bank would have immediately come to the fore. I never heard that Hussein is willing to accept the Allon Plan. I never heard of Jews who are willing to relinquish control of Jerusalem. The existing silent status quo would have been replaced by a loud debate between us and among us that would have damaged the cause of peace.[146]

Faced with an unequivocal rejection by Israel, the Palestinians, and the Arab world, Hussein attempted to clarify his position in a number of press interviews. In response to the charge that he was attempting to reach a unilateral accord with Israel, Hussein said that the plan would become operational only when "the occupied territories are liberated." Yet he concealed his desire to sign an accord with Israel and recover the territories he lost in 1967. In addition, he said that perhaps the best way to move forward would be through secret diplomacy.[147]

To further explore the prospects of a settlement with Israel, Hussein submitted a peace plan to Secretary of State Kissinger, who planned to transmit it to Israel. According to Kissinger, Hussein told him that the exact plan that had already been explored directly with the Israelis, who had rejected it, was discussed just before the 1973 war and had stipulated that "Jordan would negotiate directly with Israel about the West Bank. There would be some border changes provided the Gaza Strip was given in return [to Jordan]. If Jordanian sovereignty was restored, there could be Israeli military outposts along the Jordan River or even Israeli settlements."[148] Golda Meir's response to the proposal was negative because "she considered Israel militarily impregnable; there was, strictly speaking, no need for any change."[149] But the Israeli premier offered a counterproposal. During a debate in April 1973 in the Labor Party's Central Committee Meir outlined her position regarding a settlement: "Israel will not interfere if King Hussein decides to give expression to those Arabs who define themselves as Palestinians by amending the structure of his kingdom. After an agreement with Israel on all issues, including the eastern border, the problem of the Arabs who adhere to a Palestinian identity would be resolved in the Kingdom of Jordan."[150]

According to Mordechai Gazit, Meir understood that Israel and Jordan had a number of overlapping interests, such as the open bridges and the containment of Syria, as evidenced during the 1970 crisis. These interests existed regardless of whether a formal peace was achieved. She also understood the incompatibility of the positions of the two countries on the question of borders and, hence, she did not rush to reach a formal agreement with Jordan.[151] Indeed, if one compares Meir's proposal to that of Hussein, the only issue separating them was Israel's refusal to return to the 1967 borders. Both leaders adamantly opposed the idea of a Palestinian state.

King Hussein's United Arab Kingdom proposal, therefore, was an attempt to balance the conflicting demands made by the Palestinians, on the one hand, and the Jordanian East Bankers, on the other.[152] Hussein clearly believed that only he could reach an agreement with Israel that would satisfy Jordan's security demands and provide for Palestinian self-expression in Jordan. But such an agreement would not be compatible with Israel's demands that no Palestinian state be established on the West Bank. Israel, however, did not feel compelled to respond to Hussein because the two countries could not agree on the boundaries. It is difficult to speculate whether Hussein believed that he would be able to reach an agreement with Israel given its feeling of overconfidence. Even those in Israel who favored an agreement with Jordan did not support a total Israeli withdrawal as the king demanded.[153] It could also be argued that the Federation Plan was not aimed at Israel but at the Palestinians and the Arab states. Although the proposal did not specifically refer to peace with Israel, its intention was clear: Hussein needed the Arab world's backing and Palestinian support. But it was Israel that was in possession of the territories. In 1972 Hussein felt that his bargaining position was at its strongest point; he had just defeated the PLO in Jordan, and the Arab world was in disarray. Yet from an Israeli and American perspective the gravest danger lay on the banks of the Suez Canal and not on the West Bank. The situation of "no peace no war," which existed in the Middle East in 1972, eventually led to a renewed war with Egypt and Syria. This was of utmost concern to both Israel and the United States, which feared the danger of superpower confrontation in the wake of an Arab-Israeli war. These factors played a major role in the lack of American enthusiasm for Hussein's plan and in the fact that the United States did not press Israel on the matter.

During the 1973 Yom Kippur War Jordan did not open a third front against Israel. According to Kissinger, Jordan's symbolic dispatch of troops to the Golan Heights during the war was coordinated with Israel. Jordan relayed a message to Israel, albeit indirectly, asking that Israel not use Jordan's symbolic involvement on the Golan Heights as an excuse to attack Jordan. Israel complied with Jordan's request.[154] In another episode during the war, according to Dan Schueftan, the Israeli air force considered bombing a Syrian military installation. The air force, however, did not carry out the attack because Israeli intelligence received information that Hussein was visiting his troops at that particular military post.[155] In 1993 Israel's chief of military intelligence, Eli Ze'ira, revealed that Hussein warned Golda Meir on September 25, 1973, of the impending Yom Kippur War. Moreover, according to Aaron Kleiman, on May 13, 1973, Hussein distributed a secret memorandum among his military chiefs of staff, indicating that certain Arab countries were planning a war against Israel. A few days later the letter was leaked to a Lebanese daily and apparently was read by Israeli intelligence.[156] In addition, the Jordanian premier, Zaid Rifai, gave an interview in June 1973 to the German weekly, *Quick,* in which he said that Egypt would attack Israel that summer.[157]

After the Yom Kippur War, Labor Party leader Yisrael Galili explained why he thought Jordan did not open a third front against Israel. He attributed Jordan's behavior to Israel's policy vis-à-vis Jordan before the war: "the open bridges policy, Israel not annexing the territories, and aiding Jordan during 1970 when it faced the danger of Syrian attack. Also, successful efforts that diffused threats and misunderstandings which could have led to an Israeli-Jordanian war . . . or the Israeli aid against Palestinian activism that threatened the Jordanian Kingdom and its leaders."[158]

The 1974 Israeli-Jordanian Disengagement Plans

To understand why an Israeli-Jordanian disengagement agreement was never signed one must analyze the 1974 Israeli-Jordanian negotiations at different levels. The interplay of Israeli domestic politics, Jordanian-Palestinian rivalry, inter-Arab politics, U.S. domestic politics, and foreign policy vis-à-vis the Arab-Israeli conflict together were responsible for the fact that an agreement was never reached.

After the 1973 Yom Kippur War, three disengagement agreements were signed among Israel, Egypt, and Syria, respectively. The first was signed between Israel and Egypt on January 18, 1974 (Sinai I), the second between Israel and Syria on May 31, 1974, and the third between Israel and Egypt on September 4, 1975 (Sinai II). The three agreements were reached through the mediation of Henry Kissinger, secretary of state in the Nixon administration, who devoted much time and energy after the 1973 war to reducing tensions in the Middle East.

It was during Kissinger's shuttle diplomacy that the question of Israeli-Jordanian disengagement came to the fore. Jordanian Premier Zaid Rifai first raised the idea of disengagement during the December 1973 Arab-Israeli peace conference in Geneva.[159] The proposal was formally presented for the first time by King Hussein to Kissinger on January 19, 1974, in the Jordanian resort city of Aqaba.[160]

Two different types of Israeli-Jordanian disengagement plans were being considered: *vertical* and *horizontal* plans. *Vertical* withdrawal meant that Israel would withdraw along the Jordan River, similar to the Israeli withdrawal from the Suez Canal and the Golan Heights. According to the north-south *vertical* withdrawal plan, the Jordanians would maintain a symbolic foothold in the West Bank. The Jordanians supported the *vertical* withdrawal plan, whereas the *horizontal* withdrawal proposal, the Jericho Plan, originated during a meeting between Allon and Kissinger. The *horizontal* Jericho Plan called on Israel to withdraw from Jericho and hand it over to the Jordanian civil administration.[161]

During the Hussein-Kissinger meeting Hussein argued that he should not be punished for not participating in the 1973 war. Just like Egypt and Syria, he also wanted a *vertical* disengagement agreement with Israel. According to Kissinger, Hussein proposed that

> Jordan and Israel would each pull back eight kilometers from the river to the foothills of the mountain ranges that mark the Jordan Valley. A Jordanian civilian administration would be established in the area vacated by Israel, especially in the town of Jericho. No Jordanian armed forces would cross the river or come closer than eight kilometers. A working group should be formed as rapidly as possible to ensure Jordan's claim to represent the Palestinians.[162]

This proposal was first made public on February 14, 1974, during a speech by Hussein to the Jordanian Parliament: "For Jordan, separation of forces means the beginning of the Israeli withdrawal from the West Bank. It should be all along the front from the Dead Sea to the positions in the north. And it should be as deep as possible."[163]

Kissinger chose not to press this issue with the Israelis at the time. Israel and Syria had not yet signed a separation of troops agreement, and he wanted to complete this step before moving on to the Israeli-Jordanian question. Both Israel and Egypt thought that an Israeli agreement with Syria was more important than one with Jordan.[164]

The prospects for a *vertical* Israeli withdrawal were explored when King Hussein and Zaid Rifai met with Golda Meir and Moshe Dayan in March 1974, but no concrete results were achieved.[165] This was the last meeting between Golda Meir and King Hussein. On April 10, 1974, Meir submitted her resignation as a result of domestic pressure after the 1973 Yom Kippur "earthquake." The Israeli negotiators, while telling Hussein that the issue of Israeli withdrawal would have to be determined by the Israeli voters, had, in fact, already decided to shelve the idea. The area from which Israel was supposed to pull back (Jordan Rift) was also the most strategically important area of the West Bank according to the territorialists. Hence, Kissinger wrote in his memoirs that when he presented the Jordanian proposal to the Israeli leadership:[166]

> It had been rejected as inconsistent with the Allon Plan, according to which Israel was going to keep the Jordan Valley as a military security line. . . . I ran into a Catch-22: The Allon Plan could not be the basis of disengagement on the Jordanian front because the coalition partner, the National Religious Party, opposed giving up *any* West Bank territory at all. Thus Israel would reject a proposal inconsistent with the Allon Plan but would refuse also to negotiate the Allon Plan because it could not get the full cabinet behind it.[167]

After the Israeli-Syrian agreement was signed in May 1974, Kissinger decided to move forward with Israeli-Jordanian disengagement. He believed that unless Israel negotiated with Jordan, Israel would eventually have to face the PLO, a possibility that, according to Kissinger, would lead nowhere.

The Israeli position was somewhat precarious. Its leadership did not regard the withdrawal from the West Bank as strategically significant compared to the disengagement agreements with Egypt and Syria. There was no pressure on Israel to enter into disengagement talks with Hussein "not because it [the relationship between Israel and Jordan] was too problematic but because it did not present enough problems for the two parties."[168] After all, the two countries had reached a modus vivendi in the West Bank. In contrast, King Hussein felt mounting pressures to defend his claim that he still was the spokesman for the Palestinians in his struggle with the PLO. In addition, Meir had publicly committed herself to going to general elections and putting the issue to the Israeli public if a disengagement agreement were to require any withdrawal from the West Bank.[169] Yitzhak Rabin, who became prime minister on June 3, 1974, reiterated Golda Meir's pledge to hold elections if the issue of West Bank withdrawal became relevant. For many Israelis, territorial withdrawal from the West Bank was a very emotional issue. Deep political and ideological divisions characterized the debate over the future of the territories. This clash of perspectives was also present within the Labor Alignment.

The Israeli negotiating team included Prime Minister Yitzhak Rabin, Defense Minister Shimon Peres, and Foreign Minister Yigal Allon. They each represented a different perspective on Israeli-Jordanian negotiations. In addition to his concerns about consolidating his newly acquired power base, Rabin believed that reaching an interim agreement with Egypt would alleviate the pressures for pursuing a comprehensive settlement that included Israeli withdrawal from the West Bank. He hoped that a second Israeli-Egyptian agreement would "help the U.S. strengthen its position and reduce Soviet influence, and drive a wedge between Egypt and Syria, thus diminishing the military threat to Israel."[170]

With regard to an Israeli-Jordanian settlement, Rabin offered a proposal that was based on an Israeli military presence in the West Bank and the establishment of a Jordanian civil administration in those territories evacuated by Israel. Rabin rejected the idea of total Israeli withdrawal; he believed there had to be a fifteen to twenty-year transition period that would allow all Palestinian refugees to resettle in Jordan.[171]

This proposal, however, was insufficient as far as the Jordanians were concerned and proved to be a nonstarter for Israeli-Jordanian negotiations.

Yigal Allon, a territorialist by inclination and the more dovish member of the negotiating team, believed that Israel should pursue an agreement with Jordan before a second disengagement agreement was signed with Egypt. Allon viewed a disengagement accord with Jordan as a "preventive agreement." He argued that disengagement on the Jordanian front would help prevent the Arabs from amassing military forces on the two sides of the Jordan River and, hence, prevent a war from breaking out between Israel and Jordan. Furthermore, he said that the Israeli-Egyptian agreement had set a precedent for an open Arab-Israeli dialogue. Although he preferred a comprehensive agreement with Jordan, he did not rule out the possibility of an interim disengagement agreement that eventually would lead to a peace treaty.[172]

The third member of the team, Shimon Peres, held a functionalist view that was close to that of Moshe Dayan.[173] Even though Dayan had fallen out of grace with the Israeli public as a result of the Arab surprise attack during the Yom Kippur War, he was still influential both in and outside of government. He argued that the situation in the West Bank was not urgent because Israel and Jordan had come to a tacit understanding about the management of the West Bank affairs. Dayan favored a continuation of the status quo and thought Israel could always reach an agreement with Jordan if the status quo became untenable. He saw no need to rush into an agreement.[174] Despite the profound impact that the 1973 Yom Kippur War had on the Israeli public and elite, Dayan's views remained unchanged. He elaborated on this point during an interview with *Ha'aretz*:

> We are not engaged in a war with Jordan, and we do not have any special problems with her. We live in peace with the Palestinians in the West Bank and Gaza. Today, the situation does not require a "push" for an agreement with Jordan. If you ask me about the priorities, the agreement with Egypt comes first because Egypt is the most important country in the Arab world. Then comes Syria, with whom we recently fought a war. Only when we also reach an interim agreement with Syria will Jordan's and the other Arab countries' turns come.[175]

Like Dayan, Peres was opposed to any territorial compromise on the West Bank at that time. He was, however, favorably disposed to negotiations with Jordan regarding a West Bank condominium, which meant that the two countries would comanage the West Bank.[176] In addition, the personal rivalry between Peres and Rabin also played a role in the debate over a disengagement agreement with Jordan.[177]

As a result of these conflicting perspectives on negotiations with Jordan among the Israeli negotiators—Rabin, Allon, and Peres—

there was no movement on this front. Naturally, the question of Israeli-Jordanian negotiations was explored during President Nixon's trip to the Middle East in mid-June 1974. Nixon arrived in Israel on June 17, two weeks after the new Rabin government took office. Rabin told Nixon of the constraints that he faced in moving toward a settlement with Jordan and that it would be difficult for Israel to disengage on the Jordanian front at that time. Consequently, the United States and Israel agreed that the next step in the peace process would be an Israeli-Egyptian disengagement agreement.[178]

The "Egypt First" attitude was reinforced by Egyptian President Anwar Sadat, who was pushing for a second agreement on the Egyptian front. Sadat believed that an Israeli-Jordanian agreement was not feasible at that time and was eager to push forward in negotiating with Israel.

Kissinger's "carrot and stick" policy toward Israel, aimed at convincing the new Israeli government that Israel had to make concessions to Jordan, provided the backdrop to Nixon's visit. As a warning to Israel, Under Secretary of State Joseph Sisco said on two occasions that "there cannot be a permanent solution to the conflict unless it meets the principal concerns of the Arab states and it meets the *legitimate interests of the Palestinians*" (emphasis mine).[179] The message to Israel was clear: unless it began negotiations with Jordan, the United States would play the "PLO card," an option highly detested by an Israeli leadership hopeful that a formal American-PLO dialogue would never materialize.

The State Department sent a clarification to Israel regarding Sisco's remarks, saying that the American position on the PLO had not changed. Israel, however, still interpreted Sisco's remarks as an implicit threat.[180]

A follow-up to the American pressure on Israel occurred during Nixon's visit to Jordan. Although Kissinger did not accompany Nixon on the Jordanian leg of the trip, he still wanted to maintain the momentum. He shared neither Rabin's nor Sadat's views on bypassing Jordan in the negotiations because he feared that King Hussein faced the impending danger of losing his mandate to negotiate with Israel.[181] King Hussein seemed desperate to start negotiations with Israel.[182] When President Nixon visited Amman on June 17, 1974, the king argued that it was Jordan's turn to disengage forces with Israel.[183]

On the American side Nixon promised to try to facilitate an agreement with Israel. When the final joint communiqué was issued, however, the idea of a disengagement was not specifically mentioned; instead, "the President promised the active support of the United States for agreement between Israel and Jordan on concrete steps toward the just and durable peace."[184]

The Nixon statement was just another attempt by the administration to show Israel that it regarded the issue as worth pursuing. To place additional pressure on Israel Kissinger asked the Pentagon to delay a shipment of weapons to Israel to show American displeasure with Israel's unwillingness to negotiate with Jordan.[185] The Israeli reaction to Kissinger's maneuvers resulted in an official government communiqué that in effect killed the initiative. While the Israeli government called for "negotiations for a peace agreement with Jordan," it rejected any interim accords with it. And because it was clear to Kissinger that Rabin was unwilling at that time to call for elections, the government declaration amounted to a meaningless statement.[186] It should be noted that a minority in the Israeli cabinet, members of Mapam and the Independent Liberals, attempted to insert into the communiqué that "Israel will conduct negotiations with Jordan and with Palestinians who recognize Israel and its independence, and who are ready to reach agreements for lasting peace."[187] This attempt, however, failed.

While Israel was trying to out-maneuver the United States, both Egypt and Jordan attempted to keep the issue of negotiations with Jordan alive. From Kissinger's memoirs it is unclear what Egypt's motivations were. Kissinger states that the Egyptians were opposed to an Israeli-Jordanian accord. Perhaps Sadat felt he could not publicly refuse Hussein's requests to support him while privately he attempted to undermine the king.

Notwithstanding these ambiguous Egyptian motivations, King Hussein and President Sadat did issue a joint statement when Hussein visited Cairo on July 18, 1974. Two points in the statement are worthy of consideration: "[t]he two sides declared that the Palestine Liberation Organization is the legitimate representative of the Palestinians living inside the Hashemite Kingdom of Jordan" and "[t]he two sides also agreed that a disengagement agreement should be reached on the Jordanian front as a step towards a just peaceful resolution [of the Arab-Israeli conflict]."[188] In this communiqué Jordan and Egypt omitted the word *sole* from the statement when they referred to the PLO. This probably was a way for the Jordanian monarch to assert his position as the representative of the Palestinians. Had the word *sole* been included, it would have meant that the PLO had an exclusive mandate to represent the Palestinians. In addition, by calling for a disengagement agreement between Israel and Jordan, the two countries expressed their desire to bypass the PLO. They hoped that as a result of an interim Israeli-Jordanian agreement, the Arab League would affirm Hussein's mandate to negotiate with Israel at its upcoming summit meeting in Rabat. The PLO, indeed, interpreted the communiqué as a Jordanian ploy to undermine the Palestinian organization's improved status and growing legitimacy.

To further explore the next step in the peace process Kissinger invited the foreign ministers of Israel, Egypt, and Syria and the Jordanian king and his prime minister to separate talks in Washington. Yigal Allon arrived in Washington on July 28, 1974. During the Allon visit, the issue of an Israeli *vertical* withdrawal was considered. Prime Minister Rabin, who did not want to make any move on the Jordanian front, totally opposed this idea.[189] Allon thought that Rabin was making a mistake but did not press his case for fear of an open clash with him.[190] Yet for Kissinger the question of Israeli-Jordanian disengagement was far from resolved. When Hussein arrived in Washington for talks with the new American president, Gerald Ford, who had replaced Richard Nixon, the disengagement question was also discussed. The final joint American-Jordanian communiqué stated that "these consultations will continue with a view to addressing at an appropriately early date the issues of particular concern to Jordan, including a Jordanian-Israeli disengagement agreement."[191] This declaration was a boost to Hussein, who thought that he would be able to weather the upcoming storm at the Arab League summit scheduled for late October where the Jordanian mandate to represent the Palestinians would be considered.

Rabin reacted with anger to the joint American-Jordanian communiqué. He regarded it as a violation of the American pledge to consult Israel before making any move. He also thought that the issue of disengagement was off the agenda. Rabin publicly denounced the statement and said there was no need for an accord with Jordan because "Hussein won't run away."[192]

Shortly after Hussein's return to Amman, the king secretly flew to Israel on August 29 for his first meeting with the new Rabin government. According to Matti Golan, Rabin presented three possibilities to Hussein. First, there would be immediate negotiations toward a comprehensive settlement. Both sides agreed, however, that such negotiations involved formidable complications that made this option unrealistic at the time. Second was the idea of reaching an understanding on the principles of a comprehensive settlement and then implementing it in stages. The third possibility was to execute a functional separation of forces (no Israeli military withdrawal) or functional arrangements on the West Bank.[193]

The question of a disengagement agreement was on the agenda for the meeting. The Jordanians wanted to reach such an agreement although it was not included in the Israeli proposals. Rabin rejected the Jordanian idea of disengagement because he considered it a unilateral Israeli withdrawal.[194] Thus it became apparent to Hussein that no agreement could be reached. Peres, consistent with his functionalist position, presented to Hussein the possibility of a joint condominium over the

West Bank. None of these suggestions, however, were deemed acceptable by Hussein, who returned to Amman empty-handed. From a Jordanian perspective there were only two possibilities: either a total Israeli withdrawal from the West Bank, including East Jerusalem, or a disengagement of forces. The second option was more symbolic than substantive because it implied that a peace process had begun and eventually would lead to a comprehensive agreement. Had such a disengagement agreement been reached Hussein could have come to the Arab League and argued that the mandate for negotiations should not be taken from him and given to the PLO because he had already started the process. Yet the Israelis did not quite see the process as Hussein did, and, consequently, the negotiations got nowhere.

On the inter-Arab level, developments did not look promising for Jordan. In preparations for the upcoming Arab summit in Rabat Syrian Foreign Minister Abdel-Halim Khaddam, Egyptian Foreign Minister Ismail Fahmi, and Faruq Qaddumi, member of the PLO's Executive Committee, convened in Damascus on October 22. The statement that resulted from this meeting was a harbinger of Jordan's exclusion from the peace process and its replacement by the PLO as the representative of the Palestinians. Jordan was not even mentioned in the communiqué, which referred to the PLO as the "sole legitimate representative of the Palestinian people."[195] This statement was published only two months after Egypt and Jordan had issued a communiqué, giving the PLO secondary status vis-à-vis Jordan in the representation of the Palestinians. It was clear that Egypt's Sadat was only paying lip service to the so-called Jordanian option.[196] The official Jordanian reaction to the tripartite communiqué stated that it agreed to "freeze all Jordanian political activity undertaken on the basis of Jordan's agreement to participate in the Geneva conference. . . . Jordan hereby resolves that if the conference [the forthcoming Arab summit] adopts this communiqué, Jordan will be absolved of all political responsibility and all direct connection with the problem."[197]

Just before the Rabat summit convened, on October 19, 1974, the Israeli team met again with Hussein in an apparent last-minute effort to salvage Jordan's position. During this meeting neither the Israelis nor the Jordanians believed Jordan would lose the mandate to negotiate on behalf of the Palestinians.[198] Rabin told Hussein that it would be to Jordan's advantage if Israel moved next on the Egyptian front so "Jordan would not be burdened by the stigma of being the first [to negotiate with Israel]."[199] This, of course, was an attempt to placate the Jordanians for not reaching an agreement with Israel.

Israeli and Jordanian illusions were shattered on October 28 when the Arab summit convened in Rabat, Morocco, and declared the Palestine Liberation Organization the "sole legitimate representative of the Palestinian people." Hussein, in a last-minute appeal to the Arab summit, discussed the question of disengagement with Israel and admitted a failure.[200] The Jordanian appeal to the Arab League did not change anyone's mind. From that point onward the Arab-Israeli conflict entered a new phase in which the PLO became a major player.

In retrospect the failed 1974 Israeli-Jordanian disengagement plan was clearly a missed opportunity for the two countries. The failure of Israel and Jordan to reach an agreement had long-term implications for the course of the conflict after 1974. An agreement between Israel and Jordan could have built some momentum and enthusiasm for finding a diplomatic solution for the West Bank and Gaza. According to Kissinger, "It was an amalgam of American, Israeli, and Arab domestic politics and inhibitions in which each party for different reasons took the path of least resistance and brought about the worst possible outcome."[201]

From the American perspective the fact that President Nixon faced the Watergate scandal was probably detrimental to the outcome of the negotiations. According to Joseph Sisco, the scandal weakened Nixon and prevented the president from exerting pressure on Israel: "We [Kissinger and Sisco] felt that the President was weak and he could not have intervened like he did when the Israeli-Egyptian negotiations almost collapsed in 1974."[202] Moreover, Israel did not share with the United States the contents of its secret negotiations with Jordan.[203]

Although the American negotiators, Kissinger in particular, cannot be faulted for failing to bring about an Israeli-Jordanian agreement, perhaps they should have tried harder. George E. Gruen of the American Jewish Committee, upon visiting Jordan in 1979, was told by the Jordanians that Kissinger had admitted that he made a mistake when he did not press Israel in 1974.[204]

The Israeli government clearly was divided on this issue. Rabin did not want to pursue any agreement with Jordan because his primary objective was to reach a second agreement with Egypt, which amounted to a de facto nonbelligerency agreement. In this regard Jordan's role was minimal at best. Most importantly, the fact that Israel and Jordan were functionally cooperating in the management of the West Bank and outside the territories showed that Israel did not attach any urgency to an agreement with Hussein. The regular secret meetings between them and the Jordanians, in fact, led to forestalling an agreement. These meetings led the Israeli leadership to believe that "Hussein was tamed," and, therefore, Israel did not need to make any territorial concessions. At best, the Jordanians could be formally given the right to administer the West Bank. The Jordanians did not agree to administering the West

Bank without an Israeli withdrawal. Additionally, it seems that neither the Israelis nor the Jordanians predicted that the PLO would be accorded the status of representing the Palestinians in Rabat. During the October 19 meeting between Rabin and Hussein, Rabin told Hussein that "as far as the Palestinian problem is concerned, Israel has one and only one partner, Jordan."[205] The implications of this statement were clear. Regardless of what would be decided, Israeli and Jordanian interests were best served by the status quo.

Not everyone in the Israeli government shared this opinion. Among the proponents of negotiations with Jordan, Yigal Allon figured prominently. Abba Eban, who was not a member of the government at the time, argued for a disengagement of forces agreement with Jordan.[206]

In addition, as observed earlier, there was an attempt by a number of cabinet ministers to raise the possibility of negotiations with the Palestinians. Their views, however, were rejected. Among them were Minister of Information Aharon Yariv, who along with Minister of Health Victor Shemtov and Minister of Tourism Moshe Kol devised a formula, later known as the Yariv-Shemtov Plan, calling for negotiations with the Palestinians provided that they recognized Israel and expressed willingness to negotiate a diplomatic settlement.[207] The debate over disengagement threw into high relief the schism that had begun to divide the four positions in Israel over the question of the West Bank. What started as an ideological split in the Israeli government in the wake of the 1967 war had turned into a policy of intransigence. Rabin's argument that any return of the territories would require a national election whose outcome might not be favorable to the Labor Party was clearly a miscalculation. Although Rabin supported Allon's territorialist views in principle, in this instance the two clearly disagreed about disengagement. This contention may be attributable to the fact that Rabin was the prime minister at that time and feared a negative public reaction if he were to support the agreement. At the end of August 1974 a significant public opinion poll was published in the *Jerusalem Post*. The public's view of a disengagement agreement with Jordan was favorable: 45 percent favored a disengagement with Jordan; 36 percent opposed it; and 18.3 percent were undecided. The same poll asked about general Israeli withdrawal from the territories: 49.2 percent favored giving up the territories; 31 percent opposed; and 19 percent were undecided.[208] These two polls clearly indicated a different picture than was portrayed by Rabin. Had Rabin gone to the polls over this issue, the majority of the Israeli public probably would have supported an agreement with Jordan.

The Jordanians viewed the failure of the negotiations as spawning major implications. During the first post-Rabat meeting with the Israelis in mid-1975 Hussein accused Israel of undermining his position: "If you had consented to a separation of forces agreement, the Rabat resolution could have been averted.''[209]

Inter-Arab dynamics also played a crucial role. The Egyptian position shifted from supporting an Israeli-Jordanian agreement to a position that, in effect, undermined such an agreement. Sadat obviously did not believe that an Israeli-Jordanian agreement was feasible, and, therefore, he did not support it wholeheartedly. The Syrians did not play an obstructionist role, but neither did they actively support the agreement.

The actor that emerged victorious was the PLO. Its position in the territories, in the Arab world, and internationally was bolstered. Officially, the PLO replaced Jordan as the representative of the Palestinians, and the agenda for the peace process in the post-1974 period emerged substantially different from that of the previous period, culminating in the 1993 PLO accord with Israel. It took Jordan an additional fourteen years to accept the reality of Palestinian representation that culminated in Jordan's 1988 disengagement from the West Bank and closed a chapter in Jordanian-Palestinian and Israeli-Jordanian relations respectively.

5

From Rabat to Jordan's West Bank Disengagement, 1974–1988

It was during the 1974 Rabat Arab summit that the mandate to represent the Palestinians was taken from Jordan and given to the Palestine Liberation Organization. Fourteen years later, in the midst of the Palestinian intifadah in the West Bank and Gaza, Hussein finally accepted the fact that he no longer had a claim to the territories that Israel had occupied since the 1967 war. On July 31, 1988, he declared in a dramatic speech that Jordan would sever all legal and administrative links with the West Bank. For Israel, Jordan, and the Palestinians Hussein's declaration signaled the end of an era. No longer could Israeli leaders refer to Jordan as the only interlocutor, the key partner, for peace negotiations over the West Bank. Jordan's disengagement placed the PLO in center stage. The Palestinian uprising symbolized the rejection of Jordan's attempt to woo the Palestinians away from the PLO and to accept Jordan as their representative. It took Jordan fourteen years to act upon this reality. In 1993, five years after Jordan's disengagement, Israel and the PLO recognized each other and signed an interim accord. This agreement was, to a certain degree, facilitated by Jordan's disengagement; it paved the way, one year later, for Israel and Jordan to sign a Treaty of Peace.

The focus in this chapter is on the crucial fourteen years, 1974 to 1988, in which the dynamics of a number of key developments helped transform the Arab-Israeli conflict. These developments included Jordan's effort to regain its status in the Arab world in the wake of the Rabat decision; the exclusion of Jordan from the Camp David negotiations; the 1982 Reagan Plan; the 1983–85 Jordanian-PLO negotiations that culminated in the Amman accord and its subsequent abrogation; the April 1987 secret London agreement reached between King Hussein and Shimon Peres; and, finally, the Palestinian intifadah, which undermined Jordan's interests in the West Bank and led to the formal delinking of Jordan from the West Bank.

During these fourteen years Jordan was eclipsed by the Palestine Liberation Organization. The PLO became the symbol of Palestinian nationalism and was eventually viewed as the unchallenged representative of the Palestinians by the residents of the occupied territories, the Arab world, the international community, and, eventually, by Israel in 1993. Except for a brief interlude when Shimon Peres was prime minister in 1984–86 and foreign minister in 1986–88, Israel gave no serious consideration to peace with Jordan during the fourteen years. With the election of the Likud in May 1977, its leaders, Menachem Begin and Yitzhak Shamir, maintained the annexationist perspective that precluded formal negotiations over "Judea and Samaria"—areas they considered part of historic Israel. Jordanian involvement in the West Bank continued, however, because of the functional ties between Jordan and Israel. Likud leaders accepted these ties as the best way to maintain the status quo. Taken as a whole, the 1974–88 period reflected the gradual relegation of Jordan to a secondary role in the Arab-Israeli conflict. Although before 1974 there was no consensus in Israel regarding Jordan's role in the West Bank, there were numerous negotiations with Jordan, such as the 1974 disengagement talks. In the period after Rabat, with the focus shifting to Israeli-Egyptian relations, there was only one instance, in 1987, when Israeli-Jordanian peace negotiations actually took place (the April 1987 London agreement).

After 1974 West Bankers changed their political identification from supporting Jordan to actively promoting the PLO. The West Bank and Gaza emerged as the main foci of the Arab-Israeli conflict. Israel attempted to impose its will on the local population in the territories, and Jordan and the PLO competed for the hearts and minds of the Palestinians. All this ended, however, when the intifadah erupted in December 1987 and led to Jordan's disengagement in July 1988.

The Implications of Rabat

The Rabat summit placed Hussein in a precarious position vis-à-vis the PLO and Israel. While the king publicly supported the Rabat resolutions, privately he continued to assert his position in the West Bank via the open bridges policy. This delicate balance created a dilemma for Hussein. On the one hand, he argued that the Palestinian inhabitants of the territories would be hurt the most if Jordan renounced its ties to the West Bank. He said the PLO could not fill the vacuum that would thus be created.[1]

On the other hand, according to Dan Schueftan, Hussein regarded the "unity of the two Banks as an existential requirement; a real Jordanian departure from the West Bank could have been political suicide for the Jordanian regime."[2] Therefore, the implications of Rabat on

Jordanian-Israeli peace were profound. Because the PLO had been designated as the "sole legitimate representative of the Palestinian people," it was viewed by the Palestinians and the Arab world as the party that eventually would negotiate with Israel over the West Bank and Gaza. Jordan's position on a formal peace with Israel was also affected by these developments. Therefore, Jordan had "no interest in moderating its stance on the territorial question in order to achieve the liberation of part of the occupied territories. For as a consequence of such a deal, Jordan would be thrust back into the intra-Arab limelight as a traitorous regime responsible for selling out the Palestinians."[3] King Hussein in the post-Rabat period publicly adhered to the all-Arab position regarding the representation of the Palestinians, yet he "did not for a moment abandon his rivalry with the PLO for predominance in the determination of the political fate of the Palestinians."[4] This was true in the inter-Arab arena but, more importantly, it was evident in the West Bank. Jordan continued to pay the salaries of former Jordanian civil servants, to issue passports, and to maintain the functional relationship with Israel symbolized by the open bridges policy. As stated earlier, Hussein wanted to prove to the Palestinians that only he, not the PLO, could secure an Israeli withdrawal from the territories. As Asher Susser notes, among the factors in Jordan's favor during the post-Rabat period were "Israel's refusal to negotiate with the PLO and its policy of calling for negotiations with Jordan over the future of the West Bank with Jordan." "The political process in the Middle East remained tied to Security Council Resolutions 242 and 338, accepted by Jordan [and Israel] and rejected by the PLO."[5]

Although Hussein did not give up his eventual dream to reclaim the West Bank, he did make a number of political changes inside Jordan as a result of the new post-Rabat reality. The Rabat resolutions highlighted Hussein's predicament. Whereas idealistically he was sympathetic to the idea of Palestinian self-determination, he nevertheless saw advantages in the status quo. Lack of Israeli-Palestinian rapprochement would help him realize his aspiration to incorporate the West Bank into Jordan. The problem was how Jordan would treat its legal association with the West Bank. King Hussein's brother, Crown Prince Hassan, argued that "Jordan should cut its ties to the West Bank and that for all practical purposes, the 'unity of the two Banks' idea should be revoked."[6] The king, however, was not willing to make an official break with the West Bank. What Hussein devised was a legal-administrative solution. The Jordanian parliament, which was composed of an equal number of East and West Bankers, was dissolved on November 23, 1974. By suspending the Parliament, Hussein's implicit message to the Palestinians was that they could not be represented by the PLO and the Jordanian parliament at the same time. But the legal basis for the "unity of the two Banks"—

derived from the 1950 Jordanian annexation of the West Bank—was not altered.[7] Hussein warned the eight hundred thousand East Bank Palestinians in an interview that "they [could] choose whether they wanted to become Jordanian citizens without jeopardizing any of their basic rights in their homeland, or they could choose a Palestinian identity, in which case they [would] be free to remain here as guests with the same rights and privileges as any other Arab guests."[8]

To prove further that he did not intend to sever all ties with the West Bank, Hussein opened a new ministry, the Office of the Occupied Territories, which paid pensions to former Jordanian employees and administered economic programs with West Bank municipalities, cooperatives, and charitable societies.[9]

The 1976 Elections

Inside the West Bank, the PLO's growing stature was also evident. Unlike the 1972 municipal elections in the West Bank, which ended in a victory for the pro-Jordanian elements, the April 1976 local elections were a clear victory for pro-PLO supporters. The combination of demography and nationalism tilted the outcome of the 1976 elections in the PLO's favor. Whereas in 1972 the PLO had tried to boycott the elections, in 1976 supporters of the Palestinian organization took part in them.

The architect of the elections was Defense Minister Shimon Peres, who was responsible for the territories and who had amended the 1955 Jordanian elections law. Under the new legal provisions, all Palestinians age twenty-one and older, including women, were eligible to vote.[10] According to Moshe Maoz, Peres hoped that after the elections, a new local leadership would emerge on the West Bank who would accept his idea of Palestinian self-rule, or autonomy. The West Bank autonomy idea emanated from Peres's concept of a functional arrangement whereby either Jordan or the West Bank Palestinians, who were Jordanian citizens, would bear the responsibility for the civil administration of the West Bank.

Peres explained his basic philosophy regarding the West Bank in his book, *Kaet-machar* (Tomorrow is now).[11] He believed that a peace settlement or an interim agreement should aim to secure the following objectives: open bridges, a joint economic infrastructure, the maintenance of Jewish settlements, and an Israeli military presence in the West Bank for a long term. He presented two scenarios for a settlement. The first was a Jordanian-Palestinian federation or confederation whereby the West Bank would be demilitarized and patrolled by joint Israeli-Arab military forces. This arrangement did not preclude the possibility of a peaceful transformation of this entity from a monarchy into a republic based on a Palestinian majority in both Banks. The second possibility was either an Israeli federation or confederation that would include a "Palestinian region" in the West Bank and Gaza. Peres, however, said such a scenario would necessitate changes in the Israeli political structure and military administration of the territories, and he doubted whether this was a realistic possibility.

With neither option materializing, Peres proposed an interim agreement based on a functional arrangement whose seeds were already in place on the West Bank. This arrangement would be based on defensible borders for Israel and the transfer of the West Bank's civilian administration to Jordan. As such, West Bank Palestinians would fully participate in Jordanian political life. Peres proposed such a plan because he believed that the establishment of a Palestinian state in the West Bank would endanger Israel's security. Furthermore, he argued that Israeli and Jordanian interests converged on a number of issues, which would ease the transition into the new proposed phase.

Peres believed that self-rule for the Palestinians was of utmost importance for the success of his plan; he insisted on holding elections in the West Bank. He argued that Israel could not return to the status quo ante that existed before the 1967 war. Hence, because the "inhabitants of Judea and Samaria are Jordanian citizens, we understand Jordan's wish—and the Palestinians' desire—to be part of Jordan's political structure. Jordan must understand that Israel cannot return to a border which is 14 kilometers wide because of security reasons. *In a region which cannot be partitioned it is preferable to cooperate* [emphasis mine]."[12]

This cooperation, according to Peres, would be based on open bridges and boundaries and an Israeli military presence—perhaps a joint Israeli-Jordanian-Palestinian presence—to prevent the West Bank from becoming a springboard for political and guerrilla activities aimed at Israel and Jordan. Moreover, he proposed a joint infrastructure that would encompass transportation, communications, energy, and water regimes. The territories would be linked to Jordan economically, politically, and culturally. Many of these ideas, particularly those emphasizing Israeli-Jordanian cooperation, were later incorporated into the peace treaty signed in 1994.

By holding elections in the West Bank, Peres hoped a moderate Palestinian leadership would emerge who would help implement his plan. Like his colleague, Dayan, Peres was against drawing maps, which he believed would lead nowhere. Indeed, maps would pinpoint territorial issues that he felt should be left in abeyance. Rather, he sought to build a structure of cooperation that he thought would satisfy everybody: Israel would maintain its military control, Jordan would run the civilian administration, and the local inhabitants would have autonomy and be structurally linked to Israel and Jordan. But reality proved Peres wrong. The Palestinian nationalists who sought eventual Palestinian independence rather than dependence on Israel and Jordan had won.

A new generation of local leadership came to the fore. No longer were the fortunes of the Palestinians tied to Jordan. The newly elected mayors were younger and more educated than their predecessors. Sixty-seven percent of those elected were younger than fifty, compared to 40 percent in 1972; 10 percent were below thirty compared to 3 percent in 1972; 25 percent had a high school education (roughly the same percentage as in 1972); 40 percent were white collar professionals; 40 percent were merchants and businessmen; and 20 percent were farmers. In 1972 only 20 percent were white collar professionals.[13] The newly elected mayors, as Geoffrey Aronson noted in *Creating Facts,* "reflected the popular desire for Palestinian independence in the West Bank and Gaza Strip; but the new mayors and councilors also reflected the traditional family and class ties which defined West Bank politics. Rather than symbolizing a break with past traditions, the election of the nationalist bloc in 1976 was a bold expression of local tradition."[14]

Although certainly many prominent West Bank notables were either elected or appointed by the new West Bank mayors, the 1976 elections clearly constituted a new chapter in West Bank politics, especially with regard to Jordan's role as the custodian of the West Bank. Aronson argued that the 1976 elections "were not a radical break with the past that many Palestinians and Israelis alike took them to be."[15] Perhaps the social and class allegiance of the new leadership was similar to that of the old guard: "[T]he mayors came from the same well-to-do and socially prominent families in these towns that had always provided leadership."[16] But, the political orientation and worldview of the new elite were radically different. The identification of this new elite with the PLO was total, and even the pro-Jordanian elite "began to identify with the PLO and to regard the PLO as its sole legitimate representative."[17]

In many towns throughout the West Bank pro-PLO supporters, communists, and former members of the Arab nationalist parties gained the upper hand. For example, in Hebron Fahd Qawasmeh, an agronomist and former local civilian employee of the military government, replaced Sheikh Ja'abri, a strong pro-Jordanian supporter. In Nablus, the hotbed of West Bank nationalism, Bassam Shak'a, the pro-Ba'athist, won at the expense of Ma'azuz al Masri, a pro-Hashemite. In Ramallah and Tul Karem mayors Karim Khalaf and Hilmi Hanun, who were both closely associated with the PLO, were reelected.

In the 1972 elections the pro-Jordanians had won owing to the weakness of the PLO after the civil war in Jordan. A few years later the election results would show the growth of nationalism in the West Bank. The outcome of the elections caught Israel by surprise. For the second time in two years Israel had underestimated the strength of the PLO. In 1974 Israel had not believed that the PLO would be given the mandate to represent the Palestinians in Rabat. Now, Peres's intention to create a new independent Palestinian leadership who would participate in his Palestinian self-rule scheme went awry. It should be noted, however, that many Israeli policymakers and newspaper columnists objected to his election idea because they were worried that pro-PLO forces would triumph. Yet this resistance did not deter Peres from moving forward with his election plan.

Jordan was greatly alarmed by Israel's moves on the West Bank. It viewed Israel as pursuing a double standard. On the one hand, Peres said Jordan was the only party to the negotiations over the West Bank and conducted several clandestine meetings with Hussein. On the other hand, Israel pursued a policy that in effect gave the PLO a boost in the West Bank at Jordan's expense. Menachem Milson, the former head of the civil administration of the West Bank, wrote that Adnan Abu-Odeh, the Jordanian minister of the occupied territories, told him via a third party that Jordan could no longer coordinate policy with Israel. Abu-Odeh cited three examples of Israeli policy that ran counter to Jordan's and supported the PLO: holding the municipal elections that Jordan opposed; allowing the pro-PLO and anti-Jordanian newspaper *Al-Fajr* to operate in East Jerusalem; and appointing Shlomo Avineri, who was considered sympathetic to the Palestinians, to the position of director general of the Foreign Ministry.[18]

Despite the setback it suffered after the municipal elections Jordan still sought to maintain a modicum of influence in the West Bank. In late 1976, for example, a number of West Bank mayors began making semiofficial visits to the East Bank to discuss the resumption of economic assistance to the West Bank, which had ceased before the elections.[19] Among these mayors were Fahd Qawasmeh, the PLO supporter from Hebron, and others who were not identified as pro-Hashemites. Some analysts interpreted these visits as a sign of the PLO's weakness in the wake of its defeat at Tal al-Za'tar in Lebanon by the Maronite Lebanese Forces, who were backed by Syrian forces. This defeat signified a blow to the PLO's military and political credibility.[20] Qawasmeh explained his position regarding the resumption of economic assistance: "So long as the Jordanians keep funds flowing to the West Bank they are our allies. They may think that the PLO is finished after what happened in Lebanon. That is their privilege, but they are wrong. Meanwhile we intend to benefit from the funds they provide and their friendly inclinations."[21]

The mayors elected in 1976, however, did not stay in office very long. Mayors Qawasmeh of Hebron and Milhem of Halhoul were deported by the Israeli authorities for their pro-PLO activism on May 2, 1980. In June 1980 Karim Khalaf, mayor of Ramallah, and Bassam Shak'a of Nablus were severely wounded by bombs placed in their cars by a Jewish terrorist organization.[22] During 1982 eight mayors who were elected in 1976 were removed from office by Israel. These acts led to the de facto reversal of the 1976 elections and created a political vacuum in the territories. The result was an increased influence of the external PLO, a development that Israel certainly had not anticipated.[23]

Despite the fact that Jordan kept its links to the West Bank after the 1976 elections the local population and, more importantly, the newly elected mayors no longer viewed Jordan as the key party to a West Bank settlement. The increasing prominence of the PLO in the territories led to financial support by the PLO in the West Bank. In March 1977 the Palestine National Council decided to translate the PLO's political gains into the creation of an economic and social infrastructure in the West Bank. Israeli authorities, however, demanded that any transfer of money by non-Jordanians (from either the PLO or the Arab states) would require Jordanian approval. According to Milson, this policy was developed by those in the Israeli military government of the territories who supported the Jordanian option. In other words, Israel wanted West Bankers to give Jordan credit for any money transferred to the West Bank. Israel thought this would bolster Jordan's position against the PLO's increasing status.[24]

Jordan's attempts to cut its losses after Rabat took place in the inter-Arab political arena. Paradoxically, as Dan Schueftan points out, the Rabat resolutions and their acceptance by Jordan allowed Jordan to free itself and to compete openly with the PLO in inter-Arab politics without being accused of undermining the Palestinian cause.[25] The opportunity for Jordan to reassert itself came about as a result of the signing in 1975 of Sinai II, the second Israeli-Egyptian disengagement agreement, and the ensuing Syrian-Egyptian rift.[26] Syrian President Asad was suspicious of Egypt after Sadat signed Sinai II. Asad feared that Sadat sought a separate peace with Israel. He thought a separate peace was dangerous because it would weaken Arab solidarity and destroy the consensus that had been established after the 1973 war. For Hussein, the fact that Sadat was attempting to pursue a unilateral strategy meant that, once again, developments on the Egyptian front would eclipse Jordan's desire to regain the territories it lost in 1967. Underlying Jordan's support of Asad was Syria's conflict with the PLO in Lebanon. Indeed, earlier in Lebanon, Jordan had supported Syria's opponents—the Phalange—for precisely the same reason, and Jordanian intelligence was believed by the PLO to be actively fomenting the Lebanese conflict to weaken the Palestinian organization.

Because Syria wanted to receive the Arab world's backing for its "policing" role in Lebanon, relations with Egypt were improved toward the end of 1976. This improvement became evident during the two Arab summits held in October 1976 in Riyadh and Cairo.

During these summits Jordan's special role vis-à-vis the Palestinians was acknowledged. This, in turn, gave Jordan a boost in its quest for Arab acceptance of its role concerning the Palestinian problem.[27] Another important development in Jordan's rehabilitation occurred when Sadat declared during an interview with the *Washington Post* that any future Palestinian state should be linked to Jordan.[28]

Naturally, this was welcomed by Jordan. Its minister of information, Adnan Abu-Odeh, praised Sadat's "objectivity and his practical visualization of the desired peaceful settlement."[29] Even the PLO praised Sadat. Hani al-Hassen, a member of Fatah's Central Committee, said that "the Palestinian people believe in unity as much as they believe in liberation."[30]

During 1976 and much of 1977, until Sadat's trip to Jerusalem, Sadat sought to reconvene the Geneva conference. Sadat, however, found himself in a dilemma: he supported Jordanian participation in Geneva, but at the same time, he wanted to reward Arafat for breaking away from Egypt's rival, Syria. Sadat wanted to accomplish this dual objective by also adhering to the Rabat resolutions. He, thus, attempted to find a solution that would give Jordan the hope of becoming a party to the proposed negotiations without challenging the all-Arab consensus regarding the PLO's status as the "sole legitimate representative of the Palestinians."[31]

Sadat's dilemma became apparent when Hussein visited Cairo in January 1977 so the two leaders could coordinate their positions before the new Carter administration took office. Although the joint communiqué referred to the PLO as the sole legitimate representative of the Palestinian people, it also referred to a Jordanian-Palestinian linkage: "The form of these relations will be decided by the two people through their free choice, proceeding from unity of objectives and fate and complete identity of interests and feelings."[32] Thus, to satisfy Hussein the joint communiqué mentioned "an independent Palestinian *entity*" while mentioning "an independent Palestinian *state*" later in the text, in a less-prominent place. As a follow-up to the communiqué, Hussein offered his own interpretation of the message it contained: "The strong historic ties between the Jordanian and Palestinian people made it certain that the strongest fraternal relations must be established between Jordan and any entity that will be established in the territories."[33]

Support for a linkage between Jordan and the West Bank was also voiced by Syria. According to Adam Garfinkle, the Syrians viewed such a linkage in the context of their "greater Syria" scheme, which included Jordan and Palestine. Thus, "the Syrian effort to gain greater control of the PLO, and Jordan's general policy of striving to minimize the PLO's role in any future settlement brought to the fore the mutual interests of Hussein and Asad in undermining the existing PLO leadership."[34] It could be argued that Syria supported a linkage between the East and West banks because of its adversarial relationship with the PLO, whereas Syria was on good terms with Jordan at that time.

For Hussein the central task in the post-Rabat period had become how to neutralize the PLO while at least publicly adhering to the Rabat resolutions. These efforts continued during the initial phase of the Carter presidency and lasted until Sadat traveled to Jerusalem, changing the course of the Arab-Israeli conflict and further undermining Jordan's already fragile position.

Toward Camp David

The 1976 presidential victory of Jimmy Carter ushered in a new era in Arab-Israeli peacemaking. During Carter's tenure President Anwar Sadat made his historic trip to Jerusalem, which eventually led to the signing of the Camp David Accords and the Egyptian-Israeli Peace Treaty.

This section will address the question of why Jordan was excluded from the Camp David peace process. First, we must understand the events that led up to the Camp David Accords. The contention here is that it was largely the policies of the United States and Israel, and of Egypt to a lesser extent, that determined Jordan's exclusion. First, Carter's overtures to the PLO, which emphasized the creation of a "Palestinian homeland" not necessarily linked to Jordan, played an important role in alienating Jordan. If Jordan was no longer viewed as the custodian of the West Bank, then the incentives for Jordan to join the peace process were minimal. Second, the 1977 election of Menachem Begin with his annexationist perspective precluded an Israeli withdrawal from the West Bank. Jordan was not interested in joining a process that emphasized autonomy for the Palestinians rather than a total return of the territories to Jordan. Third, although Egypt paid lip service to Jordan's role in the peace process, Sadat apparently did not want to risk negotiations with Israel over the future of the West Bank. These three factors together explain why Jordan did not participate in the Camp David negotiations.

The Carter administration took a different approach to the Arab-Israeli conflict than did previous administrations. It supported a comprehensive settlement, abandoning Kissinger's step-by-step approach. Carter believed that if all the parties to the conflict (Egypt, Syria, Jordan, Lebanon, the PLO, and Israel) were brought together to an international conference in Geneva, then the outstanding issues, both the territorial and the Palestinian questions, could be resolved. The emphasis on a comprehensive settlement stemmed from a particular worldview held by the Carter administration, namely, that regional conflicts in the Third World benefited the Soviet Union and strengthened anti-American feelings abroad. Consequently, the administration argued, the United States must attempt to resolve the Arab-Israeli conflict to avoid a possible superpower confrontation.[35]

An important dimension of this approach was the attempt to deal with the Palestinian question. If the new strategy was aimed at a comprehensive solution, then the PLO, the representative of the Palestinians, must be included in the process as well. The American position regarding a dialogue with the PLO was based on the September 1975 Memorandum of Agreement signed by the Israeli and American governments. This agreement stipulated that the United States would not negotiate with the PLO unless the Palestinians accepted Security Council Resolutions 242 and 338 and affirmed Israel's right to exist.[36] It should be noted, however, that before Cyrus Vance became secretary of state, American officials distinguished between *negotiating* and *talking* to the PLO; although the former was forbidden, the latter was not considered taboo.

In 1975 an important statement was issued by Harold Saunders, deputy assistant secretary of state, that the "legitimate rights of the Palestinian Arabs must be taken into account" and that "the Palestinian dimension of the Arab-Israeli conflict is the heart of the conflict."[37] In 1975 a number of individuals who were to become key players in Carter's Middle East policy team issued what became known as the *Brookings Report*. The report dealt with Israeli withdrawal, Palestinian self-determination, and the U.S. role.[38]

This report could be viewed as the new administration's divining rod regarding Arab-Israeli peace. The Carter administration attempted to implement most of the recommendations of this report. The fact that the administration was not successful in bringing about a comprehensive settlement on all fronts had more to do with the politics of the conflict than with the administration's intentions. By emphasizing Palestinian self-determination the United States appeared to be relegating Jordan to a less-important position. The proposed linkage between the Palestinian state and Jordan was presented as one possible option rather than as a sine que non for a settlement. Indeed, during the first months of his presidency, Carter made several statements that were sympathetic to the notion of a Palestinian homeland. Despite the fact that he publicly made conflicting statements regarding a Palestinian homeland, Carter was clearly in favor of finding a solution to the Palestinian problem.

From an operational perspective the central task was how to reconvene the Geneva Conference and determine which parties would be represented there. The most burdensome issue was the question of PLO participation. Because at Geneva Israel had strongly objected to the formal participation of the organization, two possibilities were considered. The first called for the participation of a single Arab delegation, which would include PLO members. The second called for the inclusion of PLO representatives in the Jordanian delegation. These two possibilities were explored by Carter and Secretary of State Cyrus Vance in their various meetings with Middle Eastern leaders. But the United States was prevented from entering into a dialogue with the PLO because of its 1975 agreement with Israel. The Carter administration made several unsuccessful indirect attempts to persuade the PLO to accept 242 and to recognize Israel's right to exist.

When Secretary Vance visited the Middle East in August 1977, two issues loomed large on his agenda. The first was whether the Palestinians should participate in Geneva, and the second was what kind of transitional arrangements should be made for the West Bank—a situation that would lead to a Palestinian homeland. Before Vance's departure to the Middle East, Carter gave him a set of guidelines that, inter alia, dealt with the question of Palestinian participation in Geneva: "Arrange for the PLO to attend [Geneva], together with Arab nations, on the basis of U.N. Resolutions 242 and 338 (with refugee exception only), with the understanding that the Palestinian question will be on the agenda. . . ."[39] If the PLO will meet our requirements of recognizing Israel's right to exist, you may wish to arrange for early discussions with them—either in private or publicly acknowledged."[40] Vance took Carter's instructions to their logical conclusion and during his visit to Saudi Arabia prepared a draft document on the PLO's acceptance of the U.N. resolutions. The secretary then asked the Saudis to convince the PLO to accept it. If the PLO did accept it, the United States would immediately start a dialogue with the organization. The document contained the following: "The PLO accepts United Nations Security Council Resolution 242, with the reservation that it considers that the resolution does not make adequate reference to the question of Palestinians since it fails to make any reference to a homeland for the Palestinian people. It is recognized that the language of Resolution 242 relates to the right of all states in the Middle East to live in peace."[41]

The draft document represented a serious American overture to the PLO. Despite the fact that the 1975 American-Israeli agreement explicitly required the PLO to accept Israel's right to exist, the draft document did not require such acceptance. It only referred to 242 as entailing "the right of all states in the Middle East to live in peace." The Carter administration apparently was willing to pursue an extremely accommodationist policy vis-à-vis the PLO, in the hope that the key to a comprehensive agreement would be untying the PLO's knot, which eventually would lead to Geneva. In principle, the PLO did not reject the idea of participating in the Geneva conference. It did, however, demand that Resolution 242 be amended.[42]

Regarding transitional arrangements for the West Bank, Secretary Vance also proposed during his visit a United Nations trusteeship administered jointly by Israel and Jordan, which would then lead to the realization of Palestinian self-determination after several years.[43] Although both ideas were rejected by the concerned parties, the position of the administration became clear to the leaders of Israel, Syria, Egypt, and Jordan. For Carter and his advisers the core of the Arab-Israeli conflict was the Palestinian question. The proposal for a transitional regime gave Jordan only a secondary role as joint temporary custodian over the West Bank until the Palestinian homeland was established.

An additional element of American policy involved the Soviet Union. If the Geneva Conference was going to reconvene, the Soviet Union would have to participate as the cochair of the conference. Consequently, the two superpowers issued a joint statement on October 1, 1977, that focused on reconvening the international conference. The statement called for a "comprehensive settlement of the Middle East problem" based on Israeli withdrawal and "the resolution of the Palestinian question, including ensuring the legitimate rights of the Palestinian people; termination of the state of war and the establishment of normal peaceful relations on the basis of mutual recognition of the principles of sovereignty; territorial integrity and political independence."[44]

The October 1 agreement caused much fury among Israel's supporters in the United States and elicited a strong reaction from the Israeli government.[45] Israel objected to the inclusion of the Soviet Union in the process because the Soviets supported the Arab side. But, above all, Israel insisted that the Palestinians be represented as part of the Jordanian delegation. Moreover, the question of the West Bank, according to Israel, should be negotiated with Jordan, whereas the future of Gaza should be determined by Israel and Egypt.

After the Soviet-American proposal was issued, Israeli Foreign Minister Moshe Dayan held a number of meetings with Carter and Vance in Washington. Carter understood that without Israeli endorsement of his plan, the peace process would not move forward. The result from these discussions was two documents that created the impression that the "U.S. had abandoned the position it had just worked out with the Soviets.''[46] The first document was a joint statement that brought back to the fore Security Council Resolutions 242 and 338, neither of which had been mentioned in the joint Soviet-American statement.[47] In addition, Israel and the United States negotiated a working paper, subject to the formal endorsement of the two governments, on the procedural aspects of reconvening Geneva. According to Cyrus Vance, the main provisions of the working paper were that

> the Arabs should attend the conference in a single delegation including the Palestinians. Following an opening session, bilateral committees would be formed to negotiate bilateral peace treaties. Security Council Resolutions 242 and 338 would serve as the basis for the negotiations. The issue of the West Bank would be discussed in a separate group composed of Israel, Jordan, Egypt, and the Palestinians.[48]

Dayan interpreted the working paper as rejecting the possibility of a Palestinian homeland. Additionally, the PLO was not mentioned in the document. A major concession, however, was made by Dayan. Until the signing of the working paper, Israel had always insisted that the Palestinians be represented in a Jordanian delegation. The working paper signaled the first time that Israel recognized the Palestinians as a legitimate partner in the proposed negotiations over the West Bank separate from the Jordanians.[49] Moreover, Dayan argued, consistent with his functionalist ideas, that "[i]f we rejected foreign rule in the West Bank, and suggest an agreed means of living together with its inhabitants we needed to involve them in talking on this subject."[50]

Although Israel and the United States agreed on the principles of reconvening Geneva, it appeared that the American administration made concessions to Israel owing to domestic pressure and Israeli intransigence on the question of a Palestinian homeland. William Quandt noted that the working paper nullified the Soviet-American communiqué of October 1. In a sense, Carter's succumbing to pressure forced Sadat to search for a bilateral Israel-Egypt agreement so he would not have to rely on the United States.[51] Indeed, the Israeli-American working paper was the last episode in the search for a comprehensive breakthrough before Sadat announced on November 9, 1977, that he intended to travel to Jerusalem to address the Knesset.

The American quest for a comprehensive settlement that emphasized the centrality of the Palestinian issue led to the diminution of Jordan's role as a key actor. The various American overtures to the PLO were perceived by Jordan as attempts to undermine its already waning legitimacy among the Palestinians. Paradoxically, as Dan Schueftan notes, the consequences of such policy propelled movement on the Israeli-Egyptian bilateral level rather than on the comprehensive level that the Carter administration had intended.[52]

Sadat's decision to go to Israel undercut the American plan to reconvene the Geneva Conference. Rather than relying on the United States to mediate between Egypt and Israel, Sadat developed a secret channel directly with Israel.[53] Sadat decided to address the Israeli public directly because he regarded the technical problems associated with reconvening Geneva as too great because of the intricacies of inter-Arab politics. He feared that a stalemate would dim the chances of an Egyptian-Israeli agreement. In his November 9, 1977, speech, when he announced his intention to address the Israeli Knesset, he referred to the American-Israeli working paper as a step in the wrong direction.[54]

Two additional factors played a role in Sadat's decision. First, as in Egyptian opposition to the 1974 Israeli-Jordanian disengagement agreement, Sadat feared that bringing Jordan into the picture would detract from the prospects of successfully reaching an agreement with Israel. Second, Sadat sought to avoid going to Geneva so he could keep the Soviets out of the Middle East peace process. Soviet involvement in the process meant a return to the idea of a comprehensive settlement, an idea that Sadat rejected.

As long as the Israeli Labor party was in power, it supported an agreement with Jordan over the West Bank. When Secretary Vance visited the Middle East in February 1977, Prime Minister Rabin outlined his position on a peace settlement to Vance.[55] Rabin argued that a contractual Arab-Israeli peace must be based on normalization of relations and Arab acceptance of Israel. Rabin favored a territorial compromise if this did not lead to a return to the pre-1967 boundaries. Rabin insisted that Jerusalem be excluded from the negotiations. Moreover, he argued that the Palestinian issue did not constitute the core of the Arab-Israeli conflict, thus the PLO could not attend Geneva. He was open, however, to negotiating with a Jordanian delegation that included Palestinians: "Israel would not seek to examine the credentials of the Jordanian delegation." Rabin asserted that negotiating a territorial compromise with Jordan would rule out the possibility of establishing an independent Palestinian state, which he believed would pose a mortal danger to Israel's security. During a meeting between Vance and Israeli Foreign Minister Yigal Allon, Allon told Vance that "if the PLO would accept 242 it would no longer be the PLO." Secretary Vance referred to this exchange with Allon as a hint to the United States that it should attempt to persuade the PLO to accept 242.[56] Indeed, as discussed above, the attempt to woo the PLO became a central tenet of Carter's Middle East policy. Rabin emphasized a bilateral approach on the question of Arab representation in Geneva, namely, that Israel would negotiate with each Arab partner separately. (The only Arab leader who agreed to this approach was Sadat.)[57]

American-Israeli differences came to the fore when Rabin visited the United States in March 1977. Here again, he objected to PLO participation in the peace process. Carter notes in his memoirs that Rabin ''was adamantly opposed to any meeting if the PLO or other representatives of the Palestinians were there.''[58]

The election of Menachem Begin's Likud Party in May 1977 constituted a new chapter in Israeli politics and had wide-ranging implications for the peace process. The Likud Party was not interested in a territorial compromise on the West Bank and, hence, did not intend to pursue the Jordanian option. The principal decision makers in the new Likud cabinet were Prime Minister Begin and Foreign Minister Moshe Dayan. Although Dayan was a member of the Labor Party, he was included in the new government despite his differences with Begin, who sought to extend Israeli sovereignty over the West Bank. Begin offered the foreign ministry to Dayan for two reasons: Begin believed that only Dayan, with his extensive experience, could manage Israeli-American relations at that important juncture, and Begin felt that conditions were ripe for a peace treaty with Egypt and wanted Dayan at his side.[59] Indeed, Begin's foreign policy rested on the belief that Israel's control of the West Bank could be consolidated only if Egypt signed a peace treaty with Israel in exchange for Israeli withdrawal from the Sinai.[60]

The anti-Jordanian stance of the Begin government became apparent after a secret meeting between King Hussein and Moshe Dayan on August 22, 1977. Hussein insisted at the meeting that Israel had to withdraw to the pre-1967 lines, including East Jerusalem, if Jordan signed a peace treaty with Israel. Furthermore, the king rebuffed Dayan's suggestion that the two countries functionally divide the West Bank. Dayan recalled the meeting in his memoirs: ''I had to understand, he said, that he [Hussein], as an Arab monarch, could not propose to even a single Arab village that they cut themselves off from their brother Arabs and become Israelis. His agreement to such a plan would be regarded as treachery. He would be charged with selling Arab land to the Jews so that he could enlarge his own Kingdom.''[61]

Dayan returned to Israel with a gloomy assessment of the prospects for an Israeli-Jordanian agreement. This meeting was to become the last secret Israeli-Jordanian meeting during Begin's tenure. From that point on, all efforts were directed at reaching an agreement with Egypt.

What Begin was willing to give to the West Bank Palestinians was publicly unveiled during his December 28, 1977, Knesset speech. The plan, which was also privately presented to the Americans, was formulated after Sadat's visit to Israel. In this plan Begin called for limited self-rule for the West Bank and Gaza. According to the twenty-one-point document, the residents of the territories would elect an Administrative Council with limited responsibilities. Israel would not withdraw, and it would maintain security in the territories. The Palestinian residents could either acquire Israeli citizenship or keep their Jordanian citizenship and, thus, participate in the political life of their respective countries. Those who chose Israeli citizenship could vote in the Israeli Knesset, and those who wanted to maintain their Jordanian ties could vote for the parliament in Amman. Begin, however, left the question of sovereignty open: "Israel stands by its right and its claim of sovereignty to Judea, Samaria, and the Gaza district. In the knowledge that other claims exist, it proposes, for the sake of agreement of the peace, that the question of sovereignty in these areas be left open."[62]

Clearly, although Begin presented the autonomy proposal as a major concession, in reality, he sought to undermine Palestinian nationalism by presenting a formula for de facto Israeli annexation of the territories.[63] Neither the Americans nor the Egyptians accepted Begin's proposal. Indeed, when President Carter visited Egypt on June 4, 1978, he and President Sadat issued what became known as the Aswan Declaration. It stated that "[t]here must be a resolution of the Palestinian problem in all its aspects. The solution must recognize the legitimate rights of the Palestinian people and enable the Palestinians to participate in the determination of their own future."[64] As Adam Garfinkle notes, this formulation, which was midwifed by Carter, speaks only of "Palestinian participation" and signaled the end of Carter's attempts to woo the PLO. It also was interpreted differently by the various actors: "Begin took it to mean the 'working paper,' Sadat thought it meant U.S. support for a 'Palestinian entity,' and Hussein saw it as Washington's newly discovered 'Jordanian option'. "[65] Yet from a Jordanian perspective this formula was not sufficient incentive to join the process. The declaration was initially rejected by Israel but later incorporated into the Camp David Accords.

The Jordanian position was consistent throughout this period. Hussein was unwilling to enter into a process that relegated Jordan to a secondary role. He feared that the pro-Palestinian orientation of the American administration would eventually undermine his own position. In light of this atmosphere of uncertainty, before the signing of the Camp David Accords, Hussein preferred to close ranks with the Arab world and reiterate his long-standing demand for a full Israeli withdrawal, including from East Jerusalem.

During the period between Sadat's trip to Jerusalem and the signing of the Camp David Accords Jordan adopted a "wait and see" attitude.

It chose initially not to take sides in the emerging schism that began to divide the Arab world in the wake of Sadat's initiative.[66] Hussein was surprised by the Sadat initiative. He was not consulted before Sadat announced his intention to travel to Jerusalem.[67] Yet once Sadat had made his move, Hussein called it "courageous."[68] Hussein refused to join the Tripoli conference of December 1977—composed of Algeria, Libya, Syria, South Yemen, and the PLO—which created the rejectionist front in opposition to Sadat.[69] As Arab opposition to Sadat grew, Sadat needed Hussein to join the process. There were, however, limits to Sadat's approach toward Jordan. Sadat realized that Israel would refuse to withdraw from the West Bank, a prerequisite for Jordan to join, and that insisting on Israeli withdrawal would probably derail the peace process. Thus, when Hussein visited Cairo, he and Sadat agreed that Egypt would negotiate on Jordan's behalf over the West Bank.[70]

Once it became clear that the PLO would not make the concessions necessary to join the process, the United States attempted to convince Hussein to become a partner in the peace talks.

The Begin autonomy proposals were not sufficient as far as Jordan was concerned. The Jordanians believed this proposal would cement Israel's control of the territories rather than break the impasse. Hussein sensed his growing importance to the success of the process and increased his demands for participation. Although he told American envoy Alfred Atherton that he needed a statement of principles from Israel regarding withdrawal, this was no longer sufficient.[71] On February 9, 1978, Hussein stated that "the question now is not one of declaration of principles. . . . What is required is . . . a commitment to translate principles into fact."[72]

The Jordanian strategy on the eve of the September 1978 Camp David Accords was "to encourage Egypt, with actual U.S. support, to erode Israel's positions as far as possible *before* Hussein decided whether he would participate. And if Camp David succeeded beyond Hussein's expectations, he could still join the talks."[73] Included in this strategy was a set of constraints that both limited Jordan's freedom of action and allowed it to pursue its interests. On the one hand, Jordan was unwilling to break the Arab consensus on the question of peace for something that was less than totally acceptable. It could not join an open-ended process for fear of alienating its biggest neighbor, Syria, and the Palestinian population on the East and West Banks. On the other hand, Jordan's condemnation of Sadat did not foreclose any option to join the process in the future.[74] The signing of the Camp David Accords, however, convinced Hussein that Sadat was not interested in offering Jordan a role. Sadat had arranged to meet Hussein in Morocco after the Camp David summit. Yet when the text of the accords became public, he chose to return to

Amman. On September 14, in the midst of the Camp David negotiations, Sadat called Hussein and asked to arrange a meeting. Hussein recalled this conversation during a press interview: "I asked [Sadat] how things were going. He said, terrible. I am packing my bags and leaving tomorrow. We'll put the responsibility for the failure [of the talks] where it belongs. That was the last time I heard [from him]. I was in Spain when the announcement of the agreement was made. I was shocked. I left for home immediately."[75] The first Israeli ambassador to Egypt, Eliyahu Ben-Elissar, also confirmed the view that Sadat wanted Hussein out of the picture. He told reporter John Newhouse: "Sadat did not want Hussein involved. I heard it from Sadat."[76]

Beyond Camp David

The Camp David Accords signed by Carter, Sadat, and Begin on September 17, 1978, consisted of two separate documents: *A Framework for the Conclusion of Peace Between Israel and Egypt* and *A Framework for Peace in the Middle East*. The first dealt with peace between Israel and Egypt, and the second, considered by some an unworkable plan, focused on the establishment of a Self-Governing Authority in the West Bank and Gaza. Jordan is mentioned fifteen times in the document even though it was not a signatory to the agreement.[77] The agreement stipulated three stages. First, there would be transitional arrangements whereby the Self-Governing Authority would replace the Israeli military government "for the purpose of granting full autonomy to the Palestinian residents of the territories." Second, Egypt, Israel, and Jordan would negotiate "modalities for establishing the elected Self-Governing Authority." The Egyptian and Jordanian delegations "may include Palestinians from the West Bank and Gaza, or other Palestinians as mutually agreed." The parties then would negotiate the powers of the Self-Governing Authority, including "a strong local police force which may include Jordanian citizens."[78]

Third, a five-year transitional period would follow the establishment of the Authority. During the first three years of this period negotiations would begin to determine the final status of the territories. The agreement called for negotiations between "Egypt and Israel, and Jordan, and the elected representatives of the inhabitants of the West Bank and Gaza." At this stage the negotiations would be conducted by two separate committees. The committee, consisting of the four parties, would negotiate and agree on the final status of the West Bank and Gaza and its relationship with its neighbors. The second committee would negotiate an Israeli-Jordanian peace treaty. The parties to the second committee would be Jordan, Israel, and "the elected representatives" of the territories. The negotiations would be based on 242, 338, and the "solution from the negotiations must also recognize the legitimate rights of the Palestinian people and their just requirements. In this way, the Palestinians will participate in the determination of their own future."[79] The agreement also said that the issue of Palestinian refugees who fled the territories after the 1967 war would be resolved during the negotiations.

Jordan viewed this agreement negatively. It had no wish to participate in a process that was condemned by the Arab world and to which it was not a party. Yet it had been given a prepared script that it was not ready to follow.[80] Jordan's official reaction to the accords was that "Jordan, which is mentioned in numerous passages in the Camp David Documents, has no legal or moral obligations as regards matters it played no part in discussing, formulating, or approving."[81]

At the same time, however, Jordan wanted to clarify a number of issues pertaining to the accords in order to explore the precise implications of the agreements. After Secretary Vance's trip to Jordan on September 20, 1978, during which he tried to involve Jordan in the process, Hussein sent a list of fourteen questions to the American administration.[82] These questions focused on the American interpretation of the accords, and Hussein specifically inquired about issues such as Israeli withdrawal, East Jerusalem, the nature and power of the Self-Governing Authority, and the future of the Jewish settlements in the territories. The U.S. response was not forthcoming. The king did not believe that the United States was offering him enough incentives, especially with regard to American pressure for Israeli withdrawal. Despite repeated visits by American officials (Harold Saunders on October 16, 1978, and Vance and Brzezinski in March 1979) Hussein declined the American invitation. Instead, the king opted to join the Arab world's opposition to Sadat's separate peace bid. He attended the November 1978 Baghdad summit, which was convened to take retaliatory measures against Egypt.

From an Israeli perspective Begin presented the Camp David Accords and the autonomy framework as a complete vindication of his annexationist policies. Begin viewed the autonomy process as preventing the establishment of a Palestinian state. The autonomy negotiations between Israel and Egypt lasted from May 1979 until May 1980 when it became apparent to Sadat that Israel was bent on dragging the negotiations into a cul de sac. Egypt, however, did not want to sacrifice the newly established peace (the Israeli-Egyptian Peace Treaty was signed in March 1979) over the question of autonomy. Egypt's interpretation of autonomy was that it should lead to a Palestinian state, whereas Israel hoped to establish a limited autonomy only.[83] The differences of opinion between Israel and Egypt regarding autonomy were presented by Begin, who objected to statements made by Egyptian officials about Palestinian self-determination.

When it became apparent that Begin had no intention of making substantial progress on the autonomy talks, Foreign Minister Dayan resigned in protest in October 1979. He opposed Begin's annexationist perspective, which viewed the autonomy in the framework of a Greater Israel—autonomy for the inhabitants but not for the territory. Dayan's colleague, Defense Minister Ezer Weizman, reached the same conclusions. Weizman resigned in protest against Begin's policies seven months later.[84]

Despite the fact that the Israeli-Egyptian Peace Treaty was carried out in letter and spirit, no momentum was achieved on the question of the West Bank. Indeed, the 1981 Israeli elections resulted in another Likud victory and led to the appointment of two hard-liners in key cabinet posts: Ariel Sharon became the defense minister, and Yitzhak Shamir, the foreign minister. Both held anti-Hashemite views and sought to transform the East Bank into a Palestinian state. One of Ariel Sharon's unstated objectives during the 1982 Israeli invasion of Lebanon was to create a mass exodus of Palestinian refugees from Lebanon to Jordan and bring about the end of the Hashemite rule.

During the 1979–82 period Jordan preferred to stay on the sidelines. Not until Israel's invasion of Lebanon in June 1982 and the subsequent September 1, 1982, peace plan proposed by President Reagan did Jordan come back to the limelight.

The Reagan Plan and the Jordanian-PLO Dialogue

President Reagan's September 1, 1982, peace plan was unveiled against the background of the Israeli invasion of Lebanon. It called for West Bank and Gaza autonomy in association with Jordan. Reagan expressed his opposition to the establishment of an independent Palestinian state or annexation or permanent control by Israel.[85] Unlike his predecessor, Carter, Reagan was not committed to the idea of a Palestinian homeland. He wanted the Palestinian problem addressed in the Jordanian context. Aaron Klieman considered the plan as "the most pro-Jordanian plan ever advocated by the United States."[86] The proposed association of the West Bank with Jordan was a central component of the plan. Jordan had been excluded from the peace process at Camp David. Now Reagan attempted to rectify the situation and to offer Jordan enough incentives to join the process. In addition to making Jordan a key actor, the plan's four other objectives included gaining the approval of the Arab states, which were convening their summit in Fez, Morocco, on September 8. As noted above, one of the central tenets of Jordanian foreign policy was to refrain from making a unilateral move without Arab backing. Another objective was to get the support of the Labor Party in Israel, not in power at the time, to galvanize Israeli public opinion against Begin's annexationist policies. The Labor Party's traditional support for the Jordanian option was seen as crucial if the plan were to succeed. Also, the administration wanted to provide an opportunity for Israel's supporters in the United States, the American Jewish community in particular, to distance themselves from Begin's policies, yet still show their support for a "constructive" proposal. The timing of the plan was critical. The United States wanted to demonstrate it was capable of an independent Middle East policy in light of the charges that it had given Israel a "green light" to invade Lebanon.[87]

Of these five objectives, the first three were of utmost importance if the plan were to succeed. In one year only one objective was met. The American Jewish community began criticizing Israel's policies. The Arab states did not endorse the plan, and the Labor Party did not succeed in convincing the Israeli public or the government to support the plan. Above all, Jordan declined to participate in the negotiations.

Hussein initially endorsed the Reagan Plan, calling it "the most courageous stand taken by the American administration ever since 1956."[88] Hussein feared that if Jordan did not enter into peace negotiations under favorable terms, the West Bank soon would be totally colonized by Israeli settlements, making a territorial compromise obsolete. Further, he was afraid that Sharon's plan to transform Jordan into a Palestinian state might be made operational, and his regime would be jeopardized. To enter into negotiations Hussein needed four prerequisites.[89] First, the PLO had to agree that Jordan would represent the Palestinians in negotiations. Second, Arab backing was required to neutralize Syria's opposition to the Reagan Plan. Third, the United States had to guarantee Israeli withdrawal from the West Bank. If the United States succeeded in pressuring Israel to pull out of Lebanon, then the United States would be viewed as capable of doing the same in the West Bank. Jordan saw a linkage between the West Bank and the Lebanon issues and viewed a withdrawal from Lebanon as a litmus test. Fourth, Jordan wanted the United States to guarantee a freeze on Israeli settlements in the West Bank. Reagan pledged to Hussein during his Washington visit in December 1982 in a letter inter alia, "You will not be pressed to join negotiations on transitional arrangements until there is a freeze on new Israeli settlement activity."[90]

Hussein hoped that the Arab world, even if it did not fully endorse the Reagan Plan, would not introduce obstacles to prevent him from joining the process in the future. The Arab summit, which convened in Fez September 8–10, 1982, issued a declaration that reiterated the Arab demand for total Israeli withdrawal and called for the establishment of an independent Palestinian state. The Fez resolution also contained an item that called for "Security Council guarantees for peace for all the states of the region, including the independent Palestinian state."[91] This sentence was interpreted as a significant move forward by the Arab world because it signaled de facto acceptance of Israel's right to exist.[92] Nowhere in the Fez declaration is there a mention of the West-East Bank linkage envisaged in the Reagan Plan, nor did it endorse the Reagan proposal.

Israel's reaction to the Reagan Plan was negative. The official government communiqué stated the "position of the Government of the United States seriously deviates from the Camp David agreement, contradicts it and could create a serious danger to Israel, its security and its future. The Government of Israel has resolved that on the basis of these positions it will not enter into any negotiations with any party."[93] Although the Labor Party supported the Reagan Plan, the Knesset had a Likud majority and rejected the plan by a 50 to 36 vote.[94]

Faced with Arab ambivalence and Israeli rejection, the only available option left to Hussein was to solicit the approval of the PLO. Bound by the 1974 Rabat resolutions, Hussein needed the PLO's support to start negotiations. Hussein understood well that even if Israel entered into negotiations with Jordan, it would not relinquish its total control of the West Bank. To sign on such a concession, he needed the PLO's stamp of approval. The first phase of the Jordanian-PLO dialogue began on October 9, 1982, and lasted until April 1983 without producing any substantial results.[95] The dialogue focused on two issues: the prospects of establishing a confederal relationship between Jordan and the Palestinians and the composition of the Jordanian-PLO delegation to the peace talks. Three possibilities were considered: the "formation of a joint PLO-Jordanian delegation, the formation of a delegation of non-PLO Palestinians who would clearly reflect the PLO's political preferences and who would be selected by the PLO itself, and the creation of an Arab League delegation that would include PLO representatives."[96]

Although the Arab summit in Fez did not endorse the idea of a confederation, discussions pertaining to the proposed confederal arrangement took place in a higher committee from October 1982 until the 1983 meeting of the Palestine National Council. During this time Jordan negotiated with Arafat in an effort to enlist PLO approval to work jointly toward a Jordanian-Palestinian confederal solution as depicted in the Reagan peace initiative. Both King Hussein and Arafat met with Syrian, Soviet, and PLO opposition to the proposed confederal arrangement. During a visit to Moscow in late 1983 Hussein was told by the Soviet leader Yuri Andropov that "the Soviets would do all they could to frustrate his efforts with the PLO."[97]

A joint Jordanian-Palestinian communiqué was issued to the press in Amman on December 14, 1982. After two days of negotiations, the two parties left "with a commitment to save the occupied territories and to restore the inalienable rights of the Palestinian people."[98] Moreover, the communiqué hinted that Arafat and Hussein had been able to determine a formula to bridge the gap between the Fez declaration and the Reagan peace plan; once an independent Palestinian state was established, a referendum would be held on a confederal agreement with Jordan.

The compromise between the Fez and Reagan plans can be summarized as follows: the PLO was not to renounce its call for the establishment of an independent Palestinian state but limitations would be placed on the sovereignty of such a state, for a confederal association with Jordan had already been pledged.

At the sixteenth Palestine National Council (PNC), convened in Algiers on February 14–24, 1983, major issues pertaining to the Reagan initiative and to future relations with Jordan were to be decided. Emerging PLO pragmatism about Jordan was evident. The PNC clearly stated in its final communiqué that it "sees future relations with Jordan developing on the basis of a confederation between two independent states."[99]

Arafat was not willing to accept the Reagan proposal, yet he asked the Palestinian National Council not to condemn the plan but to agree to a confederation, as opposed to a federation, some time in the future. Furthermore, he asked the PNC to allow Hussein to open negotiations with the United States.[100] Hoping to negate any possible reemergence of King Hussein's federation plan, however, the PNC paid homage to "a special relationship between the two peoples," not within one people, as referred to by King Hussein during his 1972 speech.[101]

The confederal relationship was again discussed between March 31 and April 5 in a meeting in Amman with Arafat. A planned joint political action was agreed upon in principle but never was put into action. Thus, the initiative collapsed. Undoubtedly, the PLO's defeat in Lebanon and the growing criticism of Arafat within his organization were instrumental in preventing a Jordanian-PLO agreement. Syria also opposed the dialogue, and even the Soviets warned Hussein not to accept the Reagan Plan.[102] But, above all, Israel showed no sign of willingness to enter into a dialogue with Hussein over the question of the West Bank. The United States was perceived to be indecisive and, more importantly, it was preoccupied with the problem of Lebanon. Hussein argued that the failure of the Americans to bring about an Israeli withdrawal from Lebanon showed America's ineptitude and negligence.[103] On April 10, 1983, the Jordanian government announced an end to its dialogue with the PLO and, in effect, put an end to the Reagan initiative.

Eighteen months later King Hussein believed the time was ripe for another attempt to reach an agreement with the PLO. His assessment proved correct; Arafat was in dire need of a new course of action. For Arafat, in the aftermath of Lebanon, a partnership with Jordan was a way to regain his credibility and to maintain the PLO as a central actor in the peace process.

The most prominent feature of King Hussein's new initiative was that the PLO alone would negotiate for the Palestinians. Thereby, the Palestinians would assume direct responsibility for any risk entailed in negotiations, and the king need not require guarantees of a favorable outcome. Hussein envisioned negotiations embedded in an international conference that would include Syria and the Soviet Union. Remembering the hostility expressed by the Soviet leader, Andropov, to his 1982–83 effort, Hussein acknowledged the threat of Syria and the Soviet Union as potential spoilers. At the same time, Hussein hoped the Soviet Union's involvement would bring in both the PLO and Syria.[104]

Although King Hussein had failed in his 1982–83 effort, this time, in the aftermath of Lebanon, Arafat would be less likely to refuse. Without Arafat, Hussein's peace effort had little chance of success. At the same time, Arafat needed Jordan's cooperation; as one Jordanian observer put it, "Arafat would just be the man in the street in Tunis if the Jordanians had not given him the opportunity."[105]

Arafat had the support of the Palestinian mayors in the occupied territories to move forward in a joint Jordanian-Palestinian effort for an acceptable settlement. Former mayor of Ramallah, Karim Khalaf, stated in an interview, "We are talking about a Palestinian state within the 1967 borders . . . a state confederated with Jordan." When asked about the conditions of such a confederation, Khalaf replied, "The confederation with Jordan will come after the achievement of Palestinian independence."[106]

At the seventeenth PNC Hussein threw the confederal ball into Arafat's court. King Hussein's opening speech challenged the PLO to act. Jordan believed that the first step toward peace was the signing of the Amman accord on February 11, 1985.

The Israeli elections in July 1984 resulted in a deadlock between Labor and Likud. A Government of National Unity was formed whereby the prime minister and the foreign minister would rotate jobs after two years. During the 1984–86 period Shimon Peres served as prime minister before becoming the foreign minister in 1986. A number of important developments took place in Jordanian-Israeli relations during this period. First, Jordan and the PLO were able to reach an agreement on participation in the international conference in February 1985. Second, Peres and Hussein reached a secret agreement in their April 1987 meeting in London. Third, Israeli-Jordanian functional relations reached their zenith after the breakdown of the Jordanian-PLO dialogue in February 1986.

On February 11, 1985, Jordan and the PLO agreed on a formula known as the Amman accord. This agreement called for total Israeli withdrawal from the territories, Palestinian self-determination in a Jordanian-Palestinian confederation, resolution of the Palestinian refugee problem, and negotiations at an international conference with the five permanent members of the United Nations Security Council. The PLO would be part of a single Jordanian-Palestinian delegation.[107]

The Jordanians viewed the agreement as a "green light" given by the PLO to Jordan to become the senior partner in the representation of the Palestinians in the negotiations. Jordanian officials argued that even though the agreement called for a confederation, the PLO had agreed to a federation under Jordanian tutelage.[108] Members of the PLO, however, were sensitive to the question of Jordanian domination and feared that Hussein would not represent their interests well in negotiations. The Popular Front for the Liberation of Palestine (PFLP) and the Democratic Front for the Liberation of Palestine (DFLP) argued that by agreeing to the Amman accord Arafat betrayed the independent position of the PLO and, in effect, buried the idea of an independent state.[109] The agreement lasted only one year. By February 1986 Hussein was unable to force the PLO to accept resolutions 242 and 338 unconditionally and renounce terrorism, concessions that were necessary to attend the international conference. Hussein then abrogated the accord.

Besides disagreements within the PLO about the Amman accord, there were additional reasons why the Jordanian-PLO accord broke down. As Emile Sahliyeh notes, the October 1985 hijacking of the Italian cruise ship, the *Achille Lauro,* by a pro-Arafat group (the Palestine Liberation Front) angered Hussein. This hijacking occurred while Hussein was attempting to present to the United States a moderate PLO that was ready to participate in an international conference. Syria also opposed the accord because it viewed the new Jordanian-PLO axis as a threat to Syrian interests. Syria played an important role in cultivating opposition to Arafat's moves, which it regarded as too conciliatory toward Israel. A crucial factor that led to the breakdown of the agreement was the refusal of the United States to meet with Palestinian members of the Jordanian-Palestinian delegation. Moreover, the United States at that time opposed the idea of an international conference because of Soviet participation.[110]

Hussein's February 19, 1986, speech clearly constituted a turning point in Jordanian-Palestinian relations. During the speech Hussein blamed Arafat and the Fatah wing of the PLO for failing to endorse Resolutions 242 and 338 formally and to renounce terrorism. Hussein claimed that he had secured America's commitment to invite the PLO to the international conference if the PLO accepted these conditions.[111] Arafat insisted on American endorsement of Palestinian self-determination and a direct dialogue with the United States rather than a dialogue conducted through Jordan.[112]

By July 1986 Hussein had closed a number of the PLO's offices and all of Fatah's offices in Amman and launched an ambitious $1.3 billion development program for the territories. Other anti-PLO measures at this time included revision of the Jordanian electoral law and support for the anti-Arafat coup within Fatah led by Colonel Abu al-Zaim, who was also known as Atallah Atallah. By initiating these moves Hussein sought to co-opt the West Bank population away from the PLO and toward a pro-Jordanian stance. Israel, of course, gave the king its blessing because a reduction in PLO influence also suited its interests.

These moves, however, backfired. Hussein's hopes of cultivating a local leadership sympathetic to Jordan were dashed when Zafir al-Masri, the mayor of Nablus who had been appointed as a result of an Israeli-Jordanian agreement and was considered a moderate, was assassinated in March 2, 1987, by members of the radical PFLP wing of the PLO.[113] Al-Masri's funeral was a nationalist event, complete with Palestinian flags and portraits of Arafat. Indeed, this funeral occurred nine months before the outbreak of the intifadah and was a harbinger of events to come. Furthermore, a poll conducted in 1986 in the West Bank by the East Jerusalem paper, *Al-Fajr*, the Australian Broadcasting Authority, and the New York newspaper, *Newsday*, indicated that Hussein had lost all favor among the West Bank Palestinians: 93.5 percent regarded the PLO as the "sole legitimate representative of the Palestinian people," 77.9 percent supported the establishment of an independent Palestinian state, and 1 percent supported West Bank linkage with Jordan. Only 3.4 percent preferred Hussein as a leader, and 60 percent called for continuation of the "armed struggle" against Israel. These responses indicated that Hussein's efforts could not have achieved their intended results.[114]

Toward an Israeli-Jordanian Condominium

When Shimon Peres became prime minister in September 1984, he assembled a transition team, the "hundred day team," to coordinate and prepare policy recommendations concerning Israeli domestic and foreign policy issues. The question of peace with Jordan was a top priority. Other issues of vital importance included Israeli withdrawal from Lebanon (completed in June 1985), runaway triple-digit inflation, the staggering economy, normalization of relations with Egypt, and the extreme polarization that was affecting Israeli society in the wake of the Lebanon war.[115]

Over the next four years, two years as prime minister and two as foreign minister, Peres tried hard to inject new life into the stalled peace process. He attempted to rectify the exclusion of Hussein in the Camp David process and hoped to provide Hussein with sufficient incentives to join the negotiations. The Israeli strategy for peace with Jordan entailed a dual-track approach. Major General Avraham Tamir, the director general of the prime minister's office and one of the key strategists in Peres's team, argued that negotiations should take place in the context of an international conference, which would lead to territorial compromise based on 242. Concomitantly, a transitional agreement with Jordan was sought based on either autonomy for the Palestinians or on an Israeli-Jordanian-Palestinian condominium that would administer the West Bank. Under this plan some areas of the West Bank would be placed under Jordanian-Palestinian administration, whereas those needed for Israeli security would be under Israeli control. The goal of this strategy was to establish either a confederation with Israel or a Jordanian-Palestinian federation. Under the Jordanian-Palestinian federation the West Bank would be an autonomous region. Jerusalem would be under Israeli sovereignty, but an agreement would be sought to facilitate a solution to the status of the Muslim holy places and the political and civil rights of East Jerusalem Arabs. This scheme resembled very closely Peres's ideas regarding a functional division of the West Bank that were discussed earlier in this chapter. The aim of the plan was to establish a modus vivendi with both the Palestinians and the Jordanians that would eventually lead to a territorial solution. Unlike the Camp David autonomy this plan would give autonomy to the territories rather than to individuals. The official name that the Israelis had given to this plan was Israeli-Jordanian-Palestinian power sharing.[116]

As stated earlier, the umbrella for negotiations would be the international conference, which would be divided into three separate committees: an Israeli and a Jordanian-Palestinian single delegation; an Israeli-Syrian committee, and a delegation made up of Israel and Lebanon. The five permanent members of the Security Council would also participate, provided the Soviet Union and China established diplomatic relations with Israel. The Soviets also had to allow Soviet Jews to immigrate freely to Israel in order to participate.[117]

Israel did not agree to the participation of the PLO, only to a joint Jordanian-Palestinian delegation provided the Palestinian members were not part of the PLO. Moreover, the goal of establishing a confederation precluded the possibility of an independent Palestinian state. This was also in line with Hussein's interpretation of the Amman accord. To develop the idea of a West Bank condominium, a number of secret meetings took place between the Israeli leadership and Hussein in 1985–1986. Peres met Hussein in London in October 1985; Rabin held a meeting in Paris in March 1986; and both met the king in July 1986 in the Arava region in southern Israel.[118] During this period efforts were intense to convene an international conference, and Israeli-Jordanian functional cooperation in the territories reached its zenith. Israel and Jordan agreed to reopen the Cairo-Amman Bank, facilitated the Jordanian development plan, and agreed on the appointment of West Bank mayors, notably Zafir al-Masri, the mayor of Nablus. Israeli decision makers hoped these efforts would provide incentives for Jordan to enter formal negotiations. As Samuel Lewis, former American ambassador to Israel, notes, "lower-level Jordanians and Israelis were increasingly involved in quiet, sub-rosa coordination concerning economic and technical matters."[119] Nimrod Novik, a diplomatic adviser of Shimon Peres, stressed in an interview that Israel hoped that an increase in functional cooperation would pay dividends in the peace process.[120] Peres himself in a television interview likewise acknowledged the secret diplomacy between the two countries: "As far as Jordan is concerned, a way has been opened, conducted at this stage through secret diplomacy, and for the moment it is characterized by understanding, more than by agreement."[121]

After the February 19, 1986, rupture in Jordanian-PLO relations and the closure of the PLO offices in Amman in July 1986, Jordan initiated a policy designed to bolster its position vis-à-vis the PLO in the West Bank. The purpose of the new policy was to increase the Jordanian presence in the territories; it was coordinated with Israel, which seized the opportunity to achieve a number of objectives. First, in the absence of a political consensus on the West Bank, Israel wanted to share the burden of administering the West Bank with Jordan through a condominium arrangement. Israel hoped this would reduce Palestinian resistance to the occupation. Second, the two countries would jointly fight Palestinian activism by cultivating a leadership that would be affiliated with Jordan and would espouse anti-PLO views. In other words, this arrangement was an ideal prescription for the maintenance of the status quo, which precluded, de facto, any territorial compromise.[122] Prime Minister Peres echoed this sentiment during an interview: "They [the Jordanians] thought that they were stronger [in the West Bank] than they actually were. They will try to bolster their position and from our point of view this is O.K."[123]

The tangible benefits of the condominium idea were viewed by Jordan and Israel as follows: first, the emergence of a local leadership free of PLO influence would negotiate with Israel on the final terms of a settlement. Second, the two countries hoped that as a result of this arrangement, tranquility would be restored in the territories. Third, the Israeli military presence in the territories would guarantee that no harm would be done to Jordanian interests and clients. Israel would be in charge of security while Jordan would run the civil administration. Fourth, the formalization of such a power-sharing agreement would guarantee that Jordan would not join in a war against Israel.

The overwhelming support of the West Bank population for the PLO meant that Jordan needed an activist policy in the territories to undermine the PLO. This was based on the assumption that Jordan could offer the Palestinians financial benefits if they cooperated with Amman. Moreover, Jordan also feared that if it did not actively participate in West Bank affairs, sooner or later Israel would attempt to expel the Palestinians to Jordan and destabilize the kingdom. By "improving the quality of life in the territories, Jordan hoped that people would stay there."[124]

As part of Jordan's overall strategy, a number of practical steps were taken by the two countries. These steps included appointing Arab mayors, who were approved by Israel and Jordan, to replace the Israeli military officers who had ruled the cities since 1982. Additionally, Israel and Jordan signed an agreement to reopen the Cairo-Amman Bank, which had been closed since 1967; Jordan also announced a $1.3 billion development plan for the territories. Additionally, a new newspaper, *An-Nahar,* started publication in East Jerusalem. It was financed by Amman and espoused pro-Jordanian views.

The Jordanian Development Plan

The most visible sign that Jordan intended to increase its involvement in the affairs of the territories was an ambitious five-year development plan that called for a massive infusion of $1.292 billion into economic, social, and educational projects in the West Bank and Gaza.[125]

As Meron Benvenisti noted, the details of the plan pointed to Jordan's emphasis on developing the rural rather than the urban areas and on allocating money to the private rather than to the public sector, which was controlled by the PLO.[126] Salaries received the lion's share of the plan instead of infrastructural development. "One-third of the total went to individual salaries, mortgages, and grants, 31.5 percent to social services, 13.7 to production (agriculture and industry), 11.8 percent to physical infrastructure and 7.8 percent to financing."[127]

The emphasis on developing the rural at the expense of the urban areas was similar to Israel's attempts to cultivate the rural Village Leagues as an alternative leadership to the PLO. The fact that the Hebron region was intended to be the largest recipient of the funds attests to Jordan's political motives in issuing the plan because the Hebron area is pro-Jordanian.[128] An additional motive underlay the plan, a desire to increase the West Bank's dependence on Jordan so it could control political developments and thereby check the PLO. The Jordanian plan was denounced by most Palestinians in the territories, who regarded it as an Israeli-Jordanian ploy to undermine the PLO's legitimacy in the territories. For example, an editorial in the PFLP publication *Al-Hadaf* stated:

> What is occurring today in the territories is propelled by Jordan and Israel. This leaves no doubt that through the economic hardships inflicted on the population they are bent on creating economic facts in order to diminish the position of the PLO and to remove the obstacles facing Jordan, which has so far hesitated to enter into direct negotiations with the enemy. This is done in order to attain a final compromise agreement and to liquidate the Palestinian question.[129]

When Marwan Doudin, the former Jordanian minister of the occupied territories, visited the West Bank in June 1992, he revealed in an interview with *Yediot Ahronoth* that his office closely coordinated his moves with the Civilian Administration regarding projects that were part of the development plan. He said: "I sent my representatives to the Civilian Administration and they were received well. They [the Civilian Administration] allowed my emissaries to go out to the field and take Polaroid pictures of planned projects. I gathered that . . . Ephraim Sneh, the head of the Civil Administration, was trying to help us."[130]

By October 1987 Jordan had spent only $11.7 million on projects in three regions: $731,229 in Jerusalem; $9.2 million in the West Bank; and $1.8 million in Gaza.[131]

Jordan initially hoped that the plan would be subsidized by the oil-producing Arab states and by Western donors as well. The United States, Great Britain, and France gave only about $25 million for the plan.[132] Saudi Arabia donated $9 million, provided that the funds were dispersed by the Jordanian-PLO Joint Committee. Kuwait made a direct $5 million grant to West Bank universities despite Jordanian appeals that the funds be spent through Jordanian institutions.[133] The plan did not receive the support that Jordan had hoped for, and the Jordanian disengagement from the West Bank in July 1988 was a convenient excuse to terminate a plan that had little chance of attaining its stated objectives.

As part of the condominium strategy, Israel and Jordan cooperated in the appointment of a number of West Bank mayors who would serve as alternatives to the pro-PLO leadership in the West Bank. Among them were Khalil Musa Khalil from Ramallah, Hassan a-Tawil from El-Bireh, and Abdel Majid a-Ziv from Hebron.[134] The centerpiece of these efforts was the appointment of Zafir al-Masri as the mayor of Nablus, the largest city in the West Bank. Additional measures were taken by the two countries against PLO supporters in the West Bank. For example, Mundir Salah, the president of Al-Najah, the largest university in the West Bank, was ordered by Jordan to resign from his post, and Israel revoked his work permit because of his sympathetic views toward the PLO.[135] Akram Haniyya, the editor of the Palestinian paper *Al-Sha'ab,* whose anti-Jordanian writings annoyed the Jordanian authorities, was deported by Israel.[136] The Israeli paper *Ma'ariv* cited Israeli military sources as saying "that the decision to deport Haniyya was demanded by Jordan because Israel could not reject the hand given to it by Jordan in the fight against terrorism. We are now facing the East [Jordan] without the need for a territorial compromise."[137] Daoud Kuttab, a prominent Palestinian journalist, also cited an additional example of Israeli-Jordanian cooperation: Israel refused exit visas to Mustapha Natsha, the former acting mayor of Hebron, and Fayiz Abu Rahmah, a pro-PLO activist from Gaza who wanted to travel to an international symposium in San Diego. Kuttab quoted then Israeli Defense Minister Rabin as saying that Jordan requested that these two Palestinians not be allowed to leave the West Bank because it did not want any anti-Jordanian sentiments expressed in the United States.[138] Moreover, *Newsweek* reported that farmers in the West Bank town of Jenin were prevented from exporting their produce across the bridges because they had refused to sign a pledge of loyalty to Hussein.[139] It was also reported in the East Jerusalem press that thirty-four Palestinian journalists were blacklisted by the Jordanian authorities, who warned them that if they attempted to cross the bridges to Jordan, they would be arrested.[140]

Furthermore, the Jordanian authorities requested that Israel's Arabic-language television programs stop interviewing pro-PLO personalities in the West Bank. Consequently, Prime Minister Shamir relayed the Jordanian request to Israeli television, and his request was honored.[141] As a way of bolstering Jordan's five-year development plan, Jordanian television aired between August 1986 and the outbreak of the intifadah a weekly series in Arabic on the plan and its ramifications for West Bank development. This program also tried to discredit the PLO in the West Bank. For example, during the broadcast of the first program, Marwan Doudin, Jordan's minister of the occupied territories, accused the pro-PLO newspapers in East Jerusalem of "propagating ideological terrorism among the inhabitants of the West Bank."[142]

Jordan also increased the total number of West Bank delegates to the Jordanian Parliament and lifted the import restrictions on products from the West Bank whereby Jordan allowed the purchase of goods made by machines or raw materials imported through Israel. At the same time, Jordan restricted those who were associated with the PLO from crossing the bridges into Jordan.[143] Moreover, Jordan began financing a new daily publication in East Jerusalem, *An-Nahar,* whose editor, Othman Halaq, became the chief spokesman for Jordanian interests in the West Bank.

This "carrot and stick" policy also included attempts by the United States, with the blessings of Israel and Jordan, to "improve the quality of life" in the territories. In this context a number of businessmen cooperated, including Howard Squadron, the former chair of the Conference of Presidents of Major American Jewish Organizations, Najib Halabi, King Hussein's father-in-law, and Stephen P. Cohen from City University New York, who formed the Business Group for Middle East Peace and Development.[144] The group intended to facilitate the inflow of funds needed for West Bank development and channel them to pro-Jordanian groups to increase Jordan's influence in the territories. The failure of this group coincided with the inability of Jordan to solicit funds for its development plan.

The plan to "improve the quality of life" was coordinated with the United States by Shmuel Goren, coordinator of government activities in the territories, who was sent to Washington in March 1986 to discuss the possibility of a $500 million grant for the project. Goren also explored the possibility of involving American private voluntary organizations in the financing and implementing of the plan.[145] As did the five-year development plan, this attempt also failed to materialize owing to a lack of enthusiasm by the potential donors.

The attempts at building an Israeli-Jordanian condominium suffered a serious setback when Zafir al-Masri was murdered by members of the PFLP in early March 1987. This was the first concrete signal that there were limits to the imposition of the Israeli-Jordanian condominium idea. The murder further signified the opposition of the Palestinians to the attempts to reach a pax Israeli-Jordania. It is no coincidence, therefore, that the Palestinian uprising began after Jordan and Israel failed in their hope to inflict a fatal blow to the PLO through the condominium scheme. The Palestinian uprising was directed not only against Israel and its harsh policies in the territories but also against Jordan's attempts to co-opt the population.

The International Conference Revisited

Initially, Peres was against the idea of an international conference. His close advisers, however, Avraham Tamir and Yossi Beilin, supported the idea and eventually convinced Peres.[146] Peres hoped to persuade Hussein to enter negotiations without preconditions based on Camp David. Yet Hussein, for reasons already described, declined the offer. In a message to Israel Hussein explained why he insisted on an international conference. If Israel agreed to announce in advance its willingness to withdraw from the West Bank or to accept the PLO as a negotiating partner, then such a conference would not be needed. If, however, Israel did not agree to either of these conditions, Jordan could not afford a confrontation with the Arab world by initiating a unilateral move. Jordan would negotiate with Israel only if the Soviet Union, the major supporter of the Arab states, also participated in the process, which meant an international conference.[147]

Gradually, Peres agreed to the idea of an international conference provided that the Soviet Union reestablished diplomatic relations with Israel. Peres regarded the international conference only as an opening forum that would lead to direct bilateral Israeli-Arab negotiations; he expected that a joint Jordanian-Palestinian delegation would negotiate with Israel.[148]

Peres presented his proposal to the United Nations General Assembly; Hussein's reaction was mixed. In an interview with the *New York Times* he referred to Peres as "a man of vision" and "a bright light in an area of darkness."[149] Although he welcomed the tenor of the speech, he disagreed with its specifics in three areas. First, the Jordanians wanted the PLO included in the conference if it accepted Resolutions 242 and 338 and renounced terrorism. (The Amman accord was still valid at that time.) Israel was opposed to PLO participation under any conditions. Second, Hussein objected to Israel's insistence that the Soviet Union renew diplomatic relations with Israel before it participated in negotiations. The king regarded this as "an Israeli problem" that should not be linked to the peace process. Moreover, the stipulation that Jews be allowed to emigrate from the Soviet Union went against the Arab consensus, which objected to immigration to Israel in toto. Third, if the bilateral discussions ended in a deadlock, Hussein wanted an international conference plenum to resolve the outstanding issues. Israel viewed the latter point as an invitation to a solution imposed by the superpowers and strongly objected to it.[150]

Meanwhile, Peres sought the backing of Egypt's President Mubarak for his moves. When Peres visited Cairo in February 1987, he was able to secure Egypt's endorsement of his plan. Namely, the PLO would not participate in the initial phase of the conference but would approve the Palestinian delegates in the joint Jordanian-Palestinian delegation. Peres and Mubarak also agreed that the international conference would not impose its will on the participants in case of a deadlock.[151]

With Egypt's backing Jordan felt that it could reach an agreement with Israel and resolve the outstanding issues. On April 11, 1987, Hussein and Peres secretly concluded in London a historic agreement to convene an international conference. The king agreed to Peres's position that the conference should include separate direct negotiations between Israel and the Arab states. Further, the conference would not have the power to intervene and veto any agreement unless the parties themselves agreed to it. Thus, Jordan no longer insisted on "referring" unresolved issues to the international plenum. Israel's fears of an imposed solution were allayed. It was also agreed that the Palestinians would be represented in a single Jordanian-Palestinian delegation. Every Palestinian delegate would have to agree to Resolutions 242 and 338 and renounce terrorism. The PLO's past refusal to agree to Resolutions 242 and 338 and renounce terrorism precluded its participation in the international conference. For Peres this agreement meant that emphasis would be placed on a functional rather than on a territorial agreement. He told Aryeh Naor, the former secretary of the Israeli government under Begin, that "we are aware that they [Jordan] would start [the negotiations] with the territorial issues. They are aware that we would emphasize the functional aspect. Perhaps, eventually they would entertain the idea of a Jordanian-Israeli-Palestinian confederation."[152]

During the London meeting Peres submitted to Hussein a list of joint energy projects which he proposed that the two countries should implement together. It included storage of flood water from the Yarmuk River in the Sea of Galilee, a bilateral hydroelectric project based on either a Mediterranean–Dead Sea canal or Red Sea–Dead Sea canal, and an oil pipeline from Mafraq in northeastern Jordan to the Mediterranean port of Haifa.[153] In 1993, in an interview with *Yediot Ahronoth*, Moshe Shahal, Israel's minister of energy, confirmed that Peres submitted to Jordan a document containing a proposal to develop jointly the Red Sea–Dead Sea canal project, one in which Jordan's Crown Prince Hassan showed a great deal of interest. A team of Jordanian engineers was scheduled to arrive in Israel in January 1988 to follow up, but the intifadah caused the visit to be canceled.[154]

After the agreement was initialed, the next obstacle was to enlist the support of Yitzhak Shamir, who became the prime minister as a result of the "rotation" agreement between Labor and Likud.[155] "As long as I am the prime minister, there will not be an international conference," declared Shamir in the Knesset.[156] He considered the idea a disaster that would lead to Israel's destruction. The annexationists, led by Shamir, argued that an international conference would lead to the participation of the PLO, an imposed solution that would force Israel to return to the pre-1967 borders, and the establishment of a Palestinian state. The

Likud proposed direct negotiations with Jordan whereby the territorial status quo would be maintained and only bilateral issues such as water, tourism in the Gulf of Aqaba, and environmental issues would be discussed with Jordan. There was no mention of the need to resolve the Palestinian question outside the Camp David framework.[157]

Shamir's views on peace with Jordan were published in *Foreign Affairs:* "A de facto peace between our countries has existed for quite some time. . . . From the present conditions to a close cooperation with Jordan in a large variety of spheres is but a relatively small step. . . . There can be no doubt that an international conference would be reduced to the lowest radical denominator, and present a united front against Israel."[158] Furthermore, Shamir argued that Peres did not represent the government consensus because the Labor party was only a partner in the coalition. Indeed, Shamir dispatched Moshe Arens, Israel's ambassador to Washington and a member of the Likud Party, to convince Secretary of State George Shultz that endorsing the London Agreement would be tantamount to interfering in internal Israeli affairs. Clearly, on this issue, the United States did not wish to take the lead in attempting to push the peace process forward, given the Likud's total rejection of the London Agreement.[159] Israeli internal divisions made it apparent that no negotiations with Jordan were feasible at that time.

In an attempt to convince Jordan to abandon the idea of an international conference Yitzhak Shamir met secretly with King Hussein in London in the summer of 1987. During this first meeting between a leader of the Likud and an Arab leader, other than Egypt's, Shamir presented to Hussein the reasons for his rejection of the conference idea: "I opposed the convening of an international conference first and foremost because of the participation of the Soviet Union that was very hostile to Israel but supported the PLO and the establishment of a Palestinian state. . . . The Soviet Union also opposes Jordan ideologically and, therefore, the best chance for peace is through direct negotiations between us and Jordan, without mediators."[160] Hussein, however, was not persuaded by Shamir and maintained his support for an international conference, primarily in search of Arab and international endorsement of negotiations with Israel.

When the Palestinian uprising began in December 1987, the peace process stalled. In March 1988, however, the United States put forward a plan to address the problem of the West Bank and to reduce the growing tensions resulting from the intifadah. The Shultz Initiative called for an international conference followed by six months of negotiations between Israel and a Jordanian-Palestinian delegation on transitional arrangements for the West Bank. In the seventh month negotiations would begin on the final status of the territories. The transition period was to last up to three years, and one year was allocated for negotiations on the final status.[161]

By that time the intifadah was gaining momentum. The initiative endorsed neither PLO participation in the process nor a Palestinian state, which had been the goal of the uprising. As expected, Shamir voiced his objection to an international conference whereas Labor supported it. The Jordanians did not reject it, but the PLO did. Hussein saw no need to endorse the plan wholeheartedly because he was already contemplating disengagement from the West Bank.[162] This became evident when the king submitted to Secretary Shultz a document that contained Jordan's position on the peace process. Unlike its previous insistence on a joint Jordanian-Palestinian delegation to the international conference, Jordan left this question open. In other words, in the absence of consensus among the PLO and the Arab states on a joint delegation Jordan would talk to Israel on bilateral issues only, leaving the question of the West Bank to the Palestinians themselves.[163] This new policy meant to show to the Palestinians that Jordan no longer intended to compete with the PLO for Palestinian representation.

Just as the Reagan Plan was not implemented because of lack of a serious American commitment to move the process forward, the Shultz Plan failed because it did not address the new realities that had resulted from the uprising. The intifadah that led Shultz to draft the plan was ultimately the one that doomed it and made its realization impossible.[164]

Moreover, during the June 1988 Algiers Arab League summit it became clear to Hussein that Jordan no longer enjoyed the confidence of the Arab world on matters pertaining to Palestine. The PLO was placed squarely as the sole responsible party for the Palestinians. Jordan was not even mentioned in the final communiqué.[165] As Asher Susser notes, "Jordan now faced Arab censure, orchestrated by the PLO, for seeking to 'impose itself' on the Palestinian people. For Hussein the Algiers summit was the 'last straw'."[166] The Algiers summit stood in stark contrast to the November 1987 Amman Arab League summit, which had paid little attention to the Palestinian problem and the PLO because the Iran-Iraq war dominated the agenda. Less than one year later, in light of the intifadah, in Algiers the Arab states were forced to address the problems of the West Bank by allocating funds directly to the occupied territories and not via Jordan, thus diminishing Jordan's already precarious position. This was further proof to King Hussein that Jordan must take a drastic step to salvage its credibility among the Palestinians and the Arab states.

Hussein's Fateful Decision

Before Hussein's July 31, 1988, landmark speech in which he announced Jordan's administrative and legal disengagement from the West Bank, a Jordanian delegation visited the territories. The delegation was headed by Rateb Amar, director of Jordan's Ministry of the Occupied Territories. Its purpose was to assess the degree to which Jordan still enjoyed support among the Palestinians in the wake of the uprising. The delegation returned to Amman and reported that Jordan no longer enjoyed any support among the local population. Even traditional Jordanian supporters feared to display publicly their support for Jordan.[167]

The first concrete sign that Jordan intended to alter its relations with the occupied territories came on July 28, 1988, when Jordan canceled its ambitious five-year development plan for the territories.

Against the background of the Palestinian intifadah King Hussein made his decision. The Palestinian uprising embodied a message to Jordan that any attempt to "Jordanize" the West Bank either through unilateral actions such as the development plan or by attempting a condominium arrangement with Israel would be rejected by the West Bank population. The uprising, if anything, was a clear signal to Jordan that the Palestinians sought to disengage themselves from Jordan and to ally unequivocally with the PLO as their sole representative. This was evident in the anti-Jordanian stance taken by the intifadah's leadership. As noted by Ghada Talhami, "The intifadah was no more than the final blow to the Jordanian foundation, already riddled with holes."[168]

Several additional factors played a role in the king's decision. Hussein was unable to convince either Israel or the United States that the next step in the peace process was the convening of an international conference. This was particularly irksome to Hussein, who felt betrayed by Peres and who was unable to deliver on his commitment to have Israel join an international conference as stipulated in the secret April 1987 London Agreement. Nor was Hussein successful in his attempts to convince the PLO to give Jordan a mandate to negotiate on the Palestinians' behalf and to join a Jordanian-Palestinian delegation that would attend a future peace conference. Further, Jordan's ambitious five-year development plan, which was strongly opposed by the PLO, was not being implemented despite the promise by the oil-rich Arab states to finance the project. As Roger Owen notes, the Saudis declared that they would provide funds only to the Jordanian-Palestinian committee and not directly to Jordan. The European Economic Community preferred to deal directly with the Palestinian farmers who wanted to export to Europe rather than with Jordan or Israel.[169] The lack of movement on the development plan meant that Hussein's intentions to create an infrastructure in the West Bank tied to Jordan would not materialize. Above all, Hussein feared that the intifadah would cause unrest among the Palestinian East Bank population that possibly could lead to another civil war and the destabilization of the Hashemite regime, especially if Israel were to deport masses of Palestinians from the West to the East Bank as advocated by Ariel Sharon and other members of the Israeli Knesset. The feeling by non-Palestinian Jordanians that the government was giving the Palestinian issue too much attention while failing to address the urgent political, economic, and social problems in the East Bank played a role in the decision to disengage. As noted by Gregory Gause, these feelings of resentment came to the fore during the 1989 riots in Jordan.[170]

A combination of all these factors at domestic, regional, and international levels led to Jordan's decision. Hussein had been intimately involved with the problem of the West Bank and the Palestinians for decades yet was unable to find a solution. He finally became frustrated and gave up, vacating the center stage to the PLO. In his speech Hussein declared, "Jordan is not Palestine," and, therefore, the PLO had to bear the responsibility for the West Bank. The rationale that Hussein provided for his decision was as follows:

> Of late, it has become clear that there is a general Palestinian and Arab orientation which believes in the need to highlight the Palestinian identity in full in all efforts and activities that are related to the Palestine question and its developments. It has also become obvious that there is a general conviction that maintaining the legal and administrative relationship with the West Bank—and the consequent special Jordanian treatment of the brother Palestinians living under occupation through Jordanian institutions in the occupied territories—goes against this orientation. It would be an obstacle to the Palestinian struggle which seeks to win international support for the Palestine question, considering that it is a just national issue of a people struggling against foreign occupation.[171]

The king stated that the severance of ties was a response to the wish of the PLO to secede from Jordan and to establish an independent state. Furthermore, he made it clear that the decision would not affect the East Bank Palestinians, who "have citizenship rights and commitments just like any other citizen regardless of his origin." Concerning the "nightmare scenario" of turning Jordan into a Palestinian state, the king declared unequivocally that "Jordan is not Palestine" and that Palestinian national aspirations should be fulfilled in the West Bank rather than in Jordan as called for by some Israeli annexationists. King Hussein also maintained, however, that Jordan was not relinquishing its commitment to the peace process, and once an international conference convened, Jordan would participate but it would not represent the Palestinians.

Jordan's disengagement decision finally clarified the ambivalent state of relations that existed between the monarchy and the PLO. For the first time since the 1974 Rabat summit Jordan's rhetoric and actions were synchronized. No longer was Jordan only paying lip service to the PLO as the "sole legitimate representative" while in reality attempting to seduce the West Bankers by bestowing benefits upon the pro-Jordanians. As long as Jordan had maintained this dubious stance, neither the PLO nor the Palestinians could fully trust it. Once Jordan severed its ties Jordanian-Palestinian relations normalized. With the onset of the peace process that unfolded after the Gulf War, Jordan and the PLO coordinated their moves to participate in a joint delegation to the talks with Israel. In the wake of the September 1993 Israeli-PLO accord, discussions about a Jordanian-Palestinian confederation have assumed a new urgency. All these new developments point to a new chapter in Jordanian-Palestinian relations, one that could not have taken place without King Hussein's July 1988 declaration.

The practical ramifications of the severance of ties were considerable. About 18,000 Jordanian civil service employees in the West Bank were affected by the king's decision. Some of these employees had been receiving full salary from Jordan, whereas others had received only a supplementary salary. The total Jordanian budget allocated for these salaries was about $40 million divided among three sectors. Of 5,200 civil servants employed by the Jordanians before the 1967 war, less than one-half decided not to stop working after 1967 and continued to receive a salary. In 1988 they were forced to retire but continued to receive their pensions. Those who continued to work for the Israeli civil administration and received a double salary were cut off by Jordan or forced to retire.

The second category consisted of 14,000 employees of the civil administration who were hired after 1967, including 10,000 teachers, 1,400 health administrators, and others. Since 1986 they had received a supplemental salary. These salaries were discontinued. In the third category—2,000 employees in semiprivate institutions such as private schools, hospitals, and charitable societies, which were linked to Jordan—subsidies were severed and employees were fired. The only sector that was not affected was the Awqaf, the Supreme Muslim Council, whose 3,000 employees continued to receive full salaries from Jordan. The Awqaf became Jordan's most important link to the West Bank. All personal documents such as marriage, birth, and death certificates had to be notarized by the religious council. This, of course, combined with the Awqaf's ownership of all religious properties, continued to give Jordan leverage on the daily lives of the Palestinians. Additional measures undertaken by Jordan after the king's speech included changing the five-year Jordanian passports held by West Bank Palestinians to two-year travel documents. This meant that the Palestinians were no longer considered Jordanian citizens. All Palestinians who were working outside the West

Bank before July 31, 1988, were required to return to limit Palestinian immigration to Jordan.

Jordan's Ministry of the Occupied Territories was abolished and replaced by a Department of Palestinian Affairs at the Foreign Ministry and the parliament was dissolved because half of its members were West Bankers. By April 1989 a new election law was proclaimed in Jordan, and in November of that year, for the first time since 1950, general elections were held without the participation of West Bank Palestinians.

These measures in toto constituted a radical change for the West Bank Palestinians, who were accustomed to receiving many legal and administrative services from Jordan and for Jordan, which finally surrendered its legal claim to the West Bank.

The Jordan River bridges, however, remained open although all goods coming from the West Bank were now taxable as foreign goods. The Cairo-Amman Bank was not closed, and Jordanians continued to regulate the matriculation exams for high school graduates (Tawjihi) so they could continue to study at universities in the Arab world. Furthermore, in light of the Israeli-PLO accord and its peace treaty with Israel, Jordan agreed to reopen its banks that had been closed since 1967, to continue to use the dinar as legal tender, and to provide numerous other services to the Palestinians during the transitional stage of Palestinian self-rule.

In essence, the "unity of the two Banks" idea that dated back to the 1950 formal annexation of the West Bank and the 1972 United Arab Kingdom plan was abandoned, but not forgotten. Marwan al-Qassem, Hussein's chief of the Royal Court, succinctly summarized the new reality: "We no longer want to talk on behalf of the Palestinians. From now on, Jordan is Jordan and Palestine is Palestine."[172]

Although Hussein's move caught everybody by surprise, several signs, dating back to April 1988, had signaled that Hussein was contemplating such a move. In speeches, including a speech by Hussein at the June 1988 Algiers Arab summit, Hussein and his ministers had attempted to distance Jordan from the West Bank.[173] Chief among these signs was a statement by a senior Jordanian official on April 11, 1988, that if an international conference were to convene, Jordan would not negotiate with Israel on the West Bank but would attempt to resolve the one outstanding bilateral Jordanian-Israeli issue—Israeli withdrawal from Wadi al-Arabah (or the Arava, in Hebrew), a twenty-square-kilometer area south of the Dead Sea, and from a five-square kilometer area in the north near the Yarmuk River. Jordan claimed that Israel had occupied these areas unlawfully.[174]

Israeli officials reacted with total surprise to these demands, which had never been raised in the Israeli-Jordanian clandestine talks since

1967. Israeli sources offered two possible explanations for the Jordanian stance. The first, which was considered an "optimistic" explanation, determined that Jordan was signaling to the PLO that if "we do not reach an agreement on the establishment of a joint delegation to the [international] conference, we may participate in such a conference even without the PLO. After all, Jordan could discuss other matters besides Judea, Samaria, and the Gaza Strip with Israel." The second explanation, which closely approximated Hussein's motivations, argued that Hussein had decided to disengage from the West Bank and to have nothing to do with the Palestinian question.[175]

Yet despite this hint, when Hussein made his announcement, Israel was shocked. Initial reactions in the West Bank were mixed. Those who were paid by Jordan feared for their livelihoods and expressed anxiety for the future. The majority of the population, however, welcomed Hussein's move. Hanna Siniora, the editor of the pro-PLO newspaper, al-Fajr, said, "We are starting from ground zero. In order to reach our goal of a Palestinian state we must sacrifice."[176] In communiqué number 23 of the underground Unified National Leadership of the Uprising Hussein's decision was attributed to the success of the intifadah:

> The latest Jordanian measures to disengage legal and administrative ties with the West Bank, came as one of the most important achievements of the great popular uprising. These measures also came as a crucial step to implement the Algiers Summit resolutions and to bolster the status of the PLO and the exclusivity of its representation of our people as the only side authorized to shoulder all responsibilities toward our people in the homeland and in the diaspora.[177]

In Israel members of the Likud welcomed Hussein's move, and some even called on Prime Minister Shamir to annex the territories formally. Shamir reacted to Hussein's announcement by saying, "There is nothing revolutionary in what Hussein says. Whoever thought Hussein was a partner to the idea of a territorial compromise, now it must be evident to him that this illusion [is] totally shattered."[178] The Labor party suffered a considerable loss of credibility. The Israeli press reported that before Hussein's speech Shimon Peres contacted Hussein and asked him not to sever totally the links with the West Bank, but to no avail.[179]

For the first time since 1967 Labor's Jordanian option was devoid of meaning because it had lost its chief partner to the negotiations. Labor's inability to win in the November 1988 elections was, inter alia, linked to Hussein's decision.[180]

Jordan's decision paved the way for the Palestinians to move to center stage. In the absence of Hussein as its main partner Israel was left to address the painful reality that it had tried to avoid since 1967, namely, that if it wanted peace with the Palestinians, it would have to negotiate with them. Regional and international developments helped Israel move, albeit grudgingly, in that direction. In October 1991, three years after Jordan's disengagement, Israel, Jordan, and the Palestinians met in Madrid, and inaugurated a new era in Arab-Israeli relations, culminating in the historic agreement between Israel and the PLO that was signed on September 13, 1993, followed by the signing of an Israeli-Jordanian Treaty of Peace on October 26, 1994.

6

From De Facto to De Jure Peace

Considering the special relationship that existed between Israel and Jordan, it is not surprising that only one day after Yitzhak Rabin and Yasser Arafat shook hands at the White House the two countries signed a Common Agenda in a modest ceremony at the Department of State on September 14, 1994. They, after all, were *intimate* enemies with a history of close ties that dated back to the beginning of the twentieth century. The questions Israelis and Jordanians negotiated in Washington pertaining to water-sharing, refugees, and economic relations were the building blocks of functional cooperation that had already been secretly discussed by the two sides. During the several rounds of talks in Washington, D.C., after the October 1991 Madrid conference, each party was fully cognizant of the other's position, strengths and weaknesses, and the constraints that limited each side's ability to make concessions. The special relationship between the two formal adversaries was molded during the post-1967 period. Therefore, any examination of the 1994 formal peace treaty must include an assessment of the achievements, failures, and limitations of Jordanian-Israeli relations as they evolved over the years.

When examining Israeli-Jordanian relations in the 1967–88 period, one must first address the costs and benefits of this relationship. From a strategic perspective the greatest benefit for both countries was the fact that, except for occasional infiltrations by Palestinian guerrillas, the Israeli-Jordanian border was quiet. Even during the October 1973 war, when Egypt and Syria formed a coalition to fight Israel, Jordan chose not to participate in the war. The special relationship that emerged between the two countries after the 1967 war meant that Jordan had a stake in maintaining the status quo between the two countries. The quiet frontier allowed Israel flexibility to pursue its objectives on other fronts. During the 1973 war, for example, Israel did not need to station additional troops along the Jordanian border. It was, thus, able to counter the Egyptian and Syrian attacks. Moreover, having secured the Israeli-

Egyptian border, on the one side, with the 1979 peace treaty, and the Jordanian border on the other, with functional cooperation, Israel was able to invade Lebanon in 1982 without risking a major war on its other borders. Jordan's inferior military power vis-à-vis Israel also played a role in its cautious attitude toward its western neighbor. In the absence of a military option or Israeli willingness to withdraw from the territories Jordan felt that its interests could be best served through a policy of functional cooperation.

Notwithstanding the state of war that had existed between Israel and Jordan during the period from 1948 to 1994, the two countries' interdependence, defined in terms of common interests, over time laid the foundation for functional cooperation. As a result of myriad geographic, demographic, historical, economic, and political factors that linked it to the West Bank, Jordan felt compelled to maintain a dialogue with Israel, its formal enemy. These factors coupled with the desire by both countries to prevent the establishment of an independent Palestinian state on the West Bank were the basis of this interdependence. Although certain issues necessitated a constant Israeli-Jordanian dialogue (e.g., Eilat and Aqaba and the water issue), by themselves they were not sufficient to create a web of Israeli-Jordanian interdependence. The perceptions of their shared interests in the West Bank ultimately bound the two countries together. Certainly, had it not been for the physical proximity of Israel and Jordan and the open bridges policy—the centerpiece of the relationship—functional cooperation could not have developed.

Jordan and Israel were not the only beneficiaries of the open bridges policy. This policy allowed the Palestinians to develop and to consolidate their nationalist movement by maintaining close ties to the Arab world and the Palestinian diaspora, which enabled them to resist the occupation. A profound paradox emanates from the open bridges policy. Initially, this policy was intended by Israel to serve as a "pressure release valve," which would make the Israeli occupation tolerable. Yet the Palestinians turned this policy to their own advantage. It allowed them to maintain their ties with the outside world and permitted them to pursue a policy of *sumud*, or steadfastness, a major reason why Israel and Jordan lost the battle to "Jordanize" the West Bank Palestinians. This failure became manifest during the intifadah when Palestinians clearly expressed their intention to resist either Israeli or Jordanian attempts to impose their will. Even in the midst of the Palestinian revolt, the two countries continued to coordinate their policies in a number of areas. Israel's former president Chaim Herzog confirmed this.[1]

Between 1967 and 1987 the open bridges policy gave Israel a period of twenty years of relative tranquility on the West Bank where the costs of maintaining the occupation were manageable. Ultimately, the Palestinians demonstrated their resolve to defy any attempt to co-opt or pacify them. Had the open bridges policy not been maintained by the two countries, the Palestinian uprising might have erupted much earlier. It could also be argued that Israel without the open bridges policy would have had to come to terms with the Palestinian problem much earlier rather than maintain the status quo. Hence, Israel's open bridges policy may have delayed the outbreak of the intifadah although, paradoxically, this policy in itself contributed to the uprising.

For Jordan, attempting to support an alternative to the PLO was unsuccessful. Despite its rule over the West Bank for nineteen years before 1967 Jordan was unable to establish a powerful political and social base and to gain the loyalty of the population. The lack of Jordanian political influence became particularly apparent after Jordan's disengagement from the West Bank; most Palestinians rejoiced in the king's decision, and only a handful asked Hussein to reverse it.

When examining functional cooperation from a Jordanian perspective, it seems that Jordan took a number of risks by pursuing this policy. One of the cardinal rules of the "game" was that the substance and manner of cooperation be kept secret because the two countries were in a formal state of war. Jordan followed the pan-Arab position of "no peace" with Israel without being accused of "collaborating with the enemy." Indeed, Jordan never acknowledged its secret relationship with Israel and issued strong denials whenever a press report suggested otherwise. Israel allowed Jordan to maintain "plausible denial" of contacts with its enemy. Israeli officials, however, occasionally provided detailed accounts of Israeli-Jordanian interaction. This, in turn, embarrassed Hussein. The king felt betrayed by those who had promised to maintain silence on the matter. By meeting scores of Israeli leaders Hussein violated the Arab consensus on negotiations with Israel and exposed himself to great danger. After all, his grandfather was assassinated because of contacts with Israel. Yet the king did not pursue this policy without believing that the benefits outweighed the risks. For Hussein, however, the tangible benefits of cooperation with Israel were mixed. Above all, as stated earlier, his border with Israel remained quiet, and Israel provided Jordan with a strategic umbrella during the 1970 civil war. In the absence of Israeli willingness to relinquish control over the territories Hussein hoped to offer Israel enough incentives so it would eventually reconsider its refusal to withdraw. At the same time the king had no illusions regarding the prospects of an Israeli withdrawal. Thus, functional cooperation suited Jordanian interests as well, for much of this cooperation had taken place sub-rosa.

From Disengagement to Negotiations

Although Jordan disengaged from the West Bank politically and administratively in July 1988, it maintained some ties to the territory. For example, the Awqaf and its extensive network of religious, educational, health, social institutions, and its four thousand employees is still subject to control from Amman and now forms the formal link between the West and East Banks. Interestingly, as part of this religious network, Jordan also maintained ties to Hamas (severed in 1994), the Palestinian Islamic organization that opposes the peace process and hopes to replace Israel with an Islamic state. The Jordanian-Hamas interaction was reminiscent of previous attempts by the Hashemite Kingdom to clip the PLO's wings in the territories, albeit Jordan no longer attempted to represent the Palestinians.[2] Although Jordan used Hamas as a channel to exert its influence in the West Bank, Jordan could not afford to challenge the PLO openly; its past attempts had all failed. Now, however, that the PLO has signed an agreement with Israel, leading to a modicum of Palestinian autonomy, Jordanian-Palestinian competition in the territories has largely come to a halt. In fact, Jordan's support is essential if the autonomy is to survive the difficult tests ahead.

The Israeli-PLO Jericho-Gaza agreement led to several attempts by the Islamic organization, inside and outside the territories, to derail the agreement, mainly by launching suicide attacks against Israelis. Because one of Hamas's headquarters was located in Amman, Israel applied considerable pressure on Jordan to curtail Hamas's activities following several murderous attacks on Israelis in the spring of 1994 after the February 1994 Hebron massacre of Palestinian worshipers. Jordan agreed to curb Hamas's activities, given its special relationship with Israel. In April 1995 the Jordanian government barred Hamas members from publishing pro-Hamas statements. In addition, one month later, Jordan ordered two senior Hamas leaders, Musa Abu-Marzuk and Imad al-Alami, and their families to leave the country. The two Hamas leaders reportedly were coordinating attacks against Israeli targets.

In the sphere of education Jordan continues to supervise the Tawjihi examinations, thus giving it considerable leverage in the system. Above all, the bridges are open; people, goods, capital, and ideas continue to flow in both directions. Although Israel maintains physical control over the bridges, Palestinian police also man the border crossings to the West Bank. The Cairo-Amman Bank with its four branches was not affected by the king's decision. In fact, after the peace treaty, Jordan, Israel, and the PLO, respectively, agreed to reopen all the branches that had been closed since 1967.

Most importantly, Jordan's disengagement greatly contributed to Israel's agreement with the PLO. Jordan ceased its claims to represent the Palestinians, and, hence, it was able to reach a modus vivendi with the PLO regarding the formation of a joint Jordanian-Palestinian delegation on the eve of the October 1991 Madrid conference. The conference led to the beginning of an Israeli-Palestinian dialogue that resulted in the secret Israeli-PLO Oslo negotiations and the subsequent historic accord signed in Washington in September 1993.

Since 1967 Jordan's relations with the PLO could be characterized as both cooperative and competitive. Before 1974, when the Arab League designated the PLO as the "sole legitimate representative of the Palestinian people," the Palestinian organization did not formally challenge Jordan's claim to represent the Palestinians. But the PLO never agreed to grant Jordan such a role. Jordan had hoped that, should Israel withdraw from the West Bank, the territory would be again part of Jordan. As seen in the 1972 United Arab Kingdom plan, King Hussein proposed that an East Bank-West Bank federation, under Hashemite tutelage, was the most appropriate solution to Palestinian national aspirations. After 1974, however, the PLO openly challenged Jordan over the question of representation, and Jordan accepted the Arab League's designation of the PLO. Several attempts were made by the two sides to establish a common framework, such as the failed 1985 Amman accord. Although officially Jordan had adhered to the 1974 Rabat resolutions, in effect, it competed publicly and secretly in the West Bank with the PLO for the loyalties of the Palestinian population. During the 1974–88 period, also, Israel and Jordan attempted to form a joint condominium in the West Bank, but the intifadah and King Hussein's disengagement brought an end to these efforts to "Jordanize" it. Once the Madrid peace process was set in motion and Israel and the PLO signed the 1993 Declaration of Principles, Jordan and the PLO began again to explore the prospects for forming a confederation. With the signing of the Israeli-Jordanian peace treaty, once Israel and the PLO start negotiating the final status of the West Bank and Gaza, the question of Jordanian-Palestinian relations will become of paramount importance to all sides concerned. Although the negotiations on the final status of the territories were launched on May 5, 1996, they were suspended with the election victory of Benjamin Netanyahu and his Likud Party. It has yet to be seen when the final status talks will resume and whether the Israeli government will be willing to make significant concessions to the Palestinians so an agreement can be reached.

Regionally, between 1988 and 1991 Jordan's stature was at its nadir. While the Palestinians supported Jordan's disengagement from the West Bank as well as its pro-Iraqi stance during the Gulf War, Jordan's Arab

neighbors and the United States shunned the Hashemite Kingdom because of its support of Saddam Hussein. Yet the realization in Israel,
especially by the Likud government, in the wake of the Gulf War, that
a stable Jordan was vital to its strategic interests led to a reevaluation of
Jordan's role in Israel's grand strategy. Even Prime Minister Yitzhak
Shamir, a long-time advocate of establishing a Palestinian state on the
East Bank, altered his views during the Gulf crisis when King Hussein
faced domestic turmoil. Other members of the Likud government also
changed their minds: "I believe those who say that anything that would
replace [King] Hussein would be worse for us," said former Defense
Minister Moshe Arens. "We therefore wish him success in his fight for
his rule in Jordan."[3]

After the Gulf War Israeli public opinion, however, became less
inclined to support a territorial compromise with the Hashemite Kingdom as opposed to granting Palestinians autonomy under Israeli control
or a Palestinian-Jordanian state. This change in attitudes became clearly
visible in two public opinion surveys conducted in May 1990 before the
Gulf crisis and in June 1991 after the war.[4] In 1990, 19.6 percent of Israel's
public supported territorial compromise with Jordan as a permanent
solution (the most preferred choice among the various options presented
in the survey); after the war, however, this option received only 11.2
percent support, a 43 percent drop compared to that in 1990. The most
popular choices were autonomy under Israeli rule (16.7 percent) and
a territorial compromise leading to a Palestinian-Jordanian state (14.1
percent). As the survey's authors note, the reasons for this shift could
be attributed to Jordan's pro-Iraqi stance and to its decline in popularity
and support among the Palestinians in the occupied territories, a trend
that began after the 1988 disengagement.

During the 1967–88 period, functional cooperation inhibited progress toward a formal peace agreement. Additional factors, however, were
also responsible for the lack of movement on the peace front, such as
internal divisions in Israel regarding withdrawal and the final status of
the territories, and the Palestinian refusal to recognize Israel. Moreover,
functional cooperation made it easier for Israel to reject a diplomatic
solution. Coupled with ideological divisions inside Israel, the opportunity
costs associated with relinquishing control over the West Bank and Gaza
were perceived by Israeli leaders to be too high, leading to the paradox
of the "Jordanian option." On the one hand, those Israelis who supported the reconciliationist and territorialist positions also supported a
peace agreement with Jordan over the West Bank. On the other hand,
supporting functional cooperation with Jordan prevented Israel from
having to address the issue of a formal peace treaty, culminating in a
diplomatic stalemate that lasted until the aftermath of the Gulf War.

Functional cooperation with Jordan allowed Israel to avoid making painful political choices. De facto peace with the Hashemite Kingdom was perceived as serving Israel's interests because the two countries had cooperated to prevent the establishment of an independent Palestinian state and had addressed other issues of mutual concern without facing constraints imposed by ideology and public opinion. In other words, *functional cooperation became a substitute for the formal peace process.*

Jordan, however, short of a total Israeli withdrawal from the West Bank and East Jerusalem and without the support of the Palestinians and the Arab states, was unable to enter open diplomatic negotiations with Israel. As in Israel, public opinion in the Arab world and in Jordan also played a role. Notwithstanding Egypt's peace with Israel, the taboo on negotiations with and recognition of Israel was broken only with the convening of the Madrid conference. Despite its cooperative stance vis-à-vis Israel on a variety of issues Jordan did not give up its hope to regain the West Bank and East Jerusalem before its 1988 disengagement. Therefore, Jordan's position regarding Israeli withdrawal remained consistent: demanding a total Israeli pullout and, after 1974, officially supporting the establishment of a Palestinian state, unofficially it attempted to circumvent the materialization of a Palestinian entity. Consequently, the positions of the two parties concerning an Israeli withdrawal from the West Bank were never bridged. Once, however, the question of the West Bank was relegated to Israel and the PLO when the two signed their Declaration of Principles on September 13, 1993, a formal Israeli-Jordanian Common Agenda was signed on September 14, 1993, which constituted the blueprint for a formal peace agreement. It was followed by the signing of the Washington Declaration on July 25, 1994, that ended the state of belligerency between the two countries and led to the Israeli-Jordanian Treaty of Peace signed on October 26, 1994.

On the Road to Madrid

Barely two months from the day that Allied troops invaded Iraq in an attempt to expel Iraqi forces from Kuwait, Jordan's King Hussein commented that the war had opened a "window of opportunity" that would probably last only a short time. He would later stress in an interview with the French weekly *Le Point* that the all-Arab ban on meetings with Israelis must be ended by face-to-face encounters with Israel's leaders.[5]

Israeli Foreign Minister David Levy replied to Hussein's suggestion by inviting him to come to Jerusalem, saying that "we will gladly receive him with a red carpet and a band."[6] One week later, even Prime Minister Shamir, who had supported the "Jordan is Palestine" idea, expressed optimism that a peace treaty with Jordan might be signed during his tenure in office: "It's not a fantasy; it's not only a dream. I think it could be realistic."[7]

Six months after this Israeli-Jordanian exchange took place an international peace conference convened in Madrid in October 1991. Jordan was represented there by a joint delegation with Palestinians, and it expressed its readiness to negotiate a peace agreement with its formal enemy and tacit ally, Israel.

When the historic Madrid international peace conference convened on October 18, 1991, a joint Jordanian-Palestinian delegation was present. After a formal opening, negotiations were planned via a two-track framework: bilateral negotiations between Israel and Lebanon, Syria, and Jordan/Palestinians and multilateral negotiations involving several Middle Eastern countries and other interested parties (the European Community, the United Nations, Japan, and others) on five separate topics—water, economic development, the environment, refugees, and arms control.

As stated in the letter of invitation to the bilateral talks issued by former United States secretary of state, James Baker, although Jordan and the Palestinians formed a joint delegation, each party was to address different issues with Israel.[8] The Palestinian delegation did not include any official members of the PLO, but academicians and professionals from the West Bank and Gaza. At Israel's insistence no residents of East Jerusalem were included as official members of the delegation.[9]

With the election of Yitzhak Rabin as prime minister in June 1992 the realization grew among Israelis and Palestinians that the multiple rounds of bilateral talks had not produced any meaningful results. This, in turn, led to the opening of a secret channel in Norway where Israeli academicians and representatives of the PLO began to explore new avenues for breaking the diplomatic impasse in Washington. The result was two agreements: Israeli-Palestinian mutual recognition and an interim accord on Palestinian self-rule in the territories signed in Washington on September 13, 1993.

Israel's refusal to negotiate with the PLO before 1993 coupled with its appreciation of Jordan as a strategic buffer vis-à-vis Iraq and its insistence that the Palestinians be part of a joint delegation with Jordan, in effect, reversed Jordan's declining fortunes during the intifadah and the Gulf War. In a sense, Israel played a key role in rehabilitating Jordan after the war, which, in turn, helped the Hashemite monarchy assume a pivotal role in the peace process.

Despite its July 1988 disengagement from the West Bank, Jordan's special relationship with the Palestinians and Israel, respectively, dictated continued involvement in the peace process. In late October 1992, during the seventh round of their bilateral negotiations, Israel and Jordan agreed in Washington on a Common Agenda that included an agreement to discuss a variety of issues, including border disputes, refugees, and cooperation in areas such as natural resources, the environment, health, education, various economic areas and others. The Agenda stated that "it is anticipated that the above endeavor will ultimately, following the attainment of mutually satisfactory solutions to the elements of this agenda, culminate in a peace treaty."[10] Several issues contained in the Agenda, such as water, were previously addressed in the context of functional cooperation. This agenda, officially signed on September 14, 1993, one day after the signing of the Israeli-PLO pact, however, marked the first time that the two countries had agreed on a formal peace as a goal. This agreement ushered in a new era that contrasted with the pre-1988 period when informal understandings and tacit arrangements were the modus operandi.

Stripped from its long-held ambition to represent the Palestinians, Jordan was left to address several issues in its dealings with Israel. Some issues were linked to the question of the West Bank but most coalesced around pure Transjordanian interests. As stipulated in the letter of invitation to the Madrid conference, these issues included several border disputes (outside the West Bank), the nature of peace, water, environmental issues, waste-water management, maritime rights in the Gulf of Aqaba, tourism, refugees, and aviation, among others. Although the crucial questions of refugees and water sharing were part of the multilateral talks, Israel and Jordan agreed to discuss them also bilaterally.

The Israeli-Palestinian talks focused on the establishment of an interim self-governing authority (ISGA) in the West Bank and Gaza. The territories' final status, however, remains to be negotiated between Israel and the PLO.

The Arava Border Dispute

On April 11, 1988, Radio Monte Carlo, in Arabic, quoted a Jordanian official who said that if an international conference convened, Jordan would not negotiate the issue of the West Bank, but Israeli occupation of Jordanian lands instead.[11] The particular timing of this announcement was linked to Jordan's disengagement, which occurred later in August. The announcement was a trial balloon to gauge reactions to a possible disengagement, but it was also the first time that Jordan had officially admitted that Israel occupied Jordanian territories outside the West Bank. In the bilateral talks that followed the Madrid conference Jordan seized the opportunity to discuss this issue with Israel. But only in October 1992, during the seventh round of the bilateral talks, when a tentative agenda was agreed upon, did this issue come into the limelight.

Interestingly, when the question of Jordanian territories occupied by Israel was first publicized in 1988, Israel's leaders were embarrassed to admit that it occupied them. In April 1988, both Yitzhak Shamir and Shimon Peres evaded reporters' queries on the issue. "I did not hear such a demand," said Shamir. "One should not take every report very seriously. When we sit with King Hussein around the negotiating table, we will hear what he has to say." Likewise, Peres retorted, "Such demands have not been raised. I would not be surprised, however, if at the beginning of negotiations each side were to present its maximal demands."[12] Peres then proceeded to equate such "maximal" Jordanian demands with Sadat's early approach toward negotiations with Israel in which he demanded a total Israeli withdrawal. In fact, Israeli occupation of Jordanian lands dated back to 1950, and the most recent land "grab" took place in 1990.[13] At the end of 1950, when the Israelis paved a road leading to Eilat, part of the road passed through Jordanian territory in the east. In an attempt to halt the construction the Jordanians constructed a signpost in Arabic and Hebrew: "The Hashemite Kingdom of Jordan— Road Closed to Traffic." In addition, the Jordanian military stationed five armored personnel carriers and troops there as a warning. In reaction, the commander of the Israeli Southern Command, Moshe Dayan, was instructed on November 30, 1950, by the General Staff to commence Operation Kislev to "eradicate the enemy's forces which had infiltrated Israeli territory."[14] An Israeli-Jordanian military skirmish followed, resulting in a Jordanian retreat to an area far from the battleground. When the dispute was brought before the joint Armistice Committee chaired by the United Nations, it ruled that Israel unlawfully paved a portion of the highway to Eilat inside Jordan's territory. Israel then withdrew and completed the construction of the road in its own territory instead.

According to journalist Yehuda Litani, Israeli expansion of its border in the Arava region eastward has occurred several times since the late 1960s. Security concerns to prevent guerrilla attacks from the Jordanian borders, expansion of agricultural fields eastward, and the existence of underground water wells on the Jordanian side were the primary reasons for the Israeli expansion. At times, the various agricultural settlements and kibbutzim took unilateral action. The Israeli military was also involved, however. In the early 1970s Ariel Sharon, commander of the Southern Command, "moved the border eastward by a few kilometers [and] built a fence, thus preventing guerrilla infiltration."[15]

Jordan's demand to recover its "lost" 320 square kilometers was based on a definition of the border determined by the 1949 Israeli-Jordanian Armistice Agreement, which recognized the borders of Palestine as determined by Article 25 of the Palestine Mandate.[16]

With the signing of the peace treaty between Israel and Jordan, several kibbutzim in the Arava region were affected by the agreement to restore Jordanian sovereignty to the area: Yahel, Lotan, Grofit, Ktora, Yotvata, Pharan, Tzofar, Ein Yahav, Hatzeva, Ein Tamar, and Idan, all had part or all of their agricultural fields on the Jordanian side. Lotan, for instance, was located entirely on the Jordanian side. The treaty stipulated that Israeli farmers be allowed to farm the Jordanian land, and Jordan received 11.5 square miles of Israeli territory in exchange. The inhabitants of these kibbutzim admitted that their problem was not the land itself as much as the water aquifers located on the Jordanian side. The residents also claimed that after the Madrid conference they were contacted by the Israeli government regarding a possible withdrawal and were asked to keep a low profile on this matter.[17] Conversely, those who opposed a withdrawal based their argument on the fact that the aquifers, located in the Jordanian territories, supply the water to the kibbutzim in the Arava and to the city of Eilat. But all these issues were resolved by the signing of the peace treaty.

Jordan also claimed that Israel occupied 347.5 acres in the Yarmuk region, which prevented Jordan from using its share of the Jordan and Yarmuk rivers. The Jordanians argued that the confluence of the Jordan and Yarmuk rivers was the demarcation of the border. As a result of several floods, the two rivers changed their courses to Israel's favor, but Jordan refused to recognize the principle established by the British that a boundary must be changed to accommodate fluctuations in the direction of a river.[18] These issues, too, were resolved as a result of the peace agreement. Israeli farmers were given the right to use the land and to lease the territory from Jordan for twenty-five years.

The Washington Declaration

From a Jordanian perspective the reasons for agreeing to sign the Washington Declaration on July 25, 1994, and the peace treaty on October 26, 1994, were related to the Israel-PLO Declaration of Principles and to Jordan's economic predicament.

King Hussein, who was estranged from the United States, his longtime ally, as a result of his support for Saddam Hussein, came to the Mayo Clinic in Minnesota for cancer treatment. President Clinton agreed to meet the Jordanian king at the White House on June 18, 1993, and the meeting was characterized as successful. Hussein reciprocated by writing Clinton an emotional letter, expressing his strong desire to make peace with Israel and "fulfill that part of my grandfather's legacy and leave my own."[19] Above all, the king was concerned about Jordan's foreign debt of more than $6.5 billion, of which it owed $700 million to the United States. President Clinton became convinced that King Hussein was seriously interested in making progress, and the administration recommended that Congress approve the resumption of military aid to Jordan.

The unveiling of the secret negotiations between Israel and the PLO in Norway and the subsequent signing of the Israel-PLO Declaration of Principles convinced Hussein that a bold move was required if progress was to be made. On November 2, 1994, Foreign Minister Shimon Peres traveled to Jordan via the Allenby Bridge and initialed with King Hussein a framework for a peace treaty. However, when Shimon Peres revealed the document to the Israeli media, King Hussein decided to slow the process until the parliamentary elections in Jordan were over.

The next significant developments occurred when Israel and the PLO signed the May 4, 1994, Cairo Agreement concerning the implementation of the Gaza-Jericho autonomy, and when the two sides successfully completed the Paris talks in April 1994 aimed at regulating economic relations between Israel and the autonomous Palestinian entity. King Hussein realized that the time was ripe for an Israeli-Jordanian breakthrough. If no moves were made along the Israeli-Jordanian axis, the king feared that an Israeli-Palestinian alliance would be created to Jordan's detriment. On May 19 a Jordanian-Israeli summit was convened in London. Yitzhak Rabin was accompanied by Elyakim Rubinstein, head of the Israeli delegations to the bilateral talks with Jordan; Maj. Gen. Danni Yatom, Rabin's military aid, and now head of the Mossad; and Ephraim Halevi, deputy director of the Mossad at that time. For twenty-five years Halevi had coordinated the clandestine ties between the two countries as a representative of the Israeli government. During the London meeting a framework was agreed upon to terminate the formal state of war that had existed since 1948.

When the fourth session of the United States-Jordan-Israel Trilateral Economic Committee that met in Washington was concluded on June 7, 1994, further progress was reported. The committee composed of Israeli, Jordanian, and American representatives had agreed to form a commission to handle borders, security, water, environment, and related issues as set forth in the Common Agenda signed on September 14, 1994. The text of the press release issued by the Department of State stated inter alia that "the results of the negotiations will be incorporated into drafts which will form parts of a Treaty of Peace."[20]

Meanwhile, the intense secret negotiations taking place in a Mossad safe house outside Tel Aviv bore fruit. When King Hussein visited President Clinton again on June 22, 1994, he responded favorably to a request by Clinton for a public meeting with Yitzhak Rabin. In turn, the American president promised congressional action on debt relief to Jordan. On

July 12 King Hussein wrote a letter to Clinton in which he indicated a readiness to meet the Israeli leader on July 18 at the Jordanian-Israeli border if concrete steps were taken to forget Jordan's foreign debt. Instead, President Clinton suggested that the meeting take place in Washington, D.C., at the White House. In preparation for the Washington summit Secretary of State Warren Christopher, Foreign Minister Shimon Peres, and Prime Minister Abdel Salam al-Majali met in Ein Avrona, alongside the Israeli-Jordanian border, ten miles north of Eilat and Aqaba. Later, the talks were moved to a resort on the Jordanian side of the Dead Sea. The negotiations, involving twenty-six representatives from each country, addressed several issues that were listed in the Common Agenda and the communiqué of the Trilateral Economic Committee. Negotiations were divided among five functional areas: boundaries, security, and water, environment, and energy. Although no substantive achievements resulted from these meetings, their value was symbolic and part of the confidence-building measures that were needed in preparation for the Washington summit scheduled for July 1994.

The signing of the Washington Declaration on July 25, 1994, signaled the end of the formal state of war between the two countries. It was also the first time that the two heads of state had met in public. The declaration ushered in a new era in the two countries' relations, paving the way for the peace treaty that was to be signed on October 26, 1994.

The declaration contained both political statements about the course of future relations and a list of functional joint projects. Its main provisions included the termination of the state of war; commitment to sign a peace treaty based on Security Council Resolutions 242 and 338; and recognition of Jordan's "special role" in Muslim holy shrines in Jerusalem. In addition, the two sides agreed on a series of steps to bolster ongoing negotiations on water, borders, and security. Additional steps were meant to symbolize the new era in the relations between the two countries: opening telephone links; linking the electrical grids of the two countries as part of a regionwide electrical grid system; opening new border crossings, one near Eilat-Aqaba and the other in the north; freeing access to third-country tourists traveling between Israel and Jordan; speeding negotiations on opening an international air corridor between the two countries; cooperation between the police forces of the two countries in combating crime, especially smuggling and drug trafficking; and fostering economic cooperation in a number of areas, including the abolition of economic boycotts.

Israel's recognition of Jordan as the guardian of Jerusalem's holy sites ignited a bitter dispute between Jordan and the PLO and between Israel and the PLO. The Palestinians argued that the final status of Jerusalem ought to be determined through negotiations with Israel and that Jordan should have no formal role in the city, which is viewed by the Palestinians as their future capital. Jerusalem's Muslim holy places include the thirteen-hundred-year-old Dome of the Rock and the Al-Aqsa Mosque, the site where King Hussein's grandfather, King Abdullah, was assassinated by a Palestinian in 1951. The 1993 restoration of the Dome with personal funds of King Hussein was viewed as a reassertion by the Jordanian monarch of his country's special role in Islam's third holiest city. The Palestinians, however, did not recognize Jordan's self-appointed privileged position. After Jordan designated a pro-Jordanian Palestinian scholar Sheikh Abdel Kader Abdeen as the mufti of Jerusalem, the PLO appointed a rival mufti, Sheikh Ikirmah Sabri. For the first time in the city's history two rival muftis held the position simultaneously. The position of mufti confers political, religious, and ceremonial powers; the mufti also serves as a religious adjudicator, the court of last resort.

This dispute was finally settled in January 1995 when Jordan and the PLO reached an agreement whereby the PLO recognized Jordan's custody of the holy sites, and Jordan acknowledged the Palestinian claim for sovereignty over the city.

Israeli-Jordanian De Jure Peace

On October 26, 1994, Prime Minister Yitzhak Rabin and Prime Minister Abdul-Salam al-Majali signed the Treaty of Peace between the two countries.[21] The treaty comprised thirty articles, five annexes that addressed boundary demarcation, water issues, police cooperation, environmental issues, and mutual border crossings, and six maps. It called for the establishment of full diplomatic relations and the exchange of ambassadors and a commitment to cooperation in areas such as trade, tourism, water, economic development, security, agriculture, banking, environmental preservation, and others. The two countries referred to the mandate boundaries as their international border, and Israel acknowledged Jordanian sovereignty over the disputed territories in the Arava and near the Sea of Galilee. In the Arava, mutual border modifications enabled farmers to continue to cultivate their lands. Jordan agreed to swap 11.5 square miles and to lease to Israel two small areas of land. In the Naharayim/Baqura Area and the Zofar Area in the north Israel was given private land-use rights for twenty-five years under Jordanian sovereignty.

Each country pledged to ensure that no threats of violence against the other party would originate from within its territory and to undertake joint measures to combat terrorism. The two countries agreed to establish a Conference on Security and Cooperation in the Middle East (CSCME) to be modeled after the Organization on Security and Cooperation in

Europe (OSCE) to build a new security regime to develop confidence-building measures and to prevent conflict.

The two countries agreed upon a water-sharing regime in the Jordan and Yarmuk rivers and to provide Jordan with 1.8 mcm/yr. from the northern part of the country. In addition, the two countries pledged to cooperate to alleviate the water shortage in the region by developing existing and new water resources, by preventing contamination of water resources, and by minimizing water wastage.

With the signing of the treaty, freedom of passage was granted through border crossings, open airspace, and territorial waters. Specific agreements governing the passage of nationals and tourists and civil aviation and maritime agreements were negotiated later by joint technical committees. The two countries also declared the Strait of Tiran and the Gulf of Aqaba international waterways, open to all nations for free navigation and overflight and recognized the maritime border as their international border. (This is Israel's only recognized sea border.)

With regard to places of historical and religious significance, as stipulated in the Washington Declaration, Israel acknowledged Jordan's "special role" in Muslim holy shrines in Jerusalem. When negotiations on the permanent status, as detailed in the Declaration of Principles, take place between Israel and the PLO, Israel agreed to give "high priority to the Jordanian historic role in these shrines."

The sensitive and complex issues surrounding the plight of Palestinian refugees, or displaced persons, was to be addressed through three channels: the quadripartite committee with Egypt and the Palestinians that deals with displaced persons; the Multilateral Working Group on Refugees; and bilateral negotiations with the PLO as detailed in the Declaration of Principles.

In addition, the treaty emphasized the normalization of relations in diverse areas such as culture, education, and science, the war against crime and drugs, transportation and roads, postal services and telecommunications, tourism, the environment, energy, health, agriculture, and the development of the Jordan Rift Valley and the Aqaba/Eilat area. In the sphere of economic cooperation pledges were made to conclude agreements on the termination of the Arab boycotts against Israel, the establishment of a free trade area, joint investment, banking, industrial cooperation, and labor. In addition to direct telephone and fax lines, postal links would also be established along with wireless, cable, and television relays. Several joint projects were also outlined, including development of energy and water sources, environmental protection, joint tourism development, and the development of the Jordan Rift Valley.

After the peace treaty was signed, the two countries began to take concrete steps to implement the multifaceted peace. Thirteen follow-up agreements were signed in all areas covered by the treaty. Since 1994 Israeli and Jordanian tourists regularly cross the border. Since October 1994 approximately 200,000 Israelis traveled to Petra and to sites throughout Jordan. Jordanian tourists visiting Israel are no longer considered a novelty; over 85,000 Jordanians have visited Israel since October 1994. In June 1995 alone, 14,600 Jordanians visited Israel. Several joint Israeli-Jordanian projects, either private or public, are being implemented. In the Eilat/Aqaba region, for example, a joint science and technology college will be built; with an anticipated initial enrollment of 1,300 students, courses will be taught in Hebrew, Arabic, and English. The showpiece project, however, will be the establishment of a joint airport in the Eilat/Aqaba region—the International Peace Airport. Once this airport is built, the dream of turning the Gulf of Aqaba region into a Jordanian-Israeli Riviera will materialize. In addition, on October 25, 1995, a comprehensive bilateral trade agreement that governs all commercial transactions between the two countries was signed as called for in the Treaty of Peace. One day earlier, an agreement to cooperate in the war against crime and drugs was signed at Beit Gavriel, adjacent to the Sea of Galilee. The agreement provided for cooperation in many areas against crime: investigations, information exchanges, operational cooperation in preventive measures and forensic and identification matters, including DNA testing, and so on. In addition, a hotline connecting police headquarters in the two countries was established.

With the signing of a formal peace treaty between Jordan and Israel cooperation between the two countries is no longer a function of tacit agreements between Israeli and Jordanian leaders. But the long-term durability of the treaty is far from certain. It now depends on several factors, including the conclusion of comprehensive peace treaties between Israel, the Palestinians, Syria, and Lebanon; and above all, upon acceptance by the people of Jordan, who have been so far reluctant to embrace a treaty with Israel.

Without the breakthrough agreement between Israel and the PLO, Jordan would not have been able to sign the treaty with Israel. The PLO legitimized the idea that a separate agreement with Israel was no longer treason as was also true when Egypt made peace with Israel. But King Hussein, as did Anwar Sadat, linked peace with Israel to immediate economic prosperity and well-being, thus generating heightened expectations that have yet to be fulfilled. Most Jordanian professional associations have banned contacts with Israel, and Israeli diplomats in Amman, like their colleagues in Cairo, feel isolated.[22] Although Jordan's economic difficulties are not related to the peace treaty, many Jordanians had hoped that peace would be a panacea to all problems. Jordan's economic malaise, however, is a result of the decline in trade relations with Iraq, Jordan's largest trading partner. Before the Gulf War, Jordanian-Iraqi trade constituted 25 percent of its total exports; most of Jordan's oil was imported from Iraq, but Jordan had to look elsewhere when the United Nations imposed the embargo against Iraq. In addition, lack of significant foreign investment in Jordan since the signing of the accord is used by the opponents of normalization with Israel as "proof" that Jordanians will not reap the benefits of peace. But, above all, as long as the Palestinian issue is not fully resolved and Israel and Syria remain in a state of war, Jordanians will be reluctant to stand behind the agreement with Israel. More and more Jordanians and Israelis are meeting face to face for the first time, however, and several Israeli and Jordanian companies have begun to explore joint business ventures. There also are some indicators that Jordan's economy will improve: tourism has increased by 30 percent since the signing of the treaty, and with the July 1995 cancellation of the boycott against Israel increased economic activity is expected. When Saddam Hussein no longer rules Iraq and the United Nations embargo is lifted, Jordan will fully renew its economic ties with Iraq.

On the political level Jordanian-Israeli ties have been strengthened. Jordan, for example, was able to cause the successful reversal of a decision by the Israeli government in May 1995 to appropriate Arab land in Jerusalem. Moreover, on April 25, 1995, the two countries sent humanitarian assistance to Bosnian refugees in Jordanian and Israeli aircraft. The two governments now also coordinate policies on several regional and international issues, including the fight against Islamic militants.

King Hussein was the first Arab leader who congratulated Benjamin Netanyahu following his May 1996 election victory. Hussein expressed confidence in Netanyahu's ability to make progress in the peace process despite the Israeli leader's renunciation of the "land for peace" formula as the basis of the Arab-Israeli-Palestinian peace process. Furthermore, in July 1996, King Hussein took it upon himself to fly to Damascus in an attempt to convince President Asad to resume negotiations with Israel, but to no avail. When Netanyahu visited Jordan on August 5, 1996, King Hussein felt comfortable enough with the newly elected Israeli leader to express his dissatisfaction with the pace of normalization with Israel. He made particular references to Israeli promises to provide Jordan with additional water and expressed dissatisfaction with the slow pace of economic cooperation with Israel. During the meeting, Netanyahu pledged to act upon Israel's commitments. Among these were shortening the period for completing a project to desalinate the Jordan River channel in order to transfer 50 million cubic meters of water annually to Jordan, recommending to the IMF that it provide funding to develop water sources, reducing bureaucratic procedures on imports from Jordan, promoting the establishment of a logistics center in Eilat, establishing an agricultural cooperation committee to develop joint agriculture projects in the Jordan Valley, opening consulates in Eilat and Aqaba to facilitate border crossings and the issuing of visas, and continuing discussions on building a natural gas terminal in Aqaba for natural gas to be imported from Qatar to Israel. In line with this pro-business attitude, Netanyahu invited two leading Israeli businessmen to accompany him to Jordan: Benny Gaon, CEO and president of Koor Industries, and Shaul Eisenberg, chairman of the Israel Corporation and of the Eisenberg Group. Koor, Israel's largest corporation, expressed an interest in investing in a number of industries in Jordan including building materials, telecommunications, food, chemicals, and consumer products. Its partner in joint ventures will be Jordan's National Insurance Institute. The Eisenberg Group sought to build a power station in Jordan.[23]

On the popular level increased contacts between Jordanians and Israelis are bound to allay suspicion and fear. Once Israel and her neighbors, the Palestinians especially, resolve their outstanding issues, Jordanian-Israeli peace could be singled out as a potential model of Arab-Israeli reconciliation and prosperity.

As a result of the Madrid peace process, Jordanian-Israeli relations were fundamentally transformed. First, the Jordanian option, which viewed Jordan as Israel's chief interlocutor regarding the Palestinian question, was abandoned as a result of Jordan's disengagement, the intifadah, and Israel's agreement with the PLO. Thus, the two countries were left to address bilateral and regional issues. Second, Jordan's strategic value for Israel has increased considerably since the Gulf War. Only a handful of Israelis still support the concept of "Jordan is Palestine." Israel's "red line" now includes Jordan as a cordon sanitaire against a possible attack from the east.

Finally, with the signing of the Israeli-Jordanian Treaty of Peace, it is possible that the relationship, unlike the Israeli-Egyptian peace, will not be cold. Many Israelis have complained that aside from diplomatic formalities and political coordination at the government-to-government level, peace with Egypt did not lead to the much-anticipated increased trade, cultural ties, two-way tourism, joint economic projects, and so on. But in the Israeli-Jordanian sphere, where the two countries are interdependent in several areas, and given their record of functional cooperation, peace could become multidimensional and meaningful. The peace process, however, could not have reached this stage without King Hussein's courage, his realization of Jordanian-Israeli overlapping interests, and, above all, his willingness to be the first Arab statesman to break the wall of rejection and hatred surrounding Israel by secretly meeting Israeli leaders as early as 1963, fourteen years before Anwar Sadat made the historic journey to Jerusalem.

In the past, Israeli-Jordanian functional cooperation did not result in formal peace. But with the signing of the 1994 treaty, such cooperation provides the foundations for a durable peace. If the Oslo accords are fully implemented and the peace process moves forward, then both sides will be able to capitalize upon their rich common experiences, which constituted sub-rosa peace, and to refashion the clandestine relationship into an open and dynamic partnership that will benefit all—Jordanians, Israelis, Palestinians, and the rest of the peoples of the Middle East.

7

Afterword

Following the signing of the Israeli-PLO accords and Israel's peace treaty with Jordan, a sense of optimism prevailed among scholars, policymakers, and ordinary citizens in the Middle East about the prospects of reaching a just and durable Arab-Israeli peace. When the first major setback occurred—the assassination of Prime Minister Yitzhak Rabin—Israeli, Palestinian, Jordanian, Egyptian, and other Arab leaders hoped that his murder would not alter the basic direction of the peace process. The election of Benjamin Netanyahu in May 1996 was viewed as a reaction to the wave of suicide attacks carried out by Hamas activists against Israeli civilians. Netanyahu declared after his election that the basic tenets of the Oslo process were going to be preserved and relations with Jordan and Egypt were to be strengthened, but progress on the Palestinian track was to be more measured and Israeli security concerns would play a major role. Three years later, by the time Netanyahu was voted out of office in May 1999, the peace process with the Palestinians was derailed and Israel's relations with Jordan were near a state of crisis.

As shown throughout this book, given the remarkable level of functional cooperation that existed between Jordan and Israel under the shadow of formal war, it was expected that formal peace between the two countries would inaugurate a new era in their relations. Decades of clandestine cooperation would lay the foundation of a "warm peace." The Treaty of Peace, signed in 1994, was aimed at establishing full normalization in numerous spheres including trade, tourism, education, transportation, water-sharing, Dead Sea resource management, and joint policing efforts against drugs and crime. Yet contrary to expectations, Jordanian-Israeli peace did not materialize in a warm peace, nor was it transformed into a model of a mutually beneficial Arab-Israeli agreement. Although the two countries have implemented several agreements, the overall tenor of the relationship has deteriorated considerably, mainly as a result of misguided Israeli policies, deceit, and lost opportunities, all of which marred the relationship during Benjamin Netanyahu's tenure as prime minister.

As he assumes the post of prime minister, Barak is confronted with a relationship with Jordan that no longer mirrors the optimism and triumph that existed when the agreement was signed; disappointment and opposition to the process of normalization with Israel are now common sentiments expressed by the overwhelming majority of Jordanians, many of whom are of Palestinian origin.

What were the policies and specific actions that soured Israeli-Jordanian relations under Netanyahu? First, the stalemate in negotiations between Israel and the Palestinians had a direct negative impact on relations with Jordan. Secondly, several actions taken by the Netanyahu government severely backfired, including the opening of the "archeological" tunnel under the Temple Mount in September 1996 and the attempt to assassinate Khalid Mishal, a leader of Hamas, in Amman in September 1997. Thirdly, the persistence of powerful Israeli interests maintaining economic hegemony over the Palestinian territories while ignoring Jordan's need to export to the West Bank and Gaza was a factor. Fourthly, because of Jordan's chronic water shortage, most Jordanians had expected that Israel would be generous in establishing an equitable water-sharing regime between the two countries. Yet, despite the May 1999 water-sharing agreement, Jordanians still feel that Israel has not lived up to the spirit and letter of their agreement, especially during the severe drought of 1998 and 1999.

As argued in the concluding chapter of this book, success of Jordanian-Israeli relations, especially on the grass-roots level, has hinged upon progress in the Israeli-Palestinian negotiations. During Netanyahu's tenure, Israeli-Palestinian negotiations have slowed down considerably. Israeli redeployment from the West Bank, as stipulated in the October 1998 Wye River Memorandum, was not implemented and the final status talks that were scheduled to be completed by May 1999 have yet to be launched in earnest. Under Netanyahu, Israel continued to expand settlements in the West Bank and moved forward with building the controversial Har Homa housing project in Jabal Abu Ghunaym in East Jerusalem in violation of the Oslo Accords. The trust that slowly emerged between Rabin and Arafat dissipated during Netanyahu's rule.

Despite the fanfare that surrounded the signing of the Wye River Memorandum in October 1998—an agreement that called for further Israeli redeployment in the West Bank, establishment of a corridor between Gaza and the West Bank, opening a Palestinian airport in Gaza, and release of Palestinian prisoners held in Israeli jails—the only part of the agreement that was implemented was the opening of the

Palestinian airport. It should be noted that the negotiations leading to the signing of the Wye Memorandum were salvaged by the late King Hussein's last minute appearance and strong emotional appeal. Hussein, who flew to Maryland from the Mayo Clinic in Minnesota, where he was treated for cancer, used his moral authority to make a last-ditch effort to press the parties to sign an agreement. Yet Netanyahu's government was unable to implement the agreement because of pressure from those opposed to any further Israeli redeployment in the West Bank. The Knesset then passed a resolution calling for new elections that resulted in Barak's overwhelming victory.

Resolution of the Palestinian issue has been of utmost importance to Jordan. Given Jordan's large Palestinian population, history of Hashemite-Palestinian relations, and Jordan's interest in the West Bank, particularly in Arab-Jerusalem, these interests have meant that developments in the bilateral Israeli-Jordanian relationship are inextricably linked to the process and outcome of the Israeli-Palestinian negotiation track. Seen from Amman, as long as Israel and the PLO remained in a state of war, Jordanian-Israeli relations had to be confined to the sub rosa level. Once Israel and the PLO had recognized each other publicly, Jordan followed suit and signed a treaty with Israel. Subsequently, the Jordanian leadership hoped that successes in the Israeli-Palestinian track would help validate its new open relationship with Israel. However, each additional crisis and delay in the implementation of the Oslo Accords led to the opposite effect: more Jordanians joining the ranks of those determined to discredit the peace process with the Jewish state.

When the late King Hussein and late Prime Minister Yitzhak Rabin inked the Israeli-Jordanian Treaty of Peace on October 26, 1994, expectations ran high that the relationship between the two countries would become a shining example of Arab-Israeli partnership. Five years later, when King Abdullah II was installed as the new ruler following the death of his father, many Western media commentators speculated as to whether Jordan would continue to adhere to its peace treaty with Israel given the unpopularity of the peace agreement among Jordanians. Opposition to normalization with Israel in Jordan is widespread. It is not confined to opposition Islamist groups. Almost all professional associations, chambers of commerce, and ordinary Jordanians share this sentiment. Those who reject normalization cite Israel's continued harsh practices against the Palestinians and lack of implementation of the various agreements signed with Jordan and the Palestinians, respectively. According to a public opinion poll conducted by *Jordan Times* in 1998, Israel is still regarded by 80 percent of Jordanians as an enemy.[1] Lack of concrete "peace dividends" has led most Jordanians to point to unfulfilled promises made by King Hussein about improving their daily lives that would follow the signing of the treaty. Another survey conducted in 1997 by the Nablus-based Center for Palestine Research and Studies and the University of Jordan's Center for Strategic Studies showed that 59 percent of Jordanians were not satisfied with the expected outcome of the Israeli-Palestinian negotiations.[2]

As noted by Laurie Brand, King Hussein paradoxically responded to the growing popular opposition to the peace with Israel by reversing the process of political liberalization that began in Jordan in 1989. The king showed little tolerance for criticism of his relations with Israel. Brand cites the dismissal of Prime Minister Abd al-Karim Kabariti who strongly objected to the king's visit to Israel in March 1997. After seven Israeli school girls were killed by a Jordanian soldier while visiting a peace park along the Israeli-Jordanian border, King Hussein cut short a trip to Spain and Washington and came to express his personal condolences to the bereaved families. The king's gesture moved the entire Israeli nation. Yet, Kabariti argued against Hussein's visit, which he regarded as humiliating. The disagreement with the king cost the prime minister his job.[3] As an example of the anti-Israeli mood that has prevailed in Jordan in the past few years, many Jordanians regard Ahmed Daqamseh, the 26-year-old soldier who murdered the Israeli children, as a hero.

When Benjamin Netanyahu won the May 1996 elections, King Hussein was the only Arab leader who welcomed the newly elected Israeli leader by vouching for Netanyahu, whom Hussein trusted to continue the peace process. Soon after, Netanyahu's September 1996 decision to open an "archaeological" tunnel under the Temple Mount led to large scale Palestinian demonstrations and to fighting between the Israeli military and Palestinian police. Hussein reacted with considerable anger, saying that he viewed the Israeli action as an attempt to undermine the status quo in Jerusalem, as a disregard of Israel's pledge to safeguard the Muslim holy places in the city, and as a violation of the Israeli-Jordanian treaty. After all, Jordan's "historic role" in Jerusalem was recognized in both the July 1994 Washington Declaration and in the peace treaty. As an example of Israeli duplicity, Hussein pointed to the visit in Amman of Dore Gold, the Israeli premier's advisor, who met Hussein one day before the opening of the tunnel without even providing the monarch with advanced notice of the Israeli plan.

The violent explosion in the territories resulting from the opening of the tunnel led to a hastily arranged summit by President Bill Clinton in October 1996 and attended by Yasser Arafat, Netanyahu, and Hussein. During their meeting, the Jordanian monarch blasted the Israeli leader for his ill-conceived decision, growing intransigence, and lack of consideration of Jordanian interests. King Hussein felt that the actions of the Israeli government were jeopardizing the very delicate balance the Hashemites have maintained with the Palestinians inside and outside the monarchy, and embarrassing Hussein who had placed such blind faith in the relationship with the Israelis.

A year later, on September 25, 1997, Israeli Mossad agents bungled an assassination attempt against Khalid Mishal, one of the leaders of Hamas—the Palestinian Islamist organization responsible for numerous suicide attacks inside Israel. This episode almost led to the breaking of diplomatic relations between Jordan and Israel. It was the worst crisis between the two countries since their treaty was signed. King Hussein felt personally betrayed and humiliated by the Mossad's failed operation on Jordanian soil. Israel's attempt to inflict a blow to Hamas in fact backfired; not only did King Hussein force Israel to release Sheik Ahmed Yassin, the spiritual leader of the Palestinian Islamist organization, from jail but the little credibility Israel enjoyed in Amman clearly vanished as a result of this operation.

This event convinced even those Jordanians who were not vocal against normalization that Israel was behaving as a foe rather than a friend. Popular anger swept throughout the kingdom, and Hussein was deeply offended by what he considered to be Netanyahu's callous act. The Mossad operation made the Jordanian king vulnerable, especially given the existing domestic opposition to relations with Israel. Soon thereafter, Jordanians began referring to the peace with Israel as the "King's peace." Indeed, the Mishal affair constituted a severe crisis in the relationship, and it reinforced the perception that Netanyahu's government was trying to actively undermine the Jordanian government.

The third reason underlying the difficulties between the two countries is rooted in Israeli economic interests in the Palestinian territories. As noted in chapter 2, very shortly after the occupation of the West Bank in 1967, Israeli officials opted to turn the newly-occupied territories into a satellite of the Israeli economy—a source of cheap manual labor and a captive market for Israeli goods and services. While the number of Palestinians who work in Israel has decreased to approximately 35,000 from over 150,000 in the mid 1980s, Israel has continued to maintain an economic iron grip over the territories despite the redeployment of its troops from several areas in the West Bank and Gaza. In fact, Israeli economic interests have superseded any ideological division in Israeli society over the fate of the occupied territories. Although Israel and the PLO have signed a number of agreements, including the May 1994 trade and economic protocol, Israel still controls imports and exports to and from the West Bank and Gaza. Thus, Israel's economic hegemony over the Palestinians has hurt not only the Palestinians but also Jordan, which has been keenly interested exporting to the territories, especially in light of the United Nations embargo on Iraq which has deprived Jordan of its most important trading partner.

King Abdullah II has inherited a country with a $6.8 billion foreign debt, a colossal public sector (one out of every seven Jordanians is employed by the government) and an unemployment rate of nearly thirty percent. While Jordan's economic malaise is attributed to regional developments and domestic economic policies, Jordanians, nonetheless, had expected that the peace treaty would yield some "peace dividends." Jordanian officials point to Israel's refusal to allow Jordan to trade freely with the Palestinian territories as a clear example of Israeli protectionism intended to safeguard selfish Israeli economic interests at Jordan's expense. The discrepancy between Israeli and Jordanian annual exports to the territories is glaring: Israel exports $1.8 billion annually while Jordan exports merely $22 million, almost 100 times less than Israel's trade with the territories. The West Bank and Gaza are the second largest markets for Israeli goods after the United States.

Despite Israeli rhetoric about its close relationship with the Hashemites and the importance it attaches to its peace with Jordan, the Israeli government under Prime Minister Benjamin Netanyahu did very little to translate its rhetoric into the deeds that would benefit Jordan and restore a modicum of tranquility to the relationship. Given its control over the external boundaries of the Palestinian territories, Israel exercised a veto power on Jordanian exports by citing various security concerns. For example, Israel had required until recently that Jordanian trucks transporting goods into the West Bank use "back to back" systems requiring unloading and loading each truck to inspect its content for security reasons, thus making exports very costly, inefficient, and time consuming. In an attempt to address Israeli security requirements, Jordan had proposed a "door to door" delivery system that would expedite deliveries while safeguarding Israeli security. Jordan officials have characterized Israeli actions as protectionist rather than stemming from genuine security concerns. Even Stuart Eizenstat, Deputy Secretary of Commerce (considered one of Israel's staunchest supporters in the Clinton administration) called on Israel to act with a "sense of urgency" to address these "unacceptably low" Jordanian export levels.[4]

In light of Jordan's ailing economy and as a gesture of support towards the new monarch, the United States has granted Jordan an additional $300 million beyond the $522 million allocated as aid for 1999 and 2000. The United Arab Emirates has also transferred funds to Jordan's Central Bank in support of the dinar. Additional financial support is expected from the International Monetary Fund and the

World Bank.[5] Moreover, Abdullah has appealed to the Paris Club to reschedule even more of the kingdom's $6.8 billion debt.

Jordanians are also fearful of Israeli economic hegemony, a perception fueled by the significant gap between Israel's annual $100 billion economy per year and Jordan's minuscule $8 billion economy. When 120 Israeli firms were planning to showcase their products in a major trade fair in Amman in December 1996, members of the Islamic Action Front (IAF) and several business associations including the Amman Chamber of Commerce, the Jordanian Chamber of Industry, and the powerful Jordanian Businessmen Association (JBA) boycotted the fair. Despite the vocal opposition to the fair, the Jordanian government allowed the Israeli companies to present their products, but very few agreements resulted from the trade show.

Another bone of contention has been the establishment of a water-sharing regime. As a result of its chronic water shortage, Jordan has expected that Israel would be generous in this regard. Jordan expected Israel to transfer 150 million cubic meters as agreed to in the peace treaty. Yitzhak Rabin had originally hoped that at least 50 MC/M would come from dams built on the Yarmuk River, but Syrian opposition prevented their construction.[6] Instead, Israel has yielded 60 MC/M from the Lake of Galilee, and an additional 20 MC/M was transferred from the Yarmuk River. Jordan has contended that Israel was obligated to supply the water, while Israel has argued that it is only obligated to approach international donors to fund the project with the Hashemite Kingdom. Finally, the first concrete water project between the two countries was launched in October 1998 when the cornerstone was laid for a new dam to retain the Yarmouk's floodwaters in the Adasiya area in Jordan. In addition, the two countries have prepared a proposal submitted to the European Union to fund a wastewater treatment plant in the Jordan Valley and a desalination and conveyance system to provide Jordan with the much-need additional 50 MC/M of drinking water annually.[7] Despite a May 1998 agreement negotiated by Ariel Sharon, Israel's Minister of Agriculture, Jordan still feels that the question of water sharing is far from resolved. For example, when Netanyahu paid a visit to King Abdullah II in late February 1999, the question of water was one of the top issues in the agenda between the two leaders. Netanyahu maintained that Israel was unable to transfer 20 MC/M as Jordan has expected because of water shortages that resulted from a drought in the winter of 1998–99. In an interview with *Al-Ahram,* Jordan's Prime Minister Abdul-Ra'ouf Rawabdeh said "this is an official agreement signed between the two parties and we insist on the implementation of the agreement as it is. We will continue to demand our rights until we get them."[8] The *Al-Ahram* article has also referred to Jordanian and Israeli water experts who believe that Israel must cut its subsidies to agriculture, which uses 60 percent of the water consumption, but contributes only 2 percent to the gross domestic product. Finally, the dispute was solved when Israel agreed in May 1999 to deliver its promised water by October 1999.

The questions of water shortage and collaboration involving the governments of Israel, Jordan, and the Palestinian National Authority (TNA) to recycle waste water, to develop efficient irrigation systems, and to use the brackish water for industry and agriculture were addressed in recent study published by the National Academy of Sciences. The report's conclusions, resulting from a collaboration of Jordanian, Israeli, Palestinian, Canadian, and American scholars, portray a region plagued by chronic water shortage given the increased water use, population growth, and arid climate.[9]

Despite the difficulties of the last three years, the two countries have continued to pursue common interests. For example, *Jane's Foreign Report* contends that one of King Abdullah II's first directives was to upgrade the strategic cooperation with Israel, a cooperation that remained frozen since the September 1997 Mishal affair. The Mossad's Amman station, reported to have been one of Israel's most active espionage centers anywhere in the world, was shut down as a result of the episode. The new monarch has agreed to reopen the station, but Israel had to sign a written promise that the Khalid Mishal affair will not be repeated.[10] Other Israeli-Jordanian projects are moving forward including feasibility studies of a proposed new joint airport in Aqaba/Eilat.

Despite the low level of bilateral trade between the two countries (approximately $42 million in 1998), there are a few areas where the peace treaty has begun to yield dividends. On November 16, 1997, the Israeli and Jordanian ministers of trade and industry signed an agreement to establish a "Qualified Industrial Zone" in Irbid in northern Jordan that would allow manufacturers to ship goods duty free to the United States. The agreement established under the framework of the 1985 United States-Israel Free-Trade Area Agreement in effect enables Jordanian businesses to take advantage of the terms of the US-Israeli framework agreement. Twenty Israeli-Jordanian joint ventures, primarily in textiles, were established in Irbid to take advantage of Jordan's low wages (about 10 percent of Israeli wages). Approximately 3,000 Jordanians are employed by Jordan-based Century Investment Group (CIG) and are located in Irbid's Prince Hassan Industrial Estates. The zone also includes an Israeli customs station at the Sheikh Hussein Bridge border crossing.

The move of several Israeli textile and apparel manufacturers to Jordan resulted in large-scale demonstrations against the peace with

Jordan by those Israelis who lost their jobs as a result of moving their plant. Jordanians who oppose the Qualified Industrial Zone argue that Jordan benefits very little from the arrangement since Israel takes full advantage of Jordanian cheap labor and does little to help Jordan to advance its economy. However, notwithstanding the opposition from both Israelis and Jordanians, it is expected that new Israeli-Jordanian joint ventures will be formed in the fields of plastics, metallurgy and foodstuffs. New areas in Jordan are expected to also be considered part of the "Qualified Industrial Zone" and become eligible to export duty free to the United States. These include Mafraq and an area in the Jordan Valley south of the Sheikh Hussein border crossing point extending to the Israeli side of the border. The new expansion is part of the Jordan Gateway Projects Company, a Jordanian-Dutch joint venture.[11] While only a handful of Jordanian companies have invested in Irbid, multinational companies have shown serious interest in the zone because of the low wages and the opportunity to export duty free to the United States. According to Samir Mansour, commercial attaché at the Jordanian Embassy in Washington, D.C., there are thirty-six companies in Irbid, and new regions in Jordan, including Jordanian, Israeli, Chinese, American, Jordanian-Indian.[12]

An examination of the current state of Jordanian-Israeli relations indicates that the cascade of crises which occurred under Netanyahu has demonstrated the fragility of the relationship between the two countries. Full normalization cannot be attained—even if specific bilateral cooperative ventures are successful—unless the plurality of Jordanians are convinced that Israel is genuinely committed to a process of reconciliation with all of its neighbors. The signing of treaties is not a sufficient condition for true peace. Israel, in particular, has yet to demonstrate in concrete terms to the Jordanians and Palestinians that it is committed to opening a new chapter in their relations and in forging a real partnership for peace.

The election of Ehud Barak clearly demonstrates that despite serious setbacks under Netanyahu, most Israeli would like to resuscitate the peace process. Barak and Abdullah, both former military officers, seem to have found a common language, reminiscent of the camaraderie that existed between Hussein and Rabin. However, short of a dramatic breakthrough on the Palestinian issue, Jordanians will not warm up to Israel, even under Barak. It seems that Barak is a territorialist who favors retaining a large portion of the West Bank. He will not support a fully sovereign Palestinian state. As demonstrated throughout this work, despite the extensive overlapping of Jordanian and Israeli interests, as long as the Palestinian problem is not completely resolved, a genuine Arab-Israeli reconciliation will remain elusive.

Notes

1. Introduction

1. Corroboration of this meeting was supplied by Eli Zeira, director of Israel's military intelligence in 1973, who presented his version of the events leading to the Yom Kippur "surprise" in his book, *Milohemet Yom Kippur: mittos mul metziuut* (The Yom Kippur war: Myth versus reality) (Tel Aviv: Yediot Aharonot Books, 1993), 95–97.

2. *Yediot Aharonot,* Mar. 27, 1992, 12.

3. On Jordanian-Israeli relations see Avi Shlaim, *Collusion Across the Jordan: King Abdullah, the Zionist Movement, and the Partition of Palestine* (New York: Columbia Univ. Press, 1988); Uri Bar-Joseph, *The Best of Enemies: Israel and Transjordan in the War of 1948* (London: Frank Cass, 1987); Simha Flapan, *The Birth of Israel: Myths and Realities* (New York: Pantheon Books, 1987); Aaron S. Klieman, *Du kiyum le-lo Shalom: Yisrael, Yarden veha-Palestinaim* (Unpeaceful coexistence: Israel, Jordan, and the Palestinians) (Tel Aviv: Ma'ariv Books, 1986); idem, *Israel, Jordan, and Palestine: The Search for a Durable Peace.* Washington Papers, no. 83 (Washington, D.C.: Center for Strategic and International Studies, Georgetown Univ., 1981); idem, *Statecraft in the Dark: Israel's Practice of Quiet Diplomacy* (Boulder, Colo.: Westview Press, 1988); Yossi Melman and Dan Raviv, *Shutafut oyenet: ha-ksharim ha-sodiyim ben Yisrael ve-Yarden* (A hostile partnership: The secret relations between Israel and Jordan) (Tel Aviv: Meitam, Yediot Aharonot Books, 1987); Yossi Melman and Dan Raviv, *Behind the Uprising: Israelis, Jordanians and the Palestinians* (New York: Greenwood Press, 1989); Adam Garfinkle, *Israel and Jordan in the Shadow of War* (New York: St. Martin's Press, 1992). Ian Lustick, *Israel and Jordan: The Implications of an Adversarial Partnership,* Policy Papers in International Affairs, no. 6 (Berkeley: Institute of International Studies, Univ. of California, 1978). Dan Schueftan, *Optzia Yardenit: ha-Yishuv ha-Yehudi u-Medinat Yisrael el mul ha-mishtar ha-Hashemi veha-tnua ha-leumit ha-Palestinit* (A Jordanian option: The "Yishuv" and the State of Israel vis-à-vis the Hashemite regime and the Palestine National Movement) (Yad Tabenkin, Israel: ha-Kibbutz ha-Meuchad, 1987). Martin Sicker, *Between Hashemites and Zionists: The Struggle for Palestine. 1908–1988* (New York: Holmes and Meier, 1989). Moshe Zak, "Israeli-Jordanian Relations," *Washington Quarterly* 8, no. 1 (Winter 1985); Mary C. Wilson, *King Abdullah, Britain and the Making of Jordan* (Cambridge: Cambridge Univ. Press, 1987); and Moshe Zak, "A Survey of Israel's Contacts with Jordan," in *Israel in the Middle East,* ed. Itamar Rabinovich and Jehuda Reinharz (New York: Oxford Univ. Press, 1984), 337–42.

4. Shlaim, *Collusion Across the Jordan.*

5. Melman, *Shutafut oyenet,* 56–58.

6. Klieman, *Statecraft in the Dark,* 99–101. One of the most noted Israeli leaders who met Hussein several times, Abba Eban, recounts these meetings in *Personal Witness: Israel Through My Eyes* (New York: C. P. Putnam's Sons, 1992), 492–99.

7. Kleiman, *Statecraft in the Dark,* 95.

8. Ibid., 106.

9. The term *functional cooperation* was first used in the Israeli-Jordanian context by Klieman, *Israel, Jordan, Palestine,* 41–42.

10. John Eastby, *Functionalism and Interdependence: The Credibility of Institutions, Policies, and Leadership,* vol. 3 (Lanham, Md.: Univ. Press of America, 1985), 1–2.

11. David Mitrany, *The Functional Theory of Politics* (New York: St. Martin's Press, 1976), 253–54. See, also, idem, *A Working Peace System* (Chicago: Quadrangle Books, 1966; A. J. R. Groom and Paul Taylor, *Functionalism: Theory and Practice in International Politics* (New York: Crane, Russak, 1975).

12. Klieman, *Statecraft in the Dark,* 108.

13. For different taxonomies concerning ideological divisions inside Israel see, for example, Yehoshafat Harkabi, *Israel's Fateful Hour* (New York: Harper and Row, 1988); Rael Jean Isaac, *Party and Politics in Israel: Three Visions of a Jewish State* (New York: Longman, 1981); Rael Jean Isaac, *Israel Divided: Ideological Politics in the Jewish State* (Baltimore, Md.: Johns Hopkins Univ. Press, 1976).

14. Michael Brecher, *The Foreign Policy System of Israel: Setting, Images, Process* (New Haven, Conn.: Yale Univ. Press, 1972), 357.

15. *Ha'aretz,* Sep. 5, 1967.

16. Shabtai Teveth, *Moshe Dayan: The Soldier, the Man, the Legend* (Boston: Houghton Mifflin, 1973), 350–51; see, also, Isaac, *Israel Divided,* 115–37.

17. Isaac, *Israel Divided.* See, also, Yehudit Auerbach and Hemda Ben-Yehuda, "Attitudes Towards an Existence Conflict: Begin and Dayan on the Palestinian Issue," *International Interactions* 13, no. 4 (Sep. 1987): 339.

18. *Ma'ariv,* Apr. 25, 1993.

19. *New York Times,* Dec. 25, 1984, cited by Aaron S. Klieman, "Defense and Foreign Affairs: Holding the Line," in *Israel Faces the Future,* ed. Bernard Reich and Gershon R. Kieval (New York: Praeger, 1986), 182.

20. On Israeli and Jordanian positions regarding cooperation in the West Bank see, for example, Valerie Yorke, *Domestic Politics and Regional Security: Jordan, Syria and Israel* (Aldershot, England: Gower Publishing, 1988), 317–19.

21. For an excellent discussion of the Allon Plan see Yerucham Cohen, *Tochnit Allon* (The Allon Plan) (Tel Aviv: ha-Kibbutz ha-Meuchad, 1983), 67.

22. See Efraim Inbar, *War and Peace in Israeli Politics: Labor Party Positions on National Security* (Boulder, Colo.: Lynne Rienner Publishers, 1991), 88.

23. Melman, *Shutafut oyenet,* 71.

24. See Efraim Inbar, *War and Peace,* 88.

25. Yigal Allon, "Israel: The Case for Defensible Borders," *Foreign Affairs* 55, no. 1 (Oct. 1976): 44; see, also, Yosef Goell, "A Man and His Plan," *Jerusalem Post,* July 28, 1976.

26. Michael Brecher, *Foreign Policy System of Israel,* 366.

27. Ibid.

28. Sheila Ryan, "Plans to Regularize the Occupation," in Naseer H. Aruri, ed., *Occupation: Israel Over Palestine* (Belmont, Mass.: Association of Arab-American University Graduates, 1983), 346.

29. Yigal Allon, *Kelim shluvim* (Communicating vessels) (Tel Aviv: ha-Kibbutz ha-Me'uchad, 1980), 158.

30. Ibid., 162.

31. Ha'aretz, Sep. 7, 1967.

32. Melman, *Shutafut oyenet,* 68.

33. See Arye Naor, *Ktovet al ha-kir* (Writing on the wall), Yediot Aharonot ed. (Tel Aviv: Edanim Publishers, 1988), 40–41.

34. Isaac, *Party and Politics in Israel,* 157; see, also, Steve Heydemann, ed., *The Begin Era: Issues in Contemporary Israel* (Boulder, Colo.: Westview Press, 1984); Myron J. Aronoff, *Israeli Visions and Divisions: Cultural Change and Political Conflict* (New Brunswick, N.J.: Transaction Publishers, 1989); Amos Perlmutter, *The Life and Times of Menachem Begin* (Garden City, N.Y.: Doubleday, 1987); Eitan Haber, *Menachem Begin: The Man, and the Legend* (New York: Dell, 1979).

35. The Likud party was formed when the Herut and Liberal parties formally united, disbanding Gahal.

36. Yitzhak Shamir, "Israel's Role in a Changing Middle East," *Foreign Affairs* 60, no. 4 (Spring 1982): 791.

37. Garfinkle, *Israel and Jordan,* 171–72.

38. Benjamin Netanyahu, *A Place among the Nations: Israel and the World* (New York: Bantam, 1993), 344.

39. Ibid., 351–52.

40. Ibid., 353.

41. "Peace Monitor," *Journal of Palestine Studies* 95, no. 3 (Spring 1995): 117.

42. Shimon Peres, one of the key architects of the Israeli-PLO accord, has always been ambiguous about the extent of Israeli withdrawal. This difference notwithstanding, Peres now leads the reconciliationist camp.

43. See, also, Sicker, *Between Hashemites and Zionists,* 149–50.

44. Lilly Weissbrod, "Binationalism Reconsidered: Ideological Continuity and Change in the Begin Era," in *The Emergence of Binational Israel: The Second Republic in the Making?* ed. Ilan Peleg and Ofira Seliktar (Boulder, Colo.: Westview Press, 1989), 41–43.

45. Brecher, *Foreign Policy System of Israel,* 353–54.

46. Harkabi, *Israel's Fateful Hour,* 209.

47. Ibid., 43.

48. Don Peretz, "Israeli Policies Toward the Arab States and the Palestinians since 1967," in *The Arab-Israeli Conflict: Two Decades of Change* ed. Yehuda Lukacs and Abdalla M. Battah (Boulder, Colo.: Westview Press, 1988), 27.

49. James Lunt, *Hussein of Jordan: Searching for a Just and Lasting Peace* (New York: William Morrow, 1989), xxxiv–xxxv.

50. See, also, Klieman, *Israel, Jordan, Palestine,* 19–21.

51. Yorke, *Domestic Politics and Regional Security,* 33–35.

52. During the 1989 food riots in Jordan, the East Bank Palestinian population remained inactive. In December 1989, however, in commemoration of the uprising's second anniversary, numerous demonstrations led by Palestinians erupted in the East Bank.

53. Ali E. Hillal Dessouki and Karen Aboul Kheir, "The Politics of Vulnerability and Survival: The Foreign Policy of Jordan," in *The Foreign Policies of the Arab States,* ed. Bahgat Korany and Ali E. Hillal Dessouki, 2d ed. (Boulder, Colo.: Westview Press, 1991), 233.

54. Emile Sahliyeh, "Jordan and the Palestinians," in *The Middle East: Ten Years after Camp David,* ed. William B. Quandt (Washington, D.C.: Brookings Institution, 1988), 282–83.

55. For an overview of Jordanian interests, see King Hussein, "The Jordanian-Palestinian Peace Initiative: Mutual Recognition and Territory for Peace," *Journal of Palestine Studies* 14, no. 4 (Summer 1985): 15–22; El Hassan Bin Talal, "Jordan's Quest for Peace," *Foreign Affairs* 60, no. 4 (Spring 1982): 802–13.

56. Aaron D. Miller, "Changing Arab Attitudes Toward Israel," *Orbis* 32, no. 1 (Winter 1988): 74.

57. King Hussein told Prime Minister Yitzhak Shamir during their secret meeting in London in the summer of 1987 that he had held more than eight hundred hours of meetings with Israeli leaders; *Yediot Aharonot,* Feb. 4, 1994, weekend suppl., 4.

58. Adnan Abu Odeh, "Jordan and the Middle East Crisis," *AEI Foreign Policy and Defense Review* 3, no. 1 (1981): 12–13.

59. Hussein, "Jordanian-Palestinian Peace Initiative," 17.

60. *New York Times,* June 27, 1992, 1.

2. The Open Bridges Policy

1. Shlomo Avramovich, "The Jordan Bridges: There Is No Intifadah There," *Yediot Aharonot,* weekend suppl., Apr. 21, 1989.

2. For the best account available on the origins of the policy see Shabtai Teveth, *The Cursed Blessing: The Story of Israel's Occupation of the West Bank* (New York: Random House, 1970), 138–51. See, also, Shlomo Gazit, *ha-Makel veha-gezer: ha-mimshal ha-Yisraeli bi-Yehuda ve-Shomron* (The stick and the carrot: Israeli administration in Judea and Samaria) (Tel Aviv: Zmora, Bitan Publication, 1985), 204–22.

3. Gazit, *Hamakel veha-gezer,* 213–14.

4. See Moshe Dayan, *Mapa hadasha: yehasim aherim* (A new map: Different relations) (Tel Aviv: Ma'ariv Books, 1969). See, also, Natan Yanay, *Moshe Dayan: al tahalich ha-shalom ve-atida shel Yisrael* (Moshe Dayan: On the peace process and the future of Israel) (Tel Aviv: Ministry of Defense Publishing House, 1988), 8.

5. Teveth, *Cursed Blessing,* 32.

6. Dayan, *Mapa hadasha,* 173.

7. Samuel Sandler and Hillel Frisch, *Israel, the Palestinians and the West Bank* (Lexington, Mass.: Lexington Books, 1984), 59.

8. Gazit, *ha-Makel veha-gezer,* 205–8. See, also, Zvi Elpeleg, "West Bank Story," *Middle East Review* 13, no. 4 (Summer 1986): 8; Jerry Cheslow, "Open Bridges: The Oversight that Became Policy," *IDF Journal* 4, no. 1 (Winter 1987): 17–25.

9. Geoffrey Aronson, "Israel Trade Thrives Despite Arab League Boycott," *MidEast Markets,* June 17, 1991, 7.

10. "A Discussion," in *Israel and the Palestinians,* ed. Shlomo Avineri (New York: St. Martin's Press, 1971), 122–23.

11. Don Peretz, *The West Bank: History, Politics, Society and Economy* (Boulder, Colo.: Westview Press, 1986), 81.

12. State of Israel, Ministry of Defense, *Shalosh shnot mimshal tzva'i, 1967–1970* (Three years of military administration, 1967–1970) (Tel Aviv: Ministry of Defense Publishing House, 1971), 4–6.

13. Peretz, *West Bank,* 82.

14. Ibid., 59.

15. Meron Benvenisti, *1987 Report: Demographic, Economic, Legal, Social, and Political Developments in the West Bank* (Boulder, Colo.: Westview Press, 1987), 55–56.

16. Eram Hyatt et al., "Peace Now Settlement Watch," *New Outlook,* Mar./Apr. 1992, 16.

17. Ibid.

18. Raja Shehadeh, *Occupier's Law: Israel and the West Bank,* rev. ed. (Washington, D.C.: Institute of Palestine Studies, 1988), 6–7.

19. For the resolutions of the Amman summit see Yehuda Lukacs, ed., *The Israeli-Palestinian Conflict: A Documentary Record* (Cambridge: Cambridge Univ. Press, 1992), 517–18.

20. Larry L. Fabian, "Prologue: The Political Setting," in *Benefits and Burdens: A Report on the West Bank and Gaza Strip Economies since 1967,* ed. Brian Van Arkadie (Washington, D.C.: Carnegie Endowment for International Peace, 1977), 12.

21. Gazit, *Ha-Makel veha-gezer,* 94–95.

22. State of Israel, Prime Minister's Office, Economic Planning Authority, *ha-Gada ha-Ma'aravit: skira klalit* (The West Bank: A general overview) (Jerusalem: 1967).

23. Ibid., "Introduction."

24. Michael Bruno et al., "Summary of Recommendations for a Short-Term Economic Policy in the Administered Territories," Aug. 28, 1967. Unpublished paper.

25. Ibid., 1–2, 7.

26. Gazit, *ha-Makel veha-gezer*, 246.

27. Avraham Cohen, *Kalkalat ha-shtachim: ha-Gada ha-Ma'aravit ve-Retzuat Aza, 1922–1980* (The economy of the territories: The West Bank and the Gaza Strip, 1922–1980) (Givat Haviva, Israel: Institute of Arab Studies, 1987), 163.

28. Fawzi A. Gharaibeh, *The Economies of the West Bank and Gaza Strip* (Boulder, Colo.: Westview Press, 1985), 3–4. See, also, Vivian A. Bull, *The West Bank: Is It Viable?* (Lexington, Mass.: Lexington Books, 1975); Adel Samara, *The Political Economy of the West Bank, 1967–1987* (London: Khamsin, 1988); Eliyahu Kanovsky, *The Economic Impact of the Six-Day War: Israel, the Occupied Territories, Egypt, Jordan* (New York: Praeger, 1970).

29. State of Israel, Central Bureau of Statistics, *The National Accounts of Judea, Samaria, and Gaza Area, 1967–1986,* special ser. no. 818 (Jerusalem: Central Bureau of Statistics, 1988), 16.

30. The World Bank, *Developing the Occupied Territories: An Investment in Peace,* vol. 1, *Overview* (Washington, D.C.: World Bank, 1993), 4.

31. Ibid., vol. 2: *Economy,* 11, 14.

32. A similar pattern exists with the Gaza population. Israel, Central Bureau of Statistics, *National Accounts,* 131, 151.

33. World Bank, *Developing the Occupied Territories,* vol. 1, *Overview,* 5.

34. Isabel Kershner, "The People Behind Politics," *Jerusalem Report,* May 5, 1994, 24.

35. See, for example, Kanovsky, *Economic Impact,* 391–97.

36. Ibid.

37. *The Europa Yearbook, 1989* (London: Europa Publications, 1989), 1502.

38. Fouad Hamadi Basayso, "The Economic Implications of the Open Bridges Policy," *Shu'un Filistiniyya* 2 (1972). For a study of the Jordanian economy, see Eliyahu Kanovsky, *The Economy of Jordan: Implications for Peace in the Middle East* (Tel Aviv: Univ. Publishing Project, 1976).

39. Kanovsky, "The Economic Aftermath of the Six-Day War, II," *Middle East Journal* 22, no. 3 (Summer 1968): 293.

40. Benvenisti, *West Bank Handbook: A Political Lexicon* (Jerusalem: Jerusalem Post, 1986), 96.

41. Gharaibeh, *Economies of the West Bank and Gaza,* 107.

42. Ibid., 113.

43. David Kahan, *Agriculture and Water Resources in the West Bank and Gaza (1967–1987)* (Jerusalem: West Bank Data Project, 1987), 71.

44. Gharaibeh, *Economies,* 112.

45. State of Israel, Ministry of Defense, *An Eighteen-Year Survey of Judea, Samaria and the Gaza District (1967–1985)* (Tel Aviv: Ministry of Defense Publishing House, 1986), vii.

46. Sandler and Frisch, *Israel,* 27–42.

47. Arie Bergman, *Economic Growth in the Administered Territories, 1968–1973* (Jerusalem: Bank of Israel, Research Department, 1974), 85.

48. Avramovich, *Yediot Aharonot,* Apr. 21, 1989.

49. Ibid.

50. Ken Schachter, "Trade with Jordan is Booming," *Jerusalem Post,* Feb. 2, 1988.

51. *Ma'ariv,* Aug. 7, 1974, cited in Kanovsky, *Economy of Jordan,* 140.

52. Personal interview with David Gefen, chief supervisor of Israeli agricultural activities in the West Bank for nineteen years, Imanuel, Israel, Aug. 19, 1988; personal interview with Said Can'an, prominent Nablus businessman, Nablus, West Bank, Aug. 15, 1988.

53. Hillary Wolpert Silver, Simcha Bahiri, and Ronen Sacher, *The Economy of Jordan and Possibilities for Economic Cooperation Between Israel and Jordan: An Overview* (Tel Aviv: Armand Hammer Fund for Economic Cooperation in the Middle East, Tel Aviv Univ., 1989), 19.

54. *Israel Information Service* (on-line), "Israeli and Jordanian Trade Ministers to Sign Trade Agreement," Oct. 24, 1995. Available by e-mail: Gopher israel-info.gov.il.

55. Residents of the territories can also leave Israel via the Ben Gurion Airport or the Haifa Port.

56. *Yediot Aharonot,* July 7, 1995, 5.

57. *Jerusalem Post,* Oct. 14, 1982.

58. Ibid.

59. *Ha'aretz,* July 5, 1988.

60. Benvenisti, *West Bank Handbook,* 161.

61. Ibid.

62. Ibid.

63. Ibid.

64. Calev Ben-David, "The Haj: To Mecca and Back," *Jerusalem Post,* Sep. 4, 1986.

65. *Jerusalem Post,* Nov. 13, 1977.

66. United Nations Conference on Trade and Development (hereafter cited as UNCTAD), *The Palestinian Financial Sector under Israeli Occupation* UNCTAD/ST/SEU 3, 1987, 140.

67. Meron Benvenisti, *U.S. Government–Funded Projects in the West Bank and Gaza, 1977–1983* (Jerusalem: West Bank Data Project, 1984).

68. UNCTAD, *Palestinian Financial Sector,* 142.

69. Zvi Barel, "Holy Dinars," *Ha'aretz,* Oct. 20, 1982.

70. Ibid.

71. UNCTAD, *Palestinian Financial Sector,* 76; Lawrence Harris, "Finance and Money with Undeveloped Banking," paper presented at the symposium, "Economic Development under Prolonged Occupation: West Bank and Gaza," Oxford, Jan. 1986, 7–14.

72. Antoine S. Mansour, "Monetary Dualism: The Case of the West Bank under Occupation," *Journal of Palestine Studies* 11, no. 3 (Spring 1982): 111. The Jordanian dinar, however, was devalued considerably in 1988–89.

73. Harris, "Finance and Money," 8.

74. UNCTAD, *Palestinian Financial Sector,* 78.

75. Ibid., 79.

76. Harris, "Finance and Money," 4.

77. UNCTAD, *Palestinian Financial Sector,* 145.

78. Ibid., 144.

79. Ibid.

80. Gharaibeh, *Economies,* 121.

81. Moshe Drori, "Meafyeney ha-mishpat bi-Yehuda ve-Shomron, 1967–1977" (The characteristics of the legal system in Judea and Samaria, 1967–1977), in *Eser shnot shilton bi-Yehuda ve-Shomron* (Ten years of Israeli rule in Judea and Samaria), ed. Rafi Israeli (Jerusalem: Magnes Press, 1971), 30.

82. Raja Shehadeh and Jonathan Kuttab, *The West Bank and the Rule of Law* (New York: The International Commission of Jurists, 1980), 10–11.

83. Meir Shamgar, "The Observance of International Law in the Administered Territories," *Israel Yearbook on Human Rights, 1971* (Tel Aviv: Tel Aviv Univ., Faculty of Law, 1971), 266.

84. Peretz, *West Bank,* 80.

85. Shehadeh, *Occupier's Law,* viii.

86. Peretz, *West Bank,* 81.

87. Shehadeh, *Occupier's Law,* viii–xi.

88. Ibid.

89. Peretz, *West Bank,* 84. See, also, Geoffrey Aronson, *Creating Facts: Israel, Palestinians & the West Bank* (Washington, D.C.: Institute of Palestine Studies, 1987), 248–53.

90. *Ha'aretz,* Nov. 16, 1982.

91. Peretz, *West Bank,* 85.

92. David Richardson, "Leagues Out of Their Depth," *Jerusalem Post,* Mar. 19, 1982. See, also, Pinhas Inbari, *Meshulash al ha-Yarden: ha-magai'm ha-hashai'yim ben Artzot ha-Brit, Yarden ve-Ashaf* (Triangle on the Jordan: The secret contacts among the United States, Jordan and PLO) (Jerusalem: Cana Publishing House, 1982), 201.

93. Yosef Goell, "Milson Sums Up," *Jerusalem Post,* Nov. 11, 1982.

94. *New York Times,* May 28, 1985.

95. See Amnon Rubinstein, "The Changing Status of the 'Territories' (West Bank and Gaza): From Escrow to Legal Mongrel," *Tel Aviv University Studies in Law* 8 (1988).

96. Khalil Mahshi and Ramzi Rihan, "Education: Elementary and Secondary," in *A Palestinian Agenda for the West Bank,* ed. Emile A. Nakhleh (Washington, D.C.: American Enterprise Institute, 1980), 34.

97. Benvenisti, *West Bank Handbook,* 68.

98. See Sarah Graham-Brown, *Education, Repression and Liberation: Palestinians* (London: World Univ. Seminar, 1984), 66.

99. Michael Vinter, "Ma'arechet ha'chinuch ba-Shtachim ha-Muhzakim" (The education system in the administered territories) in *Eser shnot shilton bi-Yehudah ve-Shomron* (Ten years of rule in Judea and Samaria), ed. Rafi Israeli (Jerusalem: Magnes Books, 1971), 108.

100. Nily Mandler, "The Border Crosses the High School in Beit Tzafafa," *Ha'aretz,* Nov. 11, 1987.

101. *Ma'ariv,* May 7, 1970.

102. For a discussion of anti-Jewish material contained in Jordanian textbooks see David K. Shipler, *Arab and Jew: Wounded Spirits in a Promised Land* (New York: Times Books, 1986), 168–77.

103. Benvenisti, *West Bank Handbook,* 209–10. The sixth Palestinian university is Gaza-based Al-Azhar, which was established in 1978.

104. Ibid.

105. "The Open Bridges Policy: Revaluation and Adjustment," *Al-Ra'i,* Aug. 4, 1987, and the rebuttal by Fouad Hamadi Basayso, "Adjustment to the Open Bridges Policy," Aug. 24, 1987.

106. See Basayso, "Open Bridges Policy"; idem, "The Occupied Home: Between the Requirements of Support and the Maintenance of the Arab Boycott," *Shu'un ʿArabiyya* 42 (June 1985).

107. Basayso, "Adjustment to the Open Bridges Policy."

108. Arab League, "The Open Bridges to the West Bank and the Gaza Strip," in *Al-Watan al-Arabi* (Lebanon), Feb. 13, 1981.

109. Ibid.

110. *Divrey ha-Knesset* (The Knesset record) 12, 56, Feb. 4, 1970, 694–96.

111. Ibid., 698.

112. Zvi Elpeleg, "On Israel's Policies in Judea and Samaria," *Skira Hodshit* 5 (May 1982): 12. See, also, Elpeleg's articles in *Davar,* Aug. 17, 1975; *Ma'ariv,* July 11, 1980; *Yediot Aharonot,* May 20, 1974.

113. *Davar,* Aug. 17, 1975.

114. Elpeleg, "Israel's Policies," 15.

115. Gazit, *Ha-makel veha-gezer*, 209.
116. Reuven Mroz, *Hotam* in *Al Hamishmar*, Dec. 15, 1974.
117. Gazit, *Ha-makel veha-gezer*, 209.
118. Ibid.
119. Cheslow, "Open Bridges," 25.
120. Some of the recommendations were published by Akiva Eldar in *Ha'aretz*. These articles appeared after charges in the press that the intelligence community was caught by surprise when the uprising started. In fact, as Eldar demonstrates, the opposite was true. Parts of the minutes of the meetings were shared with this author by a person who had access to the material.
121. Akiva Eldar, "Not to Blame the Intelligence," *Ha'aretz*, Aug. 1, 1988.
122. Jerusalem Domestic Service, *FBIS*, Dec. 9, 1986.
123. Eldar, "The Recommendations to Prevent a De-Facto Annexation," *Ha'aretz*, Aug. 2, 1988.

3. De Facto Peace

1. Klieman, *Statecraft in the Dark*, 102.
2. *Ha'aretz*, Sep. 2, 1987.
3. *Ha'aretz*, Nov. 17, 1986, in Klieman, *Statecraft in the Dark*, 105.
4. Estimates of the exact number of refugees who fled to Jordan vary. Nils-Goran Gussing, a special United Nations emissary, reported that 200,000 refugees fled, 93,000 of whom were refugees from the 1948 war. The United Nations Relief and Works Agency (UNRWA) that cared for the 1948 refugees published two reports. In its October 1967 report it estimated that 200,000 refugees fled, including 100,000 refugees from 1948. By December 1967 it revised its figures, identifying 245,000 refugees, including 135,000 refugees from 1948. The latter figure included 15,000 from the Gaza Strip. Israel estimated that 130,000 refugees fled during the war and 70,000 after the war. In total, between 270,000 refugees (Israeli estimates) and 350,000 refugees (Arab estimates) fled from the West Bank to Jordan, from the Golan Heights to Syria, and from Gaza and the Sinai to Egypt. Daniel Dishon, ed., *Middle East Record, 1967* (Tel Aviv: Israeli Univ. Press, 1968), 311.
5. Gazit, *Ha-makel veha-gezer*, 57–61.
6. Dishon, *Middle East Record, 1967*, 311.
7. Ibid.
8. United Nations Document *A/6797*, in Dishon, *Middle East Recrd, 1967*, 311.
9. *Jerusalem Post*, Aug. 18, 1967.
10. Amman Domestic Service, in Arabic, Federal Broadcast and Information Service (FBIS), *Daily Report, Near East and South Asia*, July 5, 1967, D1–D2.
11. *Jerusalem Post*, July 25, 1967.
12. *Jerusalem Post*, Aug. 7, 1967.
13. *Ma'ariv*, Aug. 8, 1967.
14. *Jerusalem Post*, July 30, 1967.
15. *Jerusalem Post*, Aug. 7, 1967.
16. The Jordanians claimed that 175,000 refugees registered. See the statement by Col. Abdullah al-Rafii, secretary of the Higher Ministerial Committee for Refugee Affairs, *FBIS, Daily Report*, Aug. 21, 1967, D1. Shlomo Gazit, who was one of the senior military officers who dealt with West Bank affairs during that period, reports in his book that only 120,000 refugees applied. See Gazit, *ha-Makel veha-gezer*, 59.
17. Gazit, *ha-Makel veha-gezer*, 58–59.
18. The *Jerusalem Post* reported that the Jordanian minister of finance told the refugees on Aug. 6, 1967, that upon their return they must be "thorns in Israel's flesh." *Jerusalem Post*, Aug. 18, 1967.

19. *Ma'ariv*, Aug. 13, 1967.

20. *Jerusalem Post*, Aug. 14, 1967.

21. Touvia Navot, personal interview by author, Jan. 31, 1987, Jerusalem, Israel; and *Ma'ariv*, Aug. 21, 1967.

22. *Jerusalem Post*, Aug. 15, 1967.

23. *Jerusalem Post*, Sep. 1, 1967.

24. See the statement by the Israeli deputy minister of interior, Y. Ben Meir, *Ma'ariv*, Sep. 1, 1967.

25. *Jerusalem Post*, Aug. 30, 1967. Between 1967 and 1972 some forty-five thousand refugees were allowed to return, including for family reunification. The Israeli authorities allowed the following to return as part of family reunification: a spouse; an unmarried child under the age of sixteen; orphan grandchildren under the age of sixteen; an unmarried sister; and parents under the age of sixty. Males between the ages of sixteen and sixty were not allowed to return. During the early 1980s between nine hundred and twelve hundred applications were approved annually. Benvenisti, *West Bank Handbook*, 89.

26. *Ha'aretz*, Sep. 11, 1967.

27. *Jerusalem Post*, Sep. 11, 1967.

28. Military Headquarters, Judea and Samaria, Health Department, *Statistical Report, 1968–70* (Israel, 1971), 10–11.

29. This account is largely based on an interview given by Gazit, Dov Goldstein, "This is How the Israeli Convoys Went to Amman," in *Ma'ariv*, Sep. 30, 1970, 20–21.

30. *Davar*, Sep. 23, 1970.

31. Goldstein, *Ma'ariv*, Sep. 30, 1970.

32. *Jerusalem Post*, Oct. 13, 1970.

33. Dishon, *Middle East Record, 1969–1970* (Tel Aviv: Israeli Univ. Press, 1973), 384.

34. *Ma'ariv*, Sep. 29, 1970.

35. Dishon, *Middle East Record, 1969–1970*, 384.

36. Ibid.

37. *Ha'aretz*, Sep. 26, 1986.

38. See Gharaibeh, *Economies*, 124–25; Van Arkadie, *Benefits and Burdens*, 102–3.

39. The following account is based on Teveth, *Cursed Blessing*, 149–50.

40. Avineri, *Israel and the Palestinians*, 122–23.

41. *Ma'ariv*, Aug. 29, 1967; Oct. 9, 1967.

42. UNCTAD, *Palestinian Financial Sector*, 66.

43. Amnon Neubach, Peres's economic adviser, personal interview with author, Apr. 13, 1988, Tel Aviv, Israel.

44. Melman, *Shutafut oyenet*, 133–34; *Ha'aretz*, Sep. 26, 1986; *Jerusalem Post*, Sep. 19, 1986; *Christian Science Monitor*, Sep. 19, 1986.

45. Elie Rekhes, "The West Bank and Gaza Strip," in *Middle East Contemporary Survey*, vol. 10, ed. Itamar Rabinovich and Haim Shaked (Boulder, Colo.: Westview Press, 1986), 216.

46. *Ha'aretz*, Sep. 26, 1986.

47. James Whittington, "Jordan, P.L.O. Sign Bank Deal," *Financial Times*, Jan. 8–9, 1994.

48. Yitzhak Oked, "Drip Irrigation: A Success that May Turn Sour," *Jerusalem Post*, Aug. 19, 1984.

49. Yitzhak Oked, "Jordan Side of Border Blooming—with Israeli Help," *Jerusalem Post*, Mar. 8, 1985. This transfer of equipment was corroborated during an interview with David Gefen, coordinator of agricultural activities in the West Bank, personal interview with author, Aug. 19, 1988, Kfar Saba, Israel, and by Khalid al-Qutub, head of the largest agricultural cooperative in Jericho and a well-known businessman who lives at King Hussein's old palace in East Jerusalem. Personal interview with author, Aug. 17, 1988, Jerusalem.

50. Oked, "Drip Irrigation: A Success that May Turn Sour," *Jerusalem Post,* Aug. 19, 1984.

51. Oked, "Jordan Side of the Border Blooming—with Israeli Help," *Jerusalem Post,* Mar. 8, 1985.

52. David Gefen, personal interview with author, Imanuel, Israel, Aug. 19, 1988.

53. Oked, "Drip Irrigation: A Success that May Turn Sour," *Jerusalem Post,* Aug. 19,1984.

54. Jerusalem Post, Dec. 21, 1984.

55. Ibid.

56. Mayor Rafi Hochman, personal interview with author, Dec. 3, 1987, Tel Aviv, Israel.

57. Ibid.

58. Charles E. Ritterband, "Israel and Jordan: Peaceful Coexistence," *Swiss Review of World Affairs* (Aug. 1984): 20.

59. Yossi Melman and Dan Raviv, *Behind the Uprising,* 135–36.

60. *Ma'ariv,* Feb. 23, 1978, 7.

61. Abraham Rabinovich, "Eilat Looks North," *Jerusalem Post,* July 17, 1987.

62. Melman, *Shutafut oyenet,* 95–96.

63. Amnon Neubach, personal interview with author, Apr. 13, 1988, Tel Aviv, Israel.

64. Melman, *Shutafut oyenet,* 126, *Jerusalem Post,* July 17, 1987; Ritterband, "Israel and Jordan," 21.

65. Israeli Broadcast House, *Responses in the Arab Media,* no. 9, May 30, 1977.

66. *Al-Anbah,* May 19, 1977, in ibid.

67. Ehud Ya'ari. "The 'Common Market' of Information in the Middle East," in *Arabs, Israelis and American Media Images and the Problem of Communications,* the Shirley and Burt Harris Symposium on Middle East Communications (Washington, D.C.: Washington Institute for Near East Policy, 1987), 5.

68. Based on accounts of officials of the Israeli Broadcasting Authority.

69. *Jerusalem Post,* Jan. 19, 1986.

70. *Yediot Aharonot,* Feb. 8, 1987.

71. For a critique of Israeli Arabic language television programs, see, for example, Amira Hassan, "Israeli Arabic Radio and T.V.: Serving Official Policy," *New Outlook* (July/ Aug. 1987): 17–20; and Baher Al-Shaab, "Israeli T.V.: The Electronic Face of Occupation," *Al-Fajr,* Nov. 8, 1985.

72. *Al-Dustur,* June 7–8, 1988.

73. Dov Shinar, *Palestinian Voices: Communication and Nation Building in the West Bank* (Boulder, Colo.: Lynne Rienner Publishers, 1987), 56.

74. Ilana Basri, personal interview with author, Jan. 31, 1987, Jerusalem, Israel. See, also, Thomas L. Friedman, "Israel Medical Adviser Is Radio Envoy to Arabs," *New York Times,* Sep. 1, 1985.

75. *Maclean's,* Oct. 14, 1985.

76. *Ma'ariv,* Nov. 2, 1987.

77. Avraham Rabinovich, "High Tension in Jerusalem," *Jerusalem Post,* Feb. 23, 1979.

78. Based on a classified study, *Hevrat ha-Hashmal ha-Mizrach Yerushalmit* (East Jerusalem electric company) conducted by the Israeli military. Its contents were shared with the author by an Israeli official.

79. Rabinovich, "High Tension in Jerusalem," *Jerusalem Post,* Feb. 23, 1979.

80. Israel Defense Forces, *Minsharim, tzavim ve-minuyim,* military order no. 2 (1967).

81. Rabinovich, "High Tension in Jerusalem," *Jerusalem Post,* Feb. 23, 1979.

82. *Jerusalem Post,* Mar. 28, 1986.

83. Inbari, "Turning Off the Royal Faucets." *FBIS,* November 27, 1985, I7.

84. *Jerusalem Post,* Aug. 12, 1979.

85. *Jerusalem Post,* Dec. 31, 1980.

86. *Jerusalem Post,* Feb. 17, 1981.

87. Pinhas Inbari, "Turning Off the Royal Faucets."

88. Yehezkel Flomin, *East Jerusalem Electric Company,* submitted to Shlomo Tussie-Cohen, representing the JDEC, Mar. 9, 1986, unpublished.

89. Melman, *Shutafut oyenet,* 130.

90. *Ha'aretz,* Aug. 10, 1987.

91. *Treaty of Peace Between the State of Israel and the Hashemite Kingdom of Jordan* (Jerusalem: Israel Information Center, 1994).

92. Thomas Naff and Ruth C. Matson, eds. *Water in the Middle East: Conflict or Cooperation* (Boulder, Colo.: Westview Press, 1984), 18.

93. Ibid., 20–21.

94. Selig A. Taubenblat, "Jordan River Basin Waters: A Challenge in the 1990s," in *The Politics of Scarcity: Water in the Middle East,* ed. Joyce R. Starr and Daniel C. Stoll (Boulder, Colo.: Westview Press, 1988), 42.

95. Ibid., 43.

96. Addeane S. Caelleigh, "Middle East Water: Vital Resources, Conflict, and Cooperation," in *A Shared Destiny: Near East Regional Development and Cooperation,* ed. Joyce R. Starr (New York: Praeger, 1983), 129.

97. John Cooley, "The War over Water," *Foreign Policy,* 54 (Spring 1984): 16; Naff and Matson, *Water in the Middle East,* 43.

98. Naff and Matson, *Water in the Middle East,* 44.

99. For a discussion of the various plans see Miriam Lowi, *The Politics of Water: The Jordan River and the Riparian States,* McGill Studies in International Development, no. 35 (Montreal: McGill Univ., 1984).

100. Naff and Matson, *Water in the Middle East,* 39.

101. Lowi, *Politics of Water,* 28.

102. Cooley, "War over Water," 11–13.

103. "Whose Water?" *Economist,* Aug. 5, 1995, 41.

104. Cooley, "War over Water," 15.

105. On Israeli raids against the East Ghor Canal see, for example, *Jerusalem Post,* Apr. 21, June 24, Aug. 11, 1969.

106. Lauris Flemming, "The Secret Agreement Was Violated: The Ghor Canal Was Bombed," *Ma'ariv,* Aug. 18, 1969.

107. Moshe Zak, "Peace Without an Embassy," *Ma'ariv,* Nov. 1, 1985, in *FBIS,* Nov. 5, 1985, I3. See, also, John K. Cooley, "Success of Palestine Talks May Hinge on a Dam," *Christian Science Monitor,* July 10, 1980.

108. Naff and Matson, *Water in the Middle East,* 52.

109. *Ma'ariv,* Dec. 9, 1979.

110. Naff and Matson, *Water in the Middle East,* 52.

111. *Jerusalem Post,* Dec. 20, 1979.

112. *Jerusalem Post,* Oct. 8, 1980.

113. Ibid.

114. Selig A. Taubenblatt, telephone interview with author, July 13, 1989, Washington, D.C. Mr. Taubenblatt is a former Agency for International Development (AID) official who had principal responsibility for the Maqarin Dam negotiations.

115. Naff and Matson, *Water in the Middle East,* 53.

116. Thomas Naff, telephone interview with author, July 27, 1989.

117. Based on interviews with Israeli and American officials. Prime Minister Shamir revealed in 1984 that Israel had maintained an indirect channel to Jordan on this issue.

See *Ha'aretz,* May 13, 1984. On Israeli-Jordanian secret contacts see *Financial Times,* Dec. 15, 1986, 38.

118. Jonathan C. Randal, "Low-Key Talks Bring Opposing Sides Together," *Washington Post,* May 13, 1992, A29.

119. *Yediot Aharonot, FBIS,* Apr. 30, 1992, 7.

120. *Financial Times,* Dec. 15, 1986, 38.

121. Joyce R. Starr and Daniel C. Stoll, eds., *U.S. Foreign Policy on Water Resources in the Middle East* (Washington, D.C.: Center for Strategic and International Studies, 1987), 7.

122. Thomas Naff, telephone interview with author, July 27, 1989.

123. Naff and Matson, *Water in the Middle East,* 53.

124. *Near East Report,* Dec. 6, 1993, 214.

125. For a review of the water agreement see Sharif S. Elmusa, "The Jordan-Israel Water Agreement: A Model or an Exception," *Journal of Palestine Studies* 95, no. 3 (Spring 1995): 63–73.

126. Yehuda Lukacs, "Israel, Jordan and the Hope of Warm Peace," *Washington Times,* Nov. 2, 1994.

4. The Beginning of the Peace Process, 1967–1974

1. Yossi Beilin, *Mechiro shel ichud: mifleget ha-Avoda ad milhemet Yom ha-Kipurim* (The price of unity: The Labor Party until the Yom Kippur War) (Tel Aviv: Revivim, 1985), 20; and Melman, *Shutafut oyenet,* 66. See, also, Ilan Peleg, "The Impact of the Six Day War on the Israeli Right: A Second Republic in the Making?" in Lukacs and Battah, *The Arab-Israeli Conflict,* 58.

2. Dishon, *Middle East Record, 1967,* 70.

3. Fouad A. Jabber, ed., *International Documents on Palestine, 1967* (Beirut: Institute of Palestine Studies, 1970), 650–51.

4. *Daily Telegraph,* July 25, 1967, in Dishon, *Middle East Record, 1967,* 259.

5. Jabber, *International Documents on Palestine, 1967,* 656–57.

6. Melman, *Shutafut oyenet,* 66, and Peter Snow, *Hussein: A Biography* (Washington, D.C.: Robert B. Luce, 1972), 199.

7. *Facts on File Yearbook, 1967,* vol. 37 (New York: Facts on File, 1968), 499.

8. *Ha'aretz,* June 20, 1968.

9. *Ha'aretz,* June 24, 1968.

10. David A. Korn, *Stalemate: The War of Attrition and Great Power Diplomacy in the Middle East, 1967–1970* (Boulder, Colo.: Westview Press, 1992), 44–45.

11. *Facts On File, 1967,* 466.

12. Ibid., 467.

13. Ibid.

14. Donald Neff, *Warriors for Jerusalem: The Six Days that Changed the Middle East* (New York: Simon and Schuster, Linden Press, 1984), 341. On American pledges to King Hussein during his November 1967 visit; see, also, Korn, *Stalemate,* 36.

15. Michael Brecher, "Israel and the Rogers Peace Initiative," *Orbis* 18, no. 2 (Summer 1974): 405.

16. Kleiman, *Statecraft in the Dark,* 99; and Melman, *Shutafut oyenet,* 67–73.

17. Melman, *Shutafut oyenet,* 76.

18. Syria's formal acceptance of Resolution 242 occurred after the 1973 war when it accepted Security Council Resolution 338, which called for a cease-fire.

19. Saadia Touval, *The Peace Brokers: Mediation in the Arab-Israeli Conflict, 1948–1979* (Princeton, N.J.: Princeton Univ. Press, 1982), 136. For an illuminating account of the

Jarring mission see Gideon Rafael, *Destination Peace: Three Decades of Israeli Foreign Policy, A Personal Account* (New York: Stein and Day Publishers, 1981).

20. Touval, *The Peace Brokers,* 143.

21. Abba Eban, *Autobiography* (New York: Random House, 1977), 454.

22. *United Nations, Security Council Official Records,* Document S/10070, 19.

23. Ibid.

24. Ibid.

25. Ibid., 20.

26. Ibid., 21.

27. Eban, *Autobiography,* 455.

28. United Nations, Security Council Official Records, Document S/10070, 21.

29. Ibid.

30. *Jerusalem Post,* Aug. 16, 1968.

31. *Observer,* July 14, 1968.

32. Ibid.

33. For the text see Lukacs, *Documents on the Israeli-Palestinian Conflict, 1967–1984* (Cambridge: Cambridge University Press, 1984), 17–18.

34. Ambassador Alfred Atherton, who was then director of the State Department's Office of Arab-Israeli Affairs, accompanied Ball on the trip. Personal interview with author, Feb. 13, 1989, Washington, D.C.

35. For the full text see Lukacs, *Documents,* 80–89.

36. Nadav Safran, *Israel and Embattled Ally* (Cambridge, Mass.: Harvard Univ., Belknap Press, 1978), 431.

37. Ibid.

38. Lall, *The United Nations and the Middle East Crisis, 1967* (New York: Columbia University Press, 1970), 289.

39. Dishon, *Middle East Record, 1969–1970,* 15.

40. For a discussion of the different reasons that led to the four-power talks see Touval, *Peace Brokers,* 150.

41. United States, *Department of State Bulletin,* 60, no. 1548, Feb. 24, 1969, 159.

42. *Jerusalem Post,* Mar. 31, 1969.

43. U Thant, *View from the U.N.* (London: David and Charles, 1978), 328.

44. United States, *Department of State Bulletin,* 60, no. 1557, Apr. 28, 1969, 360.

45. Walid Khadduri, ed., *International Documents on Palestine, 1969* (Beirut: Institute of Palestine Studies, 1972), 665.

46. Ibid., 68.

47. The "oral law" never appeared in any official government documents or resolution. Yet because it was adopted by the Labor party, which controlled the government, it became part of the unofficial doctrine.

48. Shlomo Aronson, *Conflict and Bargaining in the Middle East: An Israeli Perspective* (Baltimore, Md.: Johns Hopkins Univ. Press, 1978), 107.

49. Ibid., 108.

50. *Newsweek,* Feb. 22, 1971.

51. Dishon, *Middle East Record, 1969–1970,* 30.

52. Lukacs, *Documents,* 18–22.

53. *Jerusalem Post,* Dec. 12, 1969.

54. Steven L. Spiegel, *The Other Arab-Israeli Conflict: Making America's Middle East Policy from Truman to Reagan* (Chicago: Chicago Univ. Press, 1985), 188.

55. Henry Kissinger, *White House Years* (Boston: Little, Brown, 1979), 376.

56. Ibid.

57. Quandt, *Decade of Decisions: American Policy Toward the Arab-Israeli Conflict, 1967–1976* (Berkeley, Calif.: University of California Press, 1977), 91.

58. Korn, *Stalemate,* 161.

59. Brecher, "Rogers Peace Initiative," 407.

60. For the positions of the Soviet Union and Egypt see Dishon, *Middle East Record, 1969–1970,* 35.

61. *New York Times,* Jan. 25, 1970, in Dishon, *Middle East Record, 1969–1970,* 40.

62. This exchange is based on Melman, *Shutafut oyenet,* 79–80; and Moshe Zak, "Israeli-Jordanian Negotiations," 170.

63. Ibid.

64. Ibid.

65. Brecher, "Rogers Peace Initiative," 409.

66. Safran, *Israel the Embattled Ally,* 442.

67. Ibid.; and Brecher, "Rogers Peace Initiative," 410.

68. Brecher, "Rogers Peace Initiative," 410.

69. See Bernard Reich, *Quest for Peace: United States–Israel Relations and the Arab-Israeli Conflict* (New Brunswick, N.J.: Transaction Books, 1977), 160–61.

70. United States, *Department of State Bulletin,* 63, no. 1624, Aug. 10, 1970, 178–79.

71. Brecher, "Rogers Peace Initiative," 412.

72. Aronson, *Conflict and Bargaining,* 127.

73. Brecher, "Rogers Peace Initiative," 413.

74. Aronson, *Conflict and Bargaining,* 121.

75. Ibid., 125.

76. Brecher, "Rogers Peace Initiative," 414.

77. Dishon, *Middle East Record, 1969–1970,* 77.

78. Aronson, *Conflict and Bargaining,* 131.

79. Amman Domestic Service, in Arabic, *FBIS,* July 27, 1970. D1.

80. Walid Khadduri, ed., *International Documents on Palestine, 1970* (Beirut: Institute of Palestine Studies, 1973), 885–86.

81. Ibid., 896. For additional Palestinian reactions see ibid., 889.

82. Dishon, *Middle East Record, 1969–1970,* 814.

83. A detailed description of the civil war can be found in Dishon, *Middle East Record, 1969–1970,* 789–884. See, also, Paul A. Jureidini, *Six Clashes: An Analysis of the Relationship Between Palestinian Guerrilla Movements and the Governments of Jordan and Lebanon* (Kensington, Md.: American Institutes for Research, 1971).

84. Dishon, *Middle East Record,* 789.

85. For the text of the decree see Khadduri, *International Document on Palestine, 1970,* 756–58.

86. See William B. Quandt, Fouad A. Jabber, and Ann Mosley Lesch, eds., *The Politics of Palestinian Nationalism* (Berkeley and Los Angeles: Univ of California Press, 1978), 124–28. See, also, Helena Cobban, *The Palestine Liberation Organization: People, Power, and Politics* (Cambridge: Cambridge Univ. Press, 1984), 47–49; Shemesh, *Palestinian Entity, 1954–1974: Arab Politics and the PLO* (London: Frank Cass, 1988), 133–40; Clinton Bailey, *Jordan's Palestinian Challenge, 1948–1983: A Political History* (Boulder, Colo.: Westview Press, 1984), 54–56; Asher Susser, *Ben Yarden ve-Falestin: biographia politit shel Wasfi al-Tall* (Between Jordan and Palestine: A political biography of Wasfi al-Tall) (Tel Aviv: Kav Adom, ha-Kibbutz ha-Me'uchad, 1984), 122–23.

87. Y. Cohen, *Tochnit Allon,* 147–48.

88. Henry Brandon, *The Retreat of American Power* (New York: Doubleday, 1973), 139.

89. Henry Kissinger, *White House Years,* 605.

90. Ibid., 606.

91. Marvin Kalb and Bernard Kalb, *Kissinger* (Boston: Little, Brown, 1974), 199. During a telephone interview Sisco maintained that he supported Israeli military action

rather than American intervention for the following reasons. First, Israel's security was directly threatened by the Syrian moves, and, thus, it had more at stake. Second, it would have been a "logistical nightmare" for the United States to intervene militarily in Jordan; Israel was much closer to Jordan and had its troops already deployed near the Syrian and Jordanian borders. Third, Jordan was viewed by the Arab states and the Palestinians as an "American satellite." Sending American troops to Jordan would have confirmed this perception and would have embarrassed Hussein. Telephone interview with author, Dec. 5, 1989.

92. Alan Dowty, *Middle East Crisis: U.S. Decision Making in 1958, 1970, and 1973* (Berkeley and Los Angeles: Univ. of California Press, 1984), 147. See, also, Spiegel, *Other Arab-Israeli Conflict,* 199–200.

93. See Quandt, *Decade of Decisions,* 116; and Kalb and Kalb, *Kissinger,* 202–7; Adam M. Garfinkle, "U.S. Decision Making in the Jordan Crisis: Correcting the Record," *Political Science Quarterly* 100, no. 1 (Spring 1985): 124.

94. Yitzhak Rabin, *The Rabin Memoirs* (Boston: Little, Brown, Co., 1979), 187.

95. Kalb and Kalb, *Kissinger,* 205.

96. For the full text of the agreement, see Dishon, *Middle East Record, 1969–1970,* 868–69.

97. Hussein's position with regard to the Palestinians living on the West Bank was fully articulated in his 1972 Federation Plan.

98. Quandt, *Decade of Decisions,* 122.

99. Ariel Sharon, *Warrior: An Autobiography* (New York: Simon and Schuster, 1989), 246–47.

100. Melman, *Shutafut oyenet,* 108.

101. Schueftan, *Optzia Yardenit,* 308.

102. *Ma'ariv,* Sep. 25, 1970.

103. For an excellent review of the reaction of the West Bank Palestinians, see Dishon, *Middle East Record,* 383–90.

104. *Ma'ariv,* Sep. 28, 1970.

105. Dishon, *Middle East Record,* 385.

106. *Ma'ariv,* Oct. 8, 1970.

107. *Ma'ariv,* Oct. 19, 1970.

108. Dishon, *Middle East Record, 1969–1970,* 387.

109. Jorgen S. Nielsen, ed., *International Documents on Palestine, 1972* (Beirut: Institute of Palestine Studies, 1975), 292.

110. Zvi Elpeleg, *Tochnit ha-federatzia shel Hussein: gormim u-tguvot* (Hussein's federation plan: Causes and reactions) (Tel Aviv: Shiloah Institute, Tel Aviv Univ., 1977), 1.

111. Nielsen, *International Documents on Palestine, 1972,* 290.

112. Ibid., 291.

113. Bar-Joseph, *Best of Enemies,* 138–39.

114. See, also, Shlaim, *Collusion Across the Jordan,* 359–60.

115. Shemesh, *Palestinian Entity,* 224.

116. Nielsen, *International Documents on Palestine, 1972,* 290.

117. Amman Domestic Service, in Arabic, *FBIS,* Apr. 5, 1971, D2.

118. Elpeleg, *Tochnit ha-federatzia shel Hussein,* 14.

119. Shemesh, *Palestinian Entity,* 224.

120. Nielsen, *International Documents on Palestine, 1972,* 292.

121. The idea of Gaza becoming part of Jordanian territory was first introduced by Hussein during his May 1968 meeting with the Israeli leadership.

122. *Ma'ariv,* Jan. 28, 1972.

123. Schueftan, *Optzia Yardenit,* 331.

124. Shemesh, *Palestinian Entity,* 224.

125. For the reaction of the Arab states see, also, *Washington Post,* Mar. 19, 1972, A1.; and *New York Times,* Mar. 19, 1972.

126. Elpeleg, *Tochnit ha-federatzia shel Hussein,* 17.

127. Nielsen, *International Documents on Palestine, 1972,* 300.

128. *New York Times,* Mar. 19, 1972.

129. Nielsen, *International Documents on Palestine, 1972,* 295.

130. Ibid., 311.

131. Cobban, *Palestine Liberation Organization,* 208–9. For additional Palestinian reactions, see Nielsen, *International Documents on Palestine, 1972,* 304–6, 309–17; and Shemesh, *The Palestinian Entity,* 232. See, also, *Washington Post,* Mar. 17, 1972.

132. Elpeleg, *Tochnit ha-federatzia shel Hussein,* 21–25.

133. Nielsen, *International Documents on Palestine, 1972,* 304–5.

134. Elpeleg, *Tochnit ha-federatzia shel Hussein,* 24.

135. *Ma'ariv,* Mar. 16, 1972, 2.

136. Ibid.

137. *New York Times,* Mar. 16, 1972.

138. Ibid.

139. *Jerusalem Post,* Mar. 17, 1972.

140. Ibid., 1.

141. This perspective is offered by Elpeleg, *Tochnit ha-federatzia shel Hussein,* 29.

142. *Ma'ariv,* Mar. 17, 1972.

143. Ibid.

144. *Ma'ariv,* Mar. 23, 1972.

145. See Elpeleg, *Tochnit ha-federatzia shel Hussein,* 27–29.

146. *Hitbatuyot sarim be-diyun al ha-shtachim* (Remarks by government ministers during a debate on the territories), Minutes of Meetings, Labor Party Secretariat, Oct. 5, 1972; Nov. 9, 1972; Nov. 23, 1972, 33.

147. *Ha'aretz,* Mar. 18, 1972; *Ma'ariv,* Mar. 23, 1972.

148. Henry Kissinger, *Years of Upheaval* (Boston: Little, Brown, 1982), 219–20.

149. Ibid., 221.

150. Mordechai Gazit, *Tahalich ha-shalom: 1969–1973* (The peace process: 1969–1973) (Yad Tabenkin, Israel: Kav Adom, Hakibbutz Hameuchad, 1984), 144.

151. Ibid., 155.

152. Snow, *Hussein,* 259.

153. Schueftan, *Optzia Yardenit,* 331–32.

154. Kissinger, *Years of Upheaval,* 506.

155. Schueftan, *Optzia Yardenit,* 309.

156. Kleiman, *Du kium le-lo shalom,* 157.

157. *Quick,* June 19, 1973, cited in *Ma'ariv,* June 20, 1973.

158. Yeshayahu Ben Porat, *Sihot* (Conversations) (Tel Aviv: Idanim, 1981), in Gazit, *Tahalich ha-shalom,* 146.

159. *Ma'ariv,* May 7, 1974.

160. *New York Times,* Feb. 10, 1974, 15. See, also, Edward R. F. Sheehan, *The Arabs, Israelis, and Kissinger: A Secret History of American Diplomacy in the Middle East* (New York: Reader's Digest Press, 1976), 147.

161. See Susan Hattis Rolef, "Jericho Excavations," *Jerusalem Post,* Feb. 24, 1984. Most works that discuss the 1974 Israeli-Jordanian disengagement fail to distinquish between these two types of disengagement proposals, hence, the confusion regarding the origins of the proposals.

162. Kissinger, *Years of Upheaval,* 848.

163. *New York Times,* Feb. 15, 1974, 3.

164. Safran, *Israel the Embattled Ally,* 536.

165. See Melman, *Shutafut oyenet,* 90.

166. It is not clear whether he knew of the meeting between Meir and Hussein.

167. Kissinger, *Years of Upheaval,* 847–48.

168. Safran, *Israel the Embattled Ally,* 536.

169. Matti Golan, *The Secret Conversations of Henry Kissinger: Step by Step Diplomacy in the Middle East* (New York: New York Times Book, Quadrangle Books, 1976), 217.

170. Touval, *Peace Brokers,* 260.

171. *Ha'aretz,* Jan. 8, 1974.

172. *Ma'ariv,* May 7, 1974.

173. Aronson, *Conflict and Bargaining,* 250.

174. *Ma'ariv,* Jan. 26, 1973.

175. *Ha'aretz,* Feb. 1, 1974.

176. *Jerusalem Post,* Mar. 27, 1974.

177. Golan, *Secret Conversations,* 219.

178. Rabin, *Rabin Memoirs,* 244.

179. See Joseph Sisco, interview on the *Today Show,* June 3, 1974, in *Department of State Bulletin,* July 1, 1974, 13; and Sisco's testimony before the House Foreign Affairs Committee as reported in the *Washington Post,* June 13, 1974, A2. This was confirmed by Sisco himself during an interview with the author, Jan. 6, 1989, Washington, D.C.

180. Golan, *Secret Conversations,* 219.

181. See Kissinger, *Years of Upheaval,* 1138.

182. Sisco shares the author's assessment of Hussein's desperation at that time. Personal interview with Sisco, Jan. 6, 1989.

183. *Department of State Bulletin,* July 15, 1974, 113.

184. Ibid., 119.

185. Golan, *Secret Conversations,* 219–20.

186. For the text of the communiqué, see *Jerusalem Post,* July 22, 1974.

187. Ibid.

188. Jorgan S. Nielsen, ed., *International Documents on Palestine, 1974* (Beirut: Institute of Palestine Studies, 1977), 470.

189. Golan, *Secret Conversations,* 224–26.

190. Ibid.

191. Nielsen, *International Documents on Palestine, 1974,* 318.

192. Safran, *Israel the Embattled Ally,* 538.

193. Matti Golan, *Shimon Peres: A Biography* (New York: St. Martin's Press, 1982), 151–52. See, also, Melman, *Shutafut oyenet,* 91, and Zak, "Israeli-Jordanian Negotiations," 170–71.

194. Golan, *Shimon Peres.*

195. Jorgen S. Nielsen, *International Documents on Palestine, 1974* (Beirut: Institute of Palestine Studies, 1977), 495.

196. This was also the view of Joseph Sisco, who followed these negotiations closely as a member of the American negotiating team. Joseph Sisco, interview by author, Jan. 6, 1989.

197. Nielsen, *International Documents on Palestine, 1974,* 496.

198. Golan, *Shimon Peres,* 153–54; and Melman, *Shutafut Oyenet,* 94.

199. Golan, *Shimon Peres,* 153.

200. Nielsen, *International Documents on Palestine, 1974,* 522.

201. Kissinger, *Years of Upheaval,* 1138.

202. Joseph Sisco, interview with author, Jan. 6, 1989.

203. Ibid. According to Sisco, Rabin refused to reveal anything about the meetings with Hussein when asked by American officials. The Jordanians supplied the U.S. administration with information about these meetings.

204. George E. Gruen, "Jordan's International Posture," confidential memorandum submitted to the Foreign Affairs Department, the American Jewish Congress, Sep. 6, 1979.

205. Golan, *Shimon Peres,* 154.

206. Eban, *Autobiography,* 583.

207. *Jerusalem Post,* July 22, 1974.

208. *Jerusalem Post,* Aug. 28, 1974.

209. Golan, *Shimon Peres,* 155.

5. From Rabat to Jordan's West Bank Disengagement, 1974–1988

1. *FBIS,* Oct. 31, 1974.

2. Schueftan, *Optzia Yardenit,* 344.

3. Lustick, *Israel and Jordan,* 12–13.

4. Asher Susser, "Jordan," in *Middle East Contemporary Survey,* ed. Colin Legum, vol. 1, 1976–77 (New York: Holmes and Meier, 1978), 478.

5. Asher Susser, "Jordanian Influence in the West Bank," *Jerusalem Quarterly* 8 (Summer 1978): 63.

6. Peter Gubser, *Jordan: Crossroads of Middle Eastern Events* (Boulder, Colo.: Westview Press, 1983), 109.

7. Schueftan, *Optzia Yardenit,* 344–45.

8. *New York Times,* Nov. 5, 1974.

9. Gubser, *Jordan,* 110.

10. Moshe Maoz, *Ha-Manhigut ha-Palestinit ba-Gada ha-Ma'aravit* (Palestinian leadership on the West Bank) (Tel Aviv: Reshafim, 1985), 146.

11. Shimon Peres with Hagai Eshed, *Kaet-machar* (Tomorrow is now) (Jerusalem: Keter Publishers, 1978), 256.

12. Ibid., 259.

13. Maoz, *Ha-Manhigut ha-Palestinit ba-Gada ha-Ma'aravit,* 149.

14. Geoffrey Aronson, *Creating Facts: Israel, Palestinians and the West Bank* (Washington, D.C.: Institute of Palestine Studies, 1987), 54–55.

15. Ibid., 55.

16. Emile Sahliyeh, *In Search of Leadership: West Bank Politics since 1967* (Washington, D.C.: Brookings Institution, 1988), 67.

17. Ibid. For a comparison of the 1972 and 1976 elections see Shaul Mishal and Abraham Diskin, "Palestinian Voting in the West Bank: Electoral Behavior in a Traditional Community Without Sovereignty," *Journal of Politics* 44, no. 2 (May 1982): 538–58.

18. Menachem Milson, *Yarden veha-Gada ha-Ma'aravit* (Jordan and the West Bank) (Jerusalem: Leonard Davis Institute of International Relations, Hebrew Univ., 1984), 36–37.

19. Susser, "Jordan," 483.

20. See ibid.; and Clinton Bailey, "Changing Attitudes Toward Jordan in the West Bank," *Middle East Journal* 32, no. 2 (Spring 1978): 163.

21. Bailey, "Changing Attitudes," 163.

22. Aronson, *Creating Facts,* 207; and Sahliyeh, *In Search of Leadership,* 51.

23. Sahliyeh, *In Search of Leadership,* 51.

24. Milson, *Yarden veha-Gada ha-Ma'aravit,* 38–39.

25. Schueftan, *Optzia Yardenit,* 354.

26. Adam Garfinkle, "Negotiating by Proxy: Jordanian Foreign Policy and U.S. Options in the Middle East," *Orbis* 24, no. 4 (Winter 1981): 856.

27. Susser, "Jordan," 478.

28. *Washington Post,* Dec. 30, 1976.

29. Middle East News Agency (MENA), in Arabic, *FBIS,* Jan. 3, 1977, F1.

30. Ibid., A6.

31. Schueftan, *Optzia Yardenit,* 359.

32. Ibid.

33. Ibid., D4.

34. Susser, "Jordan," 479.

35. See the following memoirs for perspectives on this issue: Cyrus Vance, *Hard Choices: Critical Years in America's Foreign Policy* (New York: Simon and Schuster, 1983), 163–64; Zbigniew Brzezinski, *Power and Principle: Memoirs of the National Security Adviser, 1977–1981* (New York: Farrar, Straus and Giroux, 1983), 83–89.

36. See Lukacs, *Documents,* 23–24, for the text of this memorandum.

37. See Yehuda Lukacs, *The Israeli-Palestinian Conflict: A Documentary Record* (Cambridge: Cambridge University Press, 1992), 61.

38. Ibid., 65.

39. The reference to "refugee exception" relates to the PLO's argument that 242 refers to the Palestinians merely as refugees and fails to accord them political rights. This argument was used by the PLO as justification for rejecting the Security Council Resolution.

40. William B. Quandt, *Camp David: Peacemaking and Politics* (Washington, D.C.: Brookings Institution, 1986), 86.

41. Vance, *Hard Choices,* 188.

42. Garfinkle, "Negotiating By Proxy," 861.

43. Vance, *Hard Choices,* 187.

44. Lukacs, *Israeli-Palestinian Conflict,* 16.

45. See Quandt, *Camp David,* 123. For the reaction of the Israeli government see *International Documents on Palestine, 1977* (Beirut: Institute of Palestine Studies, 1979), 256.

46. Quandt, *Camp David,* 131.

47. Ibid., 130.

48. Vance, *Hard Choices,* 193.

49. Moshe Dayan, *Breakthrough: A Personal Account of the Egypt-Israel Peace Negotiations* (New York: Alfred A. Knopf, 1981), 71.

50. Ibid.

51. Quandt, *Camp David,* 131.

52. Schueftan, *Optzia Yardenit,* 377.

53. A number of meetings took place between Israeli Foreign Minister Dayan and Sadat's close confidant, Tuhami. For a review of these meetings see Dayan, *Breakthrough,* 44–53.

54. *International Documents on Palestine, 1977,* 405.

55. Vance, *Hard Choices,* 168–71; Quandt, *Camp David,* 40–41.

56. Vance, *Hard Choices,* 171.

57. Ibid.

58. Jimmy Carter, *Keeping Faith: Memoirs of a President* (New York: Bantam Books, 1982), 280. See, also, Rabin's account in *Rabin Memoirs,* 293–94.

59. Ilan Peleg, *Begin's Foreign Policy, 1977–1981: Israel's Move to the Right* (Westport, Conn.: Greenwood Press, 1987), 99.

60. Ibid.

61. Dayan, *Breakthrough,* 36.

62. *International Documents on Palestine, 1977,* 315.

63. Peleg, *Begin's Foreign Policy*, 102.

64. Quandt, *Camp David*, 161; and Peleg, *Begin's Foreign Policy*, 102.

65. Garfinkle, "Negotiating By Proxy," 866.

66. Emile Sahliyeh, "Jordan and the Palestinians," in Quandt, *Middle East*, 286.

67. In 1994, when Jordan and Israel agreed to sign a peace treaty, President Mubarak, who was Sadat's deputy, was not informed in advance by King Hussein. *International Documents on Palestine, 1977*, 429.

68. Ibid., 451–53.

69. Sahliyeh, "Jordan and the Palestinians," 286.

70. *Yediot Aharonot*, Dec. 22, 1977.

71. Garfinkle, "Negotiating By Proxy," 866.

72. Moshe Gammer, "The Negotiating Process: Attitudes of Interested Parties," in Colin Legum, ed., *Middle East Contemporary Record*, vol. 2, *1977–78* (New York: Holmes and Meier, 1979), 158.

73. Garfinkle, "Negotiating By Proxy," 870.

74. See interview with Hussein, Christopher Wren, "Man on the Spot: Sadat's Peace Becomes Hussein's Trial," *New York Times Magazine*, Apr. 8, 1979.

75. John Newhouse, "Profiles: Monarch," *New Yorker* 59, no. 3, Sept. 19, 1983, 96.

76. Ibid.

77. For the text of the two agreements see United States, Department of State, *The Quest for Peace: Principal United States Statements and Related Documents on the Arab-Israeli Peace Process, 1967–1983* (Washington, D.C.: Government Printing Office, 1984), 74–83.

78. For text, see Lukacs, *Israeli-Palestinian Conflict*, 155.

79. Ibid.

80. Arthur R. Day, *East Bank/West Bank: Jordan and the Prospects for Peace* (New York: Council on Foreign Relations, 1986), 127.

81. *International Documents on Palestine, 1978* (Beirut: Institute of Palestine Studies, 1980), 507.

82. For the list of the questions and the U.S. response see Quandt, *Camp David*, 264–65, 388–96; Vance, *Hard Choices*, 229–31.

83. On the Israeli and Egyptians positions regarding West Bank autonomy see Aryeh Shalev, *The Autonomy: Problems and Possible Solutions*, Paper no. 8 (Tel Aviv: Tel Aviv Univ., Center for Strategic Studies, Jan. 1980).

84. Gershon R. Kieval, *Party Politics in Israel and the Occupied Territories* (Westport, Conn.: Greenwood Press, 1983), 162–63.

85. Lukacs, *Israeli-Palestinian Conflict*, 72.

86. Kleiman, *Du kiyum le-lo shalom*, 102.

87. Ze'ev Schiff, "Green Light, Lebanon," *Foreign Policy* 50 (Spring 1983): 73–85; and Nimrod Novik, *Encounter with Reality: Reagan and the Middle East Policy—the First Term* (Boulder, Colo.: Westview Press, 1985), 59–60.

88. BBC Television, in English, *FBIS*, Sep. 14, 1982, F3. See, also, Susser, "Jordan," in Colin Legum and Haim Shaked, eds., *Middle East Contemporary Survey*, vol. 6, 1981–82 (New York: Holmes and Meier, 1984), 631–35; and Susser, "Jordan," in *Middle East Contemporary Survey*, ed. Legum and Shaked, vol. 7, 1982–83 (New York: Holmes and Meier, 1985), 683.

89. Kleiman, *Du kiyum le-lo shalom*, 104; and Susser, "Jordan," in Legum and Shaked, eds., *Middle East Contemporary Survey*, vol. 7, 1982–83, 634.

90. For details see the two articles by Karen Elliott House, *Wall Street Journal*, Apr. 14, 15, 1983.

91. Lukacs, *Israeli-Palestinian Conflict*, 478.

92. See Henry Tanner, "Arab Moderates Offer New Proposal in New Unity," *New York Times*, Sep. 12, 1982.

93. Lukacs, *Documents*, 110.

94. Don Peretz, "Israeli Policy," in *The Middle East since Camp David*, ed. Robert O. Freedman (Boulder, Colo.: Westview Press, 1984), 167.

95. See Emile F. Sahliyeh, *The P.L.O. after the Lebanon War* (Boulder, Colo.: Westview Press, 1986), 115–38; Adam M. Garfinkle, "Jordanian Foreign Policy," *Current History* 83, no. 489 (Jan. 1984): 39.

96. Sahliyeh, *P.L.O. after Lebanon*, 127.

97. Day, *East Bank/West Bank*, 128.

98. Lukacs, *Israeli-Palestinian Conflict*, 479.

99. Ibid., 360.

100. Bailey, *Jordan's Palestinian Challenge*, 121.

101. Ibid., 121–22.

102. *Wall Street Journal*, Apr. 14, 1983, and Sahliyeh, *P.L.O. after Lebanon*, 127–36.

103. Amman Television, in Arabic, *FBIS*, May 2, 1983, F1-5. For an excellent critique of U.S. policy on this issue see Ronald J. Young, *Missed Opportunities for Peace* (Philadelphia: American Friends Service Committee, 1987), 95–118.

104. See Day, *East Bank/West Bank*, 135.

105. Ibid., 135.

106. *New Outlook*, Feb. 1984, 7.

107. Text of the accord was issued by the Jordanian Information Bureau, Washington, D.C., Feb. 25, 1985.

108. William B. Quandt, "U.S. Policy Toward the Arab-Israeli Conflict," in Quandt, *Middle East*, 369.

109. See Matti Steinberg, "Introduction," in Menachem Klein, *Du siyah ve-shivro: yahsey Ashaf ve-Yarden, 1985–1988* (Antagonistic collaboration: PLO-Jordanian Relations, 1985–1988) (Jerusalem: Leonard Davis Institute of International Relations, Hebrew Univ., 1988), 5.

110. Sahliyeh, "Jordan and the Palestinians," 299–301.

111. For Hussein's speech see Lukacs, *Israeli-Palestinian Conflict*, 499–513.

112. Quandt, "U.S. Policy," 372.

113. Personal interview with Said Kan'an, who claims to have participated in the negotiations between Israel and Jordan concerning al-Masri's appointment. Kan'an contends that Khalil al-Wazir, known as Abu Jihad, a top-ranking PLO official who was assassinated in 1988, also approved of al-Masri's appointment. Personal interview with author, Aug. 15, 1988, Nablus, West Bank. Fatah has sometimes favored pro-Jordanian figures (Elias Freij) over nationalist figures, believing that the former's weaker popular position makes them more dependent on continued Fatah support and, hence, more vulnerable to Fatah pressure.

114. The poll's results can be found in *Journal of Palestine Studies* 16, no. 2 (Winter 1987): 196–207.

115. Lewis, "Israel: The Peres Era and Its Legacies," *Foreign Affairs* 65, no. 35 (1987): 587.

116. *Ha'aretz*, Oct. 30, 1985.

117. The Labor party's strategy is discussed in Major General Avraham Tamir, *A Soldier in Search of Peace* (London: Weidenfeld and Nicolson, 1988), 92.

118. Melman, *Shutafut oyenet*, 131.

119. Lewis, "Israel," 601.

120. Nimrod Novik, personal interview with author, July 5, 1988, Jerusalem, Israel.

121. "Peres Reveals 'Secret Diplomacy' with Jordan," Agance France Presse (AFP), *FBIS*, Apr. 28, 1986.

122. "Building a Condominium," *Newsweek*, Atlantic ed., Nov. 10, 1986.

123. *Ha'aretz,* Apr. 1, 1986.

124. John Kifner, "Hussein's Gamble," *Ha'aretz,* July 21, 1986.

125. The text of the plan was published in the *Jordan Times,* July 31–Aug. 1, 1986, and reprinted in *FBIS,* Aug. 5, 1986. For a detailed analysis of the plan see Benvenisti, *1987 Report,* 24–28.

126. Benvenisti, *1987 Report,* 25.

127. Ibid.

128. Ibid., 48.

129. "Freij and Can'an are Conducting a Propaganda Campaign for the Joint Jordanian-Israeli Plan," *Al-Hadaf* 839, Nov. 3, 1986, 12–13. See, also, ibid., Aug. 18, 1986; and *Shu'un Filastiniyya,* May–June, 1986; "The Development Plan in Light of the Experience of the Joint Committee," *Al-Kateb,* Jan. 8, 1987.

130. Smadar Peri, "The Minister of the Territories," *Yediot Aharonot,* weekend suppl., July 3, 1992, 18.

131. State of Israel, Ministry of Defense, Coordinator of Activities in Judea, Samaria, and the Gaza District, "Jordanian Five-Year Development Programme for Judea, Samaria, and Gaza District," Progress report as per Oct. 31, 1987 (internal I.D.F. Memorandum). These figures, which were provided by the Israeli military in a detailed progress report, further corroborate that Israel was very closely monitoring the development plan and encouraged its implementation.

132. Benvenisti, *1987 Report,* 27.

133. Charles W. Wallace, "Jordan's West Bank Plan Faltering," *Los Angeles Times,* Mar. 4, 1987.

134. "Building a Condominium," *Newsweek,* Atlantic ed., Nov. 10, 1986, 15; John Kifner, "Hussein to Share Power with Israel," *New York Times,* Nov. 16, 1986.

135. *Ha'aretz,* Sep. 26, 1986; *Newsweek,* "Building a Condominium," Atlantic ed., Nov. 10, 1986.

136. Daoud Kuttab, *Middle East International,* Jan. 23, 1987.

137. *Ma'ariv,* Nov. 5, 1986.

138. Kuttab, *Middle East International,* Jan. 23, 1987. See, also, the article on Israeli-Jordanian cooperation in the territories in *Shu'un Filistiniyya,* 158–159 (May–June 1986). Many Palestinians who were interviewed on this subject insisted that Israel and Jordan also cooperate in exchanging intelligence information about the PLO. See, for example, an article published in the French weekly, *L'Express,* that claims that Israeli and Jordanian intelligence services exchanged information regarding PLO activists in the early 1970s. The article also reports that Israeli Chief of Military Intelligence Eliyahu Zeira met with his Jordanian counterpart, Salem Aboud, in London. "Israel-Arabes: Le Guerre de l'ombre," (Israel-Arab: War of shadows) *L'Express,* Jan. 22–28, 1973, 66–67.

139. "Building a Condominium," *Newsweek,* Atlantic ed., Nov. 10, 1986.

140. *Al-Fajr,* June 13, 1986.

141. Based on interviews with high-ranking officials at the Israeli Broadcasting Authority, Aug. 1988.

142. *Ha'aretz,* Aug. 15, 1986.

143. *Jerusalem Post,* Mar. 27, 1986; Aug. 22, 1986; Mar. 7, 1986.

144. Peretz, *West Bank,* 86; *Ma'ariv,* Oct. 23, 1984.

145. *Jerusalem Post,* Apr. 3, 1986. See, also, statement by Richard Murphy, assistant secretary of state, Bureau of Near Eastern/South Asian Affairs. Testimony before the House Subcommittee on Europe and the Middle East, Dec. 11, 1987, *American-Arab Affairs,* 23 (Winter 1987–88): 137–40; Elie Rekhes, "West Bank and Gaza Strip," in *Middle East Contemporary Survey,* vol. 10, 1986, ed. Itamar Rabinovich and Haim Shaked (Boulder, Colo.: Westview Press, 1988), 207.

146. Naor, *Ktovet al ha-kir,* 128.

147. Ibid.

148. The reference to terror was inserted to prevent PLO members who were viewed as part of a terrorist organization from participating in the conference. *Ha'aretz,* in *FBIS,* Oct. 21, 1985, 11–12.

149. *New York Times,* Oct. 25, 1985.

150. Naor, *Ktovet al ha-kir,* 156–57.

151. Shimon Shamir, "Israeli Views of Egypt and the Peace Process: The Duality of Vision," in Quandt, *Middle East,* 212.

152. Ibid., 169.

153. This information was contained in a top-secret dossier handed by Peres to Hussein in London and shown to me by an Israeli official. The idea of storing water from the Yarmuk River in the Lake of Tiberias dates back to the Johnston Plan. Hussein's response, however, to Peres's offer was negative because of the Israeli-Jordanian friction over cleaning the East Ghor Canal intake. Thomas Naff, telephone interview with author, July 1989.

154. *Yediot Aharonot,* weekend suppl., Oct. 22, 1993, 11.

155. For the text of the London Agreement see Lukacs, *Israeli-Palestinian Conflict,* 28.

156. *Ha'aretz,* Dec. 2, 1987.

157. Naor, *Ktovet al ha-kir,* 180.

158. Yitzhak Shamir, "Israel at 40: Looking Back, Looking Ahead," *Foreign Affairs, America and the World, 1987/88* 66, no. 3 (1988): 577–78.

159. For a description of the events after the signing of the London accord, including Arens's visit to the United States, see George P. Shultz, *Turmoil and Triumph: My Years as Secretary of State* (New York: Charles Scribner's Sons, 1993), 940–42.

160. *Yediot Aharonot,* Feb. 4, 1994, weekend suppl., 4–5.

161. For the text of the initiative see Lukacs, *Israeli-Palestinian Conflict,* 106.

162. Quandt, "U.S. Policy," 377.

163. See Asher Susser, *In Through the Out Door: Jordan's Disengagement and the Middle East Peace Process,* Policy papers, no. 19 (Washington, D.C.: Washington Institute for Near East Policy, 1990), 14.

164. For evaluation of Shultz's policy see Kathleen Christison, "The Arab-Israeli Policy of George Schultz," *Journal of Palestine Studies* 70, no. 2 (Winter 1989): 29–47.

165. For the text of the Algiers communiqué see Lukacs, *Israeli-Palestinian Conflict,* 518–20.

166. Susser, *In Through the Out Door,* 20.

167. *Ha'aretz,* July 24, 1988; *Ma'ariv,* Aug. 8, 1988; see, also, Don Peretz, "Intifadeh: The Palestinian Uprising," *Foreign Affairs* 66, no. 5 (Summer 1988): 978.

168. Ghada Talhami, "A Symmetry of Surrogates: Jordan's and Egypt's Response to the Intifada," in *Intifada: Palestine at the Crossroads,* ed. Jamal R. Nasser and Roger Heacock (New York: Praegar, 1990), 231.

169. Roger Owen, "Regional Order: The Palestinian Challenge," Paper delivered at the British International Studies Association (BISA), London, Mar. 1989, 5.

170. F. Gregory Gause III, "The Arab World and the Intifada," in *The Intifada: Its Impact on Israel, the Arab World, and the Superpowers,* ed. Robert O. Freedman (Miami: Florida International Univ. Press, 1991), 200.

171. Lukacs, *Israeli Palestinian Conflict,* 522.

172. *New York Times,* Oct. 18, 1988.

173. Owen, "Regional Order," 6. For Hussein's speech see Amman Domestic Service, in Arabic, *FBIS,* June 9, 1988, 5–13.

174. Paris Radio Monte Carlo, in Arabic, *FBIS,* Apr. 12, 1988, 53. During the bilateral talks Jordan had demanded an Israeli withdrawal from 320 km^2 in the Arava rather than

the 20 km^2 stipulated in 1988. Jordanian sovereignty over these territories was restored as a result of the 1994 peace treaty.

175. *Ma'ariv*, Apr. 13, 1988, *FBIS*, Apr. 13, 1988. A number of Israeli journalists speculated that Hussein might consider such a move as early as Apr. 1988. See *Yediot Aharonot*, Apr. 13, 1988; and *Al Hamishmar*, May 16, 1988.

176. *Ma'ariv*, Aug. 5, 1988.

177. Call number 23 of the Unified National Leadership of the Uprising, *FBIS*, Aug. 4, 1988, 4.

178. *Ma'ariv*, Aug. 1, 1988.

179. Ibid.

180. Robert Satloff, "Jordan and Reverberations of the Uprising," *Current History* 88, no. 535 (Feb. 1989): 105.

6. From De Facto to De Jure Peace

1. See *Al Hamishmar*, Apr. 22, 1988, 3.

2. See Clinton Bailey, "Hamas: The Fundamentalist Challenge to the P.L.O.," Research memorandum, no. 19 (Washington, D.C.: Washington Institute for Near East Policy, 1992).

3. Jerusalem Israel Television Network in Hebrew, *FBIS*, Nov. 15, 1990, 26.

4. Gad Barzilai and Efraim Inbar, "Do Wars Have an Impact?: Israeli Public Opinion after the Gulf War," *Jerusalem Journal of International Relations* 14, no. 1 (1992).

5. *Jordan Times*, *FBIS*, June 4, 1991, 20.

6. Kol Yisrael, in Hebrew, *FBIS*, June 3, 1991, 27.

7. Ibid., June 10, 1991, 31–32.

8. See "Special Document File: The Peace Process," *Journal of Palestine Studies* 21, no. 3 (Spring 1992), 130.

9. In April 1993 before the start of the ninth round, Israel agreed to allow Faisal Husseini, a resident of East Jerusalem, to become a formal member of the delegation. During the first eight rounds Husseini was the delegation's "adviser."

10. *Jordan Times*, *FBIS*, Oct. 29, 1992, 4.

11. Paris Radio Monte Carlo, in Arabic, *FBIS*, Apr. 12, 1989, 53.

12. Jerusalem Domestic Service, in Hebrew, *FBIS*, Apr. 12, 1988, 45.

13. For a detailed discussion see Israel Shahak, "Two Disputed Israeli International Borders," Report no. 113, Nov. 15, 1992. Shahak skillfully analyzes the situation on the Jordanian front and provides translation of a number of articles published in the Hebrew press, including Yehuda Litani, "The Border Was Pushed Eastward," and Akiva Eldar, "A Jordanian October Surprise," in *Ha'aretz*, Nov. 6, 1992; Ze'ev Tzahor, "It Does Not Belong to Us," *Hadashot*, Nov. 2, 1992; Yerah Tal, "The Border That Was Established by the British Was not Marked on the Ground," *Ha'aretz*, Nov. 2, 1992; Alex Fishman, "In the Very Least, Ask the Settlers," *Hadashot*, Nov. 6, 1992. For a brief Jordanian position paper see "Jordan's Occupied Land," in *Issues, Facts and Figures: A Guide*, Middle East Peace Conference, Madrid 1991 (Amman, Jordan: Jordan Media Group, 1991).

14. Litani, "Border Was Pushed Eastward."

15. Ibid.

16. "Article 25 of the Palestine Mandate," in *The Hashemite Kingdom of Jordan and the West Bank: A Handbook*, ed. Anne Sinai and Allen Pollack (New York: American Academic Association for Peace in the Middle East, 1977), 340.

17. Revital Levishtein, "The King Does Not Need These Lands," *Ha'aretz*, Nov. 1, 1992.

18. Avraham Tal, *Ha'aretz*, Nov. 1, 1992.

19. Elaine Sciolino with Thomas L. Friedman, "Crossing the River: The Israel-Jordan Pact," *New York Times,* July 31, 1994.

20. U.S. Department of State, "U.S.-Jordanian-Israeli Trilateral Economic Committee," June 7, 1994.

21. *Israel Information Service* (online), "The Middle East Peace Process," Dec. 1, 1994. Available by e-mail: Gopher Israel-info.gov.il.

22. John Snyder, "Eight Months after Pact, Jordan Still Uneasy," *Washington Jewish Week,* June 15, 1995, 15.

23. *Globes,* Aug. 6, 1996, 2.

7. Afterword

1. *Jordan Times,* Jan. 7, 1998.

2. "Joint Palestinian-Jordanian Poll on Jordanian-Palestinian Relations," Dec. 22–30, <http://www.cprs-palestine.org/polls/jointpoll/joint1a.html>.

3. Laurie Brand, "The Effects of the Peace Process on Political Liberalization in Jordan," *Journal of Palestinian Studies* 28, no. 2 (Winter 1999), 62.

4. *Ha'aretz,* Mar. 4, 1999.

5. *Ha'aretz,* Feb. 14, 1999.

6. *Ha'aretz,* Mar. 7, 1999.

7. *Jordan Times,* Mar. 2, 1999.

8. "Water Violations," *Al-Ahram Weekly,* Mar. 25–31, 1999, no. 422.

9. Water for the Future: The West Bank and Gaza Strip, Israel and Jordan (Washington, D.C.: National Academy of Sciences, 1999).

10. *Jane's Foreign Report,* Feb. 11, 1999.

11. *Jordan Times,* Mar. 2, 1999.

12. Samir Mansour, telephone interview with author, May 14, 1999, Washington, D.C.

Bibliography

Abd-Allah, Umar F. *The Islamic Struggle in Syria.* Berkeley, Calif.: Mizan Press, 1983.

Abu Odeh, Adnan. "Jordan and the Middle East Crisis." *AEI Foreign Policy and Defense Review* 3, no. 1 (1981).

Allon, Yigal. "Israel: The Case for Defensible Borders." *Foreign Affairs* 55, no. 1 (Oct. 1976): 38–53.

———. *Kelim sheluvim* (Communicating vessels). Tel Aviv: ha-Kibbutz ha-Me'uchad, 1980.

Antonius, George. *The Arab Awakening: The Story of the Arab Nationalist Movement.* London: Hamish Hamilton, 1938.

Arkadie, Brian Van. *Benefits and Burdens: A Report on the West Bank and Gaza Strip Economies since 1967.* Washington, D.C.: Carnegie Endowment for International Peace, 1977.

Aronoff, Myron J. *Israeli Visions and Divisions: Cultural Change and Political Conflict.* New Brunswick, N.J.: Transaction Publishers, 1989.

Aronson, Geoffrey. *Creating Facts: Israel, Palestinians and the West Bank.* Washington, D.C.: Institute of Palestine Studies, 1987.

Aronson, Shlomo. *Conflict and Bargaining in the Middle East: An Israeli Perspective.* Baltimore, Md.: Johns Hopkins Univ. Press, 1978.

Aruri, Naseer H., ed. *Occupation: Israel over Palestine.* Belmont, Mass.: Association of Arab-American University Graduates, 1983.

Auerbach, Yehudit, and Hemda Ben-Yehuda. "Attitudes Towards an Existence Conflict: Begin and Dayan on the Palestinian Issue." *International Interactions* 13, no. 4 (Sept. 1987): 323–51.

Avineri, Shlomo, ed. *Israel and the Palestinians.* New York: St. Martin's Press, 1971.

———. "Peacemaking: The Arab Israeli Conflict." *Foreign Affairs* 57, no. 1 (Fall 1978): 51–69.

Bailey, Clinton. "Changing Attitudes Toward Jordan in the West Bank." *Middle East Journal* 32, no. 2 (Spring 1978).

———. *Hamas: The Fundamentalist Challenge to the P.L.O.* Research memorandum, no. 19. Washington, D.C.: Washington Institute for Near East Policy, 1992.

———. *Jordan's Palestinian Challenge, 1948–1983: A Political History,* 155–66. Boulder, Colo.: Westview Press, 1984.

Baker, James A., III. *The Politics of Diplomacy: Revolution, War & Peace, 1989–1992.* New York: G. P. Putnam's Sons, 1995.

Ball, George W. *Error and Betrayal in Lebanon: An Analysis of Israel's Invasion of Lebanon and the Implication for U.S.-Israeli Relations.* Washington, D.C.: Foundation for Peace in the Middle East, 1984.

Bar-Joseph, Uri. *The Best of Enemies: Israel and Transjordan in the War of 1948.* London: Frank Cass, 1987.

Barzilai, Gad, and Inbar Efraim. "Do Wars Have an Impact? Israeli Public Opinion after the Gulf War." *Jerusalem Journal of International Relations* 14, no. 1 (1992).

Basayso, Fouad Hamadi. "The Economic Implication of the Open Bridges Policy." *Shu'un Filistiniyya* 2 (1972).

———. "The Occupied Home: Between the Requirements of Support and the Maintenance of the Arab Boycott." *Sh'un 'Arabiyya* 42 (June 1985).

Beilin, Yossi. *Mechiro shel ichud: Mifleget ha-Avoda ad milhemet Yom Hakipurim* (The price of unity: The Labor Party until the Yom Kippur war). Tel Aviv: Revivim, 1985.

Benvenisti, Meron. *1986 Report: Demographic, Economic, Legal, Social and Political Developments in the West Bank.* Jerusalem and Boulder, Colo.: Jerusalem Post and Westview Press, 1987.

———. *1987 Report: Demographic, Economic, Legal, Social and Political Developments in the West Bank.* Boulder, Colo.: Westview Press, 1987.

———. *The West Bank Handbook: A Political Lexicon.* Jerusalem: Jerusalem Post, 1986.

———. *U.S. Government–Funded Projects in the West Bank and Gaza, 1977–1983.* Jerusalem: West Bank Data Project, 1984.

Bergman, Arie. *Economic Growth in the Administered Territories, 1968–1973.* Jerusalem: Bank of Israel, Research Department, 1974.

———. *The Economy of the Administered Areas, 1974–1975.* Jerusalem: Bank of Israel, Research Department, 1976.

Bin Talal, El Hassan. "Jordan's Quest for Peace." *Foreign Affairs* 60, no. 4 (Spring 1982): 802–13.

Blum, Yehuda. "The Missing Reversioner: Reflections on the Status of Judea and Samaria." *Israel Law Review* 3 (1968).

Brandon, Henry. "Jordan: The Forgotten Crisis, Part 1, Were We Masterful . . . ." *Foreign Policy* 10 (Spring 1973): 158–70.

———. *The Retreat of American Power.* New York: Doubleday, 1973.

Brecher, Michael. *Decisions in Israeli Foreign Policy.* New Haven, Conn.: Yale Univ. Press, 1975.

———. *The Foreign Policy System of Israel: Setting, Images, Process.* New Haven, Conn.: Yale Univ. Press, 1972.

———. "Israel and the Rogers Peace Initiative." *Orbis* 18, no. 2 (Summer 1974).

Brown, Seymon. "The Changing Essence of Power." *Foreign Affairs* 51, no. 2 (Jan. 1973): 286–99.

Brzezinski, Zbigniew. *Power and Principle: Memoirs of a National Security Adviser, 1977–1981.* New York: Farrar, Straus and Giroux, 1983.

Bull, Odd. *Water and Peace in the Middle East: The Experience and Views of a U.N. Observer.* London: Leo Cooper, 1976.

Bull, Vivian A. *The West Bank: Is it Viable?* Lexington, Mass.: Lexington Books, 1975.

Caelleigh, Addeanes. "Middle East Water: Vital Resources, Conflict, and Cooperation, " in *A Shared Destiny: Near East Regional Development and Cooperation,* edited by Joyce R. Starr. New York: Praeger, 1983.

Carter, Jimmy. *Keeping Faith: Memoirs of a President.* New York: Bantam Books, 1982.

Cheslow, Jerry. "Open Bridges: The Oversight that Became Policy." *IDF Journal* 4, no. 1 (Winter 1987): 17–25.

Chomsky, Noam. *The Fateful Triangle: The United States, Israel and the Palestinians.* Boston: South End Press, 1983.

Christison, Kathleen. "The Arab-Israeli Policy of George Schultz." *Journal of Palestine Studies* 70, no. 2 (Winter 1989): 29–47.

Cobban, Helena. *The Palestine Liberation Organization: People, Power, and Politics.* Cambridge: Cambridge Univ. Press, 1984.

Cohen, Avraham. *Kalkalat ha-shtachim: ha-Gada ha-Ma'aravit ve-Retzuat Aza, 1922–1980* (The economy of the territories: The West Bank and the Gaza Strip, 1922–1980). Givat Haviva, Israel: Institute of Arab Studies, 1987.

Cohen, S., and F. E. Ntzani. "Transmission and Host Range of the Tomato Yellow Leaf Curl Virus." *Phytopathology* 58 (1966).

Cohen, Yerucham. *Tochnit Allon* (The Allon plan). Tel Aviv: Hakibbutz Hameuchad, 1983.

Cooley, John. "The War over Water." *Foreign Policy* 54 (Spring 1984): 3–26.

Davis, Uri, E. J. Antoine, and John Richardson. "Israel's Water Policies." *Journal of Palestine Studies* 9, no. 3 (Winter 1980): 3–31.

Day, Arthur R. *East Bank/West Bank: Jordan and the Prospects for Peace.* New York: Council on Foreign Relations, 1986.

Dayan, Moshe. *Breakthrough: A Personal Account of the Egypt-Israel Peace Negotiation.* New York: Alfred A. Knopf, 1981.

———. *Mapa Hadasha: yechasim aherim* (A new map: Different relations). Tel Aviv: Ma'ariv Books, 1969.

Dees, J. L. "Jordan's East Ghor Canal Project." *Middle East Journal* 13, 3 (Fall 1959): 357–71.

"The Development Plan in Light of the Experience of the Joint Committee." *Al-Katab* 8, Jan. 1987.

Dessouki, Ali E. Hillal and Karen Aboul Kheir. "The Politics of Vulnerability and Survival: The Foreign Policy of Jordan. In *The Foreign Policies of the Arab States,* 2d ed., edited by Bahgat Korany and Ali E. Hillal Dessouki. Boulder, Colo.: Westview Press, 1991.

Dishon, Daniel, ed. *Middle East Record, 1967.* Tel Aviv: Israeli Universities Press, 1968.

———. *Middle East Record, 1968.* Tel Aviv: Israeli Universities Press, 1970.

———. *Middle East Record, 1969–1970.* Tel Aviv: Israeli Universities Press, 1973.

Doherty, Kathryn B. "Jordan Waters Conflict." *International Conciliation* (1965).

Dowty, Alan. *Middle East Crisis: U.S. Decision Making in 1958, 1970, and 1973.* Berkeley and Los Angeles: Univ. of California Press, 1984.

Eastby, John. *Functionalism and Interdependence: The Credibility of Institutions, Policies, and Leadership, Vol. 3.* Lanham, Md.: Univ. Press of America, 1985.

Eban, Abba. *An Autobiography*. New York: Random House, 1977.

———. *Personal Witness: Israel Through My Eyes*. New York: G. P. Putnam's Sons, 1992.

Eilon, Joab B. *Peace Projects*. Tel Aviv: Tel Aviv Univ., Armand Hammer Fund for Economic Cooperation in the Middle East, 1993.

Elmusa, Sharifs. "The Jordan-Israel Water Agreement: A Model or an Exception." *Journal of Palestine Studies* 95, no. 3 (Spring 1995): 63–73.

Elpeleg, Zvi. *Tochnit ha-federatzia shel Hussein: gormim U-tguvot* (Hussein's federation plan: Causes and reactions). Tel Aviv: Shiloah Institute, Tel Aviv Univ., 1977.

———. "West Bank Story." *Middle East Review* 13, 4 (Summer 1986).

The Europa Yearbook, 1989. London: Europa Publications, 1989.

Evans, Rowland, Jr., and Robert B. Novak. *Nixon in the White House: The Frustrations of Power*. New York: Random House, 1971.

Fabian, Larry L. "Prologue: The Political Setting." In *Benefits and Burdens: A Report on the West Bank and Gaza Strip Economies since 1967*, edited by Brian Van Arkadie. Washington, D.C.: Carnegie Endowment for International Peace, 1977.

Facts on File Yearbook, 1967. Vol. 37. New York: Facts on File, 1968.

Fahmy, Ismail. *Negotiating for Peace in the Middle East*. Baltimore, Md.: Johns Hopkins Univ. Press, 1983.

Flapan, Simha. *The Birth of Israel: Myths and Realities*. New York: Pantheon Books, 1987.

Freedman, Robert O. *The Intifada: Its Impact on Israel, the Arab World, and the Superpowers*. Miami: Florida International University, 1991.

———. *The Middle East since Camp David*. Boulder, Colo.: Westview Press, 1984.

Garfinkle, Adam M. *Israel and Jordan in the Shadow of War*. New York: St. Martin's Press, 1992.

———. "Jordanian Foreign Policy." *Current History* 83, no. 489 (Jan. 1984): 21–24.

———. "Negotiating by Proxy: Jordanian Foreign Policy and U.S. Options in the Middle East." *Orbis* 24, no. 4 (Winter 1981): 847–880.

———. "U.S. Decision Making in the Jordan Crisis: Correcting the Record." *Political Science Quarterly* 100, no. 1 (Spring 1985).

Gause, Gregory F. III. "The Arab World and the Intifada." In *The Intifada: Its Impact on Israel, the Arab World, and the Superpowers*, edited by Robert O. Freedman. Miami: Florida International University, 1991.

Gazit, Mordechai. *Tahalich ha-shalom, 1969–1972* (The peace process, 1969–1972). Yad Tabenkin, Israel: Kav Adom, 1984.

Gazit, Shlomo. *Ha-Makel veha-gezer: ha-mimshal ha-Yisraeli bi-Yehuda ve-Shomrom* (The carrot and the stick: The Israeli administration in Judea and Samaria). Tel Aviv: Zmora, Bitan Publications, 1985.

Gerson, Allan. *Israel, the West Bank and International Law*. London: Frank Cass, 1978.

Gharaibeh, Fawzi A. *The Economies of the West Bank and Gaza Strip*. Boulder, Colo.: Westview Press, 1985.

Golan, Matti. *The Secret Conversations of Henry Kissinger: Step by Step Diplomacy in the Middle East.* New York: Quadrangle Books, 1976.

————. *Shimon Peres: A Biography.* New York: St. Martin's Press, 1982.

Graham-Brown, Sarah. *Education, Repression and Liberation: Palestinians.* London: World Univ. Seminar, 1984.

Groom, A. J. R., and Paul Taylor. *Functionalism: Theory and Practice in International Politics.* New York: Crane, Russak, 1975.

Gubser, Peter. *Jordan: Crossroads of Middle Eastern Events.* Boulder, Colo.: Westview Press, 1983.

Haber, Eitan. *Menachem Begin: The Man, and the Legend.* New York: Dell, 1979.

Harkabi, Yehoshafat. *Israel's Fateful Hour.* New York: Harper and Row, 1988.

Harris, Lawrence. "Finance and Money with Undeveloped Banking." Paper presented at the symposium Economic Development under Prolonged Occupation: West Bank and Gaza, Oxford, Jan. 1986.

————. "Money and Finance in the West Bank and Gaza." Paper presented at the Symposium Economic Development under Prolonged Occupation: West Bank and Gaza, Oxford, Nov. 1985.

Hassan, Amira. "Israeli Arabic Radio and T.V.: Serving Official Policy." *New Outlook* (July/Aug. 1987).

Hertzberg, Arthur. "The Turning Point?" *New York Review of Books* 35, no. 15, Oct. 13, 1988.

Heydemann, Steve, ed. *The Begin Era: Issues in Contemporary Israel.* Boulder, Colo.: Westview Press, 1984.

Holsti, Kal J. *International Politics: A Framework for Analysis.* Englewood Cliffs, N.J.: Prentice-Hall, 1967.

Hussein, King. "The Jordanian-Palestinian Peace Initiative: Mutual Recognition and Territory for Peace." *Journal of Palestine Studies* 14, no. 4 (Summer 1985): 15–22.

Inbar, Efraim. *War and Peace in Israeli Politics: Labor Party Positions on National Security.* Boulder, Colo.: Lynne Rienner, 1991.

Inbar, Moshe, and J. O. Maoz. "Water Resource Management in the Northern Jordan Valley." *Kidma* 7, no. 3 (1983).

Inbari, Pinhas. *Meshulash al ha-Yarden: ha-Magai'm ha-hashai'yim ben Artzot ha-Brit, Yarden ve-Ashaf* (Triangle on the Jordan: The secret contacts among the United States, Jordan, and PLO). Jerusalem: Cana Publishing House, 1982.

International Documents on Palestine, 1977. Beirut: Institute of Palestine Studies, 1979.

International Documents on Palestine, 1978. Beirut: Institute of Palestine Studies, 1980.

Isaac, Rael Jean. *Israel Divided: Ideological Politics in the Jewish State.* Baltimore, Md.: Johns Hopkins Univ. Press, 1976.

————. *Party and Politics in Israel: Three Visions of a Jewish State.* New York: Longman, 1981.

Israel Defense Forces. *Misharim, tzavim, u-minuyim shel Mifkedet kohot Tzahal be-ezor ha-gada ha-Ma'aravit* (Notices, orders, and appointments issued by the IDF headquarters in the West Bank region). Various orders.

Israel National Section of the International Commission of Jurists. *The Rule of Law in the Areas Administered by Israel.* Tel Aviv: Israel National Section of the International Commission of Jurists, 1981.

Israeli, Rafi. *Eser shnot shilton biyehuda veshomron* (Ten years of Israeli rule in Judea and Samaria). Jerusalem: Magnes Press, 1971.

Jabber, Fouad A., ed. *International Documents on Palestine, 1967.* Beirut: Institute of Palestine Studies, 1970.

Jureidini, Paul A. *Six Clashes: An Analysis of the Relationships Between Palestinian Guerrilla Movements and the Governments of Jordan and Lebanon.* Kensington, Md.: American Institutes for Research, 1971.

Kahan, David. *Agriculture and Water Resources in the West Bank and Gaza, 1967–1987.* Jerusalem: West Bank Data Project, 1987.

Kalb Marvin, and Bernard Kalb. *Kissinger.* Boston: Little, Brown, 1974.

Kally, Elisha. *A Middle East Water Plan under Peace.* Tel Aviv: Armand Hammer Fund for Economic Cooperation in the Middle East, Tel Aviv Univ., 1986.

Kanovsky, Eliyahu. "The Economic Aftermath of the Six-Day War, Part II." *Middle East Journal* 22, no. 3 (Summer 1968): 131–43.

———. *The Economic Impact of the Six-Day War: Israel, the Occupied Territories, Egypt, Jordan.* New York: Praeger, 1970.

———. *The Economy of Jordan: Implications for Peace in the Middle East.* Tel Aviv: Univ. Publishing Project, 1976.

Kellerman, Barbara, and Jeffrey Z. Rubin, eds. *Leadership and Negotiation in the Middle East.* New York: Praeger, 1988.

Keohane, Robert O. *After Hegemony: Cooperation and Discord in the World Political Economy.* Princeton, N.J.: Princeton Univ. Press, 1984.

———, ed. *International Document on Palestine, 1969.* Beirut: Institute of Palestine Studies, 1972.

Khadduri, Walid, ed. *International Document on Palestine, 1970.* Beirut: Institute of Palestine Studies, 1973.

Khalidi, Rashid. *Under Siege: P.L.O. Decision Making During the 1982 War.* New York: Columbia Univ. Press, 1986.

Kieval, Gershon R. *Party Politics in Israel and the Occupied Territories.* Westport, Conn.: Greenwood Press, 1983.

Kissinger, Henry. *White House Years.* Boston: Little, Brown, 1979.

———. *Years of Upheaval.* Boston: Little, Brown, 1982.

Klieman, Aaron S. "Defense and Foreign Affairs: Holding the Line." In *Israel Faces the Future,* edited by Bernard Reich and Gershon R. Kieval. New York: Praeger, 1986.

———. *Du kiyum le-lo shalom: Yisrael, Yarden veha-Palestinaim* (Unpeaceful coexistence: Israel, Jordan, and the Palestinians). Tel Aviv: Ma'ariv Books, 1986.

———. *Israel, Jordan, Palestine: The Search for a Durable Peace.* Washington Paper no. 83. Washington, D.C.: Center for Strategic and International Studies, Georgetown Univ., 1981.

———. *Statecraft in the Dark: Israel's Practice of Quiet Diplomacy.* Jerusalem and Boulder, Colo.: Jerusalem Post and Westview Press, 1988.

Klein, Menachem. *Du siah ve-shivro: yehsey Ashaf ve-Yarden, 1985–1988* (Antagonistic collaboration: PLO-Jordanian relations, 1985–1988). Jerusalem: Leonard Davis Institute of International Relations, Hebrew Univ., 1988.

Korany, Bahgat, and Hillal Ali E. Dessouki. *The Foreign Policies of the Arab States.* 2d ed. Boulder, Colo.: Westview Press, 1991.

Korn, David A. *Stalemate: The War of Attrition and Great Power Diplomacy in the Middle East, 1967–1970.* Boulder, Colo.: Westview Press, 1992.

Kuttab, Jonathan, and Raja Shehadeh. *Civilian Administration in the Occupied West Bank: Analysis of Israeli Military Order No. 947.* Ramallah: Law in the Service of Man and International Commission of Jurists, 1982.

Lall, Arthur. *The United Nations and the Middle East Crisis, 1967.* New York: Columbia Univ. Press, 1970.

Legum, Colin, ed. *Middle East Contemporary Survey,* Vols. 1, 1976–77; 2, 1977–78. New York: Holmes and Meier, 1978–79.

Legum, Colin, and Haim Shaked, eds. *Middle East Contemporary Survey.* Vols. 4, 1978–79; 6, 1981–82; 7, 1982–83. New York: Homes and Meier, 1982.

Lewis, Samuel W. "Israel: The Peres Era and its Legacies." *Foreign Affairs, America and the World, 1986.* 65, no. 35 (1987): 582–610.

Liden, Anders. *Security and Recognition: A Study of Change in Israel's Official Doctrine, 1967–1974.* Lund, Sweden: Studentlitteratur, 1980.

Lowi, Miriam. *The Politics of Water: The Jordan River and the Riparian States.* McGill Studies in International Development, no. 35. Montreal: McGill Univ., 1984.

Lukacs, Yehuda, ed. *Documents on the Israeli-Palestinian Conflict, 1967–1983.* Cambridge: Cambridge Univ. Press, 1984.

———, ed. *The Israeli-Palestinian Conflict: A Documentary Record.* Cambridge: Cambridge Univ. Press, 1992.

Lukacs, Yehuda, and Abdalla M. Battah, eds. *The Arab-Israeli Conflict: Two Decades of Change.* Boulder, Colo.: Westview Press, 1988.

Lunt, James. *Hussein of Jordan: Searching for a Just and Lasting Peace.* New York: William Morrow, 1989.

Lurie, Ranan B. "Israel's General Sharon: As Tough as Ever." *Playboy* (Mar. 1978).

Lustick, Ian. *Israel and Jordan: The Implications of an Adversarial Partnership.* Policy Papers in International Affairs, no. 6. Berkeley: Institute of International Studies, Univ. of California, 1978.

Mahshi, Khalil, and Ramzi Rihan. "Education Elementary and Secondary." In *A Palestinian Agenda for the West Bank,* edited by Emile A. Nakhleh. Washington, D.C.: American Enterprise Institute, 1980.

Makoud, K. M. "A Study on Tomato Viruses in the Jordan Valley with Special Emphasis on Tomato Yellow Leaf Curl." *Plant Disease Reporter* 62, no. 3 (Mar. 1978).

Mansour, Antoine S. "Monetary Dualism: The Case of the West Bank under Occupation." *Journal of Palestine Studies* 11, no. 3 (Spring 1982).

Maoz, Moshe. *Ha-Manhigut ha-Palestinait ba-Gada ha-Ma'aravit* (Palestinian leadership on the West Bank). Tel Aviv: Reshafim, 1985.

Al-Mawsuʿa al-Filistiniyya (The Palestinian encyclopedia). Damascus, Syria: Hayʾat al-Mawsuʿa al-Filistiniyya, 1984.

Melman, Yossi, and Dan Raviv. *Behind the Uprising: Israelis, Jordanians and the Palestinians.* New York: Greenwood Press, 1989.

———. *Shutafut oyenet: ha-ksharim ha-sodiyim ben Yisrael ve-Yarden* (A hostile partnership: The secret relations between Israel and Jordan). Tel Aviv: Meitam, Yediot Aharonot Books, 1987.

Meron, Raphael. *Economic Development in Judea-Samaria and the Gaza District.* Jerusalem: Bank of Israel, 1983.

Miller, Aaron David. "Changing Arab Attitudes Toward Israel." *Orbis* 32, no. 1 (Winter 1988).

————. "Jordan and the Arab-Israeli Conflict: The Hashemite Predicament." *Orbis* 29, no. 4 (Winter 1986): 795–820.

Milson, Menachem. "How to Make Peace with the Palestinians." *Commentary* 7, no. 5 (May 1981): 25–35.

————. *Yarden ve-Hagada ha-Ma'aravit* (Jordan and the West Bank). Jerusalem: Leonard Davis Institute of International Relations, Hebrew University, 1984.

Mishal, Shaul, and Abraham Diskin. "Palestinian Voting in the West Bank: Electoral Behavior in a Traditional Community Without Sovereignty." *Journal of Politics* 44, no. 2 (May 1982): 538–58.

Mitrany, David. *The Functional Theory of Politics.* New York: St. Martin's Press, 1976.

————. "The Prospect of Functional Cooperation." *Eastern Economist,* Sep. 5, 1947.

————. *A Working Peace System.* Chicago: Quandrangle Books, 1966.

Morris, Benny. *The Birth of the Palestinian Refugee Problem, 1947–1949.* New York: Cambridge Univ. Press, 1987.

Murphy, Richard. Testimony Before the House Subcommittee on Europe and the Middle East. *American-Arab Affairs* no. 23 (Winter 1987–88): 144–50.

Naff, Thomas, and Ruth C. Matson, eds. *Water in the Middle East: Conflict or Cooperation.* Boulder, Colo.: Westview Press, 1984.

Nakhleh, Emile A., ed. *A Palestinian Agenda for the West Bank.* Washington, D.C.: American Enterprise Institute, 1980.

Naor, Arye. *Ktovet al ha-kir* (Writing on the wall). Yediot Aharonot ed. Tel Aviv: Edanim Publishers, 1988.

Nasser, Jamal R., and Roger Heacock, eds. *Intifada: Palestine at the Crossroads.* New York: Praeger, 1990.

Neff, Thomas. *Warriors for Jerusalem: The Six Days that Changed the Middle East.* New York: Linden Press, Simon and Schuster, 1984.

Netanyahu, Benjamin. *A Place among Nations: Israel and the World.* New York: Bantam Books, 1993.

Newhouse, John. "Profiles: Monarch." *New Yorker* 59, no. 3 (Sep. 19, 1983): 49–120.

Nielsen, Jorgen S., ed. *International Documents on Palestine, 1972.* Beirut: Institute of Palestine Studies, 1975.

————. *International Documents on Palestine, 1974.* Beirut: Institute of Palestine Studies, 1977.

Nixon, Richard. *RN: The Memoirs of Richard Nixon.* New York: Grosset and Dunlop, 1978.

Norton, Augustus Richard, and Martin H. Greenberg. *The International Relations of the Palestine Liberation Organization.* Carbondale: Southern Illinois Univ. Press, 1989.

Novik, Nimrod. *Encounter with Reality: Reagan and the Middle East Policy—the First Term.* Boulder, Colo.: Westview Press, 1985.

Owen, Roger. "Regional Order: The Palestinian Challenge." Paper presented at the British International Studies Association (BISA), London, March 1989.

Peleg, Ilan. *Begin's Foreign Policy, 1977–1981: Israel's Move to the Right*. Westport, Conn.: Greenwood Press, 1987.

Peleg, Ilan, and Ofira Seliktar, eds. *The Emergence of Binational Israel: The Second Republic in the Making?* Boulder, Colo.: Westview Press, 1989.

Peres, Shimon, with Hagai Eshed. *Kaet-machar* (Tomorrow is now). Jerusalem: Keter Publishers, 1978.

Peres, Shimon, with Arye Naor. *The New Middle East*. New York: Henry Holt, 1993.

Peretz, Don. "Development of the Jordan Valley Waters." *Middle East Journal* 9, no. 3 (Fall 1955): 397–412.

———. "Intifadeh: The Palestinian Uprising." *Foreign Affairs* 66, no. 5 (Summer 1988): 964–80.

———. "Israeli Policies Toward the Arab States and the Palestinians since 1967." In *The Arab Israeli Conflict: Two Decades of Change*, edited by Yehuda Lukacs and Abdallam Battah. Boulder, Colo.: Westview Press, 1989.

———. "Israeli Policy." In *The Middle East since Camp David*, edited by Robert O. Freedman. Boulder, Colo.: Westview Press, 1984.

———. *The West Bank: History, Politics, Society and Economy*. Boulder, Colo.: Westview Press, 1986.

Perlmutter, Amos. *The Life and Times of Menachem Begin*. Garden City, N.Y.: Doubleday, 1987.

Public Papers of the Presidents of the United States: Jimmy Carter, Book 1: January 20 to June 24, 1977. Washington, D.C.: Government Printing Office, 1977.

Quandt, William B. *Camp David: Peacemaking and Politics*. Washington, D.C.: Brookings Institution, 1986.

———. *Decade of Decision: American Policy Toward the Arab-Israeli Conflict, 1967–1976*. Berkeley and Los Angeles: Univ. of California Press, 1977.

———, ed. *The Middle East: Ten Years after Camp David*. Washington, D.C.: Brookings Institution, 1988.

———. *Peace Process: American Diplomacy and the Arab-Israeli Conflict since 1967*. Washington, D.C., and Berkeley and Los Angeles: Brookings Institution and Univ. of California Press, 1993.

Quandt, William B., Fouad A. Jabber, and Ann Mosley Lesch, eds. *The Politics of Palestinian Nationalism*. Berkeley: Univ. of California Press, 1978.

Rabin, Yitzhak, *Pinkas sherut* (A service notebook). Tel Aviv: Ma'ariv Books, 1979.

———. *The Rabin Memoirs*. Boston: Little, Brown, 1979.

Rabinovich, Itamar. *The War for Lebanon, 1979–1983*. Ithaca, N.Y.: Cornell Univ. Press, 1984.

Rabinovich, Itamar, and Jehuda Reinharz, eds. *Israel in the Middle East*. New York: Oxford Univ. Press, 1984.

Rabinovich, Itamar, and Haim Shaked, eds. *Middle East Contemporary Survey*. Vol. 10, 1986. Boulder, Colo.: Westview Press, 1988.

Rafael, Gideon. *Destination Peace: Three Decades of Israeli Foreign Policy: A Personal Account*. New York: Stein and Day Publishers, 1981.

Randal, Jonathan. *Going All the Way: Christian Warlords, Israeli Adventurers, and the War in Lebanon*. Rev. ed. New York: Vintage Books, 1983.

Reich, Bernard. *Quest for Peace: United States–Israeli Relations and the Arab-Israeli Conflict.* New Brunswick, N.J.: Transaction Books, 1977.

Reich, Bernard, and Gershon R. Kieval, eds. *Israel Faces the Future.* New York: Praeger, 1986.

Ritterband, Charles E. "Israel and Jordan: Peaceful Coexistence." *Swiss Review of World Affairs* (Aug. 1984): 20–21.

Royal Scientific Society and Jordanian-P.L.O. Joint Committee. *Al-Ahwal al-Maliyya w-'al-masrafiyya fi'l-diffa al-gharbiyya wa-qita' gazza al-muhtalayn* (Financial and banking conditions in the occupied West Bank and Gaza Strip). Amman: Royal Scientific Society, 1985.

Rubinstein, Amnon. "The Changing Status of the 'Territories' (West Bank and Gaza): From Escrow to Legal Mongrel." *Tel Aviv University Studies in Law* 8 (1988).

Ryan, Sheila. "Plans to Regularize the Occupation." In *Occupation: Israel over Palestine,* edited by Naseer H. Aruri. Belmont, Mass.: Association of Arab-American University Graduates, 1983.

Safran, Nadav. *Israel the Embattled Ally.* Cambridge, Mass.: Harvard Univ. Press, Belknap Press, 1978.

Sahliyeh, Emile. *In Search of Leadership: West Bank Politics since 1967.* Washington, D.C.: Brookings Institution, 1988.

———. "Jordan and the Palestinians." In *The Middle East: Ten Years after Camp David,* edited by William B. Quandt. Washington, D.C.: Brookings Institution, 1988.

———. *The P.L.O. after the Lebanon War.* Boulder, Colo.: Westview Press, 1986.

Saliba, Samir N. *The Jordan Valley Dispute.* The Hague: Martinus Nijhoff, 1965.

Samara, Adel. *The Political Economy of the West Bank, 1967–1987.* London: Khamsin, 1988.

Sandler, Samuel, and Hillel Frisch. *Israel, the Palestinians and the West Bank.* Lexington, Mass.: Lexington Books, 1984.

Satloff, Robert. "Jordan and Reverberations of the Uprising." *Current History* 88, no. 535 (Feb. 1989): 85–88.

Saunders, Harold. *The Other Walls: The Arab-Israeli Peace Process in a Global Perspective.* Rev. ed. Princeton, N.J.: Princeton Univ. Press, 1991.

Sayigh, Yusuf A. "The Palestinian Economy under Occupation: Dependency and Pauperization." *Journal of Palestine Studies* 15, no. 4 (Summer 1986): 46–67.

Schiff, Ze'ev. "Green Light, Lebanon." *Foreign Policy* 50 (Spring 1983): 73–85.

Schiff, Ze'ev, and Ehud Ya'ari. *Israel's Lebanon War.* New York: Simon and Schuster, 1984.

Schoenbaum, David. "Jordan: The Forgotten Crisis (2), . . . Or Lucky." *Foreign Policy* 10 (Spring 1973): 175–81.

Schueftan, Dan. *Optzia Yardenit: ha-Yishuv ha-Yehudi u-Medinat Yisrael el-mul ha-mishtar ha-Hashemi ve-hatnua ha-leumit ha-Palastinit* (A Jordanian option: The "Yishuv" and the State of Israel vis-à-vis the Hashemite regime and the Palestinian National Movement). Yad Tabenkin, Israel: Hakibbutz Hameuchad, 1978.

Seale, Patrick. *Asad: The Struggle for the Middle East.* Berkeley and Los Angeles: Univ. of California Press, 1989.

Shalev, Aryeh. *The Autonomy: Problems and Possible Solutions.* Paper no. 8. Tel Aviv: Tel Aviv Univ., Center for Strategic Studies, January 1980.

———. *Shituf-peula be-tzel imut* (Cooperation under the shadow of conflict: The Israeli-Syrian armistice regime, 1949–1955). Tel Aviv: Ma'arachot, 1989.

Shamgar, Meir. "The Observance of International Law in the Administered Territories." In *Israel Handbook on Human Rights, 1971.* Tel Aviv: Tel Aviv Univ., 1971.

Shamir, Shimon. "Israeli Views of Egypt and the Peace Process: The Duality of Vision." In *The Middle East: Ten Years after Camp David,* edited by William B. Quandt. Washington, D.C.: Brookings Institution, 1988.

Shamir, Yitzhak. "Israel at 40: Looking Back, Looking Ahead." *Foreign Affairs, America and the World, 1987/88* 66, no. 3 (1988): 574–90.

———. "Israel's Role in a Changing Middle East." *Foreign Affairs* 60, no. 4 (Spring 1982): 789–801.

Sharon, Ariel, with David Chanoff. *Warrior: An Autobiography.* New York: Simon and Schuster, 1989.

Sheehan, Edward R.F. *The Arabs, Israelis, and Kissinger: A Secret History of American Diplomacy in the Middle East.* New York: Reader's Digest Press, 1976.

Shehadeh, Raja. *Occupiers' Law: Israel and the West Bank.* Rev. ed. Washington, D.C.: Institute of Palestine Studies, 1988.

Shehadeh, Raja, and Jonathan Kuttab. *The West Bank and the Rule of Law.* New York: International Commission of Jurists, 1980.

Shemesh, Moshe. *The Palestinian Entity, 1954–1974: Arab Politics and the P.L.O.* London: Frank Cass, 1988.

Shinar, Dov. *Palestinian Voices: Communication and Nation Building in the West Bank.* Boulder, Colo.: Lynne Rienner Publishers, 1987.

Shipler, David K. *Arab and Jew: Wounded Spirits in a Promised Land.* New York: Times Books, 1986.

Shlaim, Avi. *Collusion Across the Jordan: King Abdullah, the Zionist Movement, and the Partition of Palestine.* New York: Columbia Univ. Press, 1988.

Shultz, George P. *Turmoil and Triumph: My Years as Secretary of State.* New York: Charles Scribner's Sons, 1993.

Sicker, Martin. *Between Hashemites and Zionists: The Struggle for Palestine, 1908–1988.* New York: Holmes and Meier, 1989.

Silver, Hillary Wolpert, Simcha Bahiri, and Ronen Sacher. *The Economy of Jordan and Possibilities for Economic Cooperation Between Israel and Jordan: An Overview.* Tel Aviv: Armand Hammer Fund for Economic Cooperation in the Middle East, Tel Aviv Univ., 1989.

Sinai Anna, and Allen Pollack, eds. *The Hashemite Kingdom of Jordan and the West Bank: A Handbook.* New York: American Academic Association for Peace in the Middle East, 1977.

Snow, Peter. *Hussein: A Biography.* Washington, D.C.: Robert B. Luce, 1972.

"Special Document File: The Peace Process." *Journal of Palestine Studies* 21, no. 3 (Spring 1992).

Spiegel, Steven L. *The Other Arab-Israeli Conflict: Making America's Middle East Policy from Truman to Reagan.* Chicago: Chicago Univ. Press, 1985.

Starr, Joyce R., ed. *A Shared Destiny: Near East Regional Development and Cooperation.* New York: Praeger, 1983.

Starr, Joyce R., and Daniel C. Stoll, eds. *The Politics of Scarcity: Water in the Middle East.* Boulder, Colo.: Westview Press, 1988.

————. *U.S. Foreign Policy on Water Resources in the Middle East.* Washington, D.C.: Center for Strategic and International Studies, 1987.

State of Israel, Central Bureau of Statistics. *Administered Territories Statistical Abstract Quarterly.* Jerusalem: Central Bureau of Statistics. Various issues.

————. *The National Accounts of Judea, Samaria, and Gaza Area, 1967–1986.* Special series, no. 818. Jerusalem: Central Bureau of Statistics, 1988.

————. *Statistical Abstract of Israel.* Jerusalem: Central Bureau of Statistics. Various issues.

State of Israel, Ministry of Defense. *An Eighteen-Year Survey (1967–1985).* Tel Aviv: Ministry of Defense Publishing House, 1986.

————. Military Headquarters, Judea and Samaria, Health Department. *Statistical Report, 1968–1970,* Israel, 1971.

————. *Shalosh shnot mimshal tzva'i, 1967–1970* (Three years of military administration, 1967–1970). Tel Aviv: Ministry of Defense Publishing House, 1971.

————. Coordinator of Activities in Judea, Samaria, and the Gaza District. "Jordanian Five-Year Development Programme for Judea, Samaria, and Gaza District." Progress Report as per Oct. 31, 1987. Internal I.D.F. Memorandum.

————. Prime Minister's Office, Economic Planning Authority. *Ha-Gada ha-Ma'aravit: skira klalit* (The West Bank: A general overview). Jerusalem: 1967.

Susser, Asher. *Ben Yarden Ve-Falestin: biografia politit shel Wasfi al-Tall* (Between Jordan and Palestine: A political biography of Wasfi al-Tall). Tel Aviv: Kav Adom, Hakibbutz Hameuchad, 1984.

————. *In Through the Out Door: Jordan's Disengagment and the Middle East Peace Process.* Policy Papers, no. 19. Washington, D.C.: Washington Institute for Near East Policy, 1990.

————. "Jordanian Influence in the West Bank." *Jerusalem Quarterly* 8 (Summer 1978).

Talhami, Ghada. "A Symmetry of Surrogates: Jordan's and Egypt's Response to the Intifada." In *Intifada: Palestine at the Crossroads,* edited by Jamal R. Nasser and Roger Heacock. New York: Praeger, 1990.

Tamir, Avraham. *A Soldier in Search of Peace.* London: Weidenfeld and Nicolson, 1988.

Taubenblat, Selig A. "Jordan River Basin Waters: A Challenge in the 1990s." In *The Politics of Scarcity: Water in the Middle East,* edited by Joyce R. Starr and Daniel C. Stoll. Boulder, Colo.: Westview Press, 1988.

Thant, U. *View From the U.N.* London: David and Charles, 1978.

Taylor, Alan R. *The Arab Balance of Power.* Syracuse, N.Y.: Syracuse Univ. Press, 1982.

Teveth, Shabtai. *The Cursed Blessing: The Story of Israel's Occupation of the West Bank.* New York: Random House, 1970.

————. *Moshe Dayan: The Soldier, the Man, the Legend.* Boston: Houghton Mifflin, 1973.

Thompson, Kenneth W. *Ethics, Functionalism, and Power in International Politics: The Crisis in Values.* Baton Rouge: Louisiana State Univ. Press, 1979.

"Tomato Yellow Leaf Curl Virus." *Phytopathologia Mediterranea* 14 (1975).

Touval, Saadia. *The Peace Brokers: Mediation in the Arab-Israeli Conflict, 1948–1979.* Princeton, N.J.: Princeton Univ. Press, 1982.

United Nations Conference on Trade and Development. *The Palestinian Financial Sector under Occupation.* New York: UNCTAD/ST/SEU 3, 1987.

United Nations, Security Council Official Records. 26th yr. supplements, doc. S/10070 add. 1 and 2, July 4, 1971. New York, 1971.

United States, Department of State. *The Quest for Peace: Principal United States Statements and Related Documents on the Arab-Israeli Peace Process, 1967–1983.* Washington, D.C.: Government Printing Office, 1984.

Vance, Cyrus. *Hard Choices: Critical Years in American's Foreign Policy.* New York: Simon and Schuster, 1983.

Ward, Richard J. "Comment." *Middle East Journal* 23, no. 2 (Spring 1969): 285–86.

Weisbrod, Lilly. "Binationalism Reconsidered: Ideological Continuity and Change in the Begin Era." In *The Emergence of Binational Israel.* edited by Ilan Peleg and Ofira Seliktar. Boulder, Colo.: Westview Press, 1989.

Wilson, Mary C. "Jordan's Malaise." *Current History* 86, no. 517 (Feb. 1987): 73–76.

———. *King Abdullah, Britain and the Making of Jordan.* Cambridge: Cambridge Univ. Press, 1987.

World Bank. *Developing the Occupied Territories: An Investment in Peace.* Vols. 1–6. Washington, D.C.: World Bank, 1993.

Ya'ari, Ehud. "The 'Common Market' of Information in the Middle East." in *Arabs, Israelis and American Media Images and the Problem of Communications.* Shirley Communications. Washington, D.C.: Washington Institute for Near East Policy, 1987.

Yanay, Natan. *Moshe Dayan: al-tahalich ha-shalom ve-atida shel Yisrael* (Moshe Dayan: On the peace process and the future of Israel). Tel Aviv: Ministry of Defense Publishing House, 1988.

Yorke, Valerie. *Domestic Politics and Regional Security: Jordan, Syria and Israel.* Aldershot, England: Gower Publishing, 1988.

Young, Ronald J. *Missed Opportunities for Peace.* Philadelphia: American Friends Service Committee, 1987.

Zaghal, Ali S. "Social Change in Jordan." *Middle Eastern Studies* 20, no. 4 (Oct. 1984): 53–75.

Zak, Moshe. "Israeli-Jordanian Negotiations." *The Washington Quarterly* 8, no. 1 (Winter 1985): 167–76.

———. "A Survey of Israel's Contacts with Jordan" In *Israel in the Middle East,* edited by Itamar Rabinovich and Jehuda Reinharz. New York: Oxford Univ. Press, 1984.

Zakai, Dan. *Economic Development in Judea-Samaria and the Gaza District, 1983–1984.* Jerusalem: Bank of Israel, Research Department, 1986.

Zeira, Eli. *Milchemet Yom Kippur: mittos mul metziuut* (The Yom Kippur War: Myth versus reality). Tel Aviv: Yediot Aharonot Books, 1993.

Zion, Sidney, and Uri Dan. "Untold Story of the Mideast Talks." *New York Times Magazine*, Jan. 21, 1979: 20–53.

Zohar, Michael. "Municipal Elections in Judea and Samaria: Political Aspects." *Medina Mimshal Veyechasim Bein-Leumiyim*, no. 5 (Spring 1974).

Interviews

Mahdi Abdel-Hadi, Jerusalem, West Bank, Feb. 1988.

Alfred Atherton, Washington, D.C., Feb. 1989.

Ilana Basri, Jerusalem, Israel, Jan. 1987.

Said Can'an, Nablus, West Bank, Aug. 1988.

Ibrahim Dakak, Jerusalem, West Bank, July 1988.

Zvi Elpeleg, Tel Aviv, Israel, Apr. 1988.

Gideon Fishelzon, Tel Aviv, Israel, Dec. 1987.

David Gefen, Imanuel, Israel, Aug. 1988.

Yitzhak Glikstein, Jerusalem, Israel, May 1988.

Yair Hirshfeld, Ramat Yishai, Israel, Apr. 1988.

Rafi Hochman, Tel Aviv, Israel, Dec. 1987.

Feisal Husseini, Jerusalem, West Bank, Aug. 1988.

Eliyahu Kanovsky, Tel Aviv, Israel, Jan. 1988.

Said Kan'an, Nablus, West Bank, Aug. 1988.

Anwar Khatib, Jerusalem, West Bank, Aug. 1988.

Yoram Lass, Jerusalem, Israel, Apr. 1988.

Moshe Maoz, Jerusalem, Israel, Feb. 1988.

Aaron David Miller, Washington, D.C., Nov. 1989.

Thomas Naff, telephone interview, July 1989.

Touvia Navot, Jerusalem, Israel, Jan. 1987.

Amnon Neubach, Tel Aviv, Israel, Apr. 1988.

Nimrod Novik, Jerusalem, Israel, July 1988.

Khalid al-Qutub, Jerusalem, West Bank, Aug. 1988.

Danny Rubinstein, Jerusalem, Israel, May 1988.

Yitzhak Sever, Jerusalem, Israel, May 1988.

Ephraim Sneh, Tel Aviv, Israel, May 1988.

Selig A. Taubenblatt, telephone interview, July 1989.

Ze'ev Sher, Jerusalem, Israel, Aug. 1988.

Joseph Sisco, Washington, D.C., Jan. 1989; and telephone interview, Dec. 1989.

Brig. Gen. Fredi Zach, Tel Aviv, Israel, Feb. 1988.

Dan Zakai, Jerusalem, Israel, Aug. 1988.

Index

Syracuse Studies on Peace and Conflict Resolution
Harriet Hyman Alonso, Charles Chatfield, *and* Louis Kriesberg, *Series Editors*